Harold Washington

The Mayor, The Man

Alton Miller

Bonus Books, Inc., Chicago

©1989 by Alton Miller
All rights reserved

93   92   91   90   89   5   4   3   2   1

Library of Congress Catalog Card Number: 88-63869

International Standard Book Number: 0-933893-97-3

Bonus Books, Inc.
160 East Illinois Street
Chicago, Illinois 60611

First Edition

Composition by Point West Inc., Carol Stream, IL

Printed in the United States of America

This book is for "Charlie Green"

▢ *Contents* ▭

Someone else will write the history of the Harold Washington administration. Someone will chronicle the adventures of the "Council Wars" in Chicago, 1983–1987. Someone will probe further, into the historic social and political dynamics that defined our city at one of its most critical moments.

Someone else will write the definitive, critical biography of Harold Washington; they'll be challenged by a subject that didn't unfold his secrets easily, but they'll be rewarded by a rich complexity of material to rival the stuff of any "life and times" ever written.

Someone else will seek to catalog the "Washington legacy," and derive from the history of the Washington administration and an understanding of the man, a testament, and a blueprint for social and political action in the years to come.

I just want to take the time now, before the tapes get old, before the daily record becomes entirely illegible, before the memos and the planning papers blow away altogether, to answer the simple question:

What was it like?

1

The Day before Thanksgiving

Wednesday, Nov. 25, 1987. Overcast, a chilly Chicago morning.

Up till last week it had been a perfect November, sparkling bright, brisk but not cold. Driving down the avenue from my neighborhood to the Loop could be a treat on these late fall mornings. Through the trees and over the row houses you could see the skyline, a still life in masonry and steel except for the thin streaks of white and grey from the peaks of the tallest buildings. The juxtaposition of the neighborhood and the downtown, in one well-balanced picture, would make you glad you were up early on a Chicago morning.

But this morning was dull grey. You couldn't see the Loop through the weather. We had a groundbreaking scheduled that might be rained out. And though tomorrow was Thanksgiving, and the rest of the world was tapering off its business to prepare, we had a hell of an agenda that day.

Mayor Washington was scheduled for an 8:15 arrival at the Merchandise Mart, across the Chicago River from the Loop, for an interview with CNN, the Cable News Network. I would get there ahead of time, by 8:00. One of his security detail would be on the scene and we'd make small talk while we waited for the limousine to pull up.

The mayor had agreed to appear in a double interview with Mitch Snyder, a Washington, D.C., activist; the subject was America's public housing crisis. It was bad scheduling. He'd be driving up from his apartment at 5300 S. Lakeshore Drive to the Mart, at 400 north; then all the way back down to 4600 south for the groundbreaking at 10:00. It was exactly the kind of scheduling I raised hell about, several times a week. Yet this time it was in a sense my fault—CNN had made the request and instead of turning it down I had asked the mayor if he wanted to do it. Naturally he said he would, so here we were, starting the day too early, zigzagging the city in rush hour traffic.

I had a routine for mornings like this. First, at approximately the time when the mayor would need to be leaving, I'd call his detail in their command post at 5300—apartment 65, across the hall from the mayor in apartment 66. Just checking, I'd say, that the boss is on his way. If they hadn't spoken with him that morning, I'd call him myself. If he were going to be running late, I'd be able to call our destination and make adjustments. This morning, when I called, he was right on schedule.

Through nearly three years with Mayor Washington, I never knew him to oversleep, but he did so much business from his apartment—his friends knew that early morning was the best time to call him at home, and *everybody* had his phone number—that a series of morning telephone conversations could make him late for an early appointment.

And lately this fall he had occasionally changed his schedule at the last minute; three times he had canceled an entire day's agenda without notice. Since nearly every day's schedule included one or several public events, where TV crews and print reporters would be planning to attend, his cancellation would mean a series of calls to the media, to head them off.

But these cancellations were rare, so infrequent they hadn't attracted attention. I suspected the media were happy we'd given them a break. His secretary, Delores Woods, his scheduler, Edward Hamb, and my staff made the adjustments without resentment—after the punishing schedule he had maintained for the past five years, he had earned the right to take a break whenever he wanted one.

He had won reelection in April, and still we continued to book him in back-to-back appointments as if he were still campaigning. He would express his quiet but effective criticism by simply throwing out the entire day, from time to time.

Lately he seemed to be fighting a cold, or dealing with a touch of the flu. But I had learned during the campaign that out of nowhere he could summon reserves of energy when he needed to, then replenish them with a 15-minute nap in the limo, on the way to the next stop. He seemed to have some kind of inner circuit breaker that could just switch off when he needed to rest. He knew what he was doing.

I had made my first morning call from my own apartment. I'd also made my second routine call, checking with CNN that they were still on schedule. I had learned from experience to doublecheck these interviews, especially when the mayor's appointments were scheduled so tightly together. A 15-minute delay in taping a story might seem unimportant to the broadcasters, but it could make him late for the next event. Like falling dominoes, the whole day's appointments could be thrown out of whack.

When I placed that call, I was told that CNN might have a problem; I said I'd call back, and now, threading my way through Wells Street traffic in the three-year-old Dodge Diplomat, I tried again on the car phone. Coincidentally, CNN was on another line at the same moment, trying to reach me at home.

The producer said there had been a prison riot in Louisiana, and CNN was covering it live; that was screwing up their programming. Could the mayor's interview be postponed until later that morning?

I said I'd get back to them later to work something out. My immediate priority was to call the mayor and head him off. I knew he was already on his way, so I called the limo. I told Frank Lee, the agent in charge that day, that the 8:15 was off, so he could head back; they were on Lake Shore Drive, at McCormick Place. He handed the phone to the mayor.

I explained the situation to the mayor, who wanted to know whether we'd be able to reschedule. The interview was important to our promotion of his housing policies, which we were continuing to press on a national scale as well as in Chicago. I told him we had the option of going on to CNN and waiting around, but I didn't recommend we take the chance. It was equally important, for the same housing agenda, that the groundbreaking take place on schedule. Chicago's press corps would be waiting there.

He said he was going to breakfast, at the Hyde Park Hilton restaurant. Did I want to join him? I said I'd have to pass. I headed on in to City Hall.

Usually when he had down time between events, we used the time to talk about the issues of the day. Most of the time—today was no exception—we had three kinds of issues to consider: the ones we were trying to promote, the ones that were going to come at us whether we liked it or not, and the random issues that bubbled up from the bottom of the pot each day.

We were promoting housing. We were going to have to deal with budget issues, whether we liked it or not—the 1988 budget was being debated in City Council. Miscellaneous continuing issues that could come up at any time: an ordinance to permit night baseball at Wrigley Field, solid waste controversies, new stadiums being planned for the Bears and White Sox, education reform.

This morning, I knew, the press would swarm to cover the groundbreaking. They'd want to get their stories finished early so they could do their last-minute Thanksgiving grocery shopping. But though they'd give us a few seconds, or a few lines, on the groundbreaking as a setting, the press was not about to travel to the South Side just to cover a community event. They'd be primarily interested in a story on possible budget compromises; the way we had it planned, this would be their only shot at the mayor that day, so there would be a good turnout.

Though we needed the exposure on the housing agenda—just showing the mayor at a groundbreaking would accomplish that—we could also use the event to promote the compromise activity that was taking place in the budget issue. But we needed the latest information. The mayor's chief of staff, Ernest Barefield, had been talking with department heads and budget director Sharon Gilliam. He would have the most up-to-date list of cuts that could be made in 1988 spending, to move toward a compromise budget. I wanted to bring whatever information I could to the mayor before he encountered the press at the groundbreaking site.

Naturally he and Ernie would have spoken at length on these same matters, but not necessarily in sync with the press interest in the issue. What might seem, to people working with the nuts and bolts of any topic, too obvious, or too innocuous, or too premature, or too old hat, or otherwise immaterial to the problem at hand, might in fact be the best material for a news story that day. I wanted to pick Ernie's brain, so I skipped breakfast with Harold Washington.

Frank Lee later recalled that the mayor had a light breakfast, passing up the full buffet for fruit and coffee. He and the mayor talked—about the budget, about old times, about the mayor's father, who was a frequent subject of conversation.

"He loved his father," Lee told a reporter. "He spoke about him often and about this need for blacks and minority people to have a strong, positive male image. . . . He told me he believed that if there were more, stronger role models for the younger people, it would certainly have an impact on deterring alcoholism and narcotics dependency."

It was a typical conversation for Harold Washington to have with the officers serving on his security detail. They were men, most of them black, who had been with him since the 1970s, some of them much earlier. Most of them had fought for and had won their version of reform in the Chicago Police Department before Harold Washington began his reform of City Hall. Through organized action, and the formation of the Afro-American Police League, Howard Saffold and Renault Robinson and many other rank-and-file put their jobs and even their lives at risk. They broke the color barrier, desegregated the force.

The mayor's detail were all of above-average intelligence. They were literate, politically active men—and a few women—who enjoyed wide-ranging interests. Their commander, Howard Saffold, had run for public office; Washington's usual driver, Wilbourne Woods, a police officer who wore a dapper suit rather than a uniform, soft-spoken and deferential, with a ready smile, had also earned a college degree and a lot of postgraduate credits.

They were his first and perhaps his most important daily link with the real world. And they were his constant cushion against that world—in all the time I knew him, whether he was in Shanghai or Jerusalem, Hartford or Hollywood, the City Council or a ribbon-cutting in Uptown or on the South Side, there was nowhere Harold Washington was, where a security officer hadn't been first, waiting for his arrival. They were more than the mayor's protective ring; they were more than his ears and eyes. They were also boon companions, sounding boards, people he could argue with about sports or Chicago history or politics. Full of respect—nobody called him "Harold"—they were also people who had known him when he wasn't Mr. Mayor.

So in his leisurely breakfast with Frank Lee, in that suddenly available free time, Harold Washington was enjoying one of his favorite occupations—unaffected, free-wheeling conversation about life and its vicissitudes, with old friends who wouldn't bullshit him, and who weren't looking for favors.

After breakfast they made the short drive to the groundbreaking site on East 46th Street, where I met up with them. There was no new information from Barefield, so the mayor would have to speak in generalities. The event went well, everybody made their speeches and answered questions. Though the announcements and press Q&A were limited to the subject at hand, WLS-TV's Andy Shaw, or WBBM radio's Bob Crawford, managed to phrase a question that related to the groundbreaking but which actually probed the state of the mayor's budget negotiations. With good-natured evasiveness, the mayor bent his answer back in the direction of housing issues. We vaguely promised reporters there might be a fuller opportunity to talk about the budget later in the day. A few photos, and we were off.

I left my car at the site. Tumia Romero, my secretary, would have it picked up later in the day, by the Department of Streets and San. They'd return it to my parking place on LaSalle Street in front of City Hall; I wouldn't need it until it was time to go home. I rode back with the mayor and we used the time to get some of the day's priorities outlined.

We talked about the selling of the budget. We wanted a tax increase in 1988, because by building that increase into the base budget now, we hoped to be able to coast through the rest of the second term relying primarily on natural growth in revenues. There wouldn't be any danger of a need for election-year tax hikes.

We had developed an elaborate rationale, and a printed brochure that spelled it out. But now he was having second thoughts; he commented that we should forget all the detailed analysis and simply point out that the increases we needed, especially in the Law Department and the Department of Revenue, were an investment, an upgrade in our capacity, that would improve performance in the out-years. *Crain's Chicago Weekly* had made our case for us, he said, in that week's editorial. We should be making that case—not getting into arguments about whether we were adding 300 or 1,200 new positions to the city payroll. I pointed out that we were making the case for investment, as one in a list of some ten points or so, in fact had carried it to *Crain's* ourselves when we appeared before their editorial board. He said we should elevate it, isolate it, focus on it— not on the numbers game, which we would never win.

I had a list of other topics I needed to cover with him, and when we left the budget discussion I raised another subject: the *Chicago Tribune's* "Inc." column, a daily gossip column written jointly by several co-authors (hence the title), for political, social and entertainment items.

"Inc." had given the mayor a lot of trouble over the years. Formerly its principal writer had been a woman, Mike Sneed, who had cultivated a personal enmity with the mayor. Sneed had moved to the *Chicago Sun-Times*, with her own daily gossip column, "Sneed," and "Inc." was under new management.

I told him that maybe it was time to reconsider Kathy O'Malley and Hanke Gratteau. O'Malley, who handled mostly entertainment items, had been a co-writer with Sneed. But my wife, Cindy Bandle, who was director of press for the Goodman Theatre gave her a personal voucher; she said she was a fair reporter, favorably disposed. Gratteau currently handled most of the political material in the column, and I had known her as a good investigative journalist before she had taken over "Inc." Unlike most other gossip columnists—including a few gossipy political columnists who trafficked in hearsay, Gratteau was a reporter bound by the same standards as anyone writing for the regular news columns. She had been trained by the best—as an assistant to Mike Royko.

Just as important—this being Chicago—there was a personal voucher for Gratteau as well. Before I had known her well, she had come highly recommended by a good friend, Rick Kogan, who had been a player and an observer of the media scene in Chicago since before he was born—being the son of the respected newspaperman and Chicago historian Herman Kogan.

Gratteau was an honest columnist, I urged, who observed fair journalistic practices, even though in the past her column had been granted a dispensation from what the layman would consider basic media ethics.

The mayor listened with some impatience. We had talked about "Inc." many times—about Gratteau's "Inc." as well as Sneed's "Inc." We had always been on the same side of the discussion—clearly, "Inc." was, at one time, aligned with the political opposition, and at its worst it was, as he put it, "the bottom of the barrel" of the newspaper business. At its best, "Inc." and "Sneed" and the rest were sneaky glimpses behind all those closed doors, revealing secrets of official cover-ups. It was a tribute to their effectiveness on the political scene that the mayor would have such strong feelings and reasoned opinions; it was also the residue of years of unpleasant experience.

Now he was being pitched on an idea he viewed with distaste. Not frequently, but more and more often, I had been calling Gratteau with items of interest—always after discussion with the mayor—and I told him I thought the "experiment" was working, she was playing fair with us. Now I was suggesting that it might be time for him to sit down with her, grant her a formal interview, and see whether we might be able to turn the tables. We worked hard for a front page story; "Inc." was at least as well read as anything on the *Trib*'s front page.

Since his 1987 reelection he was mayor for life. We weren't in the desert anymore, we were in the land of milk and honey. Maybe we could begin to afford ourselves some of the luxuries of peacetime?

He looked at me sideways, with a sour look. "Harry Golden," I said, my clinching argument. He smiled at the inside joke, creasing his face with that ready grin that was always just under the surface. Then he turned serious again.

"They're all alike," he said, with a flat finality, no humor in his tone, not a hint. Flinty, cold, he would have no part of it. "You know what happens when you start playing that game," he said. "I've got better things to do. I don't want to start dealing with this shit." I suggested, with a chuckle, that I'd take it back to the drawing board and try it on him again, but he wasn't kidding. "No," he said. The subject was dead. "What else you got?"

I went on down my list, talking about tomorrow's Thanksgiving Day schedule. As usual, he would be making stops at warming centers and restaurants that were providing holiday meals for the homeless. That would mean that I would have to be there too. I actually looked forward to these events, but I'd have to figure out how Cindy and I would handle the timing of our own Thanksgiving dinner at home.

He seemed tired, his energy down, a little out of sorts. I asked him how he was feeling. He hadn't been able to shake his virus, he said. He didn't sound congested, but he said his throat was feeling a little raw. He told Frank Lee, riding up in front alongside the driver, to have someone pick him up some cough drops. They were handed to him when the limo arrived at City Hall, where he was greeted by another member of the security team.

In his office I took my usual place in the chair opposite his desk, still with my note pad of items for the day. Every day's list—accumulated from the days before, re-prioritized each morning—was longer than we could actually ever cover at one sitting. The items we didn't complete would be recycled. Most mornings we'd stretch the time a little, encroaching on his first office appointment, and I'd get as far down the list as I could. He enjoyed using that time for more general conversation as well, impressions of events, newspaper items; it was a time for generating new ideas and reassessing old ones, while he cleaned his fingernails or scoured an ear with an open paperclip, as he rummaged through his papers.

We were looking at his list of appointments for the day. Aldermen he'd be lobbying on the budget. Miscellaneous other visitors.

Delores came into the office and they exchanged their usual morning repartee. Some mornings she and I would play a silent game of tug-of-war, she trying to keep him on schedule, me trying to get as far down my list as possible before we had to get on with events. This morning, though, there was no pressure.

She had some changes in his schedule to discuss. He noted with pleasure that Robert McClory was on his list of appointments that afternoon.

The mayor had forgotten why he had wanted to see McClory, a Chicago journalist and former city editor at the *Chicago Defender*. He thought it was because McClory wanted to see him. No, Delores said, he'd told her to schedule McClory some day this week. No matter, he would have welcomed a meeting with McClory any time, he said. "You should come in for that," he said to me. "Do you know McClory?"

I said I knew him only by reputation. "You come on in for that meeting," he said. "You'll like him." Once before he had spoken appreciatively of McClory, and he repeated himself this morning, recounting the writer's background.

Delores left. I was going to have a little more free time. I looked down my list for the next priority.

Suddenly I heard a rattling, or rasping sound, a crude human noise, the sound a man might make outdoors, clearing his throat before spitting. I looked up from my note pad and saw the mayor leaning far forward in his chair, eyes straight ahead, his left cheek flat against the desk, now making no sound.

In that first instant, as my mind raced for a logical connection, it occurred to me he was reaching under his desk with his left hand for something he had dropped, something he didn't need to look for to find. Just as quickly came the crashing awareness that there *was* no logical connection, that something without reason was happening in front of me. "Heimlich maneuver" flashed through my brain.

I moved from my chair, around the desk, in an instinctive move toward him, to see whether I could respond somehow to whatever was pushing him against his desk. He was completely inert.

I didn't need to contemplate any Heimlich maneuver—there was no struggle, no gasping, no sound or sign of life. I threw open the door to the adjacent office where Frank Lee was working. "Frank! Get in here! The mayor needs you!" I barked, propping the door open with its hinged doorstop. As he crossed into the office, I turned into the outer office and told Delores to call for medical help, then went back into the mayor's office.

Michael Ceja and Phil Pence, police officers on the mayor's detail, had run in right behind Frank Lee. The mayor's dead weight had pulled him down from the chair, and he was stretched out now, the chair kicked aside. Frank had taken charge, the others were removing his shoes, undoing his belt, loosening his tie. Frank was feeling for a pulse and seemed to find one.

Frank spoke to the mayor, in quiet, confident tones. "Hang in there, mayor," he said, "hold on there, buddy." For a desperately hopeful instant I wanted to believe this was not so bad as it seemed.

In that same instant I recalled an automobile accident I'd witnessed when I was younger, working in a summer stock theater. The victim had been scalped, it appeared the top of his head had been removed, the hair and forehead flapping to one side. I'd been certain he'd been killed outright. One of our actors had been a military medic; coolly professional, he'd taken charge until the ambulance came. The next day the only reference to the accident was a local press item that said the patient suffered head lacerations, was treated and released. That macabre memory flashed back, as I was reassured by Frank Lee's cool competence.

Then Frank reacted with a start—he had lost the mayor's pulse. He continued to talk, but it was more urgent now, still insistent but almost pleading. "Come on, boss, don't leave me now, don't leave me now." He ripped his shirt open and they began a CPR procedure, Lee pounding the mayor's chest, Ceja and Phil Pence trading off in the effort to keep air moving into his lungs, and blood moving to his brain. For a moment the pulse resumed, then stopped again, forever.

Delores' first call had gone in at exactly 11:00. The police registered a call at 11:01, the fire department at 11:02. Fire Department paramedics were in the office with their equipment at 11:05. By 11:10 the Fire Department's Ron Smith had a telephone contact with the emergency room at Northwestern University

Memorial Hospital, where Dr. David Kramer took charge. Under his direction they administered epinephrine, atrophine, lidocaine, and then electric shock, to jolt the heart back into action.

"Stand clear!" they'd shout, and as the bolts of electricity racked the mayor's body, his feet would flail, jumping off the floor as though alive, and with each body motion there would be a fresh leap of hope that the inevitable, the inexorable, was not happening in front of our eyes.

For me—and after the paramedics arrived, for Frank Lee and the others as well—it was a particularly helpless moment. The one person around whom our whole life revolved was lying helpless on the floor, slipping away from us. In a moment of crisis, the security team was trained to take charge, to give orders even the mayor wouldn't countermand. That sense of responsibility remained. They still had a job to do, protecting him. But the enemy couldn't be reached.

In a similar way, I still had a job to do, advising him, covering for him, presenting him with options, at least one or two more than would otherwise be available if I weren't at hand. But at some point, the options run out.

Now we were all fully functional organs good only for transplant; the heart that kept us meaningfully functional had stopped beating.

We'd been through crises before. He had trained us, or watched us learn, as we reacted to the unexpected day in and day out. We could read each others' cues—Delores, Frank Lee and Howard Saffold, Ronnie Crawford, Al Rowe and the others on his security detail, scheduler Ed Hamb, chief of staff Ernie Barefield, aide-de-camp Chuck Kelly, I myself—we had learned to respond with alacrity, even with a certain grace, and to solve problems on the run. We had learned most of what we knew about crises from watching and working with him.

So what was my function in this one—was there to be any purposeful activity in this final crisis? I forced my mind into gear.

Who should be in the loop? Who needs to know? From the mayor's phone I called Barefield, who was summoning key staff to his office, and told him I thought he should come over and secure the mayor's papers. I was concerned that there was a break in the flow of information, in the chain of command. We had to stay in touch.

"We're going to be out of here in two minutes," I told him. "I don't know what's here that you're going to need." Whatever engine there would be running things while the mayor was incapacitated, Ernie Barefield was going to have to be the universal joint. The papers in the mayor's desk and in his briefcase would include city contracts, drafts of ordinances, memos from me and from Ernie, God knows what else. Who knew, in the confusion that we were experiencing, what might happen to them. With attention focused on the mayor, Delores certainly coming to the hospital, who knew who might try to come into the mayor's office while it was unoccupied. Even today—especially today—who could trust in luck? It was as if by keeping the office secure I'd keep a little more of the Harold Washington administration intact, for a little while longer.

Ernie said he'd be over, but I saw him only briefly, and he was gone again. I assumed all hell must be breaking loose where he was too, and he was needed in his own office.

On instructions from Dr. Kramer, the mayor was placed on a stretcher, to be moved to the hospital. I had decided that I would stay with the mayor, even if it meant crowding the ambulance, so there would be a link with Ernie at City Hall; I was grateful for the commanding tone of Frank Lee's flat statement that I would ride with them. As we wheeled the mayor down the corridor to the elevator, I was aware of a crowd of reporters and cameras. Unlike the many times we faced such a crowd, this time there was no clamor of questions, just a communal horror. I felt a rush of gratitude that the Fire Department's veteran press officer, Jerry Lawrence, had been on the scene with the paramedics in the mayor's office. He could handle their immediate questions, while we went to the hospital to look for ultimate answers.

On the street level, another crowd, mostly city workers, many faces the mayor would have known by name, or would have greeted with a smile. They were strained, many tearful, a blur of concern as we moved to the street.

Two ambulances had been provided, one facing north, one south; LaSalle Street had been completely cleared in all directions, for our rapid exit. The ambulance facing south was open, ready to roll, but it was the wrong ambulance—we needed to go north. Frank shouted orders and we moved toward the other ambulance, which was locked. After another few seconds of confusion, the other ambulance was open and we squeezed in.

We had trouble fitting everyone in, and as the rear door wouldn't close—the stretcher rolled back, nearly out the door, as the ambulance surged forward—I put my foot against the stretcher, and held the door closed as Frank held onto me.

In the emergency room, Dr. John Sanders, heart surgeon and chief of the hospital's medical staff, took charge. By a quirk of history, the 45-year-old physician had been the physician on duty 11 years earlier, when Mayor Richard J. Daley had been admitted with his fatal heart attack.

Dr. Sanders didn't condescend in his outline of the situation. It was clear the prognosis was extreme.

In addition to the medical team working on the mayor's body, Howard Saffold, Health Commissioner Dr. Lonnie Edwards and the Health Department's Dr. Linda Murray were standing in the room. Linda and Lonnie translated for Howard and me, as the hospital's new, state-of-the-art heart-lung machine was connected and procedures attempted. But I didn't need any translation; I knew that if there were a chance of saving the mayor's life, none of us, in our non-sterile street clothes, would have been in the room.

We all understood—those of us from City Hall and the hospital staff too—the importance of leaving no stone unturned. The mayor was not going to be pronounced dead until every conceivable option had been exhausted; and not until everyone who might have a justifiable reason for playing a role had played it.

But there were no life signs. The mayor was on life support, so blood was moving through his system, oxygen was being pumped into his lungs. But he was not "in a coma." He was dead.

I called Ernie Barefield, had some difficulty getting through. He was still in his office, trying to establish a command center for the aldermen who were already mobilizing for the political succession that would follow; and he was trying to provide leadership for the stunned aides, cabinet members and other employees who had congregated on the fifth floor. I asked him to have his secretary keep a line open for me. I wanted to be sure he had a direct hook-up to the scene at Northwestern, so he wouldn't be operating out of phase, or in response to what must have been fragmentary reports in the media.

During the long wait in the emergency room, I used my Day-Timer to make notes that might be necessary at the press conference. Times, doctors' mutterings, names of people who visited in the emergency room. As I jotted these entries I noticed a luncheon appointment I had made, to meet the *Sun-Times* reporter Lynn Sweet at the Wrigley Building Restaurant. I hardly ever went there—the mayor usually had soup and a sandwich in his office, and unless we were working through his lunch break, I went to Counsellor's Row across the street—but Lynn was one of the younger reporters that Harold Washington wanted to cultivate, so I had planned to treat her and myself to a grown-up business lunch. The crazy thought occurred to me that I should call Tumia and have her cancel. Then I realized that Lynn would probably know where I was.

Several times, as I went from the emergency room to the small office with the telephone, I stopped briefly to talk to the cameras outside the hospital, to give them the paltry update information available, and once to urge them to move from where they were barricading the hospital door.

I was aware they had become desperate for some word, some indication of progress, some final pronouncement. I felt responsible for providing some answers. But the mayor's family came first.

In the emergency room Dr. Sanders had suggested a suitable period to wait—against any real hope—for some return of vital signs. That provided time for members of the mayor's family to come to the deathbed before it was officially all over. As they arrived, Delores was helping to care for them in another room. His brother Ramon Price arrived and was brought into the emergency room. The Rev. B. Herbert Martin, known as "the mayor's pastor," had been called. Mary Ella Smith, the woman the mayor loved, was there and, at her request, a Catholic priest was called. Time was running out, and the announcement would have to be made—the press and public had been held in limbo for two hours. Still, it was Harold Washington's last press conference, and the city was in crisis. What I didn't want was for one TV screen to show a group of white professionals in smocks telling the people of Chicago they had lost their leader, followed by another clip from a remote location, catching Ernie off guard at City Hall, still another showing Alderman David Orr, the city's vice-mayor, reacting to the news that he would now be interim mayor.

I called Ernie and suggested that whatever he was doing, he should come directly to the hospital so we could not only formally announce the mayor's death, but also give the public confidence that the team was still in place, and the business of the city was moving forward. He should reach David Orr, I said, and arrange for him to come also. If possible the two of you should come together, in a police car. Don't get stopped by the press as you arrive, I said, and described the entrance they should use. I found a uniformed officer at the hospital and explained that Barefield and Orr would be arriving, and asked him to get them through the crowd without delay.

While I was at the phone I made a quick call to Cindy at the Goodman. Reassuring her, hearing her reassuring me, I was suddenly at the edge of tears, and I had to get off the line.

Sweeping through my field of vision, as I moved between the telephone room and the emergency room, were faces from the past, people I'd met, many only briefly, in my three years with the mayor. One I knew well was the Rev. Willie Barrow, whose face was full of both sympathy and purpose—she had placed, or received, an international call from the Rev. Jesse Jackson. She was at the pay phone in the hospital lobby. He, I understood, was calling from a U.S. ship in the Persian Gulf. I had worked with him briefly, during Mayor Washington's 1987 campaign, and again when Washington endorsed Jackson in a factory site press conference I had set up, but I didn't know him well enough to understand the thrust of his question, when he asked whether I thought he was needed back in Chicago.

I wasn't sure what he meant. "I'm one of those who believes you're doing God's work where you are, Reverend," I said.

I didn't know exactly what he was asking. If he meant did I think Chicago was going to blow up, in some inchoate rage and grief, no, I didn't. If he meant did the political crisis that would follow need some orchestration, I didn't have any idea, I didn't have an opinion.

While he was talking in my right ear, Reverend Barrow was at my left. She strongly felt he should come home, and she let me know it— she wanted me to bolster her case. I told Jackson that she thought he should cut his trip short, and hurry back, and I would rely on her insight. God knows, Jackson is a leader, and Chicago would benefit from every leader it could put into the field this day.

A number of City Council members and other city officials had collected at the hospital. We gathered them together and sent them to the small hospital auditorium where we would make the announcement. To preserve order on the street outside the hospital, I told the press that no announcement of any kind would be made there—they could go to the auditorium without fear of being scooped by anyone who lingered at the door outside the emergency entrance. I asked the hospital staff, and our own people, not to break that confidence with the press by responding to questions there.

Ernie Barefield and David Orr finally arrived. Together with hospital officials, we outlined the press conference. I would make a succinct announcement to set things up, and then Dr. Sanders, David Orr and Ernie Barefield would be there, speaking in turn, to describe the circumstances of the hour and answer questions about where we were going from here. Obviously the medical report would be essential. But it was also important for Chicagoans to see the Harold Washington team in place, men and women, blacks and whites, Latinos, Asian-Americans, assuring with whatever confidence they could muster that Chicago was still working together.

As we made final arrangements, and as Dr. Sanders proceeded to make the official pronouncement of death at 1:36, Barefield suddenly decided that Tim Evans should be present. A call went out, and we began another wait. I felt that we had stretched our time limits beyond reason already—we'd already asked the press to move, and they were undoubtedly getting desperate for news over in the auditorium, around the block from the emergency entrance, with no idea of why they were waiting. Then Roy Washington arrived, the mayor's other brother, and attention turned to the consolation of the one close family member who had not been there before Harold Washington passed.

When Tim Evans arrived we moved down an interior corridor to the press conference room, which was actually located in another building; Jerry Lawrence managed to get word to me that the press was saying the paramedics had been late in reaching Mayor Washington. He gave me a note clarifying the times of their dispatch and arrival. I took his note with me into the press conference.

The press crowded the small auditorium, and the community of Harold Washington supporters, together with the hospital staff, packed the area of the rostrum. I had been in enough chaotic events to know that you're likely to put down and forget anything you're carrying in your hands, so I was still wearing the trench coat that I had put on in the mayor's office. Now I took it off, held it clumsily, and in that moment looked down to see Ald. Anna Langford's tear-streaked face, mustering a sympathetic smile. We embraced, and she took my coat from me.

It was already 2:20 that afternoon—three hours and twenty minutes after he had been stricken. I looked around me to be certain all were in place, and faced the cameras.

"It is my sad responsibility to let you know that Mayor Washington was pronounced dead this afternoon at 1:36 p.m," I said. Dr. Kramer would provide the medical details, I said, and Interim Mayor Orr and chief of staff Ernie Barefield would also speak, before we took questions.

Dr. Kramer announced that the mayor had died of cardiac arrest, and that an autopsy would be done that evening. David Orr spoke in brief tribute to Harold Washington, saying, "We are asking everybody in the city to pull together in this very difficult time." Barefield responded to succession questions by promising a City Hall news conference the next day, on Thanksgiving. I remembered Jerry Lawrence's concern, and made a point of stressing the rapid response, the professional treatment, the state-of-the-art attempt to revive the mayor. I also mentioned, for the record, but not in response to a question, that Rev. Jesse Jackson had called from the Persian Gulf and would be returning immediately to Chicago.

That evening the hospital would be able to pinpoint a clot in a coronary artery as the cause of death. The autopsy stated that other heart arteries were 90–95 percent clogged. He was 100 pounds overweight, and his heart was enlarged to nearly three times its normal healthy size.

Nothing could have saved him, the doctors on duty agreed.

After the press conference I answered the questions of individual reporters, until everyone had what they wanted. I had repeated the same stories so often my responses were becoming mechanical. I was wearing out.

Already the medical story was becoming old news, and press attention was turning to the political story, the issue of succession. As the questions turned away from Harold Washington, I retrieved my coat from Anna Langford and disengaged from the crowd.

I didn't have my car. I hadn't eaten since early, and I was too tired to walk. I hailed a cab. The driver, a black guy named something like Charlie Green, had been crying. I slouched in the back seat and asked him to drive me to City Hall.

I called Cindy again. She said she was with our friends, Rick Kogan and Jennifer Boznos, who had come to comfort her. They knew we wouldn't want to hole up at home, and suggested we get something to eat at the Wrigley Building Restaurant—by coincidence, where I was supposed to be at lunch.

It was a somber meal, and when I had a drink it left me completely drained. The restaurant was nearly empty, and there was not much cheer among those who were there, except that occasionally there would be a short rattle of laughter from one table or another, in the normal course of dinner talk. It was anomalous, even jarring, but it was a curt reminder that life goes on.

Rick and Jennifer were solicitous, and drew me out on what I was feeling about what had happened that day. As we were finishing, a white guy came up to the table, from where he'd been sitting at the bar. I could see Rick getting tense, feeling protective. I could see him preparing for what might be a confrontation of some kind. But I knew what the guy wanted.

He mentioned his name. It was something like Charlie Green. I made a mental note that my black cabdriver had the same name. It was a day of coincidences. He moved toward me clumsily, almost abruptly, but it was to extend a hand. "I'm sorry," was what he said. "I just wanted to say it for all the rest of us."

I knew he was sorry. I knew we were all sorry. I had been with Harold Washington for one thousand days, and that was long enough to know we'd never see the likes of him again. He had changed Chicago forever, and it was not so much through his plans and his policies and his politics as it was through the force of his one-in-a-million personality.

It was a thousand days I would never forget.

2

We Took It Personal

If you lived in Harold Washington's Chicago, you took it personal. It wasn't just politics. It wasn't just government. It led the news every night for weeks on end, and dominated the front section and the business section of the papers, as well as the city section. But it wasn't just politics in the news. It was something personal.

You hated the guy, you thought he was great; you thought he was a nice, lazy politician who blundered into Chicago's best job, a fluke, and you wanted him out; or you thought he was an asshole but you wanted them to give him a chance; or you knew he was the most intelligent and most progressive mayor Chicago had seen in a generation.

He surrounded himself with the best and the brightest, he surrounded himself with amateurs and idealists; he was a crook who hired cronies, he was the first Chicago mayor in memory completely independent of the crooks and their cronies.

He was giving the city to the blacks, he was opening up the city to a new era of brotherhood.

How could you not take it personal?

He was "Harold," and he wasn't just the mayor. He wasn't just the first African-American to be elected mayor of Chicago. He was *your* mayor, or he was *their* mayor. Either way, we took it personal.

For those of us who worked for him, too, it was personal. You weren't working for the bureaucracy, and you weren't even working simply for the city of Chicago. You gave them your 40 hours, but you gave the next 20 or 30, your weekends, your heart and some of your soul, to the big guy.

You weren't there just for the "Action Agenda." You weren't submerging yourself in a faceless "Movement." You weren't slugging away because you liked the sound of his slogan, "The City that Works Together." And you weren't doing it, in one of his expressions, "because you had nothing better to do"—although in a way that was closest to the truth.

Maybe somebody, somewhere, was working for these reasons, but I never met that person. These slogans were all excuses for your wife or your family or your friends who wondered how you could get so obsessed with government work.

What were you going to tell them—it's personal? But it was.

For me, too, it was something personal. Even before I signed up in February 1985, Harold Washington had made an indelible personal impression. And when he died at his desk in November 1987, it was a loss for the city, it was a loss for the Democratic party, it was a loss for those blacks and progressives all over the country who counted him a hero, but for me and for those who worked beside him as he changed Chicago, it was a loss of a personal friend.

▢ *Open Sesame*

Of all the changes he had made, he was proudest of the fact that he had opened city government to everyone in Chicago. As he was fond of saying, he'd made it "Open, Sesame!" for all.

It occurred to me while I was on the public payroll, that only government workers who work at the municipal level are likely to enjoy the immediacy of their connection with real life government functions. Garbage collectors, bus drivers, public works employees, cops on the beat, municipal workers at O'Hare or Soldier Field or at a public parking lot—all the people who build and rebuild the city every day of our lives, collectively form a living infrastructure that simply doesn't exist at the state or federal level.

Before working for the city, I would have assumed that state or federal politics would be more rewarding, that there would be a sharper sense of having contributed to the needs of your society in your own time and place. Now that I've worked for the city I can't even remember what ever made me think such a thing. The feedback at the city level is total and instantaneous, nothing abstract or remote about it. And while I'm sure that you feel real good when you've helped improve relations with China, or retired a fraction of the federal deficit, there's nothing like being a part of the solution down on a level where people live. And at the risk of sounding corny, there really is a sense that every other city functionary, from cabinet members to transit authority tellers, is a brother or sister, part of a loose confraternity that keeps the city chugging and humming along.

Along with most community activists and civic groups, Harold Washington saw the Richard J. Daley years as years of closed government. City budgets conjured up in smoke-filled rooms. Handshake labor deals, the terms never fully disclosed. Jobs and contracts handled through an old boys' network. Minorities, women, small and emerging businesses, systematically excluded. Until Harold Washington took office, the political "Machine," which had been perfected in 19th Century urban America, but had expired almost everywhere except in Chicago, still ruled the day.

He saw the aftermath—the confused administrations of Mayor Michael Bilandic and Mayor Jane Byrne—as an attempted continuation, without the genius or the resources, of the Daley Machine.

Most of all, he saw the "Council Wars" that pitted 29 opposition aldermen against the 21 who supported him, not as an ideological conflict, not as a racial confrontation, but as a simple brute struggle for power, by politicians who hoped to motivate their public through racial fears. The archrival aldermen, Edward Vrdolyak and Edward Burke and their supporters, he knew, were not "loyal opposition" adversaries in the parliamentary political tradition, but renegades, terrorists, unable to revive the Machine, but willing to hold the city hostage until they got their personal concessions.

The old way of doing business was costly—the school system had been bankrupted, the Chicago Housing Authority was amassing hundreds of millions in deferred maintenance while its 145,000 residents watched their homes literally fall apart, and the Park District and the Port District and Chicago's other fiefdoms of patronage were bloating the public payrolls beyond all national norms, while the parks and the port deteriorated. In April 1983 Harold Washington had inherited a city deficit in excess of $100 million, a projected 1983 shortfall estimated variously at another $60 million or so, and a bond rating that was about to slip down a notch, costing the city additional millions in debt service every year.

But it was even more expensive, he believed, in what it was doing to the spirit of the city. By restricting city management to white males, Chicago was losing the talents of women, blacks, Latinos, Asian-Americans, and other minorities who could bring fresh blood to a tired body politic. By operating on wired contracts and automatic renewal of previous deals without new bids, Chicago was freezing out a new generation of entrepreneurs from city business.

By contrast, his annual budget planning was an extended public process. Community development was opened up to anyone who wanted to participate. He and his cabinet attended scores of neighborhood forums, and showed up at dozens of community meetings, block parties, businessmen's breakfasts.

The mayor made a point of traveling throughout the wards, all over the city of Chicago, planning events and making his own occasions when invitations weren't forthcoming.

And he was proud that his government leadership—commissioners, deputies, the mayor's office—was representative of many different interests and ethnic groups. He wasn't listening to those who urged that he hire only blacks in key posts. He was out to disprove those who thought he would. He was determined to recruit from business, from academe, from the arts, from areas that were previously outside the pale of politics.

And of all his appointments, probably none seemed more bizarre than when he hired me—from manager of a ballet company to press secretary to the mayor.

3

Mayor Taps Dancer

Feb. 10, 1985. "Mayor taps dancer who knows the role," read the headline in the *Chicago Tribune*.

I was never a dancer, but that was the least of the misstatements that greeted my arrival.

Another *Trib* story stated, "Miller knows the mayor's chief of staff, William Ware, from Washington, where Ware formerly lived, and Ware was one of the reasons Miller was hired as press secretary here, said Miller's acquaintances."

The stories were derisive, charged with innuendo; my appointment sparked juvenile jokes: " 'I guess he wants the press office to stay on its toes,' quipped an anti-administration alderman in one of the few comical asides that could be printed."

I had never known Bill Ware in Washington or anywhere else. To the casual reader, the misstatement was an innocent enough error. Yes, it could have been avoided simply, if the reporter had called me before writing something that was flatly untrue. But it didn't look like an item you'd consider hostile—unless you knew what was going on.

Ware had been the target of a homophobic innuendo campaign, ultimately aimed at the mayor himself. The mayor is gay, the rumors said. He had a homosexual chief of staff, they said. Now, they tried to imply, through Bill Ware's homosexual network, he's hired a homosexual press secretary as well. The *Tribune* generally, and the *Trib*'s gossip columnist, Mike Sneed, in particular, seemed especially susceptible to this campaign, one of several targeted on the mayor's character, which had tainted the 1983 election, and which would continue throughout the mayor's life.

Friends who knew more about Chicago's politics than I could have, asked me wide-eyed: "Al, do you *know* what you're getting into?"

No, but I was finding out. Though it was still a week before I was due to start, my education had begun. I learned, for instance, as I read the *Tribune* story, that I could expect as many pot shots from inside the mayor's own circles, as I could from the opposition.

"Some top administration officials. . .were taken by surprise when Miller's appointment was announced," the story said. "The mayor wants someone who will run an efficient office, someone who will get out the press releases quickly. 'The political stuff,' to use the phrase of one administration insider, will be left to Ware and Intergovernmental Affairs Director Thomas Coffey, with mayoral speechwriter Brian Boyer freed to develop and plant stories on administration accomplishments—and majority bloc failings."

There was nothing subtle about the hidden agenda of that paragraph. Ware was under attack in a guerilla war within the mayor's inner circle; and the issue of my hiring was to be one of the battlefields of that internal partisan war.

The mayor had already let me in on what was happening, in the two remarkable conversations we had before I'd been hired.

⬜ *The Shortest Conversation* ⬜⬜⬜⬜⬜

Wednesday, Feb. 6, 1985, four days before those stories appeared. I was in the waiting room outside the mayor's inner office. I was about to meet Chicago's mayor for the second time in my life. My conversation with him would be the shortest conversation I ever had with Harold Washington.

I was watching the time because I had a plane to catch, back to Akron, Ohio. He had called me in halfway through a week out of town; I'd been working with the Ohio Ballet as a management consultant.

Bill Ware had asked me to make the trip for what he promised would be "only a ten-minute conversation." Easy for him to say—for me it would require nearly eight hours of travel.

Could it wait until I returned at the end of the week? I asked. I was helping the ballet company put together a major grant proposal, and the deadline was next Monday. I couldn't cut my trip short.

Ware sounded exasperated—I was the least of his problems. "You'll be able to get right back," he promised. He added, as if it were an unusual offer: "We'll reimburse you for it."

Getting to the mayor's office from my cluttered desk in Akron meant driving an hour to Cleveland Airport, returning the rented car, making the flight to Chicago's Midway Airport, retrieving my car from the parking lot there, driving into the Loop and—this was before the city had begun to enforce parking laws downtown—parking on the street a short walk from City Hall. Then I'd have to make the return trip the same day, as soon as I'd finished.

What the hell was I doing this for, anyway?

I was skeptical of the whole process. Of course I was flattered to be recommended for the job as Harold Washington's press secretary. And it was an honor to be among the three finalists on the short list.

But I knew the search committee had to narrow it down to three names. I figured I was a ringer, one of the two extremes they needed to enhance the position of the one in the middle, the one they really wanted.

I was an arts manager. I had no political experience to speak of. My work in journalism had been brief and narrowly focused. And I was a newcomer to Chicago: Cindy and I had moved here less than a year and a half back.

We had come from Washington, D.C., but not from politics. I had been comfortable as the managing director of the flourishing Washington Ballet. Looking for more challenge, I had accepted what was described as the impossible mission of turning around the Chicago City Ballet, which was facing a debt in the order of three-quarters of a million dollars. It took me about a year to figure out that was indeed impossible, but in the meantime Cindy and I had fallen in love with Chicago. We decided to stay, and I'd become an arts consultant.

The only reason I was at City Hall now was that I had been recommended by Montgomery Ward's communications executive, Nan Kilkeary.

Mayor Washington had created "private sector resource council" groups of volunteer executives from private enterprise to provide free advice for every city department. Nan was on the advisory committee for the mayor's press office; I had met her in her other capacity, as I wandered Chicago, hat in hand, trying to raise money for the Chicago City Ballet from major corporations.

Ware had called me in on January 14 and introduced himself. He told me he'd done some research on me—with his Capitol Hill connections, Ware was able to check my Washington, D.C., credentials as well as the few references that I had in Chicago. "Everyone I've talked to gives you high marks," he said, "but I've got to tell you, I'm probably the only person in the world who would take you seriously for this job, considering your resume. You've got to tell me how I can walk into the mayor's office and recommend a ballet manager, without 'HW' thinking I'm crazy."

I was prepared for the question, of course. I stressed my press and management skills. I sold the point that there is no career field more results oriented than the performing arts.

I had worked in the theater since my teens, more than 18 years in seven different theater companies. I had done almost every job you can do in the theater, except act. Most of my time had been spent as assistant executive director at Arena Stage, the nationally respected resident theater company in Washington, D.C. I was responsible for press and public relations, with a lot of fund-raising thrown in.

You may not think about it while you're watching the play, I said, but producing theater is one of the most complicated forms of management in the world.

A theater producer has to choose a season of plays months in advance, select directors and then work with each director to cast the plays, and pick designers for the sets, the costumes, the lighting and sound; sometimes you have to line up musicians, choreographers and other collaborators. Then there's the sales effort, designing the ads and posters and fliers, planning the timing of the promotion, preparing a budget, talking to the press, pitching your stories. There are the technical considerations, ordering lumber and paint, planning the shop schedule, hiring carpenters and painters, getting everything built to specifications and on time.

Your personnel responsibilities cover the gamut—teamsters, custodians, box office personnel, secretaries, actors. There's the business manager's thankless effort, the box office ordering and handling tickets, the house manager's preparation of the theater, hiring the ushers or arranging for volunteers. There's the entire field of fund-raising, and the cultivation of the board of trustees and donors. And the whole enterprise is dependent on the changing attitudes and tastes of the general public, and your attitude toward them.

On any given day an arts manager may work with a parking lot attendant, a disgruntled carpenter, a frustrated business manager, an actor with a problem, a newspaper critic, members of the general public and the president of the board.

All this activity, I said, is targeted on one date and time, when the curtains part on opening night. Everything counts backward from that one precise moment. And then, when opening night arrives and it all comes together, you're not finished: you've only opened, you've just begun. You have to get up the next morning and start the whole process over again; for the next production is about to go into rehearsal, and the show you just opened will be in performance, night after night, for weeks.

None of that happens without solid management. My model for the consummate professional executive has always been the stage manager, the one with the clipboard, alert but cool, passionately involved but level-headed, keeping track of parallel developments in so many different areas. The best managers in any field are the kind of people who would make good stage managers.

Though I'd been a good stage manager, I was a specialist in press and public relations. That's another field, in the eye of the hurricane, where management is as important as creativity. There's about 10 percent flash, and 90 percent solid management behind the workings of a good press operation, I said. I had run a good press operation at Arena Stage. I could do it for Mayor Washington. Although the application would be different, the principles are the same. In both government and the arts, there are as many variables as there are constants, so my expertise in dealing with the unexpected would certainly apply.

And from what I'd been told, and what I'd read in the papers, and what I perceived in Harold Washington himself, he would be his own best salesman. What the mayor's press office needed more than anything was good management.

Ware asked about my politics. East Coast liberal, politically aware since the beginning of the civil rights movement back in the 1950s, and politically active since the mid-1960s, in my late teens and early twenties. I had read history and politics all my life, and though I skipped out of college before I'd finished my first year, and never returned, I was solidly self-educated in current events.

As to practical experience in politics, I didn't have much. I'd been a supporter of Mayor Marion Barry in Washington, and had worked with his transition task force, on the arts panel. I was full of energy, willing to work hard, a fast study.

Other general information? Married, one child by a previous marriage, good health; Lutheran; registered Democrat; 1963 Honorable Discharge, U.S. Marine Corps (Reserve); miscellaneous boards of directors; former drama critic for a monthly magazine, *Washington Calendar*; guest drama critic, *Washington Star*; spent a year in Europe (instead of finishing college), writing, learning languages. Except for stints as a forklift operator (in Europe), as a furniture mover (in New York) and as copy boy at the *Washington Post*, and a year and a half writing, I'd spent a lifetime in arts management.

Ware had told me he'd be in touch. I didn't count on much, but it would be a treat to meet Harold Washington, if I got that far.

I didn't take that prospect too seriously, until a week later, when Ware called to say I had an appointment with the mayor. Could I come in on the 28th?

When I came in that cold January morning to see the mayor, I assumed I'd be going in with Bill Ware, so I went to his office. He told me the mayor wanted to see me alone.

My first conversation with Harold Washington lasted a little over an hour. He began on the same note that Bill Ware had—my chief of staff has a high opinion of you, he said, but you have to explain to me why anyone with your resume should be considered for this job.

I went through the same drill: good management is good management, I was a good stage manager.

What did I think about the specifics of a press secretary's job?

I knew what little I knew about that from reading—history, current political nonfiction, the newspapers—and a book by Stephen Hess called *The Government/Press Connection*, which I had found in a Washington, D.C., bookstore shortly after Ware's first call. I knew that the bottom line for a successful press secretary is the relationship with the boss. "Reporters believe that what makes a good press secretary is access, the perceived closeness to the head of the agency. They will tolerate most faults, even arrogance, if they think the spokesman has access," Hess had written.

A press secretary, I said, should be transparent—that doesn't mean invisible, but it does mean the press secretary should be a focusing lens for his client's story, rather than the object of the story. That applied as much in the arts as in a press secretary's job, and I had always relied on the power of understatement rather than a Barnum & Bailey ballyhoo approach. In particular, the press secretary should never be a self-promoter; otherwise he or she gets in the way of the primary message. I could see by his sharpening focus that I had hit a nerve there.

How would I proceed, if I were hired? Well, I'd like to see how it's done in other cities, spend a week or two with press secretaries who run a good shop.

He interrupted me: "I've talked to mayors in just about every major city," he said. "And I've looked around for myself. There's not a well managed press office in the country." I took the statement as an exaggeration, but he'd made his point.

I said I'd spend time looking at the staff we had, assessing skills, making sure square pegs got put in square holes—Bill Ware had indicated there were some problems.

"Shit," he said, "except for one or two people, that whole shop ought to be cleaned out. Half of them came in under Jane Byrne and they aren't working for us anyway."

I said I'd outline a general game plan, together with Ware and other top staff, counting backwards from Election Day 1987. I'd develop more specific internal campaigns within that game plan, around key themes. I'd build a computer data base by issue, by constituency and interest group, by ward. I didn't know how detailed he wanted me to be that morning, but I had a lot of ideas.

He turned the conversation into more general areas. He was feeling philosophical. What did I think about what was going on in the city? In the country?

I spent a few minutes on my favorite topic: the city as the most profound expression of our culture, the city as the highest art; the great city as the masterpiece we inhabit. The urbanologist Jane Jacobs was bedtime reading for me, I told him. She had put in language what I had only felt; I knew I loved cities and she told me why. I was concerned that cities were in trouble. I wanted to share in the collaboration to make Chicago work. For its own sake, that is to say, for the sake of the people in and around Chicago who in fact are Chicago.

We talked about race relations. I believed in the "rainbow" approach to public policy, I said. We live in a pluralistic world; even though some blacks and some whites, for different reasons, might want to think of our society as a "white man's world" in which minorities cut against the grain, the truth is that we'd already begun to move into a more complex state of affairs. The journey of change was noisy at times, but the most significant transformation was happening quietly. I thought I could see the signs of change in the remarkable acceptance, in many parts of Chicago where it would have been thought impossible, of a black man as mayor. I said some whites who believed they would never "accept black people" were being won over by the personality of Harold Washington.

Don't get me wrong, I said. We haven't reached the millenium. We had plenty of problems. Coming from a black city, Washington, D.C.,

I had been shocked at the racism I discovered in Chicago—from blacks, toward me, in public encounters where I had assumed too much, behaving in Chicago as casually as I would in Washington. And I'd experienced racism from whites, surprisingly from some of the best educated and most privileged Chicago had to offer. I hadn't heard the word "nigger" since childhood, until I heard it spoken by a Loop attorney.

But never mind that; the point was that Chicago was maturing into a city neither white nor black; America was becoming a nation neither white nor black. That was the reality, whether black nationalists or the KKK liked it that way. I wanted to work in a job where I could help manage that process.

I said that I couldn't think of any point in history since World War II where you had a situation like you had here in Chicago. In politics or war, things are almost never a matter of good and evil, I said. It's almost always a question of conflicting priorities, equally valid ways of solving problems. Politics is the way you manage that conflict. "What's going on here," I said, "isn't normal politics. Here you have an old-fashioned villain. And an embattled mayor trying to bring on reform. The good guys and the bad guys. I can't imagine a more exhilarating fight," I said, "than when you know you're right and the other guy is flat wrong."

That too touched a nerve. The mayor was looking for a level of commitment rooted in personal conviction. I had that, and he could see it.

The mayor turned the discussion to his own general concerns about the press.

"We need the press," he said. "We can't live with them, but we can't live without them."

The press and a reform mayor should be natural allies, he believed. Not only because they both wanted to run the rascals out of City Hall, but also because they both had a stake in the survival and good health of the city.

"We need them to flush Vrdolyak out," he said, "and call Burke's bluff. Burke has them fooled, that he really knows what's going on. Everybody here knows that he's just a high-class ambulance chaser, and Cornelia Tuite"—a name I didn't recognize—"does all his thinking for him. But the media keeps building him up as some kind of a responsible financial manager."

"We also need them to get our story out. It's not enough to be good. People have to know you're good."

"We're going to have to rely on the neighborhood newspapers. The problem with the major media is that they're operating on so many unarticulated premises they're blind to their own racial hangups. Even the best of them, they're the first to ask for reform, but the last to stand up for you when you're taking the heat. That's what a politician does for a living—takes the heat—but it would sure help if we could get them to take sides."

He shook his head ruefully, and chuckled. It was a genuinely good-natured chuckle, no bitterness: "In this business you have to know who you are," he said. You can't go into the fray with any screaming ego needs, because you aren't going to get much sustaining feedback from the press.

"You can't play games with these guys," he said at another point. "Too many of my people think they can get in bed with these reporters, and then turn around and do the job that needs to be done." I got the clear impression that it was to my advantage that I had no connections with the Chicago media.

It was also to my advantage that I had grown up in the Washington area, and not in Chicago. There was little likelihood that I had any old-school ties that might compromise me here.

He asked if I'd ever considered running for public office. I sensed it was a trick question and the proper answer was no. In any case, that was the true answer. He asked why not. "For the same reason I'd never try to be an actor," I said. "If you're going to be any good, it's all or nothing, and there's too much I'd have to give up."

"You ought to consider it," he said. "Congress. It's a good life." I was surprised at his frank nostalgia for his stint as a congressman. "It's a great job. You're in good company there. The IQ standard is about as high as you're going to get anywhere in the world. I mean the *average* is way up there—it's not like City Council, or the state legislature, I'll guarantee you.

"But the best thing about it," he said, "is that you can carve out your own area of specialty, learn everything there is to know about it, and then lay back and let the world come to your doorstep. Everything will have to flow through you."

Maybe I reminded him of Capitol Hill: he spent five minutes recalling how he'd enjoyed the House of Representatives. Would he want to go back to Congress, I asked. He smiled—wistfully?—and said, "Ask any Chicagoan—the highest office in the land is right here in this chair."

The conversation never got down to the brass tacks of employment. We philosophized. He was mentally circling me, sizing me up. I didn't feel that I had his trust, but why should I? I was just glad for the chance to see the inside of that office.

I was impressed by his easy good nature. He made eye contact, and forced you to do the same by example and by natural magnetism. He focused. He let go of his own agenda, confident that he wouldn't lose it, and concentrated on yours. A fact I noticed later, as I watched him interact with strangers and colleagues: he fully engaged whomever he was talking to, invited the other into a closely personal conversation. It could be a political deal getting cut, or a guy asking for his autograph; it could be a governor or a "brother" on the street, it didn't matter. There was no taint of condescension, no flicker of manipulative guile. This was partly political training, but it was also natural inclination, and genuine enjoyment. He was curious about what makes people tick; there was nothing perfunctory or automatic about the exercise.

Delores Woods poked her head in the office, reminding him of appointments waiting. The conversation had run beyond its allotted time. The mayor rose, thanked me warmly for coming, shook hands. He asked if I were an athlete. No word about when I might hear about the job. I assumed the process would drag out, and in any case, I was a long shot. I was just glad for the opportunity to meet Harold Washington face to face. I was sure I'd look back on this meeting as doubtless the high point of my brush with politics. I didn't give the job much more thought.

I went back about my business as an arts consultant. I had a meeting in Washington, then had to put in a hard week in Akron, getting the foundation proposal finished. And then I got the call from Ware in the middle of the week, saying he needed me for a ten-minute meeting.

I came to City Hall straight from the airport of course. Again, I assumed I was expected to stop by Ware's office first.

Like anyone being evaluated, I was alert for signs. Martha Redhed, Ware's secretary, gave me an encouraging smile—a good sign—and interrupted him in a meeting for me. Another good sign.

Bill Ware excused himself from the folks in his office, and thanked me for coming in. He smiled, it seemed an ironic smile; or maybe a smile of satisfaction; or maybe he was just tired.

"I've got forty department heads calling me 'Bottleneck Bill'," he muttered, "all of them complaining that they never can get in to see the mayor. Now 'HW' wants to see you to tell you that he expects his press secretary to report directly to him—not through me." I smiled back at the joke, if it was a joke. "What most cabinet members would give up $20,000 a year for, he wants built into the press secretary's job."

I was still trying to figure Bill out. He gave the impression of a creative and highly educated whiz-kid, balancing both imagination and a bureaucratic bent in a to-do list so full it could never be completed. He was well-spoken, self-consciously a man of the world; he didn't do himself any favors by confiding to a reporter (the comment went straight to the gossip columns) that he was probably the only person in the Harold Washington administration who could order from a French restaurant menu without needing a translator.

He was of the sort that do very well as a Capitol Hill administrative assistant, the Congressman's right arm. In fact, that was where "HW"—sometimes Bill's language was right out of a memo—had connected with Ware. After his election to Congress in 1980, while he depended on long-time pals like Sam Patch and Clarence McClain to keep him covered in Chicago, "HW" relied on Bill Ware to run his Washington office, keep the information flow running smoothly, pre-digest his executive decisions, and do the preliminary screening of personnel.

Now Bill was looking me over like someone wondering if he'd picked the right horse. I was rumpled from the trip, living out of a suitcase in my home town.

"There's a full-court press out there, lobbying for Brian Boyer to take the job," he told me. "They're pitting me and my choice against Tom Coffey and his. What they just don't get, is that 'HW' picks his own press secretary."

He punched a number into his telephone. "Hi, Delores," he said to the mayor's secretary. "Mr. Miller is here for his 2:30. Is the boss ready?"

Back to me, Ware said, "You should go on over there. He'll be ready in a minute." He paused. "Suggestion. The glasses."

I touched the sunglasses, perched back on top of my head. Sunoco station—$6.95. They had been riding there the first time I talked to

Bill Ware, three weeks before, when he had asked me to come in and explain my resume. They were there two weeks later, when I met the mayor for the first time. What was wrong with them now?

"A little too casual," Bill suggested. "If I had my way, we'd all be wearing bluejeans, but that'll have to wait until the second term." I shrugged and pocketed the sunglasses.

So now, here I sat in the mayor's outer office on the afternoon of February 6, for what would be the shortest conversation I ever had with Harold Washington. My chief preoccupation was still the hope that I'd be able to beat the afternoon rush hour traffic back to the airport.

Looking around the large room from the vantage of my overstuffed armchair, I noted the fact that Delores Woods was assisted by a trio of mayor's secretaries—one African-American, one Latina, one Irish. All three were discreetly appraising me—another good sign—or was that my imagination?

I didn't have long to wait before Delores waved me into the inner office.

He was waiting for me, standing in front of his desk with a big smile. We shook hands. He moved behind his desk and remained standing behind his chair, while he motioned for me to sit down.

He was jammed for time today, but he was glad I could make it in. Had I had any other thoughts about the things we talked about? Any questions? No, so he got to the point.

"We talked about how a mayor and a press secretary ought to work," he said. "It's got to be clear that the press secretary reports directly to the mayor." He waited for a reaction. I nodded. "You can't have your press secretary tied up in the bureaucracy. You lose his value as an aide."

Although we hadn't made such a direct point of it, we'd already talked around that idea. I had nothing to add, waited to see what he was getting at.

But that was it. The meeting was over. He thanked me again for coming, as he gathered some papers together. He was expected in a cabinet meeting, and had to leave. He had spoken three sentences. I had said maybe ten words. He remembered something and poked into a blue paper folder on his desk for a dogeared clipping.

"Did you see this?" he asked. "This is the kind of shit we're putting up with here." And he was gone.

I went back to Ware's office. He was on his way out the door, to the cabinet meeting. He asked me how it went. "You were right," I told him. "He wanted to tell me that he thinks a press secretary should report directly to the mayor." Ware waited, a half smile. He was expecting something more. I was getting confused, and thinking about the reimbursement form I'd be wanting to file, wondering how long it took to get your money from the city.

Ware excused himself and left me standing in his office, while he darted over to the other side. He reappeared in a few minutes.

"The mayor neglected to mention it," he said, smiling, "but you're hired."

I called Cindy, a quick call on my way back out of town to finish up my work in Akron. In the plane heading back to Cleveland Airport, I pulled out the clipping the mayor had given me.

It was an article by Steve Neal of the *Chicago Tribune*. The mayor had penned "Miller" at the top.

The headline read, "Press secretaries changing beats."

I skipped past a discussion of Illinois Governor Jim Thompson's outgoing press secretary, except to note that Neal evidently agreed with my Hess book:

> As a press spokesman, [his] strength has been his ability to accurately describe Thompson's thoughts on most issues. On the few occasions when [he] didn't know, he had such ready access to Thompson that he was able to quickly find out.
>
> By contrast, Washington suggested that it is somehow his press office's fault that his message isn't getting across. Washington thinks his image has been tarnished by his political feud with Ald. Edward Vrdolyak (10th), leader of the city council's majority bloc, and that his spokesmen have spent too much time responding to the opposition. When in trouble, blame the press secretary.
>
> In losing [his current staff], however, Washington is depriving himself of two of his most astute and loyal advisers. During the battle with the City Council over the budget, [they] sent a memorandum to Washington, warning him of the political consequences of raising taxes and cutting police personnel. But their advice went against the recommendations of William Ware, the mayor's chief of staff, who had shut them out of the budgetmaking process.
>
> Had Washington been listening to [his press aides] he might have scored more points in his dispute over the budget with Ald. Edward Burke (14th), chairman of the Finance Committee. In the end, Washington compromised. But it looked more like a retreat....

> During the first year of the Washington administration, [his press sec-
> retary] had a senior policy role. As Ware consolidated his influence fol-
> lowing the forced departure of Clarence McClain as intergovernmental
> affairs chief, he began freezing [the press officers] out of policymak-
> ing, and found them convenient scapegoats for the mayor's public rela-
> tions troubles. Ware complained about their method of preparing daily
> briefing notes for the mayor, and about their use of staff. He also sug-
> gested during the budget controversy that [they] were not team players.
>
> Nothing could have been further from the truth...

The article continued, praising them as "Washington's most thoughtful and articulate defenders," "bright, hard-working, and... most dedicated." It listed a number of people who might be hired to replace them, and closed with the warning: "It's unlikely, though, that Mayor Washington will be able to sign someone of this caliber unless he is willing to give his press secretary his trust and confidence as well as a meaningful role."

I understood why the mayor had wanted me to focus on this article. As I was already coming to learn, he was alert for the diversions of others on his staff—press office or other top aides—whose agendas inclined toward self-promotion. Certainly not because he was jealous of others' public recognition.

It was more a distaste for addictions. I could see he felt that people who are hooked on seeing their name in ink, like people with any other addiction, in the long run are undependable. I felt the same way. It was the kind of reinforcing similarity of style that, twined with other strands, would ultimately form the bond between us.

4

A Tale of Two Cities

I finished the ballet foundation proposal, but most of my free time was spent clearing the decks for my new job. I read everything I could get my hands on by Chicagoans about Chicago politics. Mike Royko's *Boss*, Len O'Connor's *Clout*. I even paged through an old favorite, Ben Hecht's *Child of the Century*. I knew that the play by Hecht and Charles MacArthur, *The Front Page*, had borrowed freely from Hecht's book; and that young Chicago journalists who didn't even know why they did it, still cocked their hats and dangled their cigarettes in unconscious tribute to the spirit of that irreverent era of journalism.

I had a lot of catching up to do, a lot of East Coast prejudice to overcome. It's important—for Chicagoans as well as outsiders—to understand and reconcile the two versions of Chicago that a newcomer experiences. The view from the East Coast and the view from within are two very different pictures.

People who don't live in Chicago, people who know about us only from the stories printed in the out-of-town papers or aired on network TV or featured in the Al Capone movies from Hollywood, are stuck with a false image of our city and its people.

Most anywhere else in America, certainly on the East Coast, when you think of big city life you think of New York. The other U.S. cities are so much smaller they can't compare. To find the pizzazz and the public amenities of true metropolitan scale, you have to go to the Big Apple. But once you're there, you must train yourself to accept the poverty, the crime, the plain rudeness, the crumbling infrastructure, the deadening environment, in both the air you breathe and the alienation you experience.

Los Angeles? It's large, but it's amorphous, and a city has to have a shape, curves, edges; you can be standing in the middle of L.A. and not know where to look for it. Philadelphia and Detroit, America's other two cities of size, leave a lot to be desired. Chicago's different, but who knows it? Your first impressions are from grade school: Big shoulders, butcher of hogs. City of wind, fog on little cat feet. Remote.

Geographically, it's just a bigger bauble in a necklace of cities strung across the Great American Desert between the Appalachians and the Rockies. Pittsburgh, Cleveland, St. Louis, Kansas City, Denver—you're glad they're there but you don't need to visit.

A relatively small number of visitors get past the passenger lounge at O'Hare, and discover, with growing surprise, America's liveliest and easily its loveliest big city. A city filled with healthy people, the best and the brightest from America's heartland, pulled into Chicago as if by a great social magnet.

Imagine slicing Manhattan down the length of Broadway, revealing a cross-section of New York architecture: we have that, with better architecture, in Chicago. Lake Michigan cuts open the Chicago skyline like merchandise on display. The narrow, domesticated Chicago River cross-cuts the city, unfolding it yet again, like the Seine or the Tiber creating still more vistas in the heart of the downtown. Chicago had the good fortune to burn down in 1871, just as 20th Century architecture was coming alive. The greatest talents in the world converged on our city to compete with one another—a competition that continues to dazzle to the present day. The lakefront shows off the world's finest collection of modern architecture.

The public sculptures for which Chicago is famous—a Chagall, a Miro, a Calder, the hallmark Picasso, a dozen more—are all works of art and also placeholders, creating plazas by preempting acres that in other cities would be overbuilt. The plazas open yet more city to the sky. And then we have the awesome incidental sculptures, every time the Chicago River bridges heft their tons of steel into the air to let a tall-masted sailboat breeze by to the lake.

The litany of consumer delights is a tour-salesman's dream—from State Street that Great Street to the Magnificent Mile, all the major stores, a myriad of boutiques, restaurants, specialty shops. The term "world class" is abused, but here it applies—the Chicago Symphony Orchestra, the Lyric Opera, and the Art Institute, the museums, the aquarium, the planetarium, these can all hold their own in comparison to their counterparts anywhere in the world.

In the visual arts we're unsurpassed. There's a vital theater scene, from the Goodman Theatre to off-off Loop to the road shows at the

Shubert. Nobody does the blues like Chicago, and we near invented jazz, rock and roll, and, lately, house music.

Chicago's style, in both clothing and furniture, is world famous. Chicago's sports roster is on a scale afforded by few cities, anywhere in the world.

Out where people live, too, Chicago shines. It's one of few large cities where you can get almost anywhere by *either* rapid public transit or your own car. And for the most part, when you get there it's worth the trip. Most neighborhoods, whether upscale or modest, are centered on local shops and commercial strips, and engender a localized pride in community. Many Chicagoans never find a need to visit the Loop.

Chicagoans with their second-city inferiority complex would think you crazy for bringing it up, yet you can compare the city point for point with any other city in the world and come up looking good.

◻ *Only in Chicago* ▭

None of this is visible when you're changing planes at O'Hare. The real Chicago doesn't reach out for you—you have to find it for yourself. Not many people want to try. And when news of the 1983 Chicago election was reported world-wide during the winter of 1982–83, those who wanted to believe bad things were encouraged to believe the worst.

The election reports we got back East confirmed our picture of Chicago. To most of us, in our comparatively sleepy southern city of Washington, Chicago seemed forbidding, violent, flint-hearted and full of hostility.

The worst aspects of Chicago—the Al Capone image, the '68 riots, the grey, gritty picture of a "city that works" but only under the rod of ham-handed leadership, the citadel of corruption—all these were replayed for us as background during the election, often in condescending terms. The subtext was always, "Only in Chicago."

The tragi-comic stories were retold with relish: going back to the administration of Mike Bilandic, who became acting mayor when Daley died. His antagonist Jane Byrne disputed him and challenged him to a lie-detector test. On opposite sides of whatever the truth was, they both took the test, and both passed. Only in Chicago.

Then the stories on the Byrne administration, which staggered its way out of one of those legendary Chicago blizzards to bring reform to the Chicago "Machine." To us on the East Coast, her term seemed to be a four-year binge. The breathless, madcap mayor and her comical cronies, Eddie Vrdolyak and Eddie Burke, abandoned reform and made Chicago a laughingstock. When they were Bilandic's cronies she had called Vrdolyak and Burke the "evil cabal," but she deputized them to run the city shortly after her election. We read how they raised unprecedented millions for their warchests, much of it from companies doing business with the city, in Chicago's first "reform" government. On top of everything else, they had the names of third-graders. Where else in the world are the movers and shakers called Eddie and Richie and Janie? Only in Chicago.

There was an unfunny side to these background stories. We had heard that Chicago was the country's most racially segregated city. We had read of Martin Luther King's confrontations there, and the murder of Fred Hampton. These stories, too, were resurrected and rehashed by the press all over the world.

Then came the 1983 election itself. Once again, Chicago offered comic relief for an East Coast that had survived Jimmy Carter's malaise and was now trying to fathom Ronald Reagan. Like Americans everywhere, we participated in politics the same way we played our sports, sitting in front of the television screen. Or we read it in the papers, with our morning coffee. We watched as the players were cast in their roles, and we enjoyed the unfolding drama as an entertainment requiring only a minimum of intellectual investment.

It was all there on the tube—the hurricane of Chicago politics, and the black reform candidate with his family of supporters in their brave ship straining against the tempest.

And when the latter-day Swiss Family Washington landed safely, in April 1983, it was on an island full of cannibals. The election over, the campaign only intensified. The reports from Chicago read like scenes from a citywide theater of the absurd—a crazy nightmare drama of a metropolis gone mad, with Katzenjammer Kids in control of City Council, an unrepentant Machine, damaged but still thrashing wildly, the old guard, who lost the election, holding sway against the mayor and his team, who won.

New to Chicago in the fall of 1983, I had to reconcile the city of lights I thought I had discovered, with the city of fear I had heard about. The new mayor seemed to be facing the same challenge.

The Harold Washington we saw in news clips had become a hero to many of us in D.C., an embattled symbol of change, a clarion progressive voice cutting against the grain, a prophet trumpeting liberal values amid the babble of New Righteousness. He seemed to salvage some of what we still regarded as the Kennedy Promise. While the ideals of economic fairness and civil rights were under attack all over the country, Harold Washington had persisted.

I'd been a teenager when Kennedy was president. Old enough to keep score, but too young to play. Now Harold Washington was making history in Chicago, and now I'd be on his team.

Free Advice

When I was hired, Ware had simultaneously hired a black woman, Gladys Lindsay, as my deputy. The forced marriage was doomed from the start—Management 101 tells you the new guy has to hire his own staff—but I accepted his rationale. He said he needed to keep peace among those who had insisted that Harold Washington hire a new black press secretary to replace the outgoing black press secretary. Lindsay, from the press office of the Chicago Police Department, would "shore me up," in the parlance of the day. She wasn't due to begin for another week.

Ware took an hour or so to pass on a few words of advice. Where the mayor had said only generally that heads would have to roll, Ware was specific: Norty Kay, a wordsmith for Coffey in Intergovernmental Affairs (IGA), had to go. Coffey was spending too much time on personal promotion, he said, and that was the mayor's "pet peeve." Kay was acting as his press agent. He was out.

A number of Jane Byrne era holdovers in the press office, both black and white, had to be phased out as soon as possible. They were suspected of passing along information to the gossip columnist Mike Sneed, and some of them seemed to be reporting to Eddie Burke. I was to be the one to sever them.

He went down the list of press office aides: this one could stay, this one should go. He suggested people who should be transferred to the press office from other departments. I respected his advice, but I had been told I would have a free hand in hiring and firing, so I took everything he said as only advisory.

He also made recommendations about our mode of operation. It was most important, he said, that we stop reacting to the media efforts of others, and promote our own iniatives. The immediate project, nearly completed but currently stalled, was a Mid-Term Report. I would be expected to pick up the pieces and get it out by mid-April.

By the way, he said, he was planning to take a week or so of "combined vacation and sick time." He had been fighting a cold, or the flu, and he needed to get out of town, get away from the pressure, and take care of himself.

What that meant was that I would be coming into the new job surrounded by infighters who hadn't wanted me hired, with no deputy in place, with a demoralized and unfriendly press office staff, and without knowing anyone at City Hall. Except for the mayor and Ware, the only people I'd even spoken with briefly were Ware's secretary Martha Redhed and the mayor's secretary Delores Woods. I was reassured by Ware's observation that they expected it would be months before I would be ready to take charge, and a full year before I would be up to speed. I had time, time to learn, time to plan, time to do things right.

I arranged to come into the office over the George Washington Birthday weekend so I could get myself oriented, type up some file tabs, figure out how to work the word processor, and begin to sort through the papers I'd inherited. I also wanted to experiment with the public transportation. Now that I'd be working downtown, I should probably save on parking by leaving my car at home, and using the bus. I was pleased that it was such a straight shot on Bus Route 37, with a stop a block from my Lincoln Park apartment.

My new office was large, blandly furnished with a sofa and chair, and a government-issue cabinet with a three-screen TV set. There was an oversize roundtable, built for a conference room, that served as a desk. A low, modern sideboard with file drawers ran along the north wall. Above that, reaching wall to wall, and up to the ceiling, were plate glass windows looking from the sixth floor across Randolph Street to the modernistic State of Illinois building. I had been warned by Ware that Tom Coffey wanted to enlarge his staff and move into this suite of offices; he might have to give my office to Coffey, so I shouldn't get too used to it.

I rifled through the filing cabinets in the office. Four full drawers, but no real logic or system to them. More in the outer office, which would remain the province of the secretaries. I consolidated the contents of those four personal file drawers into three, but otherwise left them in place; maybe they'd yield their secrets later, after I had oriented myself. I started my own set of files in the single empty drawer nearest my desk.

When I finally left City Hall three years later, most of those three full drawers I had inherited were still in place, unsorted, unread, a press secretary's legacy, handed down from his predecessors. Knowing what I know of the job, I suspect they're still intact.

Brian Boyer came into the office that weekend. He had been named in the Steve Neal article the mayor had given me. And a gossip item from the *Tribune*'s "Inc." column said Boyer had been Tom Coffey's choice for the job. He had been the mayor's principal speechwriter, I'd been told.

He was offering free advice. Based on Ware's comments, I was initially skeptical, but it wouldn't kill me to listen. It didn't take me long to realize that his advice, pound for pound, was the best I got from anyone except the mayor himself. I was the more suspicious, and later the more grateful, because it had all been unsolicited.

Like Ware, he offered a capsule analysis of the press operation, including kinder and more insightful thumbnail sketches of the people in my shop. Friends, enemies. People who could be useful. Although I had read extensively in the field of general management and lately in the history and politics of Chicago, I was beginning to understand that my reading of Machiavelli was going to be more applicable.

Boyer told me the *Chicago Sun-Times'* political writer Basil Talbott had passed on the press reaction to my appointment. Talbott predicted, Boyer said, that "Lindsay will be the front person, Miller will get bogged down in the bureaucracy, and someone else will effectively run the press operation." I assumed Basil had named Boyer for that last role, and that Brian had delicately left a blank when he passed it on to me. I also suspected that Basil Talbott, and the others, assumed that Tom Coffey would neutralize Bill Ware and run all over me. I didn't take offense—why shouldn't they be skeptical of me? I'd be skeptical myself, in their position. But it also steeled me to prove them wrong.

Boyer was the one who told me that a city car came with the job. The car had a phone. By the way, that thing on the desk by my elbow was a beeper.

That weekend I still wasn't even clear what my salary was, except that it was close to what I'd been making in the ballet world, $60,000.

He told me about the car in passing, when he gave me the best advice I would ever receive on that job. It was something that would probably never have occurred to me.

"You want to know what I'd do," he said, "if I had your job? I'd drive down to Hyde Park every morning, down to the mayor's apartment. I'd leave the car, let Streets and San pick it up for you and bring it back to the Hall.

"Then I'd ride up with the mayor. That's down time for him, but for you it would be a chance to straighten out any problems with the day's agenda."

I had not yet figured out how I would regularize a daily morning contact with the mayor, especially given his unpredictable schedule. Brian's suggestion solved that for me, if the mayor didn't have a problem with it.

Since many of the mayor's days started with a morning appearance outside City Hall, this would also insure against one of the problems Ware had warned me about—a press office spending all its time playing catch-up with a mayor who has already made the day's announcements to the press.

That advice was offered on the holiday Monday. Tuesday morning the mayor's scheduler, Ed Hamb, dropped into my office shortly before 8:00 and suggested I walk with him over to the Bismarck Hotel, where the mayor was attending a business breakfast. Chicago's Bismarck, around the corner from City Hall, had become notorious as the place where the Machine cut its deals. But it was also a convenient hotel for business meetings of other kinds, and for rallies in its auditorium.

I put on my coat and followed him to the hotel. A small dining room had been arranged for a meeting to promote the annual United Way campaign. The mayor was seated near the podium. It was the first time I'd seen him since that two-minute conversation in his office.

He motioned me over and introduced me around the table. After the meeting I fell in beside him as he walked to his car, and he waved me into the limo. Though we were a half-block from the LaSalle Street entrance at City Hall, the security team preferred him to do that distance by car. As I would later find, the mayor usually preferred to walk it.

I wasn't on his schedule that day—didn't know, in fact, what his schedule was. We had maybe two minutes to talk as the car rounded the block, so I got to the point.

"Mr. Mayor," I said. "How would you feel about my coming down to Hyde Park each morning, and driving back up to the Hall with you." He looked puzzled at the thought.

"Where do you live?" he asked. "You're up north, aren't you?"

"Lincoln Park," I said, "but that's an easy commute. The time that it takes you to get to City Hall would give us a good twenty minutes every day to get our ducks in a row."

He wasn't convinced but he shrugged. "Sure," he said, "if you don't mind the drive down. We can give it a try."

I didn't see him again that day, as I spent my time trying to meet the people who now worked for me.

The press office was a shambles. There had been no press secretary for several months. The deputy press secretary, Chris Chandler, was still on the job, but on his way to another assignment with the Chicago Public Library. He was also enormously helpful, especially since his situation hardly seemed fair. He had been a supporter of Harold Washington since before the campaign, a veteran newsman, respected in both political and journalistic circles. He had put himself—or had been put—on the wrong side of the internal struggles, and was being swept out by the same broom that was sweeping me in.

He was indispensable to the operation of the office during my first week or so—but there was nothing he could do about the deflated morale in an office that had been so disorganized for so long.

I got home late that evening, and took Cindy out to dinner to celebrate my first day on the job. I told her that I planned to take it slow, get a feel for the job, reorganize the press office gradually, begin what I saw as a months-long process of "rehabilitation" of the mayor's image into something more palatable to men and women of good will than the image currently projected by the broadcast media, working reporters, and pundits.

I had no idea that even as we toasted one another at the restaurant, all hell was breaking loose at City Hall.

5

The Vrdolyak Tapes

It isn't possible to appreciate what happened on my second day on the job without some background in Chicago politics, and some background on the mayor's history with the Chicago media. Harold Washington always considered that he was in a three-way struggle—with the political opposition, the media and his administration at three corners of a triangular antagonism. All three were equal players in the events of Feb. 20, 1985.

☐ *The Eddies* ☐

The election of Harold Washington as the 43rd mayor of Chicago was, as all the world knows, not the end of his campaign for that office. It was the beginning.

The election was a study in Chicago politics.

In the 1983 Democratic primary—usually the decisive race for mayor of Chicago—the incumbent mayor Jane Byrne and her challenger Richard M. Daley, the late mayor's eldest son, had marshalled great armies of political workers in what amounted to a civil war within the remnant of Mayor Richard J. Daley's Machine.

With a 73 percent turnout in the black wards, of which 80 percent of the vote went to him, and a margin of victory among Latinos and white progressives, Congressman Harold Washington had exploited the division among the Regular Democrats to win the February primary with a 37 percent plurality. Byrne won 33 percent, Daley 30 percent.

In Chicago, in the minds of their supporters, Daley and Byrne were not so much defeated pols as chumps: some guy in his native Bridgeport neighborhood actually punched Daley out—a hand raised against the divine flesh—for "splitting the white vote."

On the other side of the street, the traditionally inconsequential Republican party of Chicago had not taken a mayoral election seriously for the better part of a generation. They had become increasingly lackadaisical about even fielding a candidate until the 1977 election, when Spanky the Clown (Ray Wardingley) made a serious effort to capture the title by default.

It would be an understatement to suggest that their 1983 candidate, Bernard Epton, was not the strongest possible contender against the now split Democratic party. Still, he was the Republican legally on the ballot, and he made it clear he wasn't about to get off. The sometimes eccentric insurance lawyer suddenly found himself championed as the Great White Hope by many Democratic leaders as well as some in his own party. Democratic committeemen, aldermen, leaders of the party offered him overt and covert help, and he won nearly 50 percent of the general vote in a bitterly contested election. His slogan was "Before it's too late," and there was little doubt what he was talking about.

All over the world, during and after the election, journalists reported the daily details of a titanic struggle between reason and chaos in Chicago.

In the *Washington Post* we read a lengthy op ed piece by the *Chicago Tribune*'s Leanita McClain, who wrote of "the vicious, psychotic events leading up to and following Harold Washington's election." In her article titled "How Chicago Taught Me To Hate Whites," she described the hate literature and the crude jokes, relics of the "Little Black Sambo" era, which she said were not spoken in some sullen corner by a hateful fringe group, but proclaimed openly and defiantly, during and after the election. "The campaign was a race war," she said. "So is the continuing feud between Harold Washington and the white aldermen usurping his authority."

This bright young black woman's painful column was made more poignant by her suicide not long after.

The leader of that continuing feud was the brash Ald. Edward Vrdolyak. He had been widely credited for losing the 1983 primary—for Byrne or for Daley depending on the point of view—with his racist rhetoric on the weekend before the election. "A vote for Daley is a vote for Washington," he was quoted. "It's a two-person race! It would be the worst thing in the history of Chicago if your candidate, the only viable candidate [meaning Byrne], was not elected. It's a racial thing! Don't kid yourself! I'm calling on you to save your city, to save your precinct! We're fighting to keep the city the way it is!"

Through the late 1960s and early 1970s, while a paternal Daley ran Chicago, he was one of two Eddies, who were the joyboys of the City Council's Young Turk movement. In a 1979 book, *Who Runs Chicago?*, the authors likened them to Chicago's other "inseparable dynamic duos," including Anselmi and Scalise of the Al Capone gang. They were called the "City Council tag team...Fast Eddie and Flashy Eddie." As they aged they never shook that Heckl and Jeckyl image.

Fast Eddie Vrdolyak started in politics in 1966, the same year that Martin Luther King had stirred up Vrdolyak's neighborhood with his anti-segregation marchers.

His first election had been as democratic committeeman in his white ethnic 10th Ward in southeasternmost Chicago, on the momentum of his vocal opposition to the city's school busing plan, in political meetings and in court.

The other Eddie, Flashy Eddie Burke, grew up in politics. He became the youngest person ever elected committeeman when he succeeded his late father in 1968.

He joined Vrdolyak to bedevil Daley, in antics that seemed more designed to exact concessions than to register real opposition.

By December 1976, on the day after Daley died, Vrdolyak was one of four aldermen who huddled in the mayor's office to cut the deal that would make Ald. Michael Bilandic acting mayor. Burke was later given credit for pulling the loose ends together. The two Eddies, joined by a third, Edmund Kelly, superintendent of the Chicago Park District, became key players in the post-Daley political tumult, attempting to run a Rube Goldberg replica of the old Regular Democratic Machine.

When Jane Byrne ran in 1979 as a reform candidate, she ran against the Machine, and the Bilandic "evil cabal" masterminded by the Eddies.

Now, in the spring of 1983, these Eddies were the ringleaders who were organizing a majority bloc of 29 aldermen to oppose Mayor Washington's programs. The "29-vs.-21" arithmetic of "Council Wars" would dominate Chicago politics for the first three years of Harold Washington's administration.

☐ *Michael Sneed* ═══════════════════

So much for the opposition. What of the neutral, objective press?

From Harold Washington's standpoint, the archetype of the *Chicago Tribune*'s journalistic power was the cynical lead writer of the well-read gossip column, "Inc." (In 1986 Sneed left that newspaper for its rival, the *Chicago Sun-Times*, where she subsequently produced a similar column five days a week, called "Sneed.")

Michael Sneed had been Jane Byrne's press secretary; her husband had been Byrne's chief of staff.

Readers could infer, from her resume, that she might be politically disposed to favor Mayor Washington's opposition. Reading a few columns would confirm the impression that she did not think highly of him. Further, she has admitted she always took an impish delight in the antics of Fast Eddie and the other "rascals." Vrdolyak was good copy, but her journalistic support for him went beyond mere appreciation of style.

The point was not missed by Neil Tesser of the *Chicago Reader*, a local ombudsman and press-watcher. "The Washington administration is consistently lambasted by INC. to the point that some people have come to wonder whether something more than the usual press-vs.-incumbents debate is going on," Tesser wrote.

In early 1985, before I was hired, Mayor Washington had asked his press office to produce a content analysis of the "Inc." column, to test the point.

Tesser reported the results of that analysis: "in 1984, Washington was mentioned 187 times in INC., 112 of them negatively (60 percent); by comparison, less than 20 percent of INC.'s references to Ed Vrdolyak (11 of 59) were negative."

The legal trade's *Chicago Lawyer* magazine that month, in "The Stink of Inc.," also noted that 29 percent of Washington's mentions were "neutral." Only 12 percent were considered "positive."

Tesser also cited an in-house study by the *Trib* done two years earlier. "The conclusion, we were told by a *Tribune* reporter, was that INC.'s political favoritism was obvious, and that 'journalistically speaking, INC. was an embarrassment.' The report sent *Tribune* editor Jim Squires—who created INC. and claims to keep a close eye on it—into a rage, and was never circulated throughout the paper. But the [staff review group] wasn't telling anybody at the *Tribune* anything new, and people there don't think anything's changed. As one *Tribune* staffer suggested to us, 'You don't need a report from the mayor. You'd have to be a raving moron not to notice that INC. is biased.' "

Tribune editor Jim Squires, quoted in the Tesser article, admitted that "Columns like INC. are vacuum cleaners that pick up every kind of thing they can pick up. If you understand that, then you understand INC."

As with the *Sun-Times'* "Sneed," only a portion of the daily column was given to politics—most was social gossip and plants from theatrical press agents. But what there was was biased.

Squires' subordinates said that he found Sneed embarrassing, but so well read that the paper couldn't do without it. Mayor Washington never accepted that simple explanation.

"If it's an embarrassment, it's an embarrassment of riches," he said. "It's at the heart of their news operation. And it infects everything else they do."

He believed that "Inc." served not so much as a vacuum cleaner as a magnet—attracting every disgruntled city employee and every political operative with a rank rumor to plant—most of which wouldn't be fit for the front page (or any other space but "Inc."), but which might sooner or later lead to a major scoop.

"They can run items that no one else would run," he would say. "They don't call to check their story. They don't tell you the story is from some geek like [Vrdolyak operative Joe] Novak. They don't give a shit if it's true or not.

"Then the next day, they'll get a front page reporter to pick up the same story, and the story will start with 'allegedly' or 'reportedly'—they'll quote themselves, they'll quote a story that didn't have enough basis to run as a front page story in the first place, and run it again, with my reaction."

Squires, in the Tesser article, supported this view: "In fact," Tesser wrote, "you'd be surprised at how often INC. prints unattributed inside info, and then quotes that same source—this time by name—as denying everything. 'We let people say in INC. that they *didn't* say something that in fact they *did* say. That's the way that works.' Squires added that he has no problem with this practice, or with publishing a signed letter in which an 'unidentified source' seeks to protect his job by going on the record as disputing a report in INC."

Tesser quoted Squires' rationale: "I'm committed to protecting sources, even to the point of reader deception, to ensure the free flow of information from government to the people."

In some sense, Mayor Washington actually agreed with this approach, in principle. "The press saved us from Watergate," he said. "It did it with leaks."

But he felt that "Inc."—and by extension the *Tribune* that encouraged Sneed's practices—had abused the principle. Further, he felt they were motivated not by muckraking zeal but by personal animosity. I was to learn how deep this vein of paranoia ran, in my first week on the job.

"Mayor Secretly Taped"

One of Sneed's biggest leaks came to her in the form of an illegal tape recording made by a long-time associate of Mayor Washington, James "Skip" Burrell.

Burrell was one of a number of candidates running in a special election in the 3rd Ward. The mayor had appointed Dorothy Tillman to fill the slot, vacant since Alderman Tyrone Kenner had been convicted in federal court for extortion and mail fraud. Mayor Washington had endorsed Tillman for election.

And now Mayor Washington was urging Burrell to pull out in the name of "community unity." He had made overtures through an aide, Sam Patch, and at a meeting in the mayor's apartment he and Patch had hoped to bring it to a conclusion.

Burrell had carried a microcassette tape recorder, hidden in a coat pocket, to that meeting on Jan. 30, 1985. He had been inspired to wear the recorder, it seemed, by the Vrdolyak camp, who had then turned the tape over to Sneed at the *Trib*. And now the story she wrote was breaking loose on the evening of February 19, my first day on the job.

Cindy and I had finished dinner and hurried home, because I had begun a project of taping and studying the 10:00 news programs. I was amazed to see that the lead story was a "major scandal" involving the mayor.

The *Tribune* was reporting in its early editions that the mayor had been bugged, and that the revelations would be embarrassing. Corporation counsel Jim Montgomery had conducted an evening press conference to respond.

The TV report previewed tomorrow morning's story (the paper's early edition was already out). It would detail the mayor's hypocrisy evidenced by his "stinging attack" on Dorothy Tillman. It would suggest the mayor had tried to "boss" Burrell out of the race. It would embarrass the mayor and cause division among his City Council allies. The *Tribune* was acknowledging that the tapes had come from Vrdolyak's operatives. Skip Burrell had been interviewed on the air, and he was admitting that he had secretly taped the mayor. Pathetic in his vaguely nonplused response to the TV reporter, when asked if he were still an aldermanic candidate, he said he guessed so, unless he were going to jail.

This had broken in the late afternoon, in a telephone call from the *Tribune* to Tom Coffey's office, but no one had thought to tell me about it. I supposed that was just as well—Ware had implied a period of apprenticeship, and I thought I'd stay in the background as this crisis unfolded, and learn by watching. I didn't call the mayor. I didn't have his number.

The next morning was the first of my new regimen: up at 5:00, read the papers and make my notes, then drive down to the mayor's apartment at 7:30 or so.

That morning the *Chicago Tribune* headlines blared in the largest type I'd seen them use: "Mayor secretly taped," by Michael Sneed. Sneed was pasted on the front page, under a straight news banner, not tucked back in the snuggery of her "Inc." column.

As promised, Sneed's scoop led with the news that the tape contained "a stinging Washington attack" on Tillman. It editorialized that "his candid assessment of Tillman is sure to widen the private but wide estrangement between the mayor and his allies on the city council, many of whom are chafing under his leadership."

It provided several examples: "Washington calls Tillman a 'loser,' 'abrasive,' and 'too loud'...;" "Washington also ridicules her knowledge of government...;" "The mayor also belittles her civil rights activities..."

Further, Sneed wrote, "In an effort to persuade Burrell to withdraw from the race, Washington tells him that if he drops out, Tillman would repay him for his campaign expenses...."

The *Sun-Times* was behind on the story, reduced to quoting the *Tribune*'s tape excerpts.

The *Sun-Times'* Basil Talbott reported that Vrdolyak had denied any role in the affair, but his ally Ald. Roman C. Pucinski "implied otherwise to a reporter who asked him, 'Why did you leak that to the wife of a consultant who does a lot of business with Vrdolyak?' To the question that referred to *Tribune* reporter Michael Sneed, wife of businessman William Griffin, Pucinski said, 'Who else could we give it to? Who else could we trust?' "

The mayor's adversaries were already being quoted with reactions ranging from scoffs at the bossism of a self-proclaimed "reformer," to charges that he was breaking the law by attempting to bribe Burrell.

I made a few notes to myself, and made the drive down to 5300. I put my city car in the only nearby space available, a no-parking area at the corner.

There was a limousine waiting in front of 5300, and the driver looked at me with what seemed to me suspicion. The mayor hadn't said anything to anybody about my plan to meet him.

The man at the front desk let me in, and I seated myself on a couch in the lobby. He said he'd let the mayor's detail know that I had arrived. A plainclothes cop sitting across the lobby looked me over and left me alone.

I pulled clippings and notes out of my briefcase, my first morning's preparation, and spread them on the couch beside me. I was definitely playing catch-up, and though I had some ideas, I wasn't sure they were necessary. In any case, they were probably hindsight, for surely the momentum of this breaking story had passed me by.

I considered the council of state that must be taking place upstairs in the mayor's apartment, right this moment. Who would be the players? Corporation counsel Jim Montgomery, certainly, and Tom Coffey. They had organized the press conference last night. Brian Boyer? Clarence McClain? I had read that McClain lived in this building.

As I sat and waited, I considered my position. Shit, this was going to be my job. Shit, it *was* my job. For better or worse, I should be up in that meeting and not cooling my heels down here. I asked the front desk to put through a call for me to the mayor's apartment.

"Mayor," I said. "This is Al Miller, down here in the lobby. I thought I should probably come on up, if I'm going to get involved in this issue today."

"Sure," he said. "Come on up."

☐ *In the Mayor's Apartment* ═══════════

As I walked up the sixth floor hallway I was aware of a TV monitor at the end of the hall. I rapped twice on the apartment door, number 66. Across the narrow corridor, number 65 opened and an impassive face sized me up, and then returned behind the door, back into a branch office of the Chicago Police Department.

At that moment the mayor opened his door, and I was admitted in. He was in shirtsleeves, no tie, suspenders flapping, not quite ready to leave for work. There was no council of state. I was the only one there.

I was standing in the apartment's entry corridor.

"Morning," he said. "Help yourself to some coffee." He padded back to the bathroom inside his bedroom, and I walked to the kitchen.

Off the corridor, to the left, was a small study, something a realtor would describe as a second bedroom, which the mayor used for reading and watching TV. A low bookcase, a sofa, an overstuffed armchair, and a television set crowded the room and gave it the look of the most-used area in the apartment. There was a small second bathroom there that looked completely unused—no shower curtain, no towels or even soap at the sink. Since I never saw anyone but the mayor go into his bedroom, this was obviously the guest bathroom, but it had as much personality as a public restroom.

As I walked down the entryway from the apartment entrance toward the living room, I moved from the bedroom door to the right, opposite the study door on the left; to the small kitchen, or "kitchen area" on the right, opposite another doorway on the left, the doors removed to reveal a walk-in closet or pantry, with a small desk and more bookshelves crowded into it. Though I was never to see the mayor working in that space, it was a handy place for papers to be stored.

The hallway itself was hung with a brass engraving of the headlines from his first inauguration, and a few other mementoes. Just past the kitchen area it opened up into a living room on the left, a dining area on the right—actually one good-sized rectangular space. Straight ahead the apartment's windows looked north, out on Hyde Park, with an overhead view of the famous nest of parrots or parakeets that had settled there.

His living room was furnished in off-white shades, several large so-
fas and matching stuffed chairs, and a wall-length mirror. It was im-
personal, especially by contrast to the warmth of the little study, and
the furniture appeared to be "coordinated," not accumulated. It was
the kind of decor you'd expect to find surrounding a younger bache-
lor who spent little time at home but had to keep up appearances.

The right-hand area of that space featured a solid oak dining table,
around which six people might eat comfortably. As I was later to
learn, as many as 15 could cluster around it for meetings, sitting in
the stacked chairs that partially blocked the entrance to the kitchen
area. This must have been where they were sitting while the mayor
was being taped.

Of greatest interest to me that first morning was not what the
apartment contained, but what it didn't: there was no planning session going on. There was no council of war. The mayor was getting
ready for work. He was wearing the light perspiration on his forehead of a man still busying himself with the shower-and-shave morning routines, and he was moving back and forth between the
bathroom inside his bedroom, and the small study where the morning papers had been discarded beside his chair.

Had I seen the newspapers? He was calm, almost bemused by
what was going on. He seemed more interested in my reaction. He
was open to suggestions. The mayor said he hadn't been meeting on
the phone that morning; he hadn't talked to anyone since after the
press conference last night, except Patch. "I was hoping he could remember all the details of what we were talking about," he said.
Though he had read the *Tribune*'s account, he hadn't studied it carefully, just garnered an impression.

He continued to move back and forth from the bedroom, as he
looped his tie around his neck and put on his shoes. I stood in the corridor as we conducted the conversation.

I had a list of notes in my notebook. I picked the most important.
"Is there anything in the tapes that wasn't in the papers, anything
that might cause real problems?" I said.

He looked a little chagrined and shook his head, uncertain. Like
anybody who had spent an hour talking into a tape machine, speaking without inhibitions on the foibles of his acquaintances, he knew
he'd end up making a lot of apologies. "You know how it is," he complained, "you're talking all up and down the wall, it's all bullshit, but
you put it in print and it looks like a goddamn indictment. There's

nothing that will give us any legal problems, if that's what you mean."

He brought an empty coffee cup from his bedroom to the kitchen. "Ain't this a bitch?" he said with a tight laugh. "This punk comes into my apartment with a tape recorder?" I thought of the atmosphere of paranoia I'd felt in some of our first conversation. Here was clear evidence that there was a point to the paranoia.

"Now we've got a whole brouhaha that we don't need, down in the 3rd Ward." He shook his head. "This is going to be a press field day."

He grinned and shook his head, as he knotted his tie at the living room mirror. "Ain't that a bitch."

Looking over my notes, and venturing to have an opinion, I said, "When we face the reporters, let's don't deal with what's on the tape." There was no way to gracefully discuss the point-by-point embarrassment of personal revelations that might be found in a private conversation, I suggested.

"Let's talk about the tapes themselves. Illegal. Dishonest. Political dirty trick. The conversation with Burrell—if it's all bullshit, let's say so." People would understand that. Ms. Tillman would understand that.

"This was a set-up," he said calmly, turning to put on his jacket. "The son of a bitch was trying to set me up." He grinned uncomfortably to himself, then paused to stare at me. "Do you know Steve Neal?" He studied my reaction. I didn't, I supposed I should have.

"He called me and tried to get me to say I knew I was being bugged."

I didn't know what the mayor was talking about. "He called me, sometime yesterday afternoon, yesterday evening, after we first heard what was going on. I think he had someone in the room with him, he must have had lawyers listening in, because he acted like he was being prompted. He said he was calling as a friendly reporter, but he found a way to ask me four or five different times if I didn't know that Burrell had a tape recorder with him." The mayor asked me again if I knew Neal, or knew who he was. I had to admit I didn't.

He shook his head and shrugged his shoulders to get comfortable in his jacket. He gathered papers on the coffee table. "Yes," he said. "We'll stay away from anything on the tapes. God knows what all's on there. They'll be dropping little bits of it all week, like the Chinese water torture."

He was ready to leave, and picked up an intercom to buzz the security detail on the other side of the hall. We continued our conversation in the car.

"What about Tillman," I said. "Have you talked to her?" He hadn't. She had been quoted in the press as being jarred by the story, but wouldn't comment until she'd talked to the mayor. There was a City Council meeting that morning, and she'd probably be caught by the media as she went in. I suggested we should call her right away and get coordinated with her, bring her to his City Hall office, eliminate any perception that they weren't getting along. The mayor agreed and said he would call when we got to the Hall.

"We can get her now, from the car phone," I urged. He was hesitant and I later understood his reluctance to talk on the car phone, which he assumed was monitored. But he did make the call, and arranged for her to come directly to his office for a meeting before City Council.

I was still going down my list of notes, emboldened by the notion that even an amateur's game plan was better than none. "We should have a press conference, first thing this morning," I said to the mayor. "Otherwise you'll be gang-banged going in and out of City Council."

Jim Montgomery, in last night's emergency press conference, had pressed two points: First, that the tapes may very likely have been doctored, thus calling into question any specifics from the tapes. Second, that obtaining and using the tapes violated state law; Illinois has one of the country's most strict wiretap laws and absent a court order all parties involved must consent to be taped. Montgomery had called for an immediate investigation.

I suggested we should continue that theme, go heavy on the legal ramifications, with Montgomery carrying the brunt of the press conference. Tillman should stand up with the mayor and belie any notion of a split between them. And we should completely refuse to discuss any of the allegations involving the contents of the tape.

He agreed, but shook his head with fresh chagrin. "I wish I knew what the hell was on that tape," he said. He was concerned that the *Tribune* might choose to use portions of the tape all week long, in a continuing series of revelations. Even though he was sure there was nothing illegal involved, he was not looking forward to being held in ridicule day after day. When we arrived at the Hall we dodged reporters with the explanation we'd have something to say a little later.

☐ *The Press Conference*

The mayor called Jim Montgomery into the office.

While we were waiting, he returned, for the second time that morning, to the question of Steve Neal's phone call. Again he fixed me with a stare. "I had the feeling," he said, "that there was someone with Neal. I had the feeling he was trying to get me to say I knew the son of a bitch was wearing a mike." I didn't understand his preoccupation with the question.

Montgomery came in and I was introduced to the city's corporation counsel. Shortly after, Tom Coffey and Brian Boyer came in.

In the presence of the group that had successfully arranged Jim Montgomery's press conference the night before, I resumed my posture as an apprentice. The consensus was to go with a press conference as soon as possible.

Conversation turned to speculation on the "other" tapes that Burrell had told newsmen that he had made. There was concern that the administration might have been compromised, in conversations other than those with the mayor.

I entered the conversation with my own speculation. I had watched the live coverage last night, I said, and I noticed that Burrell had seemed to improvise the story of the other tapes, in the later interviews, after several interviews in which they hadn't been mentioned. The threat of other tapes looked to me like a desperate attempt on his part to cover himself, and create a false concern. There might well have been conversations with Patch that he'd *wished* he'd taped, but from the *Tribune*'s description of the bugging, it sounded mightily like a first attempt. If there were other tapes, wouldn't they already be in circulation? It was just a guess, I said, but I doubted there were any other tapes, and we shouldn't restrain our reaction to *this* tape over the possibility there were others.

We talked about terminology—could we give this a spin? We agreed that we would call them the "Vrdolyak" tapes. Someone— Coffey or Montgomery?—came up with "Vrdolygate." Jim Montgomery, who would share the press conference with Mayor Washington, grinned as he mouthed the word a few times. "It doesn't exactly roll off the tongue," he said with a laugh, "but I'll give it a try."

We rehashed the contents of the day's papers. Jim Montgomery raised the question of what else might be out there, waiting to break.

Coffey suggested that the *Tribune* would likely extend the story out for a week or more, with daily doses of fresh revelations. The mayor repeated that there was nothing in the conversation to compromise him, except that he might have a few friendships to repair—as always in his private conversations, his language had been blunt, frank, quick to yield to humor, and he had peppered his dialogue with words the newspapers couldn't print.

We had been meeting on this for five minutes, perhaps a little more. Tom Coffey steered the meeting to its conclusion. "Al, you'll write a statement, and call a press conference?" I said I would, knowing very little about what would be required. Coffey added, "We're really tight on time. We should do this press conference in the next half hour, before City Council."

So our "damage control" meeting was fast and superficial; the meeting hadn't contributed much to an analysis of our situation. I was again grateful for Boyer's advice to drive to the mayor's apartment. Much more had come out of the mayor's own instincts on this issue, in the 30 minutes we had spent in the apartment and the car, than from this team effort.

I did finally learn one thing that I'd not been able to ask anyone: what do you call the mayor? Bill Ware had referred to him as "HW" in our conversations, but I had not been present at any meeting with the mayor with others in attendance. Now, for the first time, I learned that he was indeed addressed, even in casual conversation, as "Mr. Mayor." Jim Montgomery, with the familiarity of one calling him by his first name, said just "Mayor." When I first heard it, it had an artificial ring. But it quickly became the natural form of address.

In all the time I worked with him, with rare and usually contrived exceptions, although he was "Harold!" to those who greeted him on the street, he was "Mr. Mayor" to those who worked with him.

As his office cleared, I looked to the mayor questioningly. "Mr. Mayor," I asked, "how do you want to do this?" He didn't know what I was talking about, his mind already on the meeting he was about to have with Dorothy Tillman. "Should I write a statement for you?"

"Yes, put something down and let me read it over. You'll have it in—how long?"

"I'll be back in twenty minutes." I had been making notes during the meeting. Now I hurried back to my office, to see what I could do.

The statement Harold Washington would present to the cameras would be the first I'd ever written for any public official. The press

the mayor to make negative comments about Ald. Dorothy Tillman [3rd], a *Sun-Times* analysis of the recording reveals.

The tape, which Burrell said he made of a private conversation between him and Washington about the 3rd Ward aldermanic race, also shows Burrell asking the mayor for financial help.

Unlike earlier excerpts from the tape, selectively published in a gossipy style in the *Chicago Tribune*, the full transcript doesn't support Burrell's contention that Washington offered a promotion in Burrell's city employment....

Burrell repeatedly denounced Tillman and apparently attempted to get Washington to do the same. Washington offered some criticism of Tillman, but spoke in generally favorable terms of her value to the ward and City Council.

Neil Tesser in the *Chicago Reader* of March 8, 1985, commented that the *Tribune* "really did mess up the entire brouhaha.":

The paper's initial report on the bugging (February 20) was written by INC.'s Michael Sneed, who is known to be no friend of the Washington administration, and it revealed several statements of the mayor that made him seem crude, devious, and—his critique of Dorothy Tillman—supportive of a candidate for whom he held no respect.

Those quotes turned out to be sensationalized highlights taken out of context of the entire conversation. The *Tribune* itself realized as much by the next day, when it printed the full transcript of the tape—which not only changed the impact of the mayor's comments, but offered an intriguing glimpse into his private political manner.

That same day, the paper ran an editorial that seemed to reassess the previous day's front-page report, saying 'there's even something reassuring about his [Washington's] astute assessments of Alderman Tillman and the city council.' And by Sunday, February 24, a page-one analysis by political writer Steve Neal stated that in the tapes 'Washington comes across as pragmatic, self-assured, witty, intelligent, thoughtful, self-deprecating and salty.'

Why didn't the *Tribune* know all that on day one of the story? Hadn't they listened to the tapes all the way through? If not, who provided the edited highlights that formed the first reports, which were all but rebuked in the paper's subsequent accounts?

Referring to a journalists' controversy over whether Squires did the right thing in revealing that the tapes had come from Vrdolyak's camp, Tesser quoted the *Sun-Times'* Charles Nicodemus, widely regarded as an ethical journalist: "My quarrel was not with Squires naming the source in general terms. My quarrel was with the decision to first print a carefully edited and therefore inaccurate version of the transcript." Tesser noted, "Indeed, these are the matters for which the paper should be held accountable—not the dubious proposition that reporting germane facts will prevent others from surfacing."

Although our damage control efforts were effective, in retrospect there probably wasn't much chance of screwing it up. The Eddies and the *Tribune* had each shot themselves in the foot.

Although there was clearly nothing on the tape that could hurt the mayor legally, the Eddies hoped that the profanity and rough treatment of Tillman and others would be a major embarrassment.

If the *Tribune* had followed Sneed's script, she would have leaked a word here, a word there for months, bedevilling the mayor and his associates as everyone on his staff came under suspicion for the leaks, no one certain where Sneed was getting her information.

But when the full transcript was printed the next day, it went beyond simple refutation of the first story. It made a few points of its own.

For one thing, it brought Chicago into the mayor's living room to an extent that the very private mayor hadn't allowed before. It made the general public privy to his thoughts in a way that would not have been possible even if we'd tried to plant the tape ourselves.

The transcripts were probably the best-read journalism of the year, and all Chicago was treated to lines like these, spoken as the mayor commiserates with Burrell, who is being asked to pull out of the race and support Tillman:

> Burrell: I've never been this close, your honor. Never been this close. The brass ring's right across the street.
>
> Washington: Well, you never know. That's an elusive [obscenity] thing. I know the feeling. I don't take your ambition lightly. I've told you several times. One of the major criticisms people lodge against me—I don't tell people what to do. I'm too sensitive to other people's feelings, 'cause I don't buy telling me what to do. If you ask me to *think* about what I'm doing, [obscenity], you can turn me upside down. If you *tell* me what to do, I may just stand up there and let you kick my ass, I mean that's what I feel about it. So I'm sensitive to people's feelings. But I don't want to give you that impression. But my concern is selfish. I'd rather this thing would resolve without a long debate. I think it's to

the advantage of our whole movement that it be resolved quickly. That ward will be the center of a tremendous negative campaign with people coming from all over the goddamn city in there. Stirring hate, getting people upset, hell, they're going to do everything they can to, to if not win that ward, so divide the people that it will affect other wards. That's what the game plan is. That's what it's all about. They don't mind spending 50, 60, 70, 100 thousand dollars....

His primary concern was the potential for a well-financed political opposition to create racially volatile issues out of what would otherwise have remained a reasonably rational political campaign.

Again, there's a passage that sums up Burrell's situation. He became increasingly agitated as he delivered his opening lines:

Burrell: I have done, I have done what the last three white mayors have told me to do. And there ain't nothing in the world I want to do more than to do what you want me to do. I have a problem. I have a problem. I have a whole lot of people that depend, are looking for me to run for alderman of the 3rd Ward. I'm caught between a rock and a hard place. I want to do what you want me to do and I want to do what they want me to do. What the [obscenity] do I do? What do I do? Do I die?

Washington: No. Do you want me to answer?

Burrell: Yes, sir.

Washington: You do as you want to do. What you want to do depends on what you consider, consider to be your best interest. I would suggest one.

Burrell: My best interest is to keep my biggest boss happy.

Washington: [Laughs]

Burrell: [Laughs]

Washington: Well, I'm not like your white boss. I'm not going to try to tell you what to do.

Burrell: Yes, you are. In a roundabout way you are.

Patch: [Unintelligible] [Laughter by all]

Washington: No, I'm, I'm not a boss, and some people say that's a fatal flaw. I don't think so. I sleep at night. I don't [obscenity] with people. But. Ah, I think it would be a mistake for this thing to go to the wire with two strong candidates, maybe three...

Burrell: Am I one of them?

Washington: No question about it.

Burrell: Oh good.

Months later, I was still hearing from people—usually whites along the lake front—that the Burrell tapes had changed their mind about the mayor. They had been skeptical, mostly because he was such a departure from their racially insular experience. But the tapes left a number of impressions, small and large, including the reaction of a number of women who related to this line, a reference to some women's lack of enthusiasm for Tillman:

> Washington: ...We get too close to this thing. So my supporting Dorothy—some people will raise their eyebrows, some girls, some women will say, "Oh, [obscenity], she don't represent us."...

The mayor is completely uninhibited in his speaking style, his choice of subjects, even his liberal use of profanities, commonplace in City Hall. And yet he practices a totally unprompted self-censorship in his reference to women, refusing to let himself slip and call them "girls," even when his audience is limited to two long-time male cronies.

That week we discussed how to take advantage of the new momentum gained by the *Trib*'s admissions and the *Sun-Times*' points. All the weekend TV talk shows wanted the mayor to appear; we had already agreed it wouldn't make sense for him to be put in any position where he might be closely questioned about details of the conversation. Jim Montgomery was to be his surrogate for one program, perhaps for others. As to WBBM-TV's "Newsmakers," where two TV political interrogators whipsawed their weekly guests, where Walter Jacobson was regarded as the aging *enfant terrible* out to get the Washington administration, whom could we send?

"Why don't you do it, Al?" the mayor asked.

"Well, Mr. Mayor," I said, "I don't know." This was a far cry from my idea of staying in the background and soaking up impressions and information. "I'm not sure I know enough about what's going on to get involved."

"That's the idea, isn't it?" the mayor pressed. Yep, that's what I'd been saying all along, that we should keep the focus on the bugging itself, and not on details of the political race, or anything else on the tape. "You can handle that." There was a half-smile as he said it, an expression I wasn't yet used to. Was he grinning at the idea of the rookie getting raked over by two questioners who were considered the most ruthless on the air? I grinned myself, but it must have been a sickly grin.

So I finished my first week with a command performance on TV.

In all my years in the theater, as a lighting designer, as a carpenter and later as a set designer, as a stage manager, as a director, as an administrator, I had never been interested in performing. Except for one amateur performance, helping a friend with her college production, I had no experience as an actor.

As manager of the Washington Ballet I'd been interviewed once on TV. And I had been asked to audition for a TV arts program, as a potential television drama critic. My audition was embarrassingly bad, and I still winced from the experience of seeing myself on the screen. Many people—I'm one of them—find it unpleasant to hear themselves in a tape recording; the self-image just doesn't tally with the reality of what's coming out of the speaker.

I had had the same experience with video recordings. I had become used to the guy I shaved in the mirror. That was Al Miller, as far as I was concerned, and all the other angles that a TV camera will catch revealed another Al Miller, someone I didn't know and didn't find too interesting. I never got used to seeing my face on TV, mostly out of vanity—I always looked more haggard and more beleaguered on TV than the guy I shaved would admit to.

And now I had agreed to go on the air and attack the editor of the *Chicago Tribune*. What the hell. Welcome to the majors.

sume consensus on issues that should be freshly examined—he wasn't soppy with that "moist interior logic" which has defined the New Journalism. Nor was he too lazy or too busy to check his facts. And if he sometimes tested positive for that traditional malady of Chicago reporters—good healthy skepticism tending to degenerate into cynicism—he never yielded completely to the tendency. He was still practicing the "old" journalism, with a rhino's hide of reservations, and yet staying young with genuine surprise at the details of a good story, and the exuberant joy of the chase after facts that substantiate. Still, Harry had been branded an enemy, by everyone who had advised me. And in particular by the mayor.

One day, early in my new career, Harry had obliged Eddie Burke by claiming there was some minor discrepancy in our financial projections. I forget the details of the story, and research into the clippings from that period doesn't jog the memory, so it must have been truly minor. Still, at the time I was primarily concerned with the fact that he had been apparently biased on a story that had clearly been planted by the political opposition. I telephoned him from my car, on my way to the office, and questioned his facts.

He was abrupt, almost hung up on me. I must have been blunt, or he must have been busy, because though he was always quick to respond, and loud, as a rule he was a gentleman.

I had made up my mind that I wasn't going to take any shit from the "enemy" reporters. If we were going to be held accountable for our errors, the press would be held accountable too. What were they, pashas? His anger had got me angry, and I came storming into the City Hall press room on the second floor, ready to take him on.

He was just as ready, and we traded charge and countercharge in heated terms. By the time we had gone two or three rounds he was doing a furious little dance, ranting at me in a highly articulate tirade, precisely defining terms at the top of his lungs. I could see that others in the press room were familiar with this behavior, but I wasn't. Although he was all but calling me a liar, I wasn't so much offended as fascinated. I held my own, though, retreating into a controlled, emphatic conviction that he was wrong. The argument was interrupted before it was resolved.

When I saw the mayor later that morning he was angry about the same item in the paper. I told him I had already challenged Harry Golden, and recounted our exchange. The mayor was pleased that I'd taken the initiative to make an issue of it.

Later in the morning both Harry and I were calmer, though still cool toward one another. We talked about the story. Neither of us acknowledged we were wrong. Harry defended his conclusions, and I continued to maintain that he had—perhaps unintentionally—distorted their import by implying some willful deception on the mayor's part. I was impressed by his concern that the merits of the issue be clearly established; regardless of whether we were personally friendly or not, we each had professional standards to maintain. If Harry were indeed an "enemy," he was at least fastidious with his facts, and perhaps even fair in the original sense—not likely to be biased for us or against us.

I didn't have a chance to talk to the mayor about my followup conversation with Harry that morning. That afternoon, perhaps to finish up what I'd started, the mayor responded to a question from Harry—I believe it was at a Q&A session following a speech at Kent College—by castigating him for the inaccuracies of his story. The mayor's attack was laced with a bitter humor, tending toward ridicule. Harry was a proud man, and the mayor's jibes were humiliating.

Harry called me as soon as we'd all returned to City Hall. Look, he said. He didn't care if the mayor liked him or not, but in this case he was being unfair. Harry wanted to talk to the mayor about it.

I jumped at the suggestion, and urged the mayor to see him. "I think he's sure his story is solid," I told the mayor.

"Bullshit," the mayor replied.

"I don't think this is just another attack," I insisted. "I get the sense that he really cares whether his copy is right or wrong. I'll go further than that," I said. "I think your personal opinion is important to him, personally important. I think he'd respond favorably if you'd let him come in and just say his piece." The mayor was unconvinced. I took a deep breath. "I'll go even further than that," I ventured. "I'll bet you that Harry Golden will end up being one of the fairest, one of the best friends in the media that you've got."

The mayor cocked an eyebrow at me. This was crazy—Harry Golden anything but adversarial? The mayor was still forming his opinion of me, trying to figure where I was coming from, and I could see the suspicion simmering.

Still, he agreed to see him, and Harry came up. Though the mayor had asked that I always sit in when reporters meet with him, I said I thought this needed to be a more personal encounter. As I waited with Delores Woods outside the mayor's office, we listened to the same furious argument that I had heard that morning. But, as it had been in the earlier tirade, the anger was undirected, more a little dance of frustration at the unfairness of the mayor's position. Golden was venting, and it seemed to me that it was a cry for understanding rather than anger.

As I listened to Harry's voice rising in pitch and volume, with the mayor's steady tones occasionally interjected in an attempt to calm, I began to worry that I may have miscalculated. Would Harry's ire take him too far? The mayor was a proud man, too. Would he feel he had to slap Harry down? That would be lethal to any future relationship.

We could only gauge the decibel level, not hear the conversation. For a good while they were speaking in normal tones, inaudible to us. Then Harry came out and passed me with a professional smile. I went in.

The mayor was grinning, but not derisive. In fact, he was respectful. "He had some strong opinions," he said. "I still don't think he's right, but I think he wants to be fair. We'll see, Miller. You might just be right. It's crazy, but it's possible."

The mayor agreed to suspend judgment. My relationship with Harry changed immediately—I was convinced he was not "the enemy" and though he could not be expected to be "the friend," I was sure he would be straightforward with me—which was all we asked.

Before long the mayor was acknowledging publicly, not only that Harry knew the city's finances better than anyone else, but that when there was a discrepancy between our budget office's numbers and Harry's report, he'd guide on Harry's figures until the discrepancies could be resolved.

Harry became my primary source of advice on media maneuvers. And after that summer's trips to Israel, Rome, then Japan and China, when Harry covered the mayor's demanding pace for a total of over a month, up close, they had struck up a solid friendship which lasted for the rest of their lives—Harry Golden, Jr., died of cancer in May 1988, at the age of 60, a little more than five months after Harold Washington died.

They discovered they had a lot in common. The two World War II veterans were both sergeants—Harry outranked the mayor by one stripe. They were both salty, each in his own way. They were both literate, interested in the fine arts (Harry was an opera buff), but they both spoke accented, idiosyncratic English—Harry with what seemed to be a kind of Brooklynese from his native New York City, the mayor with his sometimes Mississippi-flavored South Side Chicago sound. Both were steeped in the nitty gritty of Chicago politics. They were both proud of their fathers: the late Harry Golden, Sr., had been the crusading editor and author of several best selling books, including *Only in America* and *For 2¢ Plain.* And both were complete originals, sure of their own identity, seemingly constitutionally unable to dissemble or disguise their true feelings when they spoke on any issue.

Harry would conspire with me to get the mayor committed to international trips. Each time we traveled, the bond of friendship between Harry and the mayor became stronger. And though Harry never compromised his standards to cut us any slack, he never took cheap shots either. As the mayor said all the time, "I'm not looking for any favors, I just want them to be fair." Harry was.

Steve Neal was a different story. Unlike Harry Golden, Neal was not the regular City Hall reporter. His beat was strictly political. There would be fewer opportunities for serendipity with Neal.

Still, I began with even more confidence about Neal than I had felt about Golden—not because I liked Neal (I hadn't met him) but because unlike Golden, he had come recommended. Only the mayor had problems with him.

Steve Neal had written a Sunday piece "clarifying" Sneed's Vrdolyak tapes story, showing how it had been way off point. To me, his article lent credibility to those who advised Steve was a reporter from whom we could expect a fair shake.

At the same time, I saw that the more the mayor fumed about that phone call, the angrier he got. He seemed convinced that there had been an attempt to "play me for a fool," but frustrated because he couldn't figure out what kind of fool. "All I know is that Neal was calling as part of the *Tribune's* legal protection," the mayor repeated several times that first week. "He was calling me for some lawyer in the room with him. I know it." It was as if that action was the final piece in the mayor's Steve Neal puzzle.

When Neal called to introduce himself, I was genuinely curious. This would be a test of the advice I'd been getting—from Ware, from Boyer, and from the mayor himself. Neal opened by telling me that he had an informal standing appointment with the mayor, usually in the third week of each month, when he would come in and talk to the mayor in his office, and get a story that would help put the administration across.

Sounded great to me. It jibed with the advice from Brian Boyer, that "a talk with Steve Neal in advance of the Sunday deadlines guarantees headlines." I tentatively scheduled a session with Neal for the mayor, the first interview that I had booked with a reporter.

I spoke with the mayor about it the next morning, as we went over my checklist in the limo on the way to City Hall. "I've scheduled the interview with Steve Neal for this week," I offered.

He was slightly nonplussed. Perhaps we'd spoken about an interview, and he'd forgotten about it.

"What's it about?" he asked.

"It's the monthly interview," I said, "for a Sunday piece." The mayor was perplexed but giving me the benefit of the doubt.

"What are we going to talk about?" he asked. It was my turn to be confused. I repeated what Neal had told me about his monthly arrangement with the mayor.

"That's bullshit," the mayor said. "I won't ever make any media arrangements that I don't check with you first. Never pay attention to people who say they're speaking for me."

I couldn't comprehend such a total misunderstanding—surely Neal hadn't simply fabricated the whole thing? Maybe Neal had been told by someone in the press office, before I arrived, that they were setting up such an arrangement?

I didn't look forward to telling him the interview was off—and that the "standing appointment" was not to be. I missed a breakfast I had scheduled with Neal, but when we finally did get together, we had what I thought was a good first conversation. I bit the bullet and told him candidly that the mayor was not aware of any arrangement.

He didn't seem upset. I was surprised and pleased by his equanimity; there was no further discussion of an interview (in fact I can't remember his ever having a one-on-one with the mayor though he did talk to him on the phone for one story).

Instead, to my surprise, Neal seemed to want to talk about me. He wanted to know how I'd been hired, something about my background. Did I like my job? He was clearly drawing me out, but I had no reason not to be candid with him. It was a strange interview, but, I thought, a good way to begin what would certainly be a long professional relationship.

I had had nothing but good luck with arts reporters, in Chicago as well as in Washington. I had no reason not to have confidence in my own good nature and reputation for honesty, the goodwill of reporters, and the fact that I would be learning quickly. I was completely open with him, responding to questions both professional and personal. I was hopeful and confident that we were forging a working relationship.

I didn't get to know much about him. I had expected to encounter the assertive character that his columns reflected; with a clerical tendency in his writing to catalog facts as though he were writing a list; a forced wit that didn't try for humor but did leaven his material a little.

Instead he came across as a weak type, rubber-chicken handshake, fleshy countenance, flaccid expression. I had seen that pallid presence sometimes in the theater world—an actor or ballet dancer who is strong in a macho role on stage, can be colorless without the make-up and trappings of performance. That was the impression Neal left with me.

But I didn't see the reprehensible character that the mayor had described. At worst, Neal had exaggerated the frequency with which he met with Harold Washington, or perhaps the mayor had forgotten that they'd *talked* about setting up a routine. Or perhaps Neal had been told by someone else that it was being worked out. I made my internal excuses for him, and continued to work on setting up an interview.

The next time we got to talk at any length was at the *Chicago Tribune*'s hospitality suite at the Washington, D.C., Hilton, following the annual White House Correspondents' Dinner. Neal had hoped the mayor would pay a visit there, but I hadn't been able to convince him —after dinner he'd gone back to his hotel suite for the night; he was probably playing poker with Saffold.

That was the last time I talked to Neal. But I did continue to make his case to the mayor. I suggested that even if he thought Neal were tainted by Coffey's maverick press activities—one of his objections to me was, "Coffey's always trying to get me to see him"—Neal still seemed a natural resource for us to develop. We should overlook the problems I'd inherited, treat my advent as a fresh page, start all over.

The mayor wasn't convinced, and there was no Harry Golden-type opportunity that might spark a rapprochement.

In fact, what I did accomplish was to cause the mayor to wonder whether I was falling into the Coffey orbit. The mayor's top staff was unsettled. Bill Ware was away more and more often, his health failing. Finally he disappeared altogether for a few days, and when we finally heard from him it was to learn that he was very ill, in a New York hospital, with an immune system-related disease.

The mayor was under a lot of pressure, including a vocal reaction from cabinet members to deputy chief of staff Ernie Barefield who was taking over Ware's functions. Some days it seemed the mayor's cabinet was splitting along racial lines. Had I picked sides? Was I gravitating toward a power center? Whose side was I on? I was aware, as I watched the mayor work with aldermen, advisors, even some of his aides, that he was constantly judging, evaluating, considering. It was a preoccupation of his career field, I was learning. It was disconcerting when I felt those calculating eyes on me.

I was still on trial. Not so much for my professional abilities; the mayor had no complaints, and he would be patient, in any case. I was on trial as to my loyalties. "Enemies" were everywhere, not just those who tried to undermine the mayor, but also those who were faint of heart, who paid lip service to his policies, but then developed nagging problems with his corporation counsel, or his deputy chief, or his chief of staff. All three were black men. When these problems arose among white aides, were they in fact subtly or not so subtly racially tinged? What about those white advisers who kept urging him to play more to the white lakefront and less to his black base? Was their advice valid or was it colored by their own biases? Whose side was I on?

As complacent as Harold Washington could be, and as indifferent to his personal safety or his material comforts, he could also be fiercely defensive. Sometimes he saw the universe as a we-vs.-they world. Like every great transitional figure, he had one foot planted firmly in the old environment from which he was pulling the rest of us through; and only one-half of Harold Washington was in the new environment he was trying to bring forth.

Even neutrals were suspect. Was I we? or they? Whose side was I on?

Steve Neal himself came to the rescue a few weeks later, with a scathing article about me that the mayor called "a first rate hatchet job." Unprovoked, and irrelevant to the events of the day, it ran in the *Trib* only after it had finally become clear to Neal that I wasn't having any success getting him and the mayor together.

The article was filled with half-truths and untruths, and even a few accuracies. Everything was pitched and colored to embarrass me or to question my character and credentials. Much of the material came from the candid conversations I'd had with Neal. While he was massaging me for those confidences, he had been storing up material for later use.

The *Tribune* article read:

> In his midterm report, Mayor Harold Washington brags about his efforts to open city government.
>
> But the mayor's new press secretary, Alton Miller, prefers to do things the old-fashioned way. He is attempting to reduce the flow of information from City Hall by borrowing techniques that are a throwback to the Watergate era.
>
> Miller, 41, former managing director of the Chicago City Ballet, is the weirdest press secretary since President Richard Nixon tapped Ronald Ziegler, a onetime Disneyland "Jungle Boat" guide, as his White House flack.
>
> By his own admission, Miller doesn't know very much about politics or the local news media, and sometimes he even is confused about where he lives. In a Channel 2 interview, he referred to himself as a "North Shore liberal," but then corrected himself and said that he is a resident of Chicago.
>
> In Miller's first appearance at a press conference, he announced that the mayor wouldn't take any questions. During subsequent mayoral appearances, Miller has scolded reporters for having the effrontery to ask questions about something beyond the scope of the afternoon's press release. Nor did Miller help his credibility by challenging news reports that turned out to be accurate about a Chicago City Council hearing.
>
> Even so, Miller claims he was born to be the mayor's press spokesman. Miller, whose trademark is a pair of designer sunglasses he wears on top of his head, modestly describes himself as a "celebrity" by virtue of his appointment to the $60,000-a-year job as chief of the nation's largest mayoral press office.
>
> The former ballet executive has 13 people working for him, which is two more assistants than White House press spokesman Larry Speakes is allotted. Mayor Richard Daley had a press staff of eight, and Los Angeles Mayor Tom Bradley has only three press aides.
>
> Miller did wonders for the morale of his office by publicly suggesting that some of his employees were guilty of subterfuge and disloyalty. He says that his new job is a lot like the theater, and his performance last week was right out of "The Caine Mutiny." In a May 1 memorandum to his staff that was made public last week, Miller threatened to

fire employees for attempting to be helpful to the press, and he imposed a gag rule.

"Information is our stock in trade, and if you give it away, you're stealing from the company," he told his staff.

Miller, who likes to see himself on television, declared that nobody but himself or his chief deputy is authorized to talk with reporters. Because the No. 2 slot is vacant, he has center stage all to himself.

On routine matters, "Stonewall Miller" has demanded that his staffers provide him with detailed transcripts of their conversations with reporters. If Miller keeps it up, he may soon have everyone in his office hooked up to polygraph machines.

At the same time, Miller is restricting access to top city officials. Last week, when City Hall correspondents phoned corporation counsel James Montgomery and the acting director of the Purchasing Department, Bill Spicer, they were referred to Miller.

Unhappily enough, Miller often is about as easy to find as Judge Crater. Even during his rare appearances in his office, Miller is unavailable to staffers and reporters. His associates have complained about his secretive demeanor and his habit of locking himself in his office. Gladys Lindsay, his former deputy, reportedly quit because Miller acted as if she were his secretary. Two other highly respected assistants, Chris Chandler and Dennis Church, also recently moved out.

Miller has direct access to the mayor but is aloof from Washington's other senior aides, according to administration officials. He also is negligent about returning their phone calls. David Axelrod, political advisor to U.S. Sen. Paul Simon, twice attempted to phone Miller as a professional courtesy. Miller never responded.

A survey of City Hall and political reporters gave Miller low marks for returning phone calls and showing up for appointments. It's nothing personal. Miller doesn't answer the phone for their editors, either.

One of Miller's problems is that he is attempting to do too many things at once. In addition to serving as the mayor's spokesman, Miller has become the chief speechwriter (the "resident playwright," in his words), advance man and traveling companion. Whatever Miller's shortcomings in dealing with the press, Washington is pleased with his new aide's briefing papers and speeches.

Although the mayor has been color-blind in his appointments to the press office, Miller recently confided that he is planning to use affirmative-action quotas in replacing some of his employees. Miller, who is white, said he wants to name black and Hispanic deputies, and that he has specific quotas for minorities and women.

Some critics have suggested that Miller is having problems because of inexperience. But, according to some of those who worked with him previously, Miller's performance is an encore of his brief term with the ballet here. Before quitting under fire, Miller purged the staff, ran his office behind closed doors, and left the ballet company with a $750,000 debt.

While Miller says that every day in his new job is like opening night at the theater, it could be a short season unless the imperial press secretary calls off the search for the strawberries.

Needless to add, I'd never experienced anything like it. Even with the mayor chuckling about it, and even with my own determination to let the story roll off without effect, I had to admit the shock was breathtaking.

The mayor gave me some perspective when he joked, "Welcome to the club. The *Trib* is one of the biggest-circulation newspapers in the country. Most people live their whole lives with no more than a dozen people ever seeing them get trashed like he trashed you."

Today the long article devoted to me, along with the editorial cartoons that Jack Higgins did in the *Sun-Times,* are among my framed mementoes. As the mayor said, with that wicked grin, "When you get a column like that, you've come of age."

The real reason for the mayor's relieved cheerfulness was that the article made it clear that I hadn't been co-opted into any faction. He no longer wondered whether my attempts to develop an inside vantage for Steve Neal had ulterior motives. At the time I was annoyed by what I detected to be a certain pleasure on the mayor's part that I had been bloodied. But in retrospect I owe a debt of thanks to Neal, who solidified my position at a time when it still hadn't gelled.

Golden and Neal were among several reporters who had become personal priorities, diversions in the great game. The real challenges, however, were more complex.

From our very first meeting, Mayor Washington and I were engaged in an almost continuous discussion of his game plan for promoting reform, a conversation that continued to the day he died. Every day our discussion on this subject resumed afresh. It flowed around other events, continued in the limousine between stops, got us started every morning and sometimes concluded for the day in a late telephone conversation. Often we were on the same wavelength, in easy agreement; but just as often it was a debate, or at least a Socratic examination of the issue.

Loosely, the subject was the role of the media in the development of his programs, subdivided into dozens of facets: from discussions of individual reporters to generalities about the "unarticulated premises" of the media.

Our continuous conversation sharpened at times, and one such occasion was when he took me to a meeting of his "kitchen cabinet."

Actually, the mayor had a number of "kitchen cabinets," loosely scheduled rap sessions with various collections of old friends or more recent supporters. Long-time friend Dempsey Travis recalls that he participated in a "living room cabinet" of four or five that would meet at the mayor's apartment periodically, to share their advice. Other informal groups met at the mayor's apartment from time to time, and he was always available by telephone. After his death we learned that so many of these advisers had met with or spoken with Mayor Washington so many times that their cumulative hours with him outnumbered splinters from the True Cross.

This "kitchen cabinet," however, was more formal in its organization. Delores Woods coordinated its dinner meeting on the second Wednesday of every month.

The mayor almost always did these alone. Before I knew better, I considered it a compliment that I was being asked to come. "Barefield came to one and they grilled him on his management," the mayor had said when he asked me to reserve the time. "They'll want to find out what you plan for the press office." In a careless moment once before, he had mentioned something about how they didn't have a political bone in their bodies, but they meant well.

Now that we were on our way there, he was warning me, with a half smile, that they were "going to do a job on you." He told me that I would be best advised to follow his lead, to listen, and keep my cool.

Although some of these folks were people who also worked with him on current issues, like Al Johnson and Clark Burrus, or people on whom he relied for fundraising advice, like Jacoby Dickens and Bill Berry, I had somehow gotten the strong impression that as members of his key financial support group, most of them were there because they had been offered these monthly sessions as a donor's perk.

My relationship with most of them was dicey. Some of the white advisers there seemed to consider Harold Washington their creation.

They, and some of the blacks, were defending him as "just as good as Mayor Bradley of Los Angeles," whenever they felt he needed defending. And simultaneously trying to make him more like Bradley, whatever that meant. Some cited Bradley by name as an example toward which to aspire. I was courted by these folks, who were disappointed when they learned that I wasn't among those who believed the mayor needed to be protected from himself.

They saw me as unwelcome reinforcement to certain bad tendencies in the mayor's personality, such as a ready willingness to confront rather than charm.

And there were black advisers who seemed to believe I had somehow hoodwinked the mayor—or who thought I was a necessary evil, made necessary by the greater evil of the white major media which I would somehow be controlling if I was worth anything at all. He had told me that he had been under a lot of pressure to hire a black, and in fact that issue had delayed replacing my predecessor by many weeks. "Tom Todd and the 'black nationalists' think everybody in my cabinet should be black," he said, referring to a well-known black lawyer and activist. But there were no "black nationalists" at the board table as his group sat down, and I wasn't sure why the mayor had warned me to keep my temper and listen.

These sessions, the mayor told me, started with general table talk, and then got down to a more stuctured agenda. I should come prepared for a 10–15 minute verbal presentation. The discussion would be led by one of the mayor's leading supporters, the distinguished Edwin C. "Bill" Berry, a Chicago business leader who was revered as a civil rights leader for his lifetime of commitment.

The other participants represented the mayor's bankroll and, to some extent his brain trust. On the one hand, Mayor Washington never trusted any but his own brains; on the other, he was willing to listen to anybody. But it became clear to me, from his patience and even deference as the discussion unfolded, that he treated this group with respect.

This assemblage, he had said, could give him a feel for how he was playing in the upper middleclass, black and white (no Latinos were present). He had plenty of other input from other sectors of society, but he needed this group's feedback. He wasn't merely going through the motions. Besides, the subject they wanted to deal with tonight—the mayor's press office—was of constant interest to him.

The unstructured dinner conversation set the tone: general agreement that the mayor's "image" needed professional attention. The particulars were scattershot, and represented a variety of different sentiments. While the mayor agreed easily that he had to "come across as a statesman," and that he should "avoid getting down in the gutter with Vrdolyak," he mildly reminded them that he couldn't simply roll over when attacked.

As the dinner dishes were removed, Berry began to focus the discussion. They wanted to start with a description of what I had in store for the press office. What does a press secretary do, someone asked, and how does it help the mayor's image?

I was determined to keep my cool. But I knew I wasn't going to make them happy with my approach. I wasn't interested in talking about the mayor's "image." There were two general areas where we needed a lot of work; both were equally important; neither was directed at creating an "image."

First, we needed organization, good management, a "systems approach" to the promotion of the mayor's accomplishments, and clarity on the rationale behind each of his actions. That implied we needed clarity on the overall administration, not just the press office agenda, but I didn't belabor that point. I was keeping my cool.

Second, we needed to change attitudes and orientations, about the mayor and his administration, and the importance of his reform agenda. We had to change public attitudes, and media attitudes, but we also had to change our own heads. We had to improve internal morale. The mayor himself had to operate from an attitude of confidence and optimism.

These were real objectives, substantive, not imaginary. I wasn't interested in improving the mayor's "image," I thought his "style" was just fine the way it was, and I didn't think he should worry about such cosmetics either.

What does a press secretary do?

The press secretary operates on three levels, as an aide, a cabinet member, and a department head. The principal function is that of a direct personal adviser to the mayor. When the monthly *Chicago Lawyer* created its annual "Who's Who at City Hall" in the spring of 1985, and wanted an organization chart to show the hierarchy, the mayor wanted to take a personal look at what Bill Ware planned to give them. He pulled my name out of the line-up of cabinet officers and made a box up alongside the box with his name in it—above the chief of staff and all the others. He drew a line from "mayor" directly to "press secretary." That's the way it was printed, a misleading diagram that might be understood to indicate a priority in the ranks rather than a direct line of communication. His graphic statement meant, of course, that the line of communication was unbuffered, direct.

I explained that as a principal aide, I had a responsibility for hands-on intervention at the point news was being made, as well as a role in the general planning. I made a point of being with him, seven days a week, as many hours as necessary, whenever he might be intercepted by the press. Like any other personal aide, I worked to help keep our priorities clear, present immediate options for each new situation, evaluate them against new information or changing circumstances—often in the limousine as we approached the next event, often by telephoning from the car to my office or to a trusted reporter, often by speechwriting in plain block letters, in outline form, on cards that would cue the mayor at the podium within minutes of their composition.

Chuck Kelly also rode with us, and performed even more essential services. He was dealing with the other aspect of the mayor's appearances as he criss-crossed the city: while I was solely concerned with press and public reaction, he dealt with the private side. Wherever the mayor went, he would be approached by someone. It might be a banker, or an unemployed woman on the street. The mayor would refer the person to Kelly, who would get a name and number or, if we were in a hurry, hand them a business card. After a day of traveling with the mayor, Kelly spent an equal amount of time following up on the petitioners, screening requests, deciding which could be referred to departments and which needed the mayor's attention. The press secretary, in that same sense, was a personal aide. From the mayor's standpoint, if I could perform only one function it would be that.

But I had a second role as a member of the cabinet. That is, I had an interactive role to play with other department heads and top aides. Under Ware's, and then Barefield's, direction, the cabinet had a role to play independent of the separate jobs each cabinet member had. We were the administration. We had to have our act together. Streets and San needed to know what Public Works was doing, not just on the street but in the decision-making sessions. And the press office needed to know all about it too, preferably before it showed up in the newspaper. Barefield managed by consensus, which meant a heavy dependency on meetings among all the principals. My role as a cabinet member and colleague of these line officers also meant a rapid call from them every time they got wind of a story that was about to break in their department; and every time they had a program that would soon be announced. Our rule of thumb was that the mayor announced the good news—the new library, the street construction program, the opening of shelters and warming centers in the late fall, an improvement in the crime stats—and the department head got to announce the bad news—a library construction slowdown, street cave-ins, crime stats that didn't look so good. Everyone understood I could be called at any hour, home, office, beeper, car, whenever a problem was discovered or a story was breaking.

Thirdly, I was a department head myself. The press office was something of a misnomer, because only I and my deputy press secretary, under normal circumstances, really dealt directly with the press.

Ninety-five percent of the press office's job was to prepare briefings for the mayor. For every event there was a top sheet, usually two or three pages, of who-what-where-when, which was useful to the security detail as well as the mayor; there was a section that outlined the issues that might arise, ward specifics, background on the people involved; and there were prepared remarks. We gradually improved the remarks to the point that the mayor received both an outline and a complete text. I believed he was much more effective when he spoke straight from the shoulder, using an outline as a guide, rather than when he read his remarks. I also knew that my staff would prepare more focused remarks if they outlined them first. On a busy day the mayor's briefing packet—a separate set went to me, to Delores, to Chuck Kelly, to the security detail—would be as thick as a suburban phone book. He was supposed to receive the materials 48 hours in advance, but in practice he generally got the packet the night before the events scheduled. As a practical matter, that was the only time he could focus on the next day, anyway. Material received the day of an event was almost useless—there was never enough time between events to bone up on the issues involved, and if he didn't study it the night before he would have to wing it on site.

We also prepared a packet of press releases and news items, and photographs from the mayor's photographers, and mailed them once a week to the small newspapers and selected civic leaders. The mailing, including the creation of the mailing list and the cultivation of materials from the many that circulated in the press office each week, were the responsibility of one person, Pat Michalski. The mayor had directed me to hire her, the only time he or anyone told me whom I had to hire. I had stalled, not having time to properly interview her, and he cut through the crap, signed her up and sent her to me. Along with Tumia Romero, my secretary, she was the most productive person in the office, and the most loyal to Harold Washington.

Explaining the press office to the kitchen cabinet, I told them what they already knew. It had been a mess when I arrived. We had weeded out employees who owed no allegiance to the mayor, and replaced them with good people. We weren't where I wanted to be, but we were on our way there.

There were 14 people in the press office. That included three clerical people, my deputy and myself, Michalski and one staff member who was assigned to technical TV and broadcast operations, helping with press conferences, creating public service announcements, and recording news clips. The other seven press aides worked on preparation of the mayor's daily briefings.

I planned to change the system without expanding the staff: depend more on material from the line departments, with only three briefers employed in the editing process; and put the other four press aides into a "News Team."

The "News Team" would work together with public information officers from every department, to get our story out. That effort would begin with an institutionalized, systematic, day-by-day process of determining exactly what our story would be. If we were going to try to influence the media, we had to behave like the media, in our planning.

I said that the kitchen cabinet could grasp what I was trying to do if they would imagine a daily newspaper and TV program coming out of City Hall with all the lead stories and human interest features and economic news chosen to communicate the accomplishments of the Washington administration. Daily exposure of progress, department by department, with the mayor tied in prominently wherever it was appropriate.

To exaggerate only a little, just like a newspaper we would have daily planning sessions where we'd talk about how much space to allocate to each story; we would decide what pictures should be played, which on the front page, which inside. We would plan ahead, for continuing series and related followups and features. We'd write the editorials and we'd even block in the letters to the editor. Because we were producing an imaginary TV news show as well, we would determine which stories should get special visual treatment, both in choice of location and in prepared graphics for press conferences. And we'd decide which sound bites would work best for the 15–30 second attention span to which the public has become accustomed.

The only difference between what we would do, and the real thing, would be that we would not own our own studios or printing presses. Our objective would be to take this "ideal" news output and get the major media to do it for us, through our choice of releases, leaks, press conferences, on-site events, in-depth cultivation of specialist reporters—a full tool kit of PR devices.

Planning this pro-active effort was to be the work of the "News Team." Now we were in the process of dividing the PR pie several different ways. First, we'd create a grid based on constituency groups: we'd look at every major constituency or interest group in Chicago and target each with information important to them.

Second, we would look at the city geographically, and use both the ward maps (for coordination with aldermen) and individual neighborhood maps (for more meaningful interaction with people at the level where they lived, shopped, played, went to school), and make sure that the city was covered.

Third, we would create a grid based on the current issues: since these would change, we would use the administration's division of city departments into five sub-cabinets as our guideline. Thus one person would have responsibility for issues that would be loosely grouped around Police, Fire and Safety; another for Human Services issues, including the Department of Health, and DHS; another for Economic Development, including the Planning Department.

This approach tended to be comprehensive, rather than selective—an organizing principle for the bureaucracy of PR. These procedures would guide the press office in its daily work, under the supervision of my deputy, while I concentrated on the "point of sale"—the news generated by the mayor's own contact with the press—in my capacity as a personal aide.

The kitchen cabinet listened with interest to my description of the press office. For all their concern about the mayor's treatment in the media, it was clear they'd never focused on exactly what it was that the Mayor's Press Office did.

But ultimately they weren't interested in "process." What they wanted to talk about was "product"—the mayor's "image," and the need to improve it. The conversation that followed was no more focused than our earlier dinner conversation had been. There were no specific recommendations, just complaints.

The mayor should be less combative, they said. He shouldn't be drawn into fights with the Eddies. He should be more statesmanlike, more mayoral.

I was keeping my cool, but I was frustrated with the conversation. They were making dinner conversation of a subject I had been living with, obsessed with, for weeks. This wasn't a professional analysis we were enduring, it was a gripe session.

The mayor was the one who was losing a little of his cool, I thought, as they continued to comment on his behavior. He was certainly open to specific recommendations, but he grew increasingly irritated by the generalities they were offering. Don't tell me not to fight, he said. There was no way he could avoid a conflict. He came into this job to fight. When Vrdolyak gave up trying to take charge, the fight could end—but it wouldn't end with Mayor Washington rolling over; and that included so-called "compromising."

"You can't compromise on these issues," he said. "That's not compromise, that's selling out."

One growl and they backed off. It was no fun telling the mayor that he should try harder to be something he was not; once again, they directed their complaints to me.

We had to stop reacting, and begin to "get our story out." Mayor Washington had accomplished much, but who knew it?

I tried to reply at several junctures. In fact, I said, many people knew it. Pat Michalski sowed our releases, and she reaped bushels of clippings. She gleaned the community papers every day, and she gave the mayor a ream of xeroxed articles as thick as a telephone book, every week. What they were really talking about, I suggested, was the mayor's treatment by the major media, which was all they ever saw. That was a separate, more complex issue.

"In the real world, we'll never have any ultimate control of the media," I said. "We'll never succeed in 'getting our story out' to our complete satisfaction." That wouldn't be possible unless we really did publish our own paper, or unless we spent a lot of money on paid media. Although we were in fact planning to print our own Mid-Term Report, and we were talking about a TV message to explain the budget and the G.O. bonds, as a practical matter, paid media on a continuing basis was beyond our means.

Anyone who has ever done PR is painfully familiar with the tendency to blame public relations for all the problems of an organization. We're doing our job, the reasoning goes, but our story's not getting out.

I had experienced that sentiment before this meeting, of course, but now I was getting it from the mayor's kitchen cabinet. My cool was slipping.

Finally, from the respected Bill Berry, came the comment: No reflection on you, Miller, but we believe the mayor needs professional help, professional skills, a flat out Madison Avenue approach to improve his image.

Trying not to sound sarcastic, I agreed that this wasn't something we could leave to the amateurs.

"People who wouldn't try to tell a short-order cook how to do his job, will rush to tell a PR man what he's doing wrong, and what's not getting done," I said.

One thing I had learned about PR in the last 20 years, I told them, was "the better you are, the more you realize what you could be doing that you aren't." Especially with additional staff, additional time, additional money, there was an unlimited scope for new efforts. "The better you are, the less likely you are to be satisfied with progress to date," I said. "It's an occupational hazard."

And when you're working for a guy who deserves the absolute best, a good press secretary is in a ticklish spot: would I claim that no one could do it better? No, I wouldn't.

So if the mayor felt he needed advice from a professional PR agency, I said, I knew he'd let me know. In the meantime, I said, the press office would focus on the process I'd described, without reference to the mayor's "image."

The conversation drew to a close. I was thanked for coming, and excused.

I was glad to get the hell out of there, but disturbed by what I'd experienced. It was the first time I'd been put in the boxing arena with the mayor sitting ringside and watching, making only occasional comments. Did he agree with them? Was he somehow cowed by them? Was this his way of letting me know there would be changes in the press office set-up, which so many had lobbied for?

I was appalled to think that this group could be formative in his thinking. I felt their concerns were cliche and superficial; if that was true in my field, what about the other advice they gave? Did he go for it? Did he genuinely respect their insights and opinions?

I asked him that the next day. I groped for a way to raise the question. He made it easy, by bringing it up.

"Well, what did you think?" he asked the next morning, when I met him at the limo in Hyde Park.

"That was a real experience," I said, shaking my head.

He was bemused. "They're right about the PR," he said. "We need someone to come in and sell us," he said. "We need to get our story out. That's not something the press secretary should be worrying about."

That was a new thought to me. That's precisely what the press secretary should be worrying about, I would have thought.

"You put it very well last night. The press secretary is an aide," he said. "You have to stay on top of the issues, you have to be a spokesman. Someone else has to take care of the hucksterism. Otherwise you'll lose credibility."

But I wasn't satisfied. "Mayor, when they talk about 'image making,' whatever the hell that is, they're talking about classic marketing —where one of your basic options is to change the product. That's not what we're about."

It was an important point for me. "What we're talking about is going to take a long time to accomplish. Gimmicks and trade secrets aren't going to do it. We're talking about a sea change," I said.

We had pulled up at City Hall, and his detail had opened the door for him, but he waved it closed, as he often did when we were in conversation. He had been looking at the morning's briefing while we talked, and now he peered over his glasses at me.

"I don't disagree with what you're saying," he said. "But we need to get our story out, period. When they got off on this image-making business, they were criticizing me, not you, because they want me to fit their mold.

"We're going to do what we're going to do, period. That's just the way it is. But if they tell me they know how to get our story out, I want to hear what they have to say."

He held my attention for a moment, to be sure the point had sunk in. I didn't agree with what he was saying, but I understood that he intended to reassure me.

By acceding to their recommendations, he confirmed the practice of hiring gaggles of private contractors doing occasional PR for various departments. He also set in motion a long, sputtering, start-and-stop attempt to organize what would ultimately become the "Communications Work Group." Reporting to Barefield, with the mission to "get our story out," they prepared a brochure on "Women in Government" that was never released because they left some women out; they published a "City Hall Style Book" dealing with capitalization of official titles and punctuation; they sought to organize groundbreakings and ribbon-cutting events which the mayor was sometimes able to attend; and they wrote speeches for Barefield. From time to time a reporter would discover the group and write an article about how the Mayor's Press Office—with which the Communications Work Group had no connection—was using personnel who were supposed to be working in other departments. But the group's biggest problem was the lassitude suffered by talented people with nothing meaningful to do.

In the real world of government bureaucracy, the "Communications Work Group" was inevitable, whether or not it was redundant. If the mayor's press secretary was to report directly to the mayor, and if the Mayor's Press Office were to be closely directed by the press secretary, then the bureaucracy headed by Barefield would have to get its *own* press office. Even though the last thing the mayor wanted was an independent press operation.

When Mayor Washington finally focused on the consequences of his earlier ambivalence, he ordered the unit closed down, with its employees reporting to me, and directed Barefield to stay out of PR. But in the meantime, for about a year and a half, they were an institutionalized expression of the kitchen cabinet's concern for the mayor's image.

Despite his willingness to give it a hearing, Mayor Washington never really took any interest in image cosmetics. The closest he came was when he was dressed up and photographed for campaign posters in the 1987 election, and when he allowed the "master debaters" to domesticate him for the mayoral debates.

By the last year of his life he had definitively decided against working on his image. For that matter, he had stopped going to monthly meetings with the "kitchen cabinet."

7

Mindset

The mayor didn't need an "image." He needed a "mindset." A comprehensive concept which he could use as a wrapper for the cluster of issues we were facing that spring.

This general "mindset" he was reaching for was analogous to the more specific "mindset" he wanted for every event he attended.

Clarification of a mindset for every situation freed Harold Washington to be Harold Washington, whatever the issue. Going down into a warming shelter to meet with homeless men and women and the volunteers who help them, or going into a 54th floor business breakfast with Chicago's captains of industry, he would ask—usually in the car just before we arrived, having digested all the pages of briefing materials—"What's my mindset here?"

A simple action statement, a succinct recap of those briefings into an immediate direction, would be all he needed to focus him fully on the issue at hand. Then he could put away the briefing papers, keeping only the remarks. The data he had absorbed would flow easily into his conversation, following his pursuit of ideas as they arose—ideas from a homeless woman or from a CEO—without the encumbrance of a formally prepared position. As he spoke, events from his childhood might be mixed with research from the Health Department, an anecdote from the U.S. Congress, or his (usually utilitarian) avocational reading at home—maybe Robert A. Caro's *The Power Broker* or Sen. Paul Simon's *Let's Put America Back to Work*. Not only did it get him started, not only did it free him to follow his own instincts as the event unfolded, the mindset also gave him a summation, a point at which, when he had arrived he would be able to conclude a matter coherently.

He had no lack of structured agendas, but he wanted to bring a consistency—his own personality—to every issue. What he called the "mindset" was the device that allowed him to do that.

The mindset would be developed late in the game; I asked my staff to introduce briefing papers with a topic sentence that clearly stated a reason for the event: a one-line answer to the question, "What am I doing here?" But that theme was only a guide to a mindset. The mindset itself had to be more current even than a briefing prepared the day before.

Finding (or capturing) a mindset was not always easy. The mayor's face could wrinkle in rejection of a mindset that seemed foreign to his nature, or of a mindset that didn't ring right with his current mood and tempo. No one ever could know all that he was simultaneously balancing—the need for a meeting with the Governor, or last weekend's rap session with Uptown activist Slim Coleman, or this morning's meeting with black ministers that had provided some new ideas. And a mindset was useless—it wasn't even a mindset—if he had not made it completely his own.

Sometimes he went in cold, read the material, and made his escape; or went in winging it and played off the feedback he found there. Or he settled on a suggested mindset close enough to spin off of. And of course, even without the comfort of a mindset, from the standpoint of others present he gave it his all. But he was most comfortable when we "put our finger on it," even if it was only with a single word, and gave the event relevance to the continuing cumulative developments of the day, the week, the agenda.

In performance, the difference was the gap between a dry, often hesitating reading of a prepared text, sometimes only partly audible, on the one hand; and on the other, the force of his own ideas, phrased in his own words—a difference familiar to every reporter who covered him, and to most TV viewers who lived in Chicago between 1983 and 1987.

He was a student of public administration and management; he surrounded himself with "process" people like Bill Ware and Ware's deputy Ernie Barefield; he was faithful to their plans and organization tables; he had a healthy respect for the bureaucracy even when it was frustrating. Our conversation about press office management was usually "process" talk, centered on his "agendas" (for public policy) and "themes" (for corresponding public relations initiatives). But beyond all that, the "mindset" was something personal and specific to each event.

Now he was trying to find an overarching mindset—a through-line

—to provide perspective for all his public activities in the third year of his first term.

He mentioned one cold morning that it was a good day for bad news. I asked what he meant.

"Mayors get blamed for the weather," he said. "It's subconscious, but it works. People are down, they're in a bad mood, and they're looking for someone to blame it on. This would be a good day for Eddie to come up with a hit on us."

I forget whether Eddie did. There was a hit from one Eddie or the other nearly every day, so the weather really wouldn't have made that much difference. Anyway, as I would come to learn, both sides attributed much more planning to their opponent's maneuvers than actually ever was there. Most of the time we were all improvising. Only the fact that our motivations stayed consistent created the illusion of true strategy.

But he caught my attention when he said it was a good day for bad news. Because what he was saying had a flip side. Spring was just around the corner. If mayors tend to bear the blame for bad weather —and, for that matter, in some measure take the rap when our sports teams falter—then why not take credit for spring?

If you've never celebrated April and May in Chicago you don't know the essence of spring. After months of wind, rain and cold, and well past the time you've seen spring weather on the newscasts from other parts of the country, suddenly there are the first buds on the branches, the first brave sails on the lake, the first bold colors and long legs of springtime fashion on the sidewalks. The energies of a metropolis, contained and channeled into the work of surviving the winter, break loose in those first (often false) days of spring, and blow a fresh spirit across the city. Why not take credit for those good feelings? It was clear that we needed a new tone, a new mood to get us out of the rut of "Council Wars." I was looking for a new spirit of optimism, both for internal morale and for external perceptions. Why not a "New Spirit of Chicago"?

A "New Spirit" could address another need, as well. Mayor Washington had been looking for a phrase, a concept, that would supersede the notion of "reform." Reform was the technical term, but he needed a new leitmotif. He wasn't looking for a synonym, he was looking for a shift in emphasis.

The notorious alderman Paddy Bauler said it first, but it has become a political mantra in our city: "Chicago ain't ready for reform."

Like the holy writ of other religions, in the politics of Chicago that line has been a comfort or a curse, depending on the needs of the devout. It's been used by the defenders of patronage to explain why things are and how they got that way and, by its detractors, to explain why they haven't been improved.

But if that notion once nourished a sardonic truth, by the 1980s it had become a dead husk. In a real sense, by the time Harold Washington came to the scene, Chicago *was* ready for reform. It had been ready for a long time.

The early 1980s, no less than the present times, were years of challenge for cities across the United States. The downward turn of the national economy and changing regional industrial patterns, coupled with the end of the federal partnership that had supported the cities' social and economic agendas, had drastically altered the fortunes of cities in the Midwest "Rust Belt." In Chicago, still politically torpid as the last great city to shuck its feudal Machine, the civic-minded were being rudely awakened from a long complacency.

Throughout the years of Mayor Richard J. Daley, as the steel mills closed down, as population began to decline, as public finance became overextended, Chicagoans had shrugged their big shoulders and ignored the warning signs. After all, the "Second City" was still the "City that Works." The "Boss" knew what he was doing, and every man and woman had a place within the Machine.

Yet we now know that the decades of the 1970s and 1980s were in fact years of economic decay. Shortly it would be revealed that Chicago wasn't even the second city any longer, as Los Angeles overtook us in population.

The end of complacency corresponded with a new awareness of Chicago's potential in the world marketplace, and the changes that would be necessary to realize it. The passing of Daley set the stage for the election of a reform mayor, America's first woman mayor of such a city as Chicago, the harbinger of a new era: Jane Byrne.

Chicago had made it clear that it was ready for reform. But there's another sense in which no one is ever ready.

Even Harold Washington tired of the word. Reform is not simply a condition of improvement. The verb requires an object, some would say a victim—something which must *be* "re-formed."

But people who might otherwise approve reform measures will resent being reformed. In Chicago, many of those who were losing their sense of security naturally blamed their new anxieties, not on the system that was failing them, but on the forces of reform that were coming into place. Daley had been deified; clearly, it was absence of Daley or the lack of whatever he had, that was behind our problems.

The conventional wisdom is that Jane Byrne betrayed her reform agenda when she turned City Council management over to the "evil cabal" against which she had campaigned.

Yet every mayor has two constituencies—the general electorate and the 50 members of the City Council. A slim majority of popular sentiment will get you elected, but in Chicago's "weak mayor, strong council" structure of government, your second constituency must still be reckoned with. She didn't have the votes there. In a practical political sense, Chicago wasn't ready for reform.

Harold Washington usually referred to Jane Byrne as a tragic figure. If she could have stuck to her guns, he said, he would never have been elected; he would never have been a candidate. After all, he supported her the first time around.

He wasn't being judgmental. She was more to be pitied than despised. She had been strong enough to win the office, but too weak to hold her own.

So Harold Washington saw himself as a reformer's reformer, and he tapped into a diverse reform constituency that had been developing throughout the neighborhoods of Chicago all during the manic-depressive administration of Jane Byrne.

He had mixed feelings when he talked about reform. When he was in full voice he would articulate the elements of a profound political and social change for Chicago. He wasn't kidding around.

But he tired of the sloganeering. Reform had become a code word for black patronage. It implied a set of standards which no one could codify, and yet everyone could measure him by. When all other epithets failed, he could be criticized for not being a total reformer. To him it was "the old double standard."

"I'm no Little Lord Fauntleroy," he said often. "You have to reward your friends and punish your enemies, or you can't hold your people together. And if you can't raise an average of $1,000 a day, every day of your life, you can't play in the major leagues of politics. But that doesn't mean you're untrue to reform."

While he was defending himself from the Eddies' charges that he was a phony reformer, and swatting back media stories that challenged the extent of his reform, he was simultaneously fighting a rearguard action in his own ranks.

"I've got five, ten, sometimes a dozen of my people down there," he meant the City Council, "who are giving me hell because I don't 'take it all.' They're telling me I'm crazy.

"I know what I'm doing. But they're giving me a hell of a time. Shit, half of them would be with Vrdolyak right now, if they didn't know their wards would kick their ass for it."

The solidarity of the movement, he said, had brought the black community together as a force stronger than anything else in politics, despite the inclinations of some of "his" aldermen. "If it wasn't for those ministers and those women out there, you sure as hell wouldn't see any '21' in City Council. Vrdolyak would be running the show.

"Yet and still, I'm accused of patronage, and starting my own Machine. It's insane."

There were so many fuzzy analogies drawn between the mayor's political organization and the old Machine that the mayor could be excused for believing the confusion to be willful.

Almost everyone who wrote about Chicago government or politics for a living not only ignored the distinctions that the mayor reiterated, time and time again—they also perpetuated the notion that Mayor Washington was just updating the evils of the past.

The fact is, the Machine was dead of natural causes. Harold Washington hadn't killed it, didn't claim he had. Patronage had dried up, and the Machine had atrophied.

Patronage and the Machine were mutually dependent. You couldn't have a Machine to organize your politics, without patronage to fuel it. And you couldn't have a system of patronage incentives and demerits governing your personnel system, without a Machine to perpetuate it.

U.S. Judge Nicholas Bua, in his 1979 Shakman decision, made the point (emphasis his):

> For a number of City jobs, persons normally can be hired only with regular Democratic *political sponsorship*. These include jobs with the

Department of Sanitation, the Building Department and the Bureau of Sewers.

Most of the City jobs for which such political preference is given are not policymaking or confidential in nature. These jobs include, without limitation, jobs as garbage collectors, building inspectors, street cleaners, clerks, technicians and supervisors.

The City often informs Democratic Party officials of City job openings of which public notice is not otherwise given. Persons applying for some City patronage jobs have been told by City officials that to get a job or learn about job openings the applicant must see the Democratic Party Ward Committeeman. Persons hired for City jobs with Democratic political sponsorship as described above do not have civil service, contractual or statutory protection against arbitrary discharge....

Usually, persons get sponsorship for a City, County, County officer, Park District, or Forest Preserve District job from a regular Democratic organization official either after having done or upon the expectation that they will do political precinct work (such as door to door canvassing, putting up posters, etc.) on behalf of candidates endorsed by the sponsor.

Once in awhile, in full flight at his rhetorical liveliest, Mayor Washington would chortle, "the Machine is dead, dead, dead. I killed it! I danced on its grave!" More often he would be more specific: "I didn't kill the Machine. The Machine would have been dead if I had never come along. The Machine died when the jobs ran out."

In fact, Harold Washington was not wholly opposed in principle to the "spoils system," as an American institution. Before it was clear that the Machine was obsolescent, cut off at the knees and bleeding to death, as a result of the Shakman decrees, he was arguing not that patronage should be ended, but that it should be more fairly distributed; and that the institutional corruption represented by the quid pro quos of patronage should be eliminated altogether.

But by the time he became mayor, the writing on the wall was in neon. Chicago had experienced 20 years of steady economic decline; that was worsened by a more general, nationwide economic slippage over the past decade; and it was further compounded by a gradual cutoff, beginning in the Carter presidency, of the federal funds that once poured into the big cities. Less money meant fewer jobs for mayors and party leaders to award for good service. In 1975, by Milton Rakove's estimate, there were some 30,000 political jobs. In 1983 when Washington took office, despite reform efforts there were over 42,000 city jobs—not counting the park district, county and other patronage positions—many of which were still subject to abuse despite court orders.

By this time Mayor Washington had embraced both the spirit and the letter of the Shakman decrees, and adhered to its premise: that only the top decision-making positions should be discretionary. He argued that he needed more such positions to manage well—he wanted professional administrators in the middle management positions, as well as at the top. His rationale was misrepresented as favoring a return to patronage—critics were even able to quote the "old" Harold Washington from years earlier.

As it turned out he made do with the 800 positions, which provided for department heads, their deputies and immediate staff, and the mayor's office itself. Every other job was protected civil service. By Rakove's 1975 estimate, the Machine could hardly run a ward with 800 patronage jobs, much less a city where all the middle management positions were unreconciled Byrne, Bilandic and Daley appointees.

Because the Machine was dysfunctional, active only at the ward level, and only in some wards, didn't mean that the various political camps didn't seek to create political organizations. Despite Will Rogers' famous disclaimer, all political parties, including progressive Democrats, are by definition organized—and Mayor Washington was concerned that the hodge-podge "movement" that supported him should benefit from improved political organization.

But he was frustrated by the superficial thinking that branded him a nonreformer because he was "setting up his own Machine." Pundits who wrote that were confusing political organization with the Machine structure of party politics and city management.

The mayor gave me a marked-up clipping from the *Sun-Times* of Sept. 7, 1986, the marginal notes reflecting his exasperation. No less a political expert than the *Sun-Times* political editor Basil Talbott had confused political organization with a Machine mentality, writing that the computerizing of the mayor's campaign office into "a new sophisticated organization. . . provides evidence that the mayor is turning his movement into a machine."

"No jobs!" the mayor had written in one margin. "Basil knows the difference," he complained. "You see how they have to 'balance'?— they just can't stand it if they think I'm really going to do it straight, what the others could only do crooked."

His critics pointed out that affirmative action in city hiring was good for him politically. He never disputed that. Taking a page from Daley, good government was good politics. It was also true that he insisted on 25 percent of city contracts going to minority-owned companies, 5 percent for women-owned companies.

But he believed that to confuse this policy with patronage was a deliberate lie by the Eddies, deliberate misinformation by the media. He felt it was a measure of the cynicism in the media when what he did in the name of reform was called racist, or a new form of racial patronage.

Reform wasn't the only catch-phrase he wanted to lose. In other ways, too, he wanted to break the mold, and recast himself in new terms. He hated the description of himself as an "embattled mayor." He might indeed be embattled, but the connotation was that he was crouching, defensive. He knew he was going to have to keep fighting, but he wanted his stance to be cheerfully aggressive. For a while we borrowed "the happy warrior," but he was looking for something beyond "Council Wars."

We needed a "new spirit" within our own ranks as well. There were serious morale problems within the inner circle that we had to address if we were going to communicate good vibes to the world beyond. And it had to start with the man at the top.

The internal disaffection of the mayor's team took two general forms. First, a Florentine pattern of intrigues among those at the top, which filtered down to lesser rivalries and alliances at the cabinet and deputy level, and even down into the support staff. Second, lassitude among mayoral supporters, in and out of government. The malaise I discovered in the press office when I arrived, I soon found was endemic among the fifth floor Mayor's Office staff, and among the mayor's advisers, as well.

Phil Lentz, writing for the *Tribune* that April, noted the same thing:

> His top aides, many of whom are new to government, have been ridden by petty jealousies, political naivete and a boss who seems to prefer turmoil among his underlings...
>
> The roles of the inner troika—William Ware, chief of staff; Thomas Coffey, head of intergovernmental affairs; and James Montgomery,

corporation counsel—are not well defined, which has led to battles over turf. Washington also has a penchant for criticizing his closest advisers while talking to outsiders. Taken together, these developments convince some that the mayor is using a strategy of 'creative tension' to keep his assistants in line and a bit off balance.

It's his way of not letting anyone achieve secure power in his administration," said a source close to the administration. "The mayor trusts very few people."

Harold Washington waved off the writer's observations about his own behavior and motives; if he criticized close advisers it was usually because they weren't so close as Lentz, or they, assumed.

The article piqued him as another example of a "source close to the administration" playing games with the press. Still, the writer's point was correct: the turf battles were becoming an embarrassment. Morale was being undermined.

Political writer Gary Rivlin accurately recapitulated the general mood at City Hall when he summarized 1985 politics for the *Chicago Reader* later that year. He wrote:

As the year 1985 began, some of the mayor's earliest and most dedicated supporters had lost their enthusiasm; the daily dose of news had worn them down. Washington disputed the media's portrayal of him, and blamed many of his legislative failings on the confounding ways of his foes, but that only made things worse: the image we were left with was of two cartoon characters slugging it out, an oversize Vrdolyak manhandling a child-size Washington.... The bungler image haunted this administration, to the point that a couple of people within the mayor's innermost circle confided months later that for a time they dreaded coming to work for fear of yet more of whatever would be served up, whether by the media, by Vrdolyak's forces, or God knows what.

There was a history of frustration and failure behind that dread. The administration had stumbled into many pitfalls in the first two years. Shortly after I arrived, the *Tribune* chronicled the mayor's ups and downs at midterm.

Before he'd even begun his term, the *Trib* pointed out, he had been stigmatized as bellicose and unyielding in his inaugural address.

He had inherited an artificially swollen payroll, and an accumulated deficit variously measured at around $100 million. He had begun by cutting the budget, freezing wages, and firing workers, many of them black, last-in, employees, angering many in his own voter base.

He'd been made to look inept when Vrdolyak outmaneuvered him and took control of City Council; he'd been branded a loser, and a sore loser at that, when he went to court to challenge the coup, and lost.

When he sought to restore the city's books by repealing Byrne's unwarranted election-year property tax cut, Vrdolyak forced a compromise; only half the $22 million would be collected.

One of his top aides, Clarence McClain, an associate from his days as a legislator and then considered to be the new mayor's "patronage chief," had resigned six months into the first term, when it had been revealed that McClain had "been convicted on vice charges in connection with pimping and keeping a house of prostitution."

When he attempted to pass his first budget, in December of 1983, the Eddies developed a counter-budget. Never before had the City Council developed their own budget. The "29" forced him to compromise.

A staff error in filing his ethical statements had led to a legal challenge by Burke of the mayor's right to remain in office, an additional embarrassment.

His second attempt to pass a 1985 budget, in late 1984, had resulted in what the *Trib* called a "rout." He had proposed cuts in the police department, coupled with a tax increase in a budget that was subsequently "improved" under pressure from the "29" to just a tax increase.

His staff had been ridiculed for their lack of political smarts, typified when they were on the right side legally and the wrong side politically of the move to prevent City Hall's annual display of a Christmas nativity scene.

These problems of substance, detailed in technicolor by the media, were worsened by more problems of style: The previous summer he had been embarrassed by a nationally-televised dispute with CBS-TV's Ed Bradley at the 1984 Democratic convention, when the newsman had tried to maneuver him into sharing the screen with Vrdolyak. The mayor had a strict policy of not appearing anywhere with Fast Eddie, and he was particularly unwilling to give the impression, on network TV, that Chicago had two mayors. Bradley had been tricked by Vrdolyak into playing with fire, and Washington was the one who got burned.

Earlier he'd been ridiculed in City Council when Vrdolyak questioned his masculinity—the mayor replied by threatening to punch Eddie in the mouth, in a no-win exchange.

Things got so bad, I was told, that at one point Bill Ware had dragooned the entire cabinet off to an EST session.

Creating the "New Spirit" was partly a matter of rhetoric, partly practical reality. On the rhetorical side, it was a matter of infusing his daily attitude with an upbeat point of view, rather than putting a single message into a single speech. We wrote some boilerplate paragraphs that found their way into a number of speeches. And we planned events—arts and tourism events, especially—that served as opportunities to sound upbeat and unapologetically enthusiastic about Chicago. We distinguished between "proactive" issues which we initiated, and the "reactive" responses to the Eddies' attacks. We used the "New Spirit" unabashedly in the former, more carefully but pointedly in the latter.

We sought out events like the unveiling of a new Claes Oldenburg sculpture, to provide a forum for lines like these:

> You know, there must be something in the air, in this part of the country, that stimulates the creative spirit. How else can you explain the remarkable number of writers and painters and sculptors and actors and dancers and poets and musicians who have created for Chicago such a world-wide reputation for excellence in the arts?

> There's a new feeling across the city, a sense of a new spirit of Chicago, and a sense of purpose for our creative energies.

> There's beauty in the landscape itself... And there's beauty in our people, a multi-racial, multi-ethnic mix of red and yellow, black and white, the cream of the crop from America's heartland, and from every corner of the world, working together to keep Chicago smiling and productive....

> You know, we're pleased that Chicago is on a roll, and we're pleased that the new Spirit of Chicago has resulted in so many positive economic developments, in every corner of our economy. But you don't judge a city by how much money it makes. When people praise Paris and Rome, they're not talking about industrial output. When all the money's spent, and all the shouting is done, it is in the soul of a city that you look to find its true value. The new spirit of Chicago requires fairness and freedom—but it also takes artists to celebrate it....

At a community organization's meeting, he would begin by saying,

I'm pleased to be able to spend a few minutes with you this morning, and to have an opportunity to congratulate you for the good work you're doing. This organization is a living, breathing example of the new spirit of Chicago I'm seeing everywhere I look. You are proving that it is possible to develop a city from within, from the inside out, so that the social and economic well-being of Chicago is based on a solid foundation. . . .

At a business meeting he would open his remarks by reminding his listeners that,

Chicago is on a roll, there's no question about it. All the figures are looking good—more jobs, more industrial and commercial development, more confidence in the real estate market and in the financial market. And there's a new spirit of Chicago in the faces of the people out there in the neighborhoods, a new sense of fairness and fresh opportunities.

We decided to drop "Chicago is on a roll" as a refrain. Even though that was a natural metaphor for him, and "We're on a roll" would continue to lace every speech he gave, we dropped it as a set piece because we saw the distant but distinct possibility that the *Sun-Times* cartoonist Jack Higgins would put the skyline on a hamburger bun, and we winced at the thought.

On one level I would have wanted the "New Spirit of Chicago" to become a catchphrase with a lifespan—every political writer wants to coin a logo like "New Deal" and "New Frontier." In my most lurid imagination, somewhere down the road, with a Democratic president and our own Rostenkowski as Speaker of the House, I could see a space shuttle or a moon lander or a deep sea explorer named "New Spirit of Chicago," like Lindbergh's "Spirit of St. Louis"—a national tribute to a new generation in our city. That wouldn't come to fruition until the mayor's third term, perhaps, but, I reasoned, you have to start somewhere.

But on the practical level, the point of "New Spirit" wasn't the coinage of a phrase. It was to kindle a positive mindset in the mayor himself, and those around him.

And it was also to counter an opposite impulse that had arisen. At the same time that he began using "New Spirit" in his speeches, he was also trying out another phrase that was more to his liking, one that I was trying to eradicate and replace.

He first used it in a rally of supporters, and it arose spontaneously from his exuberance as he ran down a list of improvements he had made in wards throughout the city. He was pleasantly surprised by the strong reaction he got from his listeners, when he climaxed his recital with the loud statement: "No neighborhood is safe from my fairness!"

It was a punchy line, and it had that internal reverse of direction that often makes for a memorable one-liner.

I thought it was terrible. "It makes a truncheon out of 'fairness,'" I said, miming a karate chop. "It just feeds what Vrdolyak is saying, that 'fairness' is a code word for 'black power,' and 'reform' means 'it's our turn.' It's a botched metaphor—fairness isn't something you need to be safe from."

To a lesser extent, by putting the emphasis on "neighborhood," rather than "citizen" or "ward," he was intruding on sacred ground. Citizen means John Doe; ward is neutral, jurisdictional; neighborhood is the street where you live. Don't talk about my mama and don't talk about my neighborhood, except with respect and a smile.

He wasn't convinced. He liked the sound of it, and the reaction it aroused. I was being logical, and he was going with his instinct. Maybe I was being faint of heart when strong language and bold action were needed?

No, I insisted. Sometimes political instincts are faulty, particularly when they're influenced by the good vibes that come from a crowd reaction. A crowd is more likely to be wrong than any single individual. A parallel struck me.

"I know why you like it," I said with a grin. "It's the same thing you do with the shillelagh," I told him, pointing behind his desk. In the corner of his office, behind the American flag to his right, there was a gnarled wood cudgel of genuine Shillelagh oak, a gift from Irish supporters. He carried it with glee in every St. Patrick's Day parade. The rest of the year it was propped up against the wall there, but once in a while, in a mischievous mood, he'd reach over for it, and brandish it over his head, grinning, warning, "I've got something for Eddie."

My remark connected. We talked about perceptions. Often what he intended in fun would be heard in fear. He underestimated the powerful effect his stern countenance could have on whites whose principal experience of blacks in the real world had been with janitors and busboys. He saw himself as the chuckling, good-natured, eternally tolerant bon vivant turned mayor. It rarely occurred to him that he could be fearsome.

In turn, many whites overestimated the formidable frown they saw on television and in the papers. His infinitely elastic face was so photogenic that it's hard to find a bad picture of him. And though Chicagoans were familiar with news photos of his broad, easy smile, they became just as accustomed to seeing his brows furrowed, his entire face creased in apparent anger—the kind of photo that editors would choose to illustrate a story dealing with Harold Washington defending against Vrdolyak's attack. Those photos, as often as not, weren't taken when the mayor was angry—he just looked angry. In fact, they were often taken in a moment of consternation as he considered a question. Or in the moment just before a press conference began, when he narrowed his eyes to peer back behind the TV lights to see if the camera operators were all ready.

We had talked about that, and we were on the same wavelength. He accepted the shillelagh parallel. But what really convinced him, I think, was when I pointed out that we were opening ourselves to a Vrdolyak retort—since Harold became mayor, no neighborhood is safe—period!

The rhetoric was well and good, but we had to back it up with practical reality, and support the mood with material evidence: I collected all the good news I could find—some of it garnered from city department press releases, but most of it from reading news clippings—and we elaborated it daily, in meeting after meeting and speech after speech, to sustain the mood.

The Bureau of Labor Statistics in Washington had published that the greater Chicago metro area had posted a 64,000 gain in employment in 1984, compared to 35,000 jobs lost in 1983. We cheerfully took the credit for every job, including the many beyond Chicago's borders that were included in that figure. We agreed that he'd be blamed for the loss if the figure had gone down, so why not claim the credit?

We showed that there had been a 12.3 percent increase in retail sales in Chicago over the past year—more than the increase in the suburbs, more than in the state, and more than the national rate of increase; and that this was a vast improvement over the total 1979–1983 (i.e., Byrne years) rise of only 1.4 percent.

We pointed out that there was a net increase of 103 factories in Chicago during the previous year, for the first such gain since 1969.

Manufacturing investment had gone up from $60 million in 1983 to $160 million in 1984.

There were 5 million more square feet of new office space in 1984 than in 1983, and another 3.4 million in existing office buildings.

Most important, there was a renewed business confidence among outside investors; the ultimate urban report card—cold cash from New York, say, or the Hartford insurance industry, without any influence of local chauvinism. One example we used, gleaned from our trips east that spring, was from the Travelers investors: they told us, and at my request certified a statement for us, that their mortgage investment in Chicago had grown from $650,000 in 1982, to $46.7 million in 1983, to $251.9 million in 1984. And their office building investment had shot up even more dramatically, from $14.7 million in 1983 to $248.7 million in 1984. Clear evidence of a new confidence in Chicago, despite the *Wall Street Journal*'s "Beirut on the Lake" heckling.

The City Club of Chicago had recently published a report showing that the city had just begun an upswing after two decades of steady decline. The City Club could in no way be considered a cheerleader for the Washington administration, so we accepted the evidence as unbiased reinforcement of our central point: reform was necessary, and reform was working—not just for redistribution of Chicago's assets, but for the general development of Chicago's economy.

Or, for those who probed that logic a little too vigorously, at least it was provably erroneous for anyone to say that two years of Harold Washington was hurting the economy.

Our "politics of joy" was more than morale elevation and civic boosterism. It was clear that the Eddies were using "Council Wars" to create a sense that nothing worked any more.

One of the more prominent Eddie allies, Ald. Richard Mell, said it most clearly in an indiscreet comment to Gary Rivlin, reported in the *Chicago Reader.*

The unprepossessing Rivlin, casual in his corduroys and flannel shirt, ingenuous in both his questions and his boyish manner, was often able to put government officials off guard. He was writing for an advertisers' weekly that was distributed free of charge. Mell had perhaps decided that few of his constituents ever saw the *Reader.*

But the paper is widely read, with especially high readership among Chicago's opinionmakers. Just as important, the *Reader* is well read by other journalists, so it influences news coverage in publications with even greater circulation. Thus Mell was the one who appeared unforgiveably naive, especially among his colleagues in Vrdolyak's "29," when Rivlin broadcast his analysis of their game plan. They were opposed to Harold Washington's bond proposal because, Rivlin reported:

> ...as one alderman told me in June, it would make Harold Washington look too good.

> "There are some who believe that to get rid of Harold Washington is good government because we simply can't take four more years of him," said Richard Mell, a member of the 29. "Maybe someone can make the case that, in the long run, two years of not having this [bond] is worth ten years of political stability in this city." It's a legitimate position; arguably, not voting for this bond *is* in the best interest of this city. Never mind that Mell thought the bond proposal a good one for his community; he opposed it for over a year, in the name of the Good Fight. The alderman whose ward stood to gain the most from the bond proposal—$9 million, $3 million more than any other ward—was a member of the 29, so he, too, stood in opposition to the proposal. If the 29 couldn't run things their way, better the city should crumble.

But this was no surprise to us. We knew that they were willing to hold up important bond work, tie up routine legislation, including mayoral appointments, and even sabotage the city's bond rating in the New York markets. All to the end that come election time, an "uncompromising" mayor would bear the brunt. They would be in a good position to unseat the reform mayor, and to form new alliances in a neo-Byrne/Bilandic environment where they could work their will.

8

Council Wars

To understand "Council Wars" it's important to remember, first, that they had 29 aldermen, we had 21. Early on, the mayor had desperately sought to organize at least a bare majority. Even before he was mayor, he was reaching out to the white ethnic aldermen. But Vrdolyak had already exacted pledges from 28 of them. He later claimed the "29" had organized in reaction to the mayor's "combative" First Inaugural, but Harry Golden's *Sun-Times* articles of the period show clearly that Vrdolyak's preemptive strike took place before the Inaugural.

Their 29 aldermen meant that the Eddies could pass anything they pleased in City Council. But the mayor's 21 votes meant that the Eddies could not muster the two-thirds necessary to override a veto. The result was a stalemate; nothing could move unless one side or the other could bully and bluster, and mobilize public sentiment— downtown businessmen, editors, civic leaders—to take sides. "Council Wars" become the framework of government, and the public relations battles were where the war would be won or lost.

The critical difference between our side and theirs was that we had a government to run; we would ultimately be evaluated on how well the city worked. Their mission was simpler—not to accomplish alternative objectives, but merely to prevent ours from being achieved.

Though military analogies are more applicable, I used a theater example to explain it to an actress who wanted to know why we had "Council Wars." Imagine, I said, that you run a theater company trying to produce a season of plays. You have all the problems of any theater—trying to get the word out, trying to sell tickets, trying to cast good actors and hire good directors, trying to get the sets built and the show opened on time, trying to please the critics. And now imagine that there's a rival theater company down the street, but this company doesn't produce plays. Instead, they spend their days and nights trying to think of ways to keep you from opening on time, trying to get your actors to quit, sabotaging your scenery, badmouthing you to the critics.

To further complicate matters, our governing involved two different kinds of objectives. We had a basic program agenda—city services to initiate and improve and maintain, including many that until recently had been federal government programs, now cut loose to sink or swim. Overlapping that we had a reform agenda—promoting affirmative action, opening up government, changing the contracting and purchasing procedures, clearing up a hundred million dollar deficit and cleaning up the books.

But before we could make much progress with either set of objectives, we had to win the political battles—in the media and in City Council. The show would not go on unless we could neutralize the political opposition. Though our skirmishes were purely tactical, they were essential prerequisites. What they lacked in true strategy they supplied in consistent motivations.

In our case the motivations were, on the defensive, to show that the administration was in control, on top of things, providing good city management, pursuing a coherent agenda; and on the offensive, to show that our opponents had no program, and no ability to formulate one, that they were fumblers and bumblers, destructive to no good end, blind opposition.

The motivations of the "29" were equally simple: to impugn, to deride, and to promote division and disharmony.

First, to impugn Washington's integrity, portray him as a phony reformer, brand affirmative action as just another style of patronage, and create the impression the mayor is a new "Boss" who has created a "new Machine."

Second, to deride Harold Washington, portray him as lazy and careless, and his team as stumble-bums, and demonstrate that even if they are simon-pure, they don't have the brains or the energy or that healthy larcenous appetite to take charge and run things. Though this may seem to be at cross-purposes with the first motivation—how could stumble-bums create a "new Machine"?—there was never any need for logic in this game; just good media bites.

Third, to promote division and discord, and split up all the alliances that formed the Harold Washington coalition. Divide blacks from Latinos, blacks from Jews, blacks from gays and other lakefront lifestylers, blacks from seniors—and divide blacks from blacks. And finally, in a related way, create such a turmoil in civic life that the electorate would be ready for any alternative. "A pox on both your houses," would be a victory for the Eddies.

They sought to foster discontent among Latinos by suggesting they weren't getting their proportionate share of affirmative action goals, hoping to pit the administration against the Mexican and Puerto Rican communities.

They publicized Louis Farrakhan on the front pages for months, in an attempt to embarrass Mayor Washington and cost him both Jewish support and black support as he wavered between denunciation and defense, as they expected he would.

They spread rumors that the mayor was gay, hoping he'd alienate gay rights supporters as he repudiated the rumors.

They took advantage of the complexity of purchasing and contracting issues to create the impression that Washington and his corporation counsel were steering contracts, hoping to turn off the good-government civic leaders who were key to the Washington coalition.

The object of this four-year negative campaign was to bolster public support for what would otherwise have been publicly insupportable: a nonprogram of blind opposition.

Most observers felt the "29" used the media skillfully to make their case. The mayor believed most of the media were full-fledged co-conspirators in their cause. I considered it a three-cornered relationship. It was true, of course, that the media weren't referees or dispassionate observers; but they didn't side with the Eddies, either, and it was fruitless to judge them by their unwillingness to do so. They had their own priorities, their media agenda, and in pursuing it, both sides probably came out even. The best measure of that was the number of complaints Vrdolyak lodged against media treatment— gripes against WBBM-TV's Walter Jacobson, for instance, and others—most of them the very ones that we were griping about.

Sometimes, in fact, the media were victimized themselves. They were the objects of a jiu-jitsu ploy, where their momentum in hot pursuit of the ultimate story was used to pervert that quest and mock it.

Eddie Burke was chairman of the Finance Committee, a City Council post with specified statutory perks and responsibilities. In other hands, such as those of Mayor Daley's floor leader Ald. Thomas Keane, the position has been described as that of "Chicago's other mayor." As chairman, Burke was privy to documents that even the mayor couldn't put his hands on.

Almost daily, the opposition released city documents from the Finance Committee to the media, purporting to show that friends of the mayor were getting city business, or that hiring programs employed reverse discrimination, or that someone was just plain screwing up.

From the standpoint of the news media, it was certainly news any time the chairman of the Finance Committee called the mayor of the city of Chicago a felon. So they reported each separate instance, often on page one. Any time a black contractor got city business, it could be charged—often correctly—that the contractor personally knew the mayor. As the mayor said frequently, "I've been a black public official in Chicago most of my life. I don't think there's a black corporate leader or a black banker or a leading black attorney that I don't know by name."

The news stories would report the charges by Burke or Vrdolyak, along with the standard reply—so standard and predictable it inevitably appears defensive and evasive—"the mayor's office denies the charges." The news media rarely took responsibility for evaluating the charges. It was sufficient for them that the charges were made, and denied. "Balanced reporting" required only that the administration be given an opportunity to air its response.

The general public, reading these stories, could be excused if they formed negative impressions of the administration. John F. Kennedy once said of politics that where there's smoke there's often a smoke-generating machine. But few casual readers could read stories day after day, claiming chicanery in high places, supplemented by TV clips of an earnest Eddie Burke waving papers and charging illegal behavior, without becoming suspicious of the mayor's administration. At the very least, the average citizen might adopt the "pox on both your houses" attitude toward the fuss, and wish for a fresh start.

Mayor Washington believed that the only real answer to four years of day-in, day-out negative campaigning by the Eddies would be remedial action on the part of journalists. Don't just report the charges, he'd say; report the motivation for the charges, and report that the charges are unfounded. "Take sides," he demanded. And then, after a series of charges had proven to be totally unfounded, cease reporting the charges at all. That, believed the mayor, would be responsible journalism.

But few reporters or editors considered themselves employed in the business of remedial journalism. Their point was that it would be highly improper for them to "take sides." That was fine for columnists and for editorial writers, but not for the people who put the stories and the photos on the front pages. Many journalists, editors mostly, were defiant in asserting their priorities: if it's a good story, we'll use it. True? False? Don't be simplistic. Responsible journalism? That's a slippery concept, as useful to a Hitler or a Stalin as to a reformer. A story is true if it happened, false only if it didn't. Did or did not Burke charge that the contract was wired? If he did, that's a story, that Burke made the charge, that the mayor denied it.

Absent any remediation by journalists, we had only a few options, and we played them all.

One was to continue to plug away with our own direct promotion, getting the word out (along with photos) to the hundreds of community newspapers that proliferate in Chicago. We did a weekly mailing to them, sending every newspaper a packet of materials that resulted in scores of favorable articles each week.

Another was to exploit the mayor's affable availability to press—he was game for almost any interview, for rap sessions on radio talk shows, for press conferences (sometimes several a day), even for impromptu "ambushes" as he entered or left a building, or got in and out of his car. Just as he never took a bad photo, he also never gave a bad sound bite, and reporters were eager to follow him almost anywhere he went. In time he would sour on the decision to be so available, but during the critical months of 1985's "Council Wars," this availability was important.

Another was to shape the mayor's remarks, regardless of the events at which he spoke, to send and reinforce the messages we wanted publicized. If he could keep his speeches—and his response to questions—consistently motivated, then the media couldn't help but get our message out. That approach was only marginally effective, but every little bit helped.

We tried to pick events carefully so that his association with them sent a message and established his priorities. That meant, of course, limiting his appearances at other events, to force the spotlight on our issues. It was never possible for scheduler Ed Hamb to adhere to any such tight focus, so this approach too was of limited effectiveness.

We made an effort to multiply our spokespersons by using surrogates, sending department heads and articulate aldermen allied with the mayor to a secondary selection of public events, to help press our points. Again, useful but not decisive.

Our most visible PR programs were devised for specific legislative initiatives—a bus tour of Chicago neighborhoods to promote a bond issue, or a comprehensive media program for the selling of each budget. These campaigns brought together the entire cabinet, and used the entire PR arsenal: meetings with editorial boards and constituency groups; scene-setting leaks of information (where a press release wouldn't be read, the same information presented in memo form, ostensibly from me or Ernie to the mayor, judiciously leaked, would make front page news); a series of press conferences, sometimes with elaborate charts and graphs and studies prepared to buttress our points; individual ward brochures, patterned after similar brochures that Mayor Daley had distributed, outlining city services and capital improvements, neighborhood by neighborhood; letter-writing campaigns to newspaper editors; and regular weekly informational releases to black ministers and other civic leaders who could be counted on to underscore our message. In all these ways we could work beyond the headlines, or sometimes through them, to say what we wanted to say.

Probably our most effective PR was done in the many business breakfasts and civic organization luncheons where the mayor appeared in person to press his case. From the annual State of the City address to private sessions at the Merchandise Mart, the power of his own presentation had the long, slow effect of converting the skeptical and building confidence.

And in addition to all the promotional efforts, the biggest newsmakers were still the mayor's retorts to the Eddies' attacks. He was a firm believer that after 24 hours, any unchallenged rumor becomes "the truth." And although he tried to adopt the attitude that he wouldn't contribute to the headlines by responding to charges, he just couldn't keep himself from it. He was constitutionally unable to take a slap without punching back. Even though the continued scrapping might work to the Eddies' advantage, and even though he knew he was being manipulated by TV reporters who could count on a pungent response just by mentioning Vrdolyak's name when posing a question, he gave them what they came for, and made news with his counter-attack.

⬜ *In Council Chambers* ⸤━━━━━━━━━⸥

Of all the arenas for acting out the dramas of "Council Wars," there was none superior to the City Council meetings themselves.

City Council chambers are on the second floor of City Hall, not far from the press room (not to be confused with the mayor's press office on the sixth floor), where City Hall reporters had their desks.

The public is invited to attend City Council meetings, seated on the main floor and in a gallery. Attendance is free, of course, on a first-come, first-served basis. Frequently during the mid-1980s, City Council audiences were treated to the liveliest theater in town.

Chicago's mayor presides over these meetings. As the presiding officer, the mayor recognizes speakers, announces votes and when necessary rules on their results, or on other points of law or parliamentary procedure. To assist him he has, seated to his left, the City Council parliamentarian, and to his right, the city's principal lawyer and head of the Law Department, the corporation counsel.

The chambers include four long arcs of desks, 51 in all, numbered left to right from the mayor's point of view; except that the alderman who has been elected Finance Committee Chairman by his peers, regardless of his ward number, sits in a favored location in the front row, on an aisle.

The location is favored by tradition and also by the angle of the TV cameras, as the press box, with cameras from at least four stations and numerous print reporters, is positioned in the front corner of the chambers, at the mayor's extreme left. The aldermen from certain wards, when they face the presiding officer or turn to their colleagues, will be looking away from the cameras. But the Finance Committee Chairman and his staff assistant—the 51st seat is provided for the Finance Committee Chairman's chief of staff—are situated in perfect camera position.

By his good fortune, so is the alderman from the 10th Ward. Seated at the mayor's right, across the chambers from the press box, Ald. Edward Vrdolyak faced the mayor, the body assembled, and the TV audience all at the same time.

Occasionally a camera will be placed in the gallery, where it will pick up the mayor full-face; more commonly, the mayor is portrayed in profile, from the press box cameras.

One of the regular highlights of "Council Wars" was the TV coverage of City Council meetings. The ordinary business of Chicago's City Council is as dull as the ordinary business of any legislative body. But for every Council meeting, something would be planned by one side, or both, to promote their cause. It might be the eruption of the only Latino alderman, a Vrdolyak ally, who could be prompted to heave a stack of papers into the air, in protest of a policy. Or a scathing attack by Burke on contracting procedures, delivered toward the cameras. Or a taunting, invariably witty chastisement of the mayor by Vrdolyak, who was so well placed that he didn't need to "cheat" toward the camera and could concentrate on his target.

On our side, only a few aldermen could be counted on for "good theater" in their comeback. The mayor himself would be limited to brief asides as he recognized speakers and announced rulings of the chair—if he wanted to address the body he was required to step down from his rostrum and take a position at floor level, too cumbersome a procedure for routine business.

Nonetheless, for every major issue we prepared talking points that could be used by selected aldermen in their floor debate. We continued to hope that our spokespersons would air some of our best arguments forcefully enough to make the evening news, and often they did. The talking points also helped to keep the party line consistent among the "21."

Tim Evans, the mayor's floor leader and later the head of his political office, was the most dependable. He and two other aldermen, Wilson Frost and Larry Bloom, were each squadron leaders of one-third the mayor's troops. By using Evans, Frost and Bloom as liaisons in this way, when necessary the "21" could meet in three groups without triggering the open meetings act, which required that press could attend any meeting of 13 or more aldermen. He could count on the three of them to make a powerful statement, or to cue others for action.

The mayor also depended on David Orr, who would later be his vice-mayor. Orr was not only ideologically committed to the reform agenda, but also articulate and earnest on the issues he promoted, and so squeaky-clean in his personal motivations for public office that he rankled many professional pols—his allies as well as his enemies.

"Did you ever notice that Vrdolyak won't stay in the room when Orr gets up to speak?" the mayor pointed out to me, with a grin. "He can't take him. He just doesn't know how to handle him, because the dude's got no handles." The mayor took delight in recognizing Orr to speak just after Vrodolyak had finished, which, as the mayor noted, had the effect of driving Fast Eddie out of the room when he might otherwise be following up his oratory with personal arm-twisting.

He also had high regard for Dorothy Tillman, his personal choice for alderman in the Third Ward. He told me, on more than one occasion, that Tillman was one of the brightest aldermen on the floor. "She'll surprise you," he said, of the young woman who was chiefly known for her stylish, sometimes flashy hats and her outspoken command of the South Side Chicago idiom. "She's already running one of the best ward organizations in the city. She drives these downtown types crazy, but they better take a closer look."

But as effective as our best speakers were, we couldn't compete with the two Eddies. Only the mayor could outweigh them, and he didn't get to open up until after City Council had ended, when we would usually hold an impromptu press conference.

While City Council meetings progressed, the mayor's legal and legislative team—Coffey for awhile, later Tim Wright, always with veteran legislative aide Ed Bell and Law Department attorneys—would mill around the floor area under the mayor's rostrum, ready to do the bidding of the mayor or corporation counsel, to provide answers or get answers to questions that arose. They were also invaluable in briefing me, or sometimes the press directly, on the import of what was happening.

I too moved from my position with them, to the mayor's side at the rostrum, to the telephone located in the parliamentarian's desk, to the press box. Often I had papers prepared on the issue—to be distributed to the press or to the aldermen. But my chief function, as I saw it, was to be a second pair of eyes and ears for the mayor, on the one hand, and to collect and find answers for the continual questions of reporters, on the other.

The competition was busy, too. Cornelia Tuite, widely respected at City Hall as the "brains behind Eddie Burke," not only kept track of the Finance Committee but also ran a professional press operation. One of her most competent operatives was an attorney, Lisa Rubel, an attractive young woman whose perkiness and apparent preoccupation with the legal aspects of Burke's changing tactics disguised a sharp awareness of what made good copy, or good TV. Stationed as she was in the press area, with her reams of legal papers, she was a ready reference for media questions, well-positioned to give their sto-

ries an Eddie Burke spin. Dennis Church, formerly of the Mayor's
Press Office, also lurked in that area, chewing a cigar and making
wisecracks, but he was generally dismissed by reporters. "He never
knows what he's talking about," one told me.

During one of my first City Council meetings, I picked up on the
theatrical aspect of the proceedings, and made my own small contribution.

I noticed that a dramatic structure had developed in these meetings. On any issue, whether introduced by our side or the opposition,
a certain amount of preparation would have been done and releases
or straight photocopies of resolutions would have been distributed to
the media. The sponsoring alderman would speak to the issue, and
debate would follow.

Eddie Burke would have his say, in colorful and usually mocking
language—good stuff for the cameras. He was articulate and his
manner and style suggested he knew the issues better than anyone
else in the room.

The mayor would call on aldermen from both sides to make their
case. As the speeches were made by those who were accustomed to
speaking on the issues—less than a third of the aldermen ever did so
—other aldermen would mill around on the Council floor, moving
from one group to another, from claque to claque, dealing with nuances of the issue at hand or meeting on completely unrelated issues,
sometimes leaving for the restrooms, to grab a cup of coffee in the
"backstage" area behind Council chambers, or to talk to reporters.
Cutting a sharp figure among the background forms arranged in
their clusters, would be the strident, purposeful Eddie Vrdolyak,
moving from deal to deal, or just prowling the aisles like a panther,
grinning confidently, very much the maestro of the "29."

But then, when the discussion had matured to a state of readiness,
Eddie Vrdolyak would return to his seat and ask to be recognized.
The bustle of City Council would come to a stop, aldermen who had
gone "backstage" would return to their seats, staff and even audience in the gallery who might have been maintaining a steady mur-
mur of background noise, all would become still.

In the press box, normally a beehive of running commentary, the
only sound would be the muttering of TV reporters to their camera
operators: "Get Eddie," or "Eddie's going to speak." Even Mayor
Washington would settle back into his seat as if the overture had finished, and the performance was about to begin.

Vrdolyak didn't disappoint. He wasn't a classic orator, of course. But a classic orator couldn't have played that house. He was sharp when he needed to be, and blunt when that worked better. He was clear on the points he needed to score, and he knew how to make them penetrate—steel-jacketed bullets that drilled through the blandness of city business on the evening news, and got you in the gut. His admirers saw him as Mack the Knife, the rascal of City Hall, more mischievous than malicious, a taunting antidote to the bombastic mayor or the tiresome seriousness of purpose in the mayor's crowd. At least one Chicago reporter, Susan Axelrod, was unabashedly infatuated. She called Eddie "one of the sexiest men in Chicago. . . . Face it," she wrote, "if Eddie Vrdolyak were a quiet alderman who did his homework and voted his conscience, he'd be a good public servant but not a lust object." So when Vrdolyak got up to speak, even his opponents—even the mayor himself—seemed to pause to enjoy his performance.

My small contribution followed that observation. Just as Vrdolyak was once again commanding the attention of everyone in the room, I interrupted the mayor's own enjoyment to ask him why we were all hushing to hear Fast Eddie speak. "Everything else in this room happens with people milling around," I said.

He took my point immediately, glanced up past me and motioned to Dorothy Tillman. "Get Dorothy's attention," he asked. He suggested her moves, and she picked right up on it. Ald. Anna Langford was seated behind Vrdolyak, so Tillman, in one of the stylish, colorful hats she always wore, strode past Eddie, through his camera shot, and took a position over his shoulder where she could chitchat with Langford. It was unusual enough to distract the alderman, who paused briefly to glance over his shoulder. Then Tillman had a question for an alderman behind Anna, and then a point of order with which she interrupted Fast Eddie. It cut into his cadence and rattled his performance, and in its small way served to blunt a few of his one liners.

We didn't always remember to produce this nuisance—sometimes we were just too damn interested in whatever it was Eddie was coming up with—but we did it often enough to begin to dispel some of the Eddie mystique among our own troops, at least. And I'd like to think we cost him a few good moments on the evening news.

There was no love lost between Mayor Washington and either Eddie Vrdolyak or Eddie Burke. Theirs was not an artificial politicians' rivalry that gave way to good cheer when the cameras weren't looking. They were enemies, 24 hours a day, each side committed to the political extinction of the other. Vrdolyak wouldn't hesitate to slander the mayor, impugn his morals and his lifestyle. Mayor Washington was only slightly less reluctant to bring up Vrdolyak's tax problems, or his brother who was doing time in Florida; or to charge that Burke was a draft-dodger who had used connections to avoid the military, which occurred to the mayor every Veterans Day.

He avoided ever being photographed with either of the two, and would not appear on television with them. It was important to the mayor that his supporters understood the political confrontation was not a joking matter. He didn't want to allow anyone to harbor the impression that this was not a serious conflict, with everything at stake.

I assumed he felt the same about both of them, and I was surprised to learn otherwise.

"I've known guys like Eddie all my life," he told me, speaking of Vrdolyak. "I grew up with them. He's not a racist. He's a bully. He'll use race, hell, he'll use anything, he'll use his own grandmother to get what he wants. But that doesn't make him a bad guy in my book. Amoral, yes. Racist, uh uh."

"Burke is a racist," he told me. Like many people who followed "Council Wars" from the outside, I would have assumed the mayor's opinion of the two of them would have been just the opposite. Vrdolyak, not Burke, was the one who'd been stirring up racial unrest wherever he could. But the mayor insisted on his analysis without providing more details. "I know these guys," was all he'd say.

There are a few rare photos that show the mayor together with one Eddie or the other. It does appear he could have a good laugh, matching wits with Fast Eddie. But there's no joy to be found in his regard for Flashy Eddie.

For Mayor Washington, the most grating irritant in "Council Wars" was the term itself. Running a close second was the pundits' assertions that he enjoyed or benefited from "Council Wars."

Chicago comedian Aaron Freeman, who created the revue sketch called "Council Wars" as a stand-up act, gave the Chicago news media their latest byword.

He had developed a *Star Wars* satire in which Vrdolyak was the Darth Vader character, the mayor cast as a chubby Luke Skywalker.

Though the act was short-lived, the Chicago comedian had created a metaphor for an era. The mayor was not pleased, and considered the term "Council Wars" as destructive as "Beirut on the Lake" to the self-image of the city.

By making the mayor's political struggles the object of ridicule, the satire provided an excuse for the retreat of media and citizens who might otherwise be encouraged to take sides. This wasn't *his* fight. This was their fight, and he was taking all the blows. Sometimes he would laugh ruefully about the situation. Sometimes he would be openly bitter.

He was all the more bitter because some pundits conjectured that he was deliberately fostering "Council Wars" as a dodge. Vrdolyak and Burke promoted this notion, and it gained some credence. His bitterness usually came through only in short bursts, but occasionally a reporter's question would prompt a more detailed look at his feelings.

Financial reporter Merrill Goozner, then writing for *Crain's Chicago Weekly*, posed a question:

> I hear this from some business leaders, you get high marks throughout the business community, but I think if there's one criticism that's out there, they lament—not necessarily even blaming you—they lament the divisiveness in the city and they worry about the image that projects beyond our borders, and they wish that Harold Washington would do more to overcome that kind of divisiveness. They feel that you're a politician, you like to get down there, whether you're dragged down there or you jumped down there, it doesn't really matter. You're down there in the gutter with these guys, and...they wish you wouldn't do that, or they wish that somehow we had the kind of mayor that could somehow bring this city together again. What do you—

Harold Washington interrupted:

> They can wish unto hell. Let me tell you something very bluntly. You've had two kinds of mayors in this city. One who watered the Machine, fomented the Machine, incubated it, patted it, squeezed it, developed it, and milked this city dry. The others were like me, trying to clean it up.
>
> Now you cannot clean it up unless you get down in the mud with these suckers and fight 'em. You cannot deal with these people.
>
> I'm not crazy, I know how to make accommodations, I know how to compromise. That's the essence of my life. But you cannot compro-

mise with a person who says give me all of it. You can't do that. And the sooner the media in this city understand that, and the sooner the business people understand that, the sooner we can get over that hump.

These people are wrong, absolutely wrong. You think I want to spend four years with this mess? I don't enjoy this. I'd much rather have a City Council I could work with. They don't want to work with me. They want to bring this city to its knees so that in 1987 they can say I failed as a mayor. It's just that simple. It isn't any more complicated than that.

And for me to get peace in City Council I'd have to capitulate as Byrne did. I feel sorry for Ms. Byrne. She walked in this office, sat down, these knuckleheads beat her across her skull, scared the hell out of her, she looked around and said I can't handle this, I don't have the tensile strength for it. I want to give in. And she gave in.

And then old Harold came along. I'm not going to do that. So it's not a question of me being recalcitrant or hardheaded or intractable or uncompromising, that's not it at all, these people are nuts. They want to run this city under the same old system they had before and won't compromise with anything less. So the business community—God bless 'em— [He shook his head in exasperation.]

Instead of standing back and suggesting that you all make peace, why don't they just say, you're wrong today, Eddie, and you're right, Harold. Don't play games about it. You serve no purpose by standing up there like a spectator that says you all fight or you all solve the problem. It's not going to happen that way. There are rights and wrongs.

The business community in this city has refused to do what the business communities have done in almost every other city in this country —they've refused to be the referee. If you look at these major cities that have had reformations, the mayor didn't do it, the business community did it. This is one of the few cities where the mayor has tried to reform the city, with almost no help from the business community.

Even if they sided with the opposition, that'd be better than doing nothing. But that just couldn't happen. That just couldn't happen. Some of the reforms that we advocate came out of the business community. I'm called conservative because I want to balance budgets, don't spend money we don't have, lay off people we can't pay. Those came not from me, those came from the business standard.

We have management teams trying to improve government. These aren't my ideas, these are private sector people. These are their standards. That was the definition of reform for years: business standards.

We've gone a bit further than that, but certainly, to reform a government you've got to at least have acceptable business standards.

So I accept the criticism, but I say I've heard it too often. It doesn't mean anything any more.

In another taped conversation, with the *Washington Post*'s Kevin Klose, he went further. Klose had asked whether it were possible that "Council Wars" would cease. The mayor replied, "Certainly it's possible." What would it take? "Simple: Act like a human being." The mayor continued:

I've made it very clear that I'm a practical politician. I've been one all my life. I know what it is to make do and get along and work with people. I've got no problem with that. I've seldom gone into a situation and come out with 100 percent of what I wanted. That's not expected and never bothers me. But there are certain fundamental issues about running government that you cannot give up. Otherwise, why even be there?

There are certain things that were wrong with this city that have to be changed. And one of the things wrong with this city is that the wrong people were running it for the wrong reasons, and in the wrong way.

And I just said, "You can't do that any more. And if you do it, it won't be with my help. And as a matter of fact, over my opposition." Beyond that, we can talk. Instead, they're adopting an attitude—they would try to stop everything I tried to do. It's just that simple.

If they stopped doing that, no problem. They're going to run us through a budget process, just playing games, and trying to obstruct and divide and waste and irritate; they'll continue to do that. It's something like children playing with a toy. They have no conception of government, what it's all about, what it's designed to do, nor do they care.

To them it's a toy, it's a tool, to become more affluent and assist their friends to become more affluent. My two major opponents owe every dime they've got to this city. They got it *from* the city. Every damn dime! They never had any job, never been out there working. These cats don't know what work is. They just came in here and picked up the city as a fountainhead of money, and got rich, both of them...they got rich here. Never done a damn thing for themselves. Matter of fact, Burke goes back a couple generations.

For us to get along they simply have to stop doing what they're doing. Sit down and discuss problems as competitors, and as people who are concerned about a city, do. As politicians do everywhere else.

I have served on some tough bodies of rough tough people, in Illinois and otherwise. I have never seen people whose whole design was to destroy. That's what their purpose is. They go beyond the pale, one step too far. Most politicians won't do that, they'll stop short of that.

The mayor continued on the subject of "Council Wars" news coverage:

I have some strong feelings about people who imply equal guilt.

People say why don't you all solve this problem. Why don't you all do this. Why don't Council Wars stop. Well, I resent very much the two parties not being able to sit down and resolve this. But hell, I'm not at fault.

There seems to be a fear of pointing the finger in this case. Is the mayor wrong when he puts appointments before the Council? No. Then why do you blame him when the Council won't function. What do you want him to do other than what he's done—cajole, entice, talk, public discussion. What am I supposed to do? They just refuse to move on them and they'll even tell you flat out the real reason *why* they won't move on them. So is the mayor wrong on that? No. So why not say it— just say, "You gentlemen are *wrong*"? They're not going to saddle the mayor with that. They tried to obstruct the O'Hare Airport bonds—it was clear that's what they were doing. Why not just say so?

That's no longer loyal opposition or the legitimate political opposition. This is just an attempt to destroy, to stop things. There seems to be this hesitancy on the part of many, many people to point things out. In the main it's the media, but not exclusively. To a great extent, but not all.

But clearly the media does that. The editorials do it, the stories do it, it's gotten to be a thing: "Council Wars include the mayor and the Council, wrapped in an interminable struggle. Both are wrong." Not true at all. Absolutely untrue. And that's not the way you make man better.

The mayor paused in his invective, gave a self-conscious laugh at what he had just said. Klose, with an instinct for the essence of his interviewee, asked him how you "make man better."
Mayor Washington answered:

By punishing those who are wrong, and rewarding those who are right. Making distinctions. Not only is that the way to do it, but that's *intelligence*. Don't just say, You all do this. You have to make distinctions. The press is, generally speaking, not inclined to do it, for whatever reasons. The net result is there's still some confusion in people's minds about who's at fault.

He was particularly unhappy when civic leaders and the media allowed "Council Wars" to be further confused with racism and racial division. He was looking for an opportunity to deal publicly with the issue, and it came in April, less than two months after I'd been on the job.

We had wanted to take the offensive, move confidently out on the open field rather than hunker inside the fortress. We had wanted to get away from any idea that "Council Wars" was somehow a racial confrontation. And we had wanted to appeal to the sense of well-being about Chicago that we knew was latent, just under the surface and waiting to be invited out into the clear spring air.

The opportunity was provided by New York mayor Ed Koch's attack on Jesse Jackson, in the course of which Koch called Chicago "the most racially divided city in the country." The *Sun-Times* called to ask if we'd like to respond, in an open letter to Koch. They promised to give the article good play.

The mayor had misgivings about getting involved in a Jesse Jackson altercation. I promised we could give the newspaper an article which would be launched from the issue they were interested in, but which would make the points we wanted to make. Further, as he had told me, you never lose when you "stand up for Chicago," and even whites who had no use for Harold Washington would stand a little closer to him on this issue. In the article he wrote:

> I sympathize with anyone who has to tangle with the Rev. Jesse L. Jackson, but I take issue with Koch's tactics... He calls us one of the most racially divided cities in the country. I suggest what he means is that we are the most upfront city in the country when it comes to dealing with our racial diversity.
>
> It is true that we are making up for lost time in our social education and in healing wounds between various ethnic groups—not just black and white... We're confronting our problems directly and in a healthy way. Naturally, this produces a good deal of spirited dialogue. That's a symptom not of racial division but of racial diversity.
>
> Further, I hope Koch is not making a mistake of superficial perception, that our *political* problems are *racial* problems....
>
> I have a problem with the term "Council Wars." Some people—in the press, in public office and in private life, and even, incredibly, the president of our Chamber of Commerce—take a perverse delight in focusing on the colorful and the chaotic. I doubt that Chicago ever had more gangsters than other major cities, but somehow we got stuck with the

Al Capone image, no doubt in large part due to the delight to be found in writing and talking about such escapades. It gave our city a reputation we've been stuck with for 50 years.

Today the same people like to talk about and write about "Council Wars" and unless we're careful to keep such foolishness in its place, they might be sticking our city with another 50 years of mistaken identity.

Now, make no mistake, we have been experiencing a well-organized, deliberately disruptive program of *civic sabotage* in City Council.

One of the most stabilizing influences in parliamentary democracy—the concept of a "loyal opposition"—is completely absent here in Chicago. Its absence represents a serious problem that should concern every Chicagoan.

In 17 years as a legislator in Springfield, and through two terms in the U.S. House of Representatives, and in my extensive reading of American and British parliamentary history, never have I encountered a pattern of abuse of democracy within a legislative body such as we are witnessing here in Chicago. The American way, the democratic way of behavior, is for the opposition to make its case and use its parliamentary options to push its programs, but to stop short of sabotaging the system itself.

Yet [here] we have cynical, sometimes desperate members of the opposition who would rather see not a pothole filled, not a bond passed, not a library built, not an appointment approved and not a single step forward taken by the city of Chicago during the administration of this mayor. And who, therefore, have tried to hold the business of the city of Chicago as their political hostage.

Now, I object to glamorizing this kind of behavior by calling it "Council Wars," implying some kind of struggle between equals on a darkling plain where enemies clash by night. But neither do I call it "racist." I characterize it for what it is, a kind of low-grade parliamentary "terrorism," an attempt to frighten businessmen, families, tourists and international trade with the idea that Chicago has frozen its gears for four years; in order that the old patronage system might gain tolerance, despite its corruption, as "the only way that works."

You don't have to be a racist to be greedy, and I resent Koch bringing that element into a city that is doing so much to preserve and celebrate diversity, and to provide fairness to all sides. . . .

Yes, we're sometimes a rough-and-tumble bunch, we Chicagoans. We're the City of the Big Shoulders, the City that Works, and we're proud of our multi-national, multi-ethnic heritage. We have our contradictions (can you imagine any other city where the president of the chamber of commerce would run down his city?) But when the chips are down, we stick together, from the man in the street to the mayor's seat. So, Mr. Koch, when you run down Chicago, you're walking up the wrong side of me.

He continued to press the point in his State of the City speech that year. "Those who don't know us well consider Chicago a city rife with racial divisions," he said. "But we celebrate Chicago as a city rich with racial and ethnic and cultural *diversity.* . . .

"My election was not the beginning of cultural or racial divisions in our city. My election was the beginning of a process of reconstruction, of new focus on the real problems confronting Chicago, a new opportunity to bring us all back together after long years of tragic separation. . . ."

By the fall, in his annual speech to the Academy of Television Arts and Sciences, at which he traditionally evaluated the Chicago press corps for their handling of City Hall stories, he would be fancifully pronouncing "Council Wars" dead and gone.

Borrowing some of his themes from the letter to Koch, he would say:

> I never did believe there ever was such a thing as "Council Wars". . . but there were two small minority groups who had a vested interest in the concept of "Council Wars," who kept the fiction alive: the last-ditch defenders of the bad old days. . .and the Press, who benefited enormously from the game of pitting those last-ditch defenders against the forces of reform. These same newsmen and women were the same types who, a generation earlier, when Italians were the offended minority, took great delight in writing up the gang wars of the Al Capone days—they called it "good copy," even though we now know that to focus so much on the low-lifes in our society was extremely damaging, not only to Chicago's self-esteem and morale, and to our system of values, but also to our image across the country and around the world. Now we see that same small group getting the same delight —and financial reward—from its portrayal of city government as a fight between pit dogs. They are just as misdirected in their focus, and they are doing just as much damage not only to Chicago's image, but even to its self-esteem, and its system of values.

Harold Washington never got down off his bully pulpit—he considered his opportunity to change attitudes to be one of the most important missions of his mayoralty.

But he knew that the "New Spirit," and all it connoted, was only background music to the real drama.

He would somehow have to achieve a series of parliamentary objectives—despite being outnumbered 29 to 21. Those objectives were specific and clear-cut, and each had its place in the game plan for 1985. They were all likely to become confused in the eye of the press and public—he thought deliberately confused—but they had to be accomplished, even if the sparks they threw threatened to fire up "Council Wars" even more.

He had to prevail in his affirmative action policies, in all city hiring but especially in the world's largest airport project, at O'Hare.

He had to successfully negotiate the largest contract in the history of the city of Chicago, for a People Mover at O'Hare.

He was facing the City Council showdown over the annual appropriations for Community Development Block Grant funds. He had to end the stalemate over the "G.O. bonds" for neighborhood improvements. And he faced his third major budget battle.

At the same time he had to persevere with the changes he was trying to make in the Revenue, Purchasing and Law Departments, not only to institute responsible management and reform their practices, but also because those changes were necessary to accomplish his other ends.

And after all those challenges were met, he would still be only halfway to his goal. In the course of meeting these challenges he would stoke up "Council Wars" to a fever pitch, and year's end could find him with a Pyrrhic victory. He might win "Council Wars" and lose all.

The only way he was going to win reelection, and prevail in his reforms, was if he took charge of city government.

The "New Spirit" was a precondition to "Council Wars" success, but winning "Council Wars" was itself only a precondition to the real objective: taking charge.

9

Winning Council Wars

Mayor Washington would have to "beat their ass," and win undisputed control of city government. That was what we were about in the spring, summer and fall of 1985.

He might reassure and fortify the public and the press with the merits of his cause and he might achieve significant accomplishments that would impress professional politicians. But he would not be reelected without a highly visible showdown. As much as political peoples anywhere, Chicagoans love a winner, and deride a loser, even if he's a good guy.

The polls reflected this. The spring, summer and fall of 1985 did indeed produce a string of substantive victories that enhanced his position and contributed to the success of the final showdown, in 1986.

But the superficial pyrotechnics of "Council Wars" continued unabated: Vrdolyak succeeded in tactics like stirring up controversies between Jews and blacks over Louis Farrakhan, and between Latinos and blacks over affirmative action goals. So even though the mayor was "beating their ass" in the real world, Vrdolyak was still moving toward the opposition's long-term objectives: to tire the public of "Council Wars," oust Harold Washington, and return the city to a neo-Daley era of Bilandic and Byrne—under a white mayor or perhaps a Latino or even a black that they would be able to control as they had controlled Byrne.

Polls supported both premises of his concern. A poll taken for the *Chicago Tribune* in March of 1985 measuring relative satisfaction with Harold Washington's handling of his job showed that only 35 percent rated him as excellent or good. By November, the number was up to 49 percent. And a full 60 percent gave a thumbs-up when asked the yes-or-no question of whether they approved the way he was doing his job—including 42 percent of whites.

Relative to Vrdolyak, Washington did far better: "Polled

Chicagoans gave Vrdolyak only a 21 percent approval rating for his city leadership role, and he trails Washington even among whites—only 30 percent of whom said they approve of Vrdolyak's performance," the *Trib* reported.

The mayor was getting high marks for the "New Spirit" he'd been selling. And yet Gallup polls measuring electability made the opposite point: people were apparently deciding that, good or bad, a politically impotent Harold Washington meant more "Council Wars." Chicago might benefit from a change. An April 1985 tally showed young Richie Daley beating Harold Washington in a one-on-one race, 49–43, with a clear majority of Latino votes and even 18 percent of blacks. The same poll showed disaffection among Washington's black supporters.

And in December of that year, after a string of PR victories, which nonetheless stopped far short of a climactic showdown, Gallup still showed Daley leading 50–46, with almost one-fourth of the black vote.

But by September 1986, the mayor had taken charge. After a year and a half of neighborhood rebuilding, victory in the ward remap case and special elections, and "beating their ass" in the media, the *Sun-Times* printed a Gallup poll that showed Washington clearly out in front of the competition, with a commanding lead over Daley (50–42), and everyone else who might run against him.

Shortly after I was hired, in March 1985, Ed Burke floated the notion of running Congressman Dan Rostenkowski for mayor. The *Sun-Times* gave the idea banner coverage, quoting Chicago pols in support, and political observer Don Rose, "close to Washington," as saying "No doubt Rostenkowski would be the strongest candidate." As it turned out, in polls the next month, Washington trounced him, 53–36, but Burke had demonstrated the opposition's active hunt for a stop-Harold candidate, a search that never ended.

The winning of "Council Wars" probably began with the Burrell tapes. The "New Spirit" dovetailed with a public relations campaign, with community relations aide Jetta Jones on point, to embarrass the Eddies for their opposition to the mayor's appointments. As many as 80 nominees were being prevented from serving on boards and commissions, and you didn't have to love Harold Washington to know this was silly.

A steady campaign was being waged against the mayor's affirmative action program. There were many small MBE skirmishes in the form of anecdotal evidence that minority business enterprises were sometimes less qualified than the white-owned firms they underbid. And there was one sustained major battle, over the People Mover.

In the skirmishes, both newspapers printed the almost daily Eddie Burke charges of favoritism, cronies getting business, bid-winning black contractors who had not submitted the lowest bid, relatives on the payroll, a scattershot attack always based on a grain of truth, always misleading. Burke, as chairman of the Finance Committee, had access to bushels of the city's financial documents. His staff could leak papers to a credulous reporter who lacked the legal training to know what he or she was reading; then, under deadline pressure, the reporter could be counted on to go with a story that was literally true and yet essentially wrong.

The Washington administration's O'Hare parking attendants were under investigation for skimming (yes, but the Washington administration had initiated the investigation; and the employees had been in place when Mayor Washington took office); a black company had not been the lowest bidder (yes, but the lowest bid had been a company with a history of low-balling, underbidding and then, under pressure of a job half-done, pressing for and winning an upward adjustment); a black bond counsel was less experienced than the white bond counsel who had lost the contract (yes, the black counsel was less *experienced* in this field—in the past, blacks were cut out of city bond work—but he was amply *qualified* to do the work); the black company that won the contract was an acquaintance of Harold Washington, a contributor in fact (yes, but where in the city of Chicago was there a black businessman that Mayor Washington did not know? The point is that the contract was competitively let, in a fishbowl of scrutiny; moreover, the mayor had voluntarily committed that he would accept no more than $1,500 annually in contributions from anyone doing business with the city).

The *Sun Times'* Fran Spielman was one of the regular recipients of Burke's documents. She didn't have much time to check her facts—she'd be scooped by whomever else Burke might be feeding, including Sneed who would be the newsperson of last resort for factually shaky stories. So Spielman would rush into print with the fat headlines that the *Sun-Times'* owner Rupert Murdoch was famous for. She would call at 3:00 p.m. for reaction, which was not enough time to track down the details of the matter. The only rebuttal that made the story, too often, was the evasive conditional denial of someone who wasn't familiar with the issue.

The skirmishes hurt, but it was in the major battle around the People Mover at O'Hare Airport that we fought most fiercely. The People Mover was a closed rail system to move passengers between air terminals and parking facilities at O'Hare. Bidders had been asked to design and quote a price for the system—the city had not provided specs, since we were looking for the best feasible design.

In accordance with proper procedures—as later confirmed in court —corporation counsel Jim Montgomery and the panel he chaired opened and reviewed the proposals in a closed session.

In the dog days of late August, Burke charged through Spielman, with Murdoch's Mack Truck front page headlines, "O'HARE BIDS OPENED IN SECRET—Sealed bids for the largest single contract in the city's history were opened by the Washington administration behind closed doors, despite a state law requiring that bids be opened in public." A small portrait of Burke was captioned, "Bids can be rigged." Alongside Montgomery's portrait: "It's perfectly legal."

The story was kept alive for weeks. "VRDOLYAK RIPS PACT," with a portrait of Fast Eddie saying "That is discrimination," against a portrait of Montgomery looking stressed, saying, "I do not steer contracts." The intelligent reader of the *Sun-Times* could be excused for concluding that there must be at least some fire under all that smoke, and that the Washington administration had finally been caught red-handed. Even members of the cabinet were claiming Montgomery had been guilty of bad judgment, and City Council allies were calling for an investigation.

Burke was given a platform for sustained invective against the city's handling of not just the People Mover, but the entire O'Hare development. The largest project of its kind in the world, it involved $1.5 billion in contracts and thousands of jobs. Burke was mounting a campaign to win City Council veto rights over O'Hare construction contracts, a power grab that would have put the Vrdolyak "29" in the management of executive responsibilities, seriously undercutting the Washington administration. By "proving" foul play in the People Mover, he was strengthening his case. "As far as I'm concerned," he told the *Sun-Times*, there will be no people-mover system. . . . The process was tainted. It cannot be rehabilitated."

The *Sun-Times* added editorials to its news stories: "Throw the bids out," read one, which concluded by saying, "The point is, Burke happens to be 100 percent on target, whatever his motivations. The blame is yours, Jim Montgomery." The editorial chided him:

> Sealed bids for construction of the controversial people-mover system for O'Hare Airport should not have been opened in secrecy. . . . You say the state law that requires public bid openings is "not black and white, cut and dried and simple." You imply there are circumstances that require scrutiny of bids under cover of darkness. Baloney . . . Playing with words. Double bull. . . . You do not help matters, Jim Montgomery, by vowing full and complete disclosure *"after the decision is made."* No, sir. The public is entitled to know what the sealed bids offer *before the decision is made.* That's why the law requires at least 48 hours between the opening of bids and the awarding of a contract. [original emphasis]

This singularly uninformed editorial completely ignored the city's attempts to explain that the People Mover contract had nothing to do with sealed bids. The controversial people-mover—controversial because Burke had been successful in his manipulation of the media—was not using what they called the sealed bid process because it was not obliged to use the sealed bid process: in fact the sealed bid process would have been completely inappropriate to the unprecedented nature of the People Mover contract. Our arguments went unheard and unprinted, though they were outlined in press releases and detailed in press conferences, and though the *Sun-Times* devoted barrels of ink to this story, heaping insult upon misinformation, castigating the corporation counsel for his handling. It wasn't until late the following November that the *Sun-Times* reported, in a small story buried among the turkey ads on page 34, that the city had been right all along.

The article quoted Judge David J. Shields, who acknowledged that "with the need for design and engineering skills, cost questions, the quality of the companies involved, the conduct of the negotiations, the use of consultants, the fact that price was not the sole consideration, and the uniqueness of the proposals, I don't think the situation was compatible with competitive bidding." In other words, Jim Montgomery had been completely correct in how he handled the negotiations, and how he processed the submitted designs and price quotations. In the course of his negotiations he saved the city of Chicago $20 million.

There was no editorial acknowledging the point, but the city had persevered. It was an important victory.

It came along with a string of City Council victories. All the dominoes were falling our way.

We had been successful in standing up to the attacks on affirmative action, and on the mayor's prerogatives in city contracting.

Next in turn was the confrontation over federal Community Development Block Grants. Under the CDBG program, the federal government earmarked a total dollar amount for each locality in the country, and required local jurisdictions to legislate a package of grants to local agencies totaling no more than the dollar figure allocated. Federal guidelines allowed Chicago to decide how the money would be used (i.e., to evaluate grant requests and make awards), but required that the money be used only in lower income neighborhoods. It further required concurrence by the City Council and the mayor. Both sides understood that if we failed to arrive at an agreement, the federal funds could be lost.

Members of the "29" from middleclass wards were engaging in simple demagoguery by insisting that their neighborhoods should receive their "fair share" of this money. They were using Mayor Washington's theme to stir up anti-Washington sentiments. They knew full well that even if the City Council approved, the federal government might disallow any such grants—it had happened under Byrne—and the funding would be returned to the federal treasury, forever lost to Chicago.

That was our first showdown, and we took our lumps. The Eddies committed a gaffe or two along the way. In their move to eliminate Washington-recommended Latino agencies, they made the error of removing *every* Latino agency. That damaged their efforts to woo Latino support away from the administration. We took the initiative when they were forced to back off. The CDBG fight wasn't a total victory, but it gave us valuable experience in marshalling our troops, and the self-confidence we gained helped in the G.O. bonds contest.

The Eddies had sworn to prevent the mayor from launching a major neighborhood improvement program to be funded by general obligation bonds. Those G.O. bonds were the difference between a year of ribbon cuttings and a year of further neighborhood decline. In some parts of Chicago the streets had not been improved since they were first graded and covered under the Roosevelt-era WPA program. These WPA streets, many cracked and potholed, had no gutters for water run-off, and would cause floods at intersections and in people's yards.

In many parts of Chicago the sidewalks had been constructed eight feet above grade, on vaulted brick spans that were now giving way—a cracked sidewalk could mean a fatal fall for a small child. To make these and other repairs to alleyways and gutters, the G.O. bonds were needed—but the Eddies had publicly sworn that no bond issue would be allowed to pass.

Yet it was passed, after Tom Coffey took his legislative lobbying to the streets. While the mayor and a small contingent of us were in Israel and Italy in the summer of 1985, Coffey's staff and the press office began organizing a media bus tour to key wards. When we returned, the mayor led the tour, greeted local aldermen—members of the "29"—and walked along the sites where we were proposing reconstruction. The white residents of the wards came out and met with the mayor and their alderman, agreed that we needed to fix the sidewalks and repave the streets, and said so to the news media who accompanied us—and in no uncertain terms, to their aldermen.

It was all very cordial, the aldermen a little sheepish but good sports, and the mayor completely successful in making his point: the G.O. bond program was a "nonpartisan" priority. Interest rates were low, and together with the refinancing of a 1982 bond issue, originally financed when rates were high, we could undertake some $130 million in improvements with no increase in taxes.

We coupled the CDBG and G.O. bond campaigns in the popular imagination, even though they were generally unrelated in their effects and in their timetable. We showed that the G.O. bonds would be evenly distributed among all 50 wards; in fact, because some city-wide projects like sewer repairs fell within certain wards more than others, some of the "29" wards would come out way ahead.

☐ *Turning the Tide*

By summer's end, thanks to Coffey's lobbying, our improving morale and coordination, our steadily developing hard-headedness, and the growing public impatience with Vrdolyak's obstructionism, we had passed both the CDBG and the G.O. bonds, and by late fall we had succeeded in winning the People Mover case in court. Mayor Washington believed that a critical factor in winning the hearts and minds was the Eddies' tendency to overkill.

Not content merely to fight the parliamentary battles over the bonds, the block grants, and O'Hare development, they harassed the mayor and called attention to their unsavory motives with a number of trivial spats they would have been better off ignoring.

For over a year they refused to confirm the appointment of William Spicer as the mayor's choice for Director of Purchasing. As it happened, the mayor decided Spicer had to go. "He's fully credentialed to run a modern, professional purchasing department," the mayor contended, "but we need a different kind of problem solver to sort out the mess we inherited in that department. Spicer's not the man." Yet when the mayor replaced him with Mary Skipton, the Eddies rushed through a confirmation of *Spicer's* appointment, even luring Spicer into the controversy briefly, in opposition to the mayor.

That confirmation of Spicer was the more conspicuous by contrast with the scores of other appointments they were holding up. They became at times haughty about their intentions to "protect" the city institutions from the mayor, and though that played well in some wards, it was irritating to the business and civic interests who were slowly coming around to express an opinion.

In another example, when the city tried to collect parking fines that had gone uncollected for years by previous administrations—in fact, had been written off the books—the Eddies took advantage of public confusion to urge that scofflaws not pay their fines. A few media folk, notably WMAQ-TV's Jim Ruddle, enthusiastically got on the bandwagon and virtually told viewers they'd be suckers to pay up, given the confusion at City Hall. The resultant loss of revenues hurt the city, which is just what the Eddies had in mind.

And Vrdolyak reached down to the bottom of the barrel to incite a riot in City Council, by goading Slim Coleman into a threatened fist fight. Coleman had helped a young man break away from a neo-Nazi street gang, and then had sadly helped the young man's parents bury the boy when he was gunned down, presumably in retribution. Vrdolyak had verbally assaulted him as "the funeral director of the Nazi party," spurring Coleman to leap from the press box and threaten the alderman. Murdoch's *Sun-Times* exulted "OH SCRAPPY DAY!" in giant headlines that filled the front page. Vrdolyak intended them to remind lakefront liberals that "radicals" like Coleman were important members of the mayor's coalition.

But all these headlines also reminded Chicagoans that Vrdolyak was wild and irresponsible, that apparently nothing was off limits in the pursuit of his objectives. Simultaneously, the mayor was sounding more and more responsible. What many had feared would be a black-take-all administration was settling into a familiar pattern of Chicago ethnic politics.

☐ *Ethnic Politics* ━━━━━━━━━━━━━━

Harold Washington took pains to make sure I understood Chicago's distinctive history of ethnic politics. Too many non-Chicagoans misunderstand the city's ethnic politics as evidence of racism, and an historical perspective is needed to dispel the notion that Chicago is simply racist.

Mayor Washington tried to clarify the difference in his speeches and press conferences, but without much success. I used to wonder whether the press heard him on the subject and disregarded what they heard, or whether they simply tuned him out when he spoke about the absence of racism in politics. Yet for all the media complaints, during his first two years as mayor, that he used race as a lever, he tried to be careful to maintain the distinction.

Chicago is without a doubt the most European of major American cities. From any of the towers in the built-up central city area, the "City of Neighborhoods" spreads as far as the eye can see, with church spires punctuating the cityscape, giving some idea of the parishes into which the city has been divided. Never mind that what was consecrated as a German-speaking Catholic church now offers services only in the Spanish language. The specifics have changed, but the essential quality remains.

For most of its history, throughout its neighborhoods, Chicago has been a city of immigrants forming almost self-sufficient communities, attracting greater and greater numbers of their fellow countrymen. Nearly a century ago it was already "the second American city of the globe, the fifth German city, the third Swedish, the second Polish"—a tradition it has maintained.

Out-of-towners are often surprised by the ethnic consciousness of Chicagoans, who are likely to think of themselves, and not just their adversaries, in terms of their ancestry. It's not considered impolite or unduly curious to wonder out loud where a person's parents came from. Harold Washington, who was a practiced politician in asking well-wishers their names, would frequently try to guess their cultural background from the surname.

To pick one example, the late historian Milton L. Rakove, in his "Oral History of the Daley Years," *We Don't Want Nobody Nobody Sent,* profiled some 40 players of the period, and was careful to identify each by ethnic background: Mexican, Jewish, Croatian, White Protestant.

Mayor Washington gave me a book published for the Institute of Race Relations in London, making his point. I'll quote the entire passage he was referring to, from Ira Katznelson's *Black Men, White Cities,* because it clarifies where he was coming from:

> As a consequence of the mosaic pattern of ethnic settlement in Chicago, the city's political parties, to win elections, had to put together electoral majorities composed of blocs of ethnic groups; as a result, the ethnic group, "as a group," functioned as a pressure group that could bargain and threaten sanctions. In turn, the opportunity for ethnic communities to enter the political process acted to solidify group consciousness and to perpetuate the division of the city, demographically and politically, into ethnic components.
>
> Chicago's ethnic enclaves largely coincided with the political unit of the ward. Compared with New York's, Chicago's wards (fifty after 1921) were small and compact, hence for the most part ethnically homogeneous. The multitude of national groups in Chicago had, as a result of this institutional feature of the city's politics, a political base from which to bargain, to attain access to the decision makers, or become decision makers themselves. The politics of Chicago were the politics of boundary management and direct ethnic group bargaining. In terms of numbers, the city's black population was one of many ethnic groups . . . ; in Chicago, blacks could not only vote, but almost from the onset of the migration, could, in realistic fashion, fight for political control of at least two of the [wards] as well.

Mayor Washington picked up that mosaic motif, and used it throughout his mayoral career. He preferred it to the "melting pot" metaphor. "I don't know that I believe in the melting-pot concept," he told a group of reporters in the fall of 1985. "I'm not sure that it's necessary for any of us to have our sharp flavors cooked away. I prefer the vitality and lusty differences of the Mexican and Jewish and black and Caribbean and Polish and German and Irish and Puerto Rican, and all the rest. And I think what makes Chicago such an exciting city, and what makes our era such an exciting moment in history, is that we are proving you don't have to give up anything of your own identity in order to be a part of the great mosaic of colors and tongues that we know as Chicago."

When he defended Jesse Jackson's 1983 pronouncement that "it's our turn," he was careful to explain the context, at least from his point of view. He didn't endorse that statement as a defiant claim that the blacks were in and the whites may as well pack up.

In speech after speech, and session after session—notably at Loop College in late February 1985—he carefully outlined the progress of ethnic groups in Chicago. When the Irish were no longer outcasts and when the Germans stopped being the "niggers" of Chicago, their ascendance didn't mean displacement of the previous in-groups. It simply meant that the Irish, or the Germans, or the Polish could assume a leadership role in the governance of the city, alongside those already in place. Harold Washington believed that blacks were now finally coming into their own, and he hoped to lead black and Irish and Polish and Croatian alike into a new mentality that saw not black vs. white, but black—or African-American, if you will—among a full spectrum of ethnic diversity.

He grew increasingly confident that he was winning the hearts and minds of the city. He believed that the Eddies had greatly overestimated Chicago's racism. He saw the polls showing steady improvement, the economic stats were all on the upswing, and the major political battles had been won—we were in position to spend 1986 cutting ribbons and breaking ground.

And even more importantly, the mayor had won a major battle in the ward remap issue.

One of the most nationally notorious facts of Chicago politics had been the gerrymandering of the wards by Mayor Byrne and the people who ran her city for her. As the mayor constantly maintained, there would be no 29–21 split if the ward lines had been fairly drawn to reflect the black and Latino populations of Chicago; the mathematics would be improved to at least 25–25.

The opposition had resisted legal challenges and court orders for years, but in November 1985, under pressure from U.S. District Judge Charles Norgle, they were forced to accept a new map of ward boundaries.

And their worst fears were realized when a special election was ordered for the spring of 1986. Seven new wards would be created.

Harold Washington victories in any four would mean that the mayor would be able to break City Council ties.

That would mean a flood of stalled appointments, passing through City Council. Which in turn would mean that boards would be able to take care of postponed business. For example, the venerable Edmund Kelly would be out of a job at the Park District, and that patronage-rich enterprise would be subjected to the same reform that had arrived at City Hall.

It would mean that the city budgets could be planned around the city's needs, and not the pyrotechnics of "Council Wars."

It would mean that the City Council committees would be reorganized, chairmanships would be reassigned to the mayor's allies. Which in turn would mean that former members of the "29" would make their accommodations, come around, and the City Council would more nearly approximate a normal legislative body.

That by itself would go far toward restoring confidence in Chicago. It would help Chicago restore the bond rating, lost by Mayor Byrne's financial irresponsibility. It would clinch the "new spirit" the mayor had been talking about.

"You see," Mayor Washington said, "it's hard enough to discipline a legislative body in the first place, because the responsibility is so diffused. Every legislator says 'The hell with you,' in the final analysis, 'if they love me at home, I don't give a damn what you think.' And when the media lumps me in there with them, that makes it even more difficult to discipline.

"But with a legislature that works, you're going to automatically restore confidence in government. We're getting there, you'll see."

It was a good year, but there were two issues where Vrdolyak stymied us. They were particularly frustrating to the mayor for similar reasons: both involved charges that were not only false but contrary to his deepest nature; and both were no-win situations where Vrdolyak scored if they were even debated, whether anyone won a "victory" or not. Vrdolyak succeeded simply by getting the media to pay attention.

One was the "Vrdolyak-Farrakhan debacle." The other was the charge that the mayor was a homosexual.

10

Farrakhan

In October 1985, Minister Louis Farrakhan of the Nation of Islam harangued an estimated 20,000 followers in New York's Madison Square Garden, where he was winding up a national tour. He was quoted as calling New York the "capital city of Jews," and making a number of anti-Semitic statements. He defended his position by comparing himself to Jesus: "Jesus had a controversy with the Jews," he said. "Farrakhan had a controversy with the Jews. Jesus was hated by the Jews. Farrakhan was hated by the Jews."

Louis Farrakhan preached separatism and economic independence from the white power structure. He had first made national headlines the previous year, during Jesse Jackson's 1984 campaign, when he focused his anti-white sentiments on Jews. He made several sensational speeches, including one where he called Judaism a "dirty religion." (The line was transformed, in the course of reporting, to "gutter religion," and that misquote became a metaphor for Farrakhan's anti-Semitism.)

For good measure he threw in another seeming tribute to Adolf Hitler: Hitler was a great man—not one Farrakhan could endorse, of course, but still, "wickedly great." He made headlines all over the country.

Many blacks, for various reasons, were attracted and mesmerized. Louis Farrakhan was a speaker of charismatic force, a spellbinder, an entertainer. In fact, 30 years earlier he had been "The Charmer," a calypso singer on Chicago's Rush Street. Added to the smoothness of his delivery was the passion of an Old Testament prophet, and the articulate argumentation of an imam. His message, for all its venom, still had the force of a religious proclamation for many of his hearers.

Moreover, he provided a focus for the active black racism of many in his audience, and an outlet for the frustrations of many more.

The *Tribune*'s Clarence Page, in a column labeled "Conversations with my own self," answered his own question, Why is he so popular: "He stands up to the white man in a way a lot of black folks would like to. He articulates our frustrations and offers us a feather of confidence. Farrakhan challenges us. If Arabs and Asians, especially the Japanese, can develop themselves economically without government help, he says, why not black folks?. . . He gets credibility from the fact that he angers white people."

And the Rev. B. Herbert Martin, "the mayor's pastor," attempted to explain the appeal of the man. "I understand how the remarks Farrakhan has made [about Jews] could be easily offensive," he was quoted as saying, "but once you get past all that, the man has a tremendous message. He was working in poor black communities teaching people to hold their heads high before whites even knew his name. I doubt that it's 20,000 anti-Semites who are showing up to hear him speak."

The week of the Madison Square Garden rally, Vrdolyak began a campaign of race-baiting in Chicago designed to pit Jews against blacks, and to split the mayor's base of support among both groups. He began by introducing a nonbinding resolution in City Council "jamming" the mayor—asking Mayor Washington to condemn Farrakhan. Never mind the incendiary potential—Vrdolyak was playing politics with a history of anti-Semitism in Chicago—the ploy was welcomed with glee by his light-hearted followers as a clever new twist to "Council Wars."

Ald. Bernard L. Stone, a Jewish member of the "29," was needed to provide the issue some gravity, and obliged by drawing on a reservoir of righteous indignation for the cameras. Allan Streeter, the black alderman of the 17th Ward where the Nation of Islam was headquartered responded with equally emotional resentment, in support of Farrakhan. In the subsequent vote the blacks voted as a bloc against Vrdolyak's resolution. A new black-vs.-Jew controversy had been conjured up, and the mayor had been maneuvered into the center of it. Vrdolyak could claim he hadn't invented black anti-Semitism, merely exposed it.

It was an off-again, on-again controversy that Vrdolyak managed to keep in the news for weeks, through the end of the year. In its way this issue demonstrated the poverty of the opposition's politics: the mayor was finishing up 1985 with a series of clear wins on the real issues, and Vrdolyak had to resort to gutter demagoguery to stay in the headlines. But we took scant comfort from that awareness.

Mayor Washington was frustrated and angry—as much at the media for giving Vrdolyak (and Farrakhan) coverage, as he was at Vrdolyak himself.

Vrdolyak's ploy worked. And while we all winced as out-of-town papers used the "Black anti-Semitism" to write more unfavorable Chicago stories, Jewish friends and non-Jews, white and black alike, were building up pressure on the mayor to denounce Farrakhan. He was advised that such a statement would be a litmus test, a barometer of his friendship, on a par with support for Israel.

He wasn't the only American mayor being pressured. Mayor Tom Bradley of Los Angeles had at first refused to publicly denounce Farrakhan, preferring to attempt to persuade the Black Muslim leader to moderate his speech. He finally denounced Farrakhan's anti-Semitism, reportedly after being pressured by the Jewish community in Los Angeles.

But Harold Washington was not about to be boxed in—by Vrdolyak or anyone else; he would not be forced to denounce Louis Farrakhan —or anyone else. He knew a denunciation would have been counterproductive, would have achieved the opposite effect. Partly because Farrakhan was more than a preacher. "These guys have been running social programs," the mayor said. "People depend on them. There are neighborhoods where the kids wouldn't be eating breakfast if they weren't around. You've got a lot of mothers in some of those neighborhoods telling you 'Don't you mess with this man. You may not like the way he sounds, but he's taking care of us—the city never did.' "

"He gets these young men in there," the mayor told me, "and he gets their act together. They quit drinking, doing dope, gang-banging. He puts them to work."

And partly because the mayor was opposed to such litmus tests on principle. The *Tribune*'s Clarence Page made the point best: "Repudiation is an alien game to blacks," he wrote. "When one black leader criticizes another, it triggers memories among blacks of 'house slaves,' who curried the favor of whites, as opposed to 'field slaves,' who were ennobled by their refusal to 'act white.' "

Harold Washington was even more blunt. "They've got to be crazy," he said of writers who were claiming he had a responsibility to undermine Farrakhan by denouncing him. "The whole point of this guy, his whole message, is that black politicians are getting their strings pulled by whites—bankers, corporations, the media. So I'm going to prove Farrakhan wrong by jumping up and denouncing him—because the bankers and corporations and media say I have to? Because Eddie Vrdolyak says I have to? Shit. . . ." He doubted the sincerity of those in the media who were joining Vrdolyak's call.

As he put it, Louis Farrakhan filled a lot of needs, in politics and in journalism, as well as among his followers.

The same newspapers and magazines who are still, 45 years later, capitalizing on the drawing power of a front page portrait of Adolf Hitler, or a swastika or other "wickedly great" icons that repel and fascinate, were able to make the same use of Louis Farrakhan. Farrakhan served their sales purposes, an important criterion for any celebrity. Two months after Vrdolyak had started things rolling, Farrakhan was still the lead front page story in the Sunday *Sun-Times*.

The white major media, in their scandalized attention to him, were making Louis Farrakhan rich and famous. In another *Sun-Times* item, Vernon Jarrett wrote of a time, not long before, ". . . when Minister Farrakhan was lucky to have 300 to 400 followers on hand at any regular worship in his Chicago mosque. . . . Today [in 1985, he] can earn from $5,000 to $7,000 for a speech at a white institution, I am told.

"Although he has never won or sought elective office, nor ever built a plant or founded a major black institution, he was invited to address the prestigious luncheon of the National Press Club in Washington."

The nationally-syndicated black columnist Carl T. Rowan had written:

"I have come to view all this [publicity for Farrakhan] as just another part of the tragedy of race relations in America. White people in the media have insisted that they make black heroes and villains. They made Stokeley Carmichael and H. Rap Brown pop celebrities. I want to say, with certainty, that Farrakhan is not the spokesman for black America, and I resent the fact that he is made to appear so."

The mayor clipped these and other articles, key passages marked and circled. He was pained that some of his supporters didn't understand his position, and he was groping for an explanation that would make sense to them. On the Carl Rowan clipping, he had noted in the margin, "Not black issue."

Not a black issue? Black anti-Semitism is not a black issue? *"That's* not the issue," he said. "Why are we talking about '*black* anti-Semitism' now? There's a Big Lie here, and Eddie's getting away with murder. Rowan's right—what you have here is white writers trying to characterize black leaders by setting up Farrakhan as a spokesman for blacks."

Who gave Vrdolyak—or the pundits whose buttons he was pushing —the right to demand from blacks an accounting for anti-Semitism? The very idea incensed Harold Washington.

He told me that blacks historically have identified their fortunes with the Jews in bondage under Pharoah, or wandering in the wilderness, struggling toward the promised land. American black gospel music is Christian in theme but Israelite in mood. "Let my people go" is as much a black American phrase as an ancient Hebrew one. The everyday metaphor of the black ministry is as much Old Testament as New.

The contrast "is insane," he said to me, "Your tribe [he knew, because we'd talked about it, I'm a Lutheran of German heritage] has done just about everything it could to kill off the Jews." Not just the Holocaust, he said, but the persecution of Jews all across Europe— "especially in Croatia." He laughed.

The reference was to Vrdolyak's Croatian heritage; I don't know if he was historically accurate about anti-Semitism in Croatia, but I got the drift. He had pressed the point to me, more than once before, that the white ethnic population of Chicago for the most part represented those areas of eastern and central Europe where anti-Semitism over the centuries had been most intense, and most lethal.

And not just the white ethnic, and not just in Middle Europe. "You have no-Jews-allowed clubs here," he said. "You have no-Jews-allowed neighborhoods. You want to find anti-Semitism, you don't have to go down to 79th street."

Washington wasn't the only politician to recognize that white anti-Semitism in Chicago isn't limited to the crackpot neo-Nazis who occasionally put us in the national headlines with their marches in Skokie or Marquette Park. Ed Burke referred to the "latent anti-Semitism in Chicago and a large population that will never vote for a Jew. They would vote for anybody before a Jew," he said. (The statement was made in 1976; in 1983 he would probably want to say "almost anybody," since the Jewish Bernard Epton polled almost half the vote against Harold Washington.)

Speaking of that prejudice (and, outside of Cook County, a Protestant prejudice against Catholics as well), Burke described it accurately: "It may be latent, it may be the kind of prejudice that would not come to the surface in a business, professional or personal relationship, but when that individual gets behind that curtain on election day, and he sees that name on the ballot, he has an opportunity to satisfy his latent biases or prejudices."

Another prominent Chicagoan, Marshall Korshak, summed it up with understatement: "I never was inhibited because I was Jewish, but I will say if there is a highly competent Christian and an equally highly competent person of the Jewish faith, and both aspiring to it, I think it is practical politics that the Christian will get it. It's unfortunate that living in perhaps the most enlightened period in the history of civilization, there is a great deal of prejudice. We have made the atom bomb and we landed on the moon, but in man's relationship to man, we still have a long way to go."

So why the concentrated attention on the phenomenon of "*black* anti-Semitism"? the mayor asked. "I'm not saying the guy's not anti-Semitic," he said of Farrakhan, "but what's the motive for giving Vrdolyak all this attention." He questioned whether Fast Eddie was alone in wanting to drive a wedge between black and Jew, or whether there was a more deep-seated malevolent force at work.

"Why the hell aren't they attacking white anti-Semites?" he asked. "Do they think blacks are a cheaper target? Do they think I'm a noodle they can push around with this phony sanctimonious bullshit?" It was clear that on this issue he had backed into a corner and no amount of coercion or suasion was going to get him out of it.

His usual response to attack was counter-attack, and so he did, even though he was fighting with both hands tied behind his back.

On the one hand, to keep the story alive was to lose on the issue. Any fighting was worse than none. On the other hand, he couldn't use the historical argument, because he would be fanning more flames of disharmony by appearing to be attacking white ethnics in Chicago.

He had to settle for halfway measures. As we had with the "Vrdolyak Tapes," we tried to use nomenclature to turn the whole issue back on Vrdolyak. Even though we might not be able to change the tenor of the reporting, we might be able to reach some percentage of the public with the reminder that it was Vrdolyak, not Harold Washington, giving Farrakhan such publicity. It was Vrdolyak, not Harold Washington, putting Farrakhan's picture on the front pages. Our unwieldy terminology was "the Vrdolyak-Farrakhan debacle," which writers occasionally picked up.

Mayor Washington criticized both Vrdolyak and the media together when he said the Vrdolyak-Farrakhan debacle was one of the lowest points in the history of Council Wars. By that time Stone and Streeter had done their Punch and Judy show, shouting and poking their fingers at one another. Wisecracks from other aldermen had prompted the mayor to reprimand them from the presiding officer's chair: "We don't need any smart-ass remarks from anybody else." It was not the City Council's finest moment. The media accurately portrayed a grinning Vrdolyak, prowling the aisles during the debacle, surveying the pandemonium he'd unleashed by pushing Stone's and Streeter's buttons.

The next day, Mayor Washington charged that Vrdolyak's success in injecting the issues of racism and anti-Semitism into the Council proceedings "will live in infamy." He told the press that the Vrdolyak-Farrakhan debacle "will be remembered as a low point in city history."

He also stressed his own lifelong commitment to the causes of the Jewish community, through the General Assembly and the U.S. Congress, as well as the Mayor's Office. His commitment was not directed to the appreciation of his own voter base; it was heartfelt and born of his wider world view.

He believed he had a responsibility to work for closer ties between Jews and blacks, and responded whenever his Jewish advisers made recommendations: to place phone calls and sponsor Jewish "refuseniks" in the Soviet Union; to visit Jewish neighborhoods where acts of (white) anti-Semitism had taken place; to commemorate the Holocaust each year; to participate in Jewish programs and religious services; and to lead a Chicago delegation to Israel in the summer of 1985. When he joined a Jewish demonstration against President Reagan's visit to the S.S. gravesites in Bitburg, West Germany, he spoke eloquently about the meaning of the Holocaust:

> The Holocaust is not simply a Jewish observance. The fact of the Holocaust is overwhelmingly powerful to the people who lost six million of their own—men, women and baby children, grandmothers and favorite uncles, doctors and lawyers, farmers and merchants, laborers, dock workers, newspaper editors and newspaper vendors—people like you,

people like me—average people who might not make much of an impression as they pass you on the street—as well as the best and brightest of a generation of Europeans, writers, poets, artists, philosophers— all swept away in a factory of death that could process a trainload of human beings into ashes before the factory whistle blew for lunch. It has personal meaning to our Jewish brothers and sisters. But it has profound meaning to all of us. The Holocaust is a fact of our modern history that has meaning to Jews and Gentiles alike.

None of that made a difference, in the end. He was sometimes bitter toward Jewish advisers who would accept no explanation for his silence on Farrakhan. He felt they were applying the "phony litmus test" instead of giving him credit for what he stood for.

Farrakhan, he said, was the polar opposite of everything Harold Washington represented. Farrakhan's political strategy aimed to exclude. "You want a minority, and you want them stirred up," he said. "You might say it's the opposite of what black politicians want"—a majority, coalitions, inclusion, practical power to change the system and not rhetorical opportunities to excoriate it.

He stressed that it was not a matter of two black leaders trying to do the same thing in different ways. "We're doing entirely different things. If they [his Jewish critics] can't see that, well later for them."

11

Rumors of Homosexuality

The other no-win issue was the long-lived rumor that Harold Washington was a homosexual.

When I first came to Chicago I had been told, matter-of-factly, that the mayor was gay. My informant was a politically connected board member of the Chicago City Ballet who seemed to know his way around. It was common knowledge, he said. No big scandal, just a fact.

The circumstantial evidence was in place: he was unmarried, and had been single for years. He had a fine looking young man, Bill Walls, as his personal aide, later replaced by another, Chuck Kelly. His chief of staff, Bill Ware, was said to be gay. The woman he loved, Mary Ella Smith, had been described by his campaign staff as his "fiancee" during the 1983 election, and the status seemed permanent, artificial.

Familiar with my informant's racial preferences, and reasonably satisfied that his familiarity with the subject was not at first hand, I disregarded his statement. I recognized that it belonged in the category of "personal sexual defensiveness expressed offensively," familiar to every boy and girl of seven or so. At about that age, sexual anxieties combine with sexual mystification to create preoccupations that some people never outgrow. At one level, "fag" is intended as a specific charge; at another level it's a generalized epithet, like "motherfucker." Most "motherfuckers" are not really being accused of having performed the act that the word would seem to indicate.

As I was later to learn, *every* politician is gay, to listen to their opponents. Gov. Jim Thompson had to endure a rumor campaign early in his administration. Former alderman Leon Despres told me that he was simultaneously accused of being a homosexual and having a mistress, in the same election.

The difference was, the mayor told me, that when rumors about candidates surfaced in other elections, newsmen dismissed them for what they were. But in his case, he said, the rumors were given credence.

Such rumors have appeal to even those with high credulity thresholds, and they have an amazing staying power. A full 13 months after the mayor's death I was still to meet an intelligent, politically and socially aware Chicagoan who matter-of-factly repeated what he'd heard—that a police officer routinely watched young boys troop into and out of the mayor's apartment.

What bothered him was not just that the attempt to smear him was treated as news. That didn't happen often in such cases, but it was not unheard of. What bothered him was that in the case of Harold Washington the rumors were exhaustively researched.

The rumors were not merely whispers, but forged photographs, with the mayor's face crudely spliced onto pornographic pictures.

TV reporter Dick Kay told the mayor that WMAQ-TV had sent investigators to Washington, and to visit Harold Washington's ex-wife in Alabama, in an effort to prove the rumors—it was the mayor's conclusion they were trying to *prove* the rumors since obviously such rumors can never be absolutely disproved. WMAQ-TV spent thousands of dollars and it was ultimately satisfied there was no truth to the stories.

He believed that the problem was worsened by a homophobic bent on the part of the *Chicago Tribune.* And he said that a white candidate would not suffer the same indignity. Yet it must be noted that the rumors were spread throughout the black community as well as the white; and like all such rumors, they stuck.

When I was hired, the rumors revived. The implication that I was gay—my association with the ballet world was cited—didn't make things easier for him. And Bill Ware became a fresh target when he became ill, early in 1985. Ware's illness became a pathetic sidebar to the continuing effort to refute rumors about the mayor.

There were almost daily references to Ware's health in the gossip columns, and he considered them to be a program of deliberate innuendo. "They're implying I have AIDS," he told me. "I'm not the real target. This is aimed at the mayor."

One morning after another such item appeared in Irv Kupcinet's *Sun-Times* column, Bill called me to ask how the rumors might be confronted. I had already decided they couldn't be, short of a counterproductive lawsuit, but he was determined to take some kind of direct action. The only approach I could suggest was to visit the columnist in person. "Kup's fair," I said. "Let's go over and you look him in the face and let's settle this once and for all."

That's what we did. Kup invited us in, gave Bill a hearing, and said he understood Bill's concern. The next day he printed a short item to the effect that despite the rumors, Ware was up and around and felt fine. What I didn't realize is that I had never seen Bill Ware in good health. The Ware I brought to visit Kup was a shadow of his normal self. The trip must have confirmed Kup's concerns. Still, he gave Ware the benefit of the doubt. In a few weeks, Ware was dead of an immune system disease.

The rumors of homosexuality resurfaced regularly. The first time we talked about them was in connection with a Vernon Jarrett article which made reference to the slanders. The mayor was upset with Jarrett for giving them another cycle of life, though the columnist had run the story to refute them.

"You don't refute those stories," the mayor said. "You ignore them. The damage is done when the stories appear, no matter what they say."

"The worst part of it is that you don't want to offend the gays," he said. It didn't bother Vrdolyak or Burke that their flunkies were characterizing gays' sexual preference in a negative way, by using it in a derogatory manner—they had nothing to lose. But the mayor, personally and philosophically committed to gays and lesbians as full partners in his coalition of minorities, could not even acknowledge that he had been insulted.

I thought I was helping him to articulate that frustration when I searched for the words to frame his situation. "I've been around gays all my adult life," I told him, "and I don't attach any particular stigma to that label. Why not just laugh it off—say something like, 'No, I'm not gay, but if I were I'd come over there and beat the shit out of you.'"

I was reiterating what I took to be his own position on it when I added, "I just let it roll off me, water off a duck's back—if there's no way to deal with the Vrdolyak lies, don't worry about them. Let them say what they want. I don't give a shit."

When I said that, his frustration broke through, an outburst of pent-up anger. "Well *I* give a shit," he said, angry, as though I'd made a concession. "I'm a man, goddamnit. In *my* family, it makes a big difference. It makes me want to punch him in the mouth." The response, in turn, offended me.

"Don't get me wrong," I said, now sticking up for my upbringing. "*My* family would be offended too. But"—I was quoting him back to himself—"what's the point of keeping the issue alive?" Later, smoldering, I realized again how difficult it was to deal with this kind of rumor, how loaded it was with overtones, how difficult to handle— even talking between ourselves.

The stories didn't inhibit the mayor from backing a gay rights ordinance, or appearing at "gay pride" rallies, and occasional other events in support of gay rights. The mayor insisted, whether talking to gays or about them, that he was for "human rights, including rights for gays and lesbians." That clarification was a concession to those, especially blacks, who believed in a Biblical injunction against homosexuality; it was his reminder to them that civil rights and human rights had to be protected in all quarters.

The issue arose again when former school board superintendent Ruth Love, taping a TV talk show for WLS-TV, made a rude remark between takes, when she thought the cameras weren't rolling. WLS-TV aired the clip, enhanced by subtitles because Ms. Love's body mike had been turned off, in which she referred to the mayor and the current superintendent, among others, as "a bunch of gays." When the mayor went to WBBM radio to tape an interview, a WBBM-TV reporter, Phil Ponce, flanked by his camera operator and sound person, surprised the mayor with the sudden question: "Ruth Love says you're gay—do you have a response?"

In July of 1986, reporting on the progress of the gay rights ordinance, the *Chicago Tribune* embellished its story with a recounting of the rumors. The mayor was not alone in considering the material totally gratuitous to the reporting of the gay rights story. The *Trib's* City Hall reporters were upset that their story had been tampered with, and assured me the additional material had been inserted by editors without their knowledge or over their objections. The mayor was indignant, but of course unwilling to prolong the issue by commenting.

The usual generous and supportive response to rumors was the standard disclaimer, uttered by even his closest supporters: "The mayor's private life is none of my concern," or "They shouldn't deal in those rumors; whether he's homosexual or not has nothing to do with the conduct of his job." He couldn't complain about that response without sounding as if he were offending gays as he did so. If the rumor-mongers succeeded in bringing public opinion to that point of "acceptance" of "whatever his sexual preference," the rumors had succeeded, the mayor had lost. It was bitterly frustrating to him.

The truth is that Mayor Washington was anything but gay. And despite his demanding schedule it would seem he had a pretty active social life. Specifically what things he did in his free time is something I wasn't privy to, but I know he did them with a number of attractive women.

Mayor Washington's professional and formal relationships with women were typical of many men his age. He had an automatic deference to "the ladies"—some complained that he tended to put them on a pedestal. When meeting an attractive younger woman he could be openly flirtatious, but when meeting one closer to his age he could be respectful and, if he were attracted to her, almost shy. He was the door-holder type, as one woman told me. I noticed that his manner changed and his language cleaned up whenever a woman was present in a meeting, and there's no denying that he was more comfortable in his work when he was dealing with men— unfortunately a not uncommon liability for women in business who, like men, benefit from easy dealings with the boss.

And it must be acknowledged that he was capable of the most outrageous momentary lapses. Kari Moe, one of his top aides, an attractive and energetic younger woman, daily had to grit her teeth as he greeted her with lines like, "How're you doing, little one?" It was, as she knew, not only a term of affection but even a flirtation. As far as I could tell, she enjoyed it in the spirit in which it was offered. But she also knew that she, like the rest of us, had to help break him of that easygoing manner of address, because it was considered a political liability. Another woman who gently but firmly took the mayor to task for pleasant but ultimately patronizing comments was deputy chief of staff Brenda Gaines.

Frequently, in off-the-cuff speeches describing the dramatic progress in his administration's hiring of women, and the important cabinet posts to which women had been appointed, he would say, summing up, "We've got women squirreling around all over the government," and we'd *all* grit our teeth.

Liz Hollander was another who asked me to remind him that these expressions might be as offensive to some women as racial stereotypes would be to other minorities. He was reminded, but I doubt anyone considered it a fatal flaw.

More likely, they gave him the benefit of the doubt, because when he could be made conscious of his slip, he took it seriously and made a note not to make the same error again. And, even more important, he had kept his promise to open city government, at the top decision-making levels, to women appointees. Some 40 percent of his top appointments were women.

In his personal life, Mary Ella Smith was clearly the woman he loved, and a good deal of his free time was devoted to her. He not only obviously enjoyed her company, but also sought her advice for personal decisions—buying clothing, attending social functions—as well as professional matters. He respected her intelligence and her insights and would ask for her comment both on speeches he was to deliver, and on gifts he had to present, and other issues of style.

She was a familiar sight in the mayor's outer office, waiting with Delores Woods until he'd finished his late afternoon business. When he realized she'd been waiting, he'd visibly relax, welcome her in, engage in the light banter of two people restraining their familiarity in public.

"Smiff," he would call her in a playfully gruff voice, when he was able to leave, "let's get out of here." And they'd leave City Hall together in the limo. The affection was natural and easy, and clearly a mutual relationship of real devotion.

He was solicitous of her needs, attentive to her when she was in his company, and careful to insure that she was included in the logistics when he was attending an evening function with her; the mayor's security detail followed suit, and she was embraced under their contingency plans every bit as much as if she'd been Chicago's first lady as Mrs. Harold Washington.

But at the same time, she was not the only lady in his life. No one had much time at City Hall for extracurricular adventures with the opposite sex, but whenever word came to the mayor of interoffice romance, he'd say with a grin that "Everybody's getting something out of this job but me." I don't know who was "getting something," but I know he wasn't left out.

It was clear when we traveled that he had access to admirers almost everywhere we went—though only occasionally time to take advantage of their admiration. And there were periods in Chicago when he was by prearrangement unavailable for staff phone calls due to a day out of town for "creature comforts," as he put it. If a staff member innocently assumed from his intimations that he was traveling somewhere with Mary Ella, he discreetly avoided being specific, but cautioned that Mary Ella didn't know and didn't need to learn that he was making this trip.

He had a roving eye, but not a leer. Even in his ogling, he was a gentleman, but he had a knack for encouraging a woman of initiative. Once after I had seen him flirting for 15 minutes with a clearly attracted stewardess, he turned to me with a grin and said, "It's not the man, it's the office."

More than one sultry voice had his phone number, and I'm not the only aide who had the experience of answering his phone during a meeting at his apartment, and having to disappoint one of those sultry voices with the fact that he was in conference. Occasionally he would be alert for the call, and would ask to have it transferred to another room. Not much later we'd be informed, sometimes with that grin, that the meeting was about to conclude, it was time for us to leave.

David Canter, a long-time friend of the mayor, and a Hyde Park neighbor, occasionally met with Mayor Washington early in the morning, before the mayor's schedule for the day had begun. He remembers one morning, when he had statistical data the mayor had been anxious to see, he came in early, was shown into the living room rather than the small study the mayor usually used, and seated on a couch tucked back into a recess of the room. "I wanted to spread my papers out on the coffee table so I sat myself on the other couch, opposite. It was at an angle where I could glance down the hall, and while I was doing my work I saw an attractive female form slipping out of the mayor's bedroom. Naturally, I didn't bring it up."

The women I'm speaking of were black women, those I saw and so far as I could tell those whose voices I heard. But he did remark to a young black aide, on an appropriate occasion, "My boy, every man needs to have a Swedish woman, once in his life."

The mayor also apparently suffered some of the anxieties not uncommon to a sexually active man of his age and physical condition. As we were settling into our seats en route to Washington, D.C., in the summer of 1987, he loosened his tie and ordered a vodka tonic, arranged his reading material, and smiled over at me. I noticed that he looked more relaxed than he had been in several weeks, and I commented on it.

"I've just seen the doctor, had a check-up," he told me. I took him to mean an annual physical. "I'm just glad to know that everything works." Howard Saffold was sitting in first class with us, across the aisle, and the mayor made some remark to him that I didn't catch. Saffold laughed.

The mayor turned back to me, paused, then explained. "I was taking a medication for high blood pressure," he said, "and it interfered with my—creature comforts. I couldn't figure out what was going wrong, and I thought, oh shit, I'm getting too old. But the doctor changed the prescription, and now I'm doing just fine." He smiled to himself, shook his head. "I've gotta tell you," he said, "you go through something like that, and it makes you a little short-tempered sometimes."

One's sex life is the ultimate privacy, and there should be a reluctance to be specific about someone else's. In the matter of the rumors that he was gay, his second, and real, concern would be to avoid offending any homosexual who regards reaction to those rumors as offensive. But I know his first concern would be to make it clear that "He was a man, goddamnit."

12

Clarence McClain

The triumph of symbol over substance in the "Council Wars" era was personified in one individual who would certainly have been Chicago's "Man of the Year" in 1985, if we awarded such dubious honors.

I never met Clarence McClain. I never talked to him. In a thousand days of work with Mayor Washington, I never knew the mayor to meet with or talk with McClain socially or professionally, in person or on the phone.

I knew Clarence McClain the way most Chicagoans knew Clarence McClain, as the media-sponsored bugbear of the Washington administration.

With his much-ridiculed woolly wig, his distinctive, cruelly mimicked style of speech, and his advertised lack of formal education, this black man was tailor-made for bigots who wanted to characterize the new mayor's team as an "Amos and Andy" show. Coming into City Hall in mid-1983, two months after the inauguration, (he had been in the hospital for 70 days following an auto accident in early April), with the racist jokes of the campaign still ringing in the public's ears, he seemed to confirm the prejudices of those who feared the worst from Chicago's first "black administration."

He was there for the summer, then forced to resign when his police record—two vice convictions—and some tax problems were made public. But the Eddies and a fascinated, some would say obsessed, media kept him at center stage in the Washington administration throughout most of the first term.

To some journalists McClain was "the mayor's closest personal friend," but in City Hall he was what Mayor Washington referred to as "the cheshire cat—there's nothing to him but his grin."

I found out nearly everything I know about McClain from reading the papers—two self-promoting profiles that appeared in the *Trib* and *Sun-Times* in the fall of 1985, and Robert Tuohy's detailed article in the January 1987 issue of *Chicago Lawyer.*

The mayor was impressed with Tuohy's article, so I read it carefully. Had I not, my impressions of McClain would be based on the major media coverage he got, and on libelous statements like that of Eddie Burke, who called him a pimp, a panderer and a child molester. Linking Washington ally Ald. Larry Bloom, for some forgotten reason, and probably trying to cast further aspersions on Washington's sexuality, the chairman of the Finance Committee said, "When the Washington-Bloom-McClain political caravan comes around to your neighborhood, the mothers and fathers of Chicago children better lock them up and keep them out of the way."

McClain's early resume, garnering from the Tuohy article, would be considered exemplary, the kind of record you'd cite to show what a child of the projects can attain with hard work:

Born: June 13, 1941

Family: mother a cook and caterer, working out of the home; stepfather a butcher at the stockyards; brother John now a Chicago cop.

Education: Dropped out of high school during his junior year (1958). After the army, attended Washburne Trade School, 1964–65, learning the tool-and-die-making trade.

Military: Honorable discharge, U.S. Army (1960); served stateside and in Korea, where he was company clerk (90-wpm typing speed); still sharp at the typewriter and word processor.

Employment history: After army discharge, worked two full-time jobs, testing tractors at International Harvester (nights), and X-ray technician at Billings Hospital (days). Left to enroll at Washburne. Soon making good money, working 60 hours a week at General Electric, 1965–1971.

In 1968 he departed from the script, taking a leave of absence from GE, to try his hand at promoting musical acts. By his account he did well. He booked black performers who had previously been self-managed, or managed by whites, in small clubs and in major venues like the Howard Theater in Washington, D.C. He even managed the "Jackson 5" for a time in 1970–71, before Diana Ross discovered them.

Still in his twenties, promoter McClain moved to Grace Street on Chicago's North Side, living a colorful life far removed from the Harold Ickes public housing highrise at 22nd and State, where he'd lived as a child. He was considering managing strippers in the Uptown area, "more for the socializing it offered, than for the money," he told Tuohy.

"McClain said one of his two vice convictions occurred during this period, a charge of patronizing a prostitute," Tuohy writes. Tuohy covers the episodes carefully, and the details are important in light of the libels McClain—and by association, the mayor—later suffered. Tuohy noted:

> His [McClain's] version is: "I was on the street one evening near where I lived and I saw an officer was harassing a black girl and I interceded and I got arrested for being a patron of a prostitute."
>
> He was fined $25. The other arrest for which he was convicted was in 1965. "I managed an apartment building and had an office in an apartment in the building," McClain said. "This was on the South Side. There were two girls who shared an apartment and another girl, a neighbor, complained about them. Two white cops answered the call and I went down there. The cops had searched the place for drugs and found nothing. There were no men there. The girls said they were being accused of prostitution. I told the girls not to say anything until you get a lawyer. The cops knocked me down and handcuffed me and arrested me on suspicion of being the keeper of a disorderly house. I put up a $25 bond. I had the choice of forfeiting my $25 bond or taking a day off the job, paying for a lawyer, and putting my faith in the courts. I took the easiest way out for me."
>
> Published reports on the arrests would indicate that McClain may have had the dates of the two incidents flip-flopped. . . . McClain said it's possible he might have the dates wrong but he recalls clearly the circumstances.

The alleged child molestation simply never happened, Tuohy indicates:

> The accusation that drove Burke to call for protective custody for the city's children was a pandering and contributing to the delinquency of a minor charge, ultimately dropped. The alleged victim was supposed to be a young male from Grand Rapids, Michigan. When reporters checked, they found that the McClain allegedly involved was not Clarence.

McClain moved from promoting performers to promoting a politician. His booking office was adjacent to the legal offices of Charles E. Freeman, later to become the judge who swore in Harold Washington at both his inaugurals. Through Freeman he met 16th Ward committeeman and state representative James C. "Bulljive" Taylor, and suggested that his promotional abilities could enhance Taylor's political career. He seems to have flourished as a one-man legislative office, organizing community events, raising funds, helping to coordinate legislation, and doing public relations.

Harold Washington told me that he met McClain at about this time, through Freeman. He was impressed, he said, with his native intelligence and his street smarts. "McClain is one of those few people who always know what's happening, down on the street, in the 'hood—what he doesn't know, he knows how to find out, he knows who to ask," Mayor Washington told me. "He has an uncanny sense, a feel for what's going on, a feel for what works, an instinct. I don't have enough people around me with that instinct, and McClain was invaluable."

McClain left Taylor to do volunteer work for Harold Washington in late 1971. He says he saw in Washington the principled independent that machine hack Taylor would never be. (In fact, Taylor and Washington were bitter enemies; Taylor is the only person, of all his adversaries, that I ever heard the mayor speak of in a tone of hatred. Taylor apparently felt the mayor was a phony; the mayor thought he was "the bottom of the barrel," and "completely bad news.")

Tuohy quotes McClain:

"I was very impressed by Harold, very impressed. He never took three days off in a row. Never took a long weekend, never really took a weekend. He was usually doing something. I liked the way he stood up to the currency exchange lobby." He stayed with Washington through his Springfield career, in the house and Senate, and went on the payroll when Harold Washington went to Congress in 1980.

In the summer of 1983 he came into the new administration as a dependable, savvy aide who could help with the initial rough sorting of City Hall personnel and issues into "We" and "They."

For those who supported Harold Washington but wished he had fewer rough edges, Clarence McClain was their worst nightmare. Even to other top staff, McClain was a reminder of the mayor's unruly, uncouth side. McClain and Bill Ware were opposite poles of the new order, appealing to opposite impulses in Washington's personality, and McClain suffered by comparison.

The mayor was perfectly happy with the dichotomy. He knew he needed the input of both, particularly as he began to assign the scant

800 first- and second-level management positions over which he had discretionary hiring rights. These were the people he would depend upon to conduct the administration's business as the new term began.

He wanted Bill Ware to set up a management structure, recruit and hire professional personnel, marry the business sector to government, bring in the computers, revise the systems, guarantee the integrity of personnel and purchasing and finance departments. And he wanted Clarence McClain to be in a position to review, criticize, recommend, keep an eye on the process, be an open ear to anyone who was being "professionalized" out of access to City Hall, and give the mayor his gut reactions to how things were going.

Mayor Washington felt that although he couldn't have set up shop without Bill Ware, he needed someone of McClain's perception and intelligence to review the proceedings from the perspective of the base—as high Episcopalian Bill Ware would never be able to do.

As McClain later told the *Trib's* John Kass, "He [Ware] wanted to bring in academics who eventually stagnated some things. I wanted to bring in qualified people, yes, but they first had to prove their loyalty to the mayor. That they should get a position, that's fine. But let them be loyal first. There are a lot of eggheads and Ivy League types who don't know how to get things done," he said, "who've stagnated this administration. I'm not smooth. I'm South Side. But I know who to talk to and how to talk to them. That's what I do best. That's one reason I'm the mayor's friend. We've been friends for 15 years, and that's not going to stop. I'm loyal."

McClain's title had been Freedom of Information officer, a position that gave him plenty of elbow room, since the real clerical work of FOI was done by clerks. At $69,001, he was the highest-paid official in the mayor's office—he had asked for a token $1 more than any other employee in the top rank (the mayor's salary, set by the budget ordinance, was only $60,000). He was top man on the totem pole.

For the four brief months that he was on the scene, McClain was the administration's lightning rod. Want to attack affirmative action? Want to ridicule blacks in high places? Want to know what "black reform" is really all about? Look who the mayor has put in charge. Critics were not about to let his dismissal rob them of a target. The Eddies said it, the media repeated it, and just about everyone believed it: even after he was fired, throughout the first term, McClain was the Rasputin behind Harold Washington, he was the fixer for contracts, he was "the mayor's longest, deepest, closest friend." Didn't he live (he did) in the apartment building where Harold Washington lived? Didn't they cut their deals there? Wasn't he still the man who called the shots?

Mayor Washington was almost 20 years older than Clarence Mc-Clain, and sometimes seemed to have a mentor's concern for his welfare. Precisely because McClain had been singled out by the opposition as the administration's most vulnerable victim, and by friends as the administration's most expendable scapegoat, the mayor was inclined to give him the benefit of the doubt. Never one to denounce on demand, Mayor Washington refused to join the fray.

The mayor knew that McClain had no nefarious role to play in city contracts. But just to make sure, because of the allegations, Mayor Washington reminded each top level employee, as she or he was hired, that they were supposed to operate by the book, no one was due any favors; above all, no one spoke for the mayor. That didn't mean that McClain couldn't make a living as a consultant to small black companies that were trying to figure out how to get a foot in the door at City Hall. There was nothing wrong with that—how else do small companies get started?—so long as the "clout" was "clean." So long as it derived from McClain's expertise and experience, and it didn't depend on illegal shortcuts through the carefully elaborated process that Bill Ware was supervising. The mayor was confident that Bill Ware would see to that.

In the meantime, the mayor seemed to be amused by the idea that McClain might be lining up white clients who thought he knew some secret password for getting work at City Hall. He told me the apocryphal story of the man who stood outside traffic court; as defendants filed past he would offer to fix their case for $25, and he did a brisk business. Then he'd watch the proceedings, and he'd refund the $25 to all those who lost their case. "He never had to do anything," the mayor said. He made his living on gullibility. McClain could offer more substantive assistance than that, of course; but the mayor was confident he couldn't fix a contract, nor that he'd try to.

Because he had been close to the mayor, and because he was who he was, Clarence McClain was an easy target for the Eddies. And he also bore the brunt of all the arguments against affirmative action. Where more sophisticated arguments might get lost in the details, he was easy to caricature and criticize, a perfect target for those who

considered affirmative action a process of stealing from more qualified whites.

For reporters and editors he was never simply "Clarence McClain,"
but "the mayor's closest personal friend, Clarence McClain," until I
called both newspapers to complain. The mayor wasn't denying his
association, but was irked by the presumption of the young reporters
who made such an attribution.

It was accepted as fact by the media that although McClain had
been forced out, he was still an eminence at City Hall, he was still the
man to see if you were black and you wanted a piece of the action, or
if you were a white businessman trying to learn the new rules of the
game.

Why won't you simply disown him, many black advisers urged. Reporters badgered the mayor and me with the same question, as
though all he had to do was make some kind of formal recantation
and they'd back off. But he accurately predicted that it wouldn't
make any difference what he said, and when he finally was driven to
clarify McClain's role, in the heat of "Molescam," he was proven
right.

"You have to know who you are." The mayor would say that with
an easy smile. Or he'd say it with a bitter smile. He'd say it when he
was under siege—as much a reminder to himself as advice to me—
and he'd say it to fortify me when I was taking the brunt of the press
reaction. It may have been advice from his father; it had that mantric
quality when he said it. And he said it again as he reacted to the pressure to denounce. "I'm a man, not a noodle," he said.

Why should he insult one who had been his loyal associate, whose
only failing, despite the successful propaganda campaign by the Eddies, had been his victimless misdemeanors of 15 years earlier, by
singling him out and repudiating him? No, he wasn't going to do it,
and if that were a political liability, well we all have a few.

And yet he did, ultimately, denounce Clarence McClain.

McClain himself set the process in motion, when he too obviously
encouraged the perception that he had an inside track on contracts
and jobs at City Hall. A *Sun-Times* reporter who interviewed him
wrote, "Since leaving the administration, McClain said, he never
talks to the mayor. He took the statement back a few minutes later,
saying, 'I had to say that.'" I would suggest the gullible reporter got
it right the first time; I doubt that McClain had second thoughts

about shading the truth; it's more likely that he realized such an acknowledgement could cost him business.

The reporter also writes that an associate "suggested some of McClain's purported clout may be a bluff, inadvertently furthered by the news media...He's got the best public relations in town...The image [the news media] has created is of an ex-pimp, who is the man to see if you want a contract. He has the appearance of influence... maybe even greater than his actual influence."

He fostered that impression. After a period of badgering by the Eddies, who called him in to testify before a City Council committee on his clout, sizeable stories appeared in each of Chicago's dailies the same week, in November 1985. That was the first time that I saw Mayor Washington's irritation directed toward McClain and not the media. He recognized that McClain was feeding their curiosity. At that point he felt that they were working at cross-purposes, McClain encouraging the very speculation the mayor had been seeking to discourage. Still, he continued to resist the suggestion that he disown McClain.

McClain had been making a living as a consultant working with black firms, helping them get certified for MBE assistance, helping them understand how City Hall works; it was good business for him to be acknowledged as a former top city aide, a long-time associate of the new mayor. He certainly knew the players, and he knew his way around the red tape. Of course, the fact that he was persona non grata to Bill Ware, who as chief of staff actually controlled all city contracting, was omitted from the equation, as reporters, following up leads from the Eddies, assumed McClain to have a pipeline into City Hall.

The quality of the "McClain Scare" reporting was perfectly exemplified in the *Sun-Times* of Oct. 5, 1985. A banner headline stretching from margin to margin proclaimed, "McClain talks revealed," with a subhead stating, "O'Hare ex-chief says formal mayoral aide sought contract data." Unless you had time and interest to read the story, you would miss the details.

> James A. Wilhelm, 31, who resigned this week as O'Hare Airport operations manager after a shakeup ordered by the Washington administration, said McClain made no attempt to steer contracts to specific companies.
>
> "The guy never tried to intimidate me," the "ex-chief" was quoted as

saying. "He never suggested that I do anything wrong or that he was about to do anything wrong. He just represented himself as someone who could solve problems."

Naturally, the story had the two obligatory paragraphs that we on the fifth floor could recite by heart, one to further sully McClain, the other to sully the mayor:

> Majority bloc aldermen have maintained for months that McClain holds a crucial behind-the-scenes role in city government. [Burke] charged earlier yesterday that Wilhelm was one of several city official McClain had contacted recently in attempts to influence city contracts. . . .
>
> McClain resigned his $69,000-a-year job as a Washington aide in 1983 after disclosures that he had failed to pay property taxes and had three misdemeanor vice convictions dating to 1965.

I suggested to the mayor that McClain was called a hustler, but if he were white, he'd be called a lobbyist. I once referred to McClain as a hustler myself, using the word in the "white" sense—a man who never rested, a man who knew all the angles and all the (legal) short-cuts. The mayor made sure I understood that McClain was no hustler in the other, pejorative sense—the penny-ante con man pulling a dodge on the street.

"He's a bright young man who didn't get any breaks," the mayor told me. "He had one chance in a thousand of getting off the streets and into a position where he could make something of himself. And he took it. And he got himself all the way to the fifth floor at City Hall. Nobody gave him a thing. He made it happen." And then, on the threshold of glory, if you will, he was caught up by misdemeanors of his youth.

"McClain is a tragic figure," he told me. "He's a guy who worked his way, rung by rung, all the way to the top, all the way from public housing to top job at City Hall.

"But he could never outrun his past." Not that he had a vile past, just that he had been careless about it.

When McClain left City Hall, the mayor told me, he went out "with a 21-gun salute. I said all those good things you say about a man who's given you good service. 'Fine, upstanding young man, good advice, always be my friend.' Now the media blows that up and quotes it back to me and uses it as evidence that he's still running things at City Hall."

Mayor Washington didn't want to begrudge McClain whatever might assuage his self-esteem. "Clarence has a lot to be proud of," he said. And he didn't want to buckle under the Eddies' personal attacks on the man. But he did realize that the attacks on McClain were in reality very effective attacks on his affirmative action program. And he was increasingly aware that he was going to have to take a position.

☐ *Affirmative Action* ☐ ═══════════

Mayor Washington once paraphrased Winston Churchill in describing affirmative action as a remedy for generations of inequity: It's the worst solution, he said, except for all the others.

He believed he had a double responsibility in the area of affirmative action: first to make it work in Chicago, as an integral part of his reform program; and then to defend it in principle, at a time when its detractors included the U.S. attorney general, the Justice Department, the White House, the president himself.

Chicago had long been considered the nation's most racially segregated city. Even before Lorraine Hansberry's *A Raisin in the Sun*, set in Chicago, the city had earned a reputation comparable to that of the deep South. And it was broadcast nationally: Martin Luther King's reception in 1966; the murder of Fred Hampton in 1969; and Daley's 1972 delegation to the National Democratic Convention being turned away because it was not adequately representational in its composition of women, of Latinos, of blacks. Bilandic had his confrontation with the federal government over the issue of segregation within the police department. Then Byrne, who had received a winning margin from black voters, offended them with her policies and appointments aimed at holding on to white ethnic voters she feared losing to Richard M. Daley.

Chicago's reputation for segregation was comprehensive: in terms of residential segregation, in terms of attitudes, and in terms of distribution of jobs and contracts.

Residential segregation was an issue on which Mayor Washington had many misgivings. He took pains to explain to me the history of block-busting in Chicago, and was sympathetic to the concerns of homeowners whose life savings, invested in their homes, could be wiped out through market manipulation by those who played to racial anxieties. He respected the community cohesion of our "city of neighborhoods" and while he could not countenance illegal restrictions to home ownership, he never concerned himself with any ideal of racial residential homogenization.

Racial attitudes—that was a vineyard where he toiled continuously.

But it was in the area of jobs and contracts where he could make a practical difference.

When he first took office, he established affirmative action guidelines for the Purchasing Department, and for other city departments in their routine procurements—25 percent to companies owned by blacks, Latinos and other minorities, and 5 percent to women-owned companies, for a total of 30 percent of the city business. These were not formal set-asides, or quotas that must be met; they were the target figures by which progress would be measured. By the same token, they weren't abstract goals; department heads were held accountable and were expected to be able to explain themselves if the goals weren't met.

He expected the totals to be exceeded eventually, as the capacity of MBEs improved. Ultimately—not "someday," but during his administration—"capacity-building" and public policy would have the combined effect of bringing city hiring and contracts in line with city population figures. That was the whole idea behind affirmative action, and it was a goal that he expected all men and women of good will to subscribe to. At the same time, though he could be publicly irascible on the subject, privately he was patient with media and business critics. He knew he was right, and he would go ahead despite the criticism, but he allowed that there could be a reasonable difference of opinion on procedure.

In March 1985, one of the first public statements I drafted for him from Jim Montgomery's legal language was his announcement of the "MBE/WBE/small business" executive order. In establishing the 25-5 formula as official city policy, he was not only formalizing city policy, but also joining issue with the Reagan administration's attack on affirmative action.

With his executive order he created a certification process to guarantee that phony MBE or WBE "fronts" could not take advantage of the program, and that they would be subject to liquidated damages if any slipped through. And he pointed out that the new procedures were shaking up the applecart to the advantage of every supplier, white, black or otherwise, who had previously been cut out by the wired contracts and old-boy arrangements that had prevailed.

He stressed that his policies were directing more city contracts to small businesses, both black and white, and that he had reversed a trend toward contracting outside the city. Before he was elected, he said, about 60 percent of the city's business came from outside Chicago. Since his "Buy Chicago" policies were implemented, buying from vendors within the city had grown to 62 percent, only 38 percent coming from outside.

Throughout his years on the fifth floor he continued to attack President Reagan's anti-affirmative action policies, and in particular the work of the chief of the Justice Department's civil rights division, William Bradford Reynolds.

"Make no mistake about it," he said, "they're working overtime to kill affirmative action. The only thing preventing them is a thin margin in the Supreme Court." For that reason he was among the first public figures to attack the Supreme Court nomination of Robert Bork.

He had reason to be proud of his accomplishments in affirmative action. After his second inauguration, concerned about that "thin margin," he led the fight against Brad Reynolds. As one observer wrote, his City Hall was "one of the few institutions in the country putting the rhetoric of affirmative action into policy."

He quoted Rosalynn Carter's observation that Ronald Reagan had made it respectable again to be anti-civil rights, and attacked three fallacies he said Reagan's team were promoting:

"The first," he said, "is ideological, or perhaps just superstitious. It's the idea that a social conscience isn't necessary." He said the neo-conservatives seemed to believe in an "invisible hand" that would sort things out, if everyone simply worked solely in self-interest. "According to this theory, your own 'private conscience' will suffice, so long as you're God-fearing and a good person. That fallacy should be called 'the new selfishness.' "

The second fallacy, he said, "is the idea that we have reached a kind of plateau, economically and socially, where there is no longer a need for affirmative action, no need for righting the balance. As one writer put it, 'the white guilt trip is over.' " That fallacy, as he pointed out, flies in the face of everything we're learning about the growing disparities between black and white, between haves and have-nots, as America becomes an ever-more divided society.

"The third fallacy is that affirmative action doesn't work," he said, and set out to prove his point, using Chicago as a case study.

In hiring, he said, "the city work force I inherited was 27 percent black, 68 percent white. We've brought those numbers almost in line with Chicago's private sector work force. We're now at 31 percent black (the private sector is 32 percent), and 63 percent white. That was achieved despite 8,000 layoffs by affirmative action—over the past three years we averaged 58 percent black new hires, 29 percent white."

In city contracts he had exceeded his goals. "Last year we awarded minority businesses $116 million in contracts, a figure that represents 27 percent of total city procurement. And we awarded over $34 million to women-owned businesses, almost 8 percent. The total for MBEs and WBEs, 35 percent." He noted that the city had put teeth in his executive order, as well, collecting some $900,000 in liquidated damages from companies who had broken their promises to comply.

He was especially pleased that Chicago's private sector was heeding his example, and not Reagan's. "Perceptions and practices are changing," he said. "A number of major employers have voluntarily adopted our affirmative action goals in their hiring practices."

He chided "the old cliches, the 'common-sense' argument that affirmative action will cost more and produce lower standards."

"To that common-sense argument, let me suggest another way to look it it," he said. "Every member of a minority at one time or another has reflected on the hard fact that, as an unproven and untried competitor, he or she has to work harder, has to pay even more attention, has to adhere to even higher standards. That's a fact of life.

"With affirmative action policies in place, the minority competitor finally has the opportunity to see the hard work rewarded. Now the old-line firms realize that they too must gear up for a new level of competition. They have to raise *their* standards, pay more attention, work harder. With the old deals no longer in place, with everyone working harder, the industry as a whole becomes more competitive. That is what we are beginning to see among city suppliers in Chicago."

He cited as evidence a cost savings to the city of $24,300,000 in 1986, representing the difference between cost estimates based on previous years' experience, and the actual contract bids that were signed. In one example, the contract for the city audit was awarded to a consortium led by Touche Ross, with 55 percent going to minority and women-owned accounting firms, at a cost of only $850,000 for what had cost a cool million just the year before.

Critics of affirmative action carped that contracts were sometimes not awarded to the lowest bidder. The mayor's comeback was that "lowballing"—deliberately bidding low and then negotiating a change-order later with the job half-done and the city dependent on the firm—had been a notorious problem in previous administrations.

Often the "low bid" was far from the best bid. "You've got two guys telling you they'll fix the dent in your car—one asks for twenty-five bucks, the other says it'll cost a hundred. Who in this room is going to jump at the twenty-five dollar bid? Yet and still, if the city doesn't pick the 'low bidder' we get more headlines."

The proof was in the $24 million net savings to the city, after eliminating all the proprietary bidding and "emergency contracts" which short-circuited the bid process.

Other critics complained that better qualified whites were sometimes passed over for less qualified blacks. Mayor Washington insisted that this principle was the most frequently abused. "You've got a job that requires training and a year's on-the-job experience. You've got two applicants, a white with training and three year's experience, and a black with training and one year's experience. Which is better qualified—for that job?" he said, poking a finger at me. His answer was that they were obviously equally qualified, since the specs called for just one year's experience. "Qualifications have been drawn up to exclude minorities for years," he said. "All we're saying is you take the pool of *qualified* people, and then get your minority goals out of that pool.

In his last year he was under fire from Latinos who brought him statistics showing they were underrepresented in jobs and contracts. His response surprised me: he thought they were too pushy, aggressive beyond their readiness to compete.

In that confrontation, Harold Washington the politician was defensive. Harold Washington the tactician was reactionary. Too often he'd been confronted by what he called "the Byrne Hispanics," who he believed were not so much identifying with minority causes (and in fact resented being identified as "people of color"), as they were muscling in to what they saw as just another turn of the Machine. I think he misunderstood the Latino protests of 1987 as purely political pressure, using inflated population or work-force statistics. "They're mau-mauing us, and I'm getting tired of it," he complained.

He was also concerned that blacks and Hispanics could be divided by greed and envy, and resisted any attempt to create a formula to further specify a breakdown of the 25 percent for minorities. "That's where goals become quotas," he said. "You can't put in there Hispanics so much, Asian-Americans so much—where does it stop? Mexicans as over and against Puerto Ricans and Cubans, you know. I mean we lose the ballgame before we start."

He was concerned, too, that the black reaction to Hispanics getting more than their share was never far below the surface, and in fact bubbled over frequently.

He ruffled feathers when he made the ill-advised statement that "We haven't been able to attract Latinos who are qualified." He repeated the statement and defended it—he pointed to the city's active recruitment efforts in Latino communities and insisted that while we hadn't been able to steal professionals away from the corporate world, on the other end of the employment spectrum the city had fewer and fewer jobs for unskilled workers. It was a no-win argument and though we had his office full of community activitists in prolonged discussions, with charts and graphs supporting his argument, he recognized that it was the kind of argument that would never end.

"We'll always have arguments about who's getting the biggest share," he said. But he seemed impatient that the Latinos weren't keeping the argument "within the family." In fact, it was probably a tribute to him and the changes he'd wrought that they were so outspoken.

He never wavered in the conviction that affirmative action was helping the society as a whole. Sometimes he talked the practical language of redistribution. "Blacks are going to get into the action. Make no mistake about it, Bunky. Blacks are going to get their share of the pie. Period." And just as often, in his private considerations as well as his public rhetoric, he talked the philosophy and principle of fairness as the only way to sustain a healthy body politic, for whites as well as blacks. The occasion was a private criticism of Walter Mondale's 1984 campaign—he called him "Willy Lump-Lump" for fearing to stick up for liberal principles—but he intended a more general application, when he said that "People won't even admit it but they want fairness. You can't get your ass comfortable if you're sitting on all the goodies."

Of course, the most telling argument against affirmative action was in the human stories of those who claimed to be fired or displaced by minorities. The mayor flatly denied that ever happened. "That's the oldest song in the world," he said. "I didn't get my job because. I don't think there's a single valid case of that. I damn sure know we didn't fire anybody to put in a black. Sure, we have to hire minorities and women at higher rates, but the majority's still the majority."

Jesse Hoskins, Mayor Washington's Personnel Department commissioner, told a reporter, "It was never our intention to just sweep people out of their jobs. The mayor's goal is to ensure that there is parity in the work place. That means that the work force reflect the numbers of the city. To get there, we have to hire at a higher percentage of minorities, otherwise we won't reach this goal until sometime in the next century."

Redressing the balance just wasn't going to happen by itself—not in Chicago and not anywhere else. The affirmations made in the 1960s—that government would actively seek more equal distribution of jobs and contracts—were promises that Harold Washington took seriously. As mayor of Chicago he was in a position to do something about those promises, and he intended to.

He was proud that it could be said that during his administration, City Hall was "one of the few institutions in the country putting the rhetoric of affirmative action into policy."

13

The Mayor and the Media

The mayor had made it clear, before I was hired, that he wanted to utterly destroy the informal press channels that had developed. He wanted to dry up Sneed's sources. He asked that I establish tight controls of the press office—"if I can't control my own goddamned press office, then I might as well give it up, trying to control the rest of government."

He wanted a highly visible, well-publicized crackdown on leaks in government. He suggested that my firings in the press office be connected to specific leaks, if possible, so the point could be clarified. He encouraged my publication of an in-house memo for cabinet members outlining press policies, clarifying that only the press secretary and his deputy were authorized to speak for the administration. He wanted something written with the press corps in mind, that would "shake their cage," so that in their editorial reaction they would publicize a "crackdown on leakers."

Even as late as the fall of 1987, he was still looking for opportunities to fire people for leaking, to make that point.

However, that tendency was in apparent conflict with the freedom-of-information, open-government thrust of his administration, and he understood that there was no way to promote the premise—certainly not through the mass media—that it was good government to fire people who leak stories to the mass media.

Further, it was city policy not to discuss confidential personnel matters when terminating an employee. So public hangings were difficult to pull off. Though journalists often got the message, that only meant more grief for me. And the severity of the public example was never communicated to other employees or to the public at large except once, when Sneed, writing in the *Trib's* "Inc." column, suggested that she'd heard a reason for Tom Coffey's 1986 severance was the mayor's impatience with stories leaked from Coffey's camp. She solemnly assured the world that such had never happened, thereby confirming the mayor's suspicions—and satisfying him that she had helped to spread the word.

He remained adamant that "you can't manage even a Ma and Pa store if your employees are disloyal," and believed that leaking damaging information was the ultimate disloyalty. He never lightened on that subject. "It isn't like they can't bring their problems to me, or Bill [Ware], or their department heads," he said. "There's no excuse for leaking. There's no excuse for disloyalty."

About this time I gave him a copy of the Stephen Hess book, *The Government/Press Connection*, which I had been using as a reference, with a book mark at the chapter headed "Leaks and Other Informal Communications."

Hess provides a "typology of why leakers leak," including the Ego Leak ("I am important because I can give you information that is important"); the Goodwill Leak ("a play for a future favor"); the Policy Leak (sometimes when promoting a policy by press release would get no attention, leaking it will produce a headline); the Animus Leak ("used to settle grudges" or to embarrass); the Trial-Balloon Leak ("revealing a proposal that is under consideration in order to assess its assets and liabilities," most often used by those opposed to the proposal); the Whistle-Blower Leak ("the last resort of frustrated civil servants").

The morality of leaks is no different from any other moral question. At one end it is as much a tool of press communication as a press release, upon which both press and public official are mutually dependent. At the opposite end it is a caviling resort of a sneak, even of a thief, if the information is sold (no matter what the currency) or if the information is proprietary. In a public office, the information generated in the process of decision-making is not only the "private property" of those participating, but can be even personal and privileged, for example the circumstances of severance for such personal reasons as health. Looked at from a different cut, a "good" leak can expose a national hazard, a "bad" leak can unfairly tarnish a public career.

The issue of leaks to the press is one area of principle where the press, generally speaking, seems incapable of coherent, dispassionate appraisal. So much newsgathering is apparently dependent on leaks that it is hard to find an editorial supportive of the right of a public official to conduct his or her business in private— that is, to decide when a process has been brought to the stage where information is ready to be made public. Taking another tack, some have defended the right to privacy, but have also defended a journalist's right to invade privacy in the pursuit of a good story, if he or she can get away with it.

Mayor Washington was even more adamant in safeguarding the right of government officials to confidentiality during the process of decision-making on account of his "open sesame" policy of freedom of information. By executive order he had declared the city's files open to all. The policy under previous mayors had been to keep everything under wraps, and even those few materials legally obtainable were in practice made very difficult to get in a timely fashion. Mayor Washington was guaranteeing that nothing would be hidden from the public—everything would ultimately be available for inspection—with the understanding that the city managers could conduct each stage of their business without the disruption that would be caused by disclosure of matters under consideration.

If the official media positions were predictably inhospitable to that line of reasoning, many individual journalists had no problem admitting to me off the record that the mayor had that right of self-preservation. And when they inveighed against us in editorials and articles and cartoons about "muzzling" and "Ron Ziegler tactics," we took satisfaction from the awareness that we'd struck a nerve. After the press office staff changes, there was a brief frenzy of editorials and articles emphasizing our new policy. The mayor was mildly disappointed that the clamor died down as quickly as it did.

The "education of the media" was more than a side track for Harold Washington. It was a major continuing preoccupation for him.

And the chief priority in that education was making clear his discontent with the very concept of "Council Wars." He pressed his case every chance he got. If only a small percentage of his critique of the media's handling made it through to the public at large, he still felt it was important that he continue to try to impress the media.

One indelible lesson from politics for anyone who spends any time in that environment, is that there are no monoliths—none. Anywhere.

Whenever you speak about "the *Tribune*" or "Channel 7" or "the Department of Economic Development," you are using abstract concepts. You can discuss Managing Editor Dick Ciccone at the *Trib*; you can talk about General Manager Joe Ahern at Channel 7; you can analyze the planning commissioner's position on an issue. But you can't speak meaningfully about the *Trib*, Channel 7, or the Department of Planning, if you're working for results.

For you are simultaneously aware of a counterforce in the person of individual *Trib* reporters and members of the editorial board, with their own strong opinions; or of Andy Shaw's or Jay Levine's independent streak over at Channel 7; or of staff members at the Planning Department, with a contrary point of view, a "minority opinion" that may be tomorrow's new direction.

Parties interact, not infrequently in conflict, within even the smallest organs of society. One may appeal to the factions in a large group, the splits between principals, even the ambiguities within an individual's process of reasoning.

And so he did, as Mayor Washington drummed his opposition to "Council Wars," and characterized Vrdolyak as a "terrorist." Reporter by reporter, issue by issue, he worked on "changing their heads." Particularly with younger reporters, I sometimes got the impression that he thought he could save them from the tendencies of their employers if he could individually persuade them of his points. He told me he'd purchased some 20 copies of a book on the difference between how blacks and whites communicate, and had made presents of them to the City Hall press. "It didn't take," he said, "but it was worth the try."

Particularly with the *Chicago Tribune*, he believed changing their heads to be an important part of his mission.

He spoke in terms of the "Good Trib, Bad Trib" syndrome. The "Bad Trib" was the flagship metropolitan newspaper of the Reagan and Republican and conservative cause. He perceived links between the *Tribune* and the Reagan White House, and while he sometimes reacted outwardly to the local or immediate effects of a *Tribune* story, he also analyzed the larger-scale implications, looking for the connections to Attorney General Ed Meese, or to HUD's Jim Pierce, or to Education Secretary William Bennett, or to Reagan himself. He believed that the "Bad Trib" served the ideology and the ambition of those at the very top, to play an active role in the advancement of a conservative agenda, often to the embarrassment of its finest writers.

The "Good Trib" had put together a thoroughbred stable of the country's best civic-minded writers, dedicated to solving the problems of one of the world's most important cities. The politics of this group were nonpartisan, often nonspecific, submerged in the more immediate priorities of each issue.

He believed that the newspaper suffered a split personality. He recognized that its owners and editor and writers alike, were compelled by ethics and professional standards to be fair, objective, responsive—after all, although the *Trib* endorsed Richie Daley in the primary, they weighed in for Washington in the general election rather than sit it out or endorse Epton. At the same time, he felt, they aspired to be a "great" newspaper in another sense—to exercise their role as a counterweight to the other "great" newspapers of liberal bent, in other cities across the country.

Very often he played directly to the "Good Trib" group of writers, understanding their justifiable pride in the paper's civic record and implicitly refusing to believe they were going along with the "Bad Trib."

He believed it made sense to "work on" reporters and members of the editorial board, both veterans and youngsters. "You have to talk to each one of them as if they worked for the 'Good Trib,' " he'd remind himself by way of saying it to me. "You'll be wrong most of the time, but when you're right you'll score."

This approach made good sense to me. I had become personally convinced that anyone exposed to Harold Washington on a good day would come away a convert; I attributed most of his problems with the media to misunderstandings about the man, which would be cleared up in even a brief meeting. Although I was naive about the depth of cynicism in some parts, and perhaps naive about the inflexible assignments burdening some of the reporters we invited in, I sold him on one reporter after another, always using the Harry Golden case as an example.

He thought John Kass was anti-Washington, tainted by his reputed 10th Ward origins and his reputed acquaintanceship with Vrdolyak? Not true, I argued, he just didn't know the mayor well enough to appreciate him. Dean Baquet was "a snake in the grass" and had come to the *Tribune* from New Orleans with a warning—"don't trust him"—from Mayor Ernest "Dutch" Morial? That was then and this is now, I reminded him, Baquet seems sincere.

Ann Marie Lipinski suspect? Give her a chance, she's not looking to do us in, she just wants a good story, she's trying to get ahead, I had lunch with her, she's our kind of people. "Bad Tribune" doing a major, Pulitzer-quality series on "The Wall," the shame of Chicago's public housing? No, that's the "Good Tribune." This is not another Sneed-style attack on the administration, the reporters are serious journalists, not out to do a hatchet job, let's talk. Bruce Dold trying to get an inside look at government and politics? Trust him, at least once.

Of course, he was equally suspicious of Chicago reporters in other venues. Tom Fitzpatrick at the *Sun-Times*, writing nasty stuff, sneaking in sexual innuendoes—still, isn't it likely that his biggest problem is that all his information about you comes from Ed Kelly and his flacks? Basil Talbott is terminally cynical, the *Sun-Times'* mirror image of Steve Neal (then at the *Trib*)? Not so; he's no friend of mine but he's clearly a professional journalist and doesn't work out any neuroses in print.

Vernon Jarrett was the one journalist that Harold Washington most nearly trusted.

He first mentioned Jarrett to me in connection with the brief mention he'd written on the homosexuality rumors. He was unhappy that Jarrett had dealt with the issue at all—whether he thought he was being helpful or not—and he told Jarrett so.

He told me that he and the columnist were not seeing eye-to-eye just then, that they had "gone round and round about Ruth Love." Jarrett, for reasons that he couldn't fathom, had defended the former school superintendent in her squabbles with the Board of Education. Since Ruth Love and Mayor Washington had become antagonists over that issue, she was a point of friction between the columnist and the mayor.

Some weeks later, the mayor agreed to participate in a "roast" for Jarrett, at the Drake Hotel. I had prepared some notes for him, and suggested a line that punned on the word "love"—the line escapes me now—something along the lines of ". . . although on some issues there is no Love lost between us. . . ". He scratched it out with a grin, shaking his head. He didn't feel he was ready to take a chance on levity with that issue. But as he was making his remarks, when the moment came he used the line, and though probably only he and Jarrett knew what they were talking about, they both laughed a good laugh that was picked up by the other guests.

Knowing what I know now about their long history together, the friction over Ruth Love couldn't have been serious. At some point in my first few months, Jarrett and the mayor met for lunch on the South Side, and the mayor asked me to come along. "You have to meet Vernon," he said. "He's about the best we got."

I made some naive reference to his friendship or support for the mayor, and he cautioned me, "Now don't let your guard down. He's still a reporter, don't forget that." I wasn't to talk about anything we didn't want any other reporter to hear.

He added with a grin, "He doesn't trust you, by the way. He's warned me, he says you're just in this to write a book." I grinned back. "I could think of worse things to write about," I said.

If the mayor was cautious with Jarrett during that period, their relationship became much more comfortable once Ruth Love had finally left the scene. And when "Raymond the Mole" stories exploded in the press, it seemed to me that Jarrett made a conscious decision: screw the liabilities and the professional dangers and take sides. Where he had walked a fine line before, as a "balanced" reporter, he became an outspoken supporter of the mayor and his policies. "If they're going to fire me, they're going to fire me," he told me, "but I'm probably *more* secure by taking a position than I would be playing it safe."

It seemed to me that by throwing away the wraps of journalistic "objectivity" without abandoning the standards of journalistic fairness, Vernon found his voice, and connected his newspaper and TV work with his real core as a lifelong activist in civil rights and black consciousness-raising. Whatever the cause, I saw a new vitality in his political commentary, beginning about that time.

During the final two years of the mayor's life, Jarrett was one of the few people of any profession—certainly the only journalist—who could show up at the mayor's office any time without an appointment and get as much time as he needed. And of course, my office was open sesame to him as well.

Almost all the TV and radio reporters were suspect, but aren't we all about fairness, and wouldn't it be inherently unfair to write them off without a full trial?

Mayor Washington saw in the suburban-squeaky-clean video persona of WLS-TV's Andy Shaw and WBBM-TV's Mike Flannery an ingrained bias that he could never hope to overcome. Yet both were: (a) not suburbanites; they were fully invested in the city personally and professionally; (b) not lazy or seduced by the hand-outs they accepted from the Eddies; and (c) fair-minded, nonracist, ideologically in line with the mayor's own reforms. Shaw was one of my best barometers of media fluctuations and in our conversations Flannery demonstrated real insight into the complexities of Washington's situation. Even WBBM-TV's commentator Walter Jacobson, vicious as he could be, was not a mortal enemy. He saw his profession to be the cooking and carving of mayors, and we shouldn't take it personally. Perhaps needless to note, that was a point that got nowhere.

I always thought that was one of the mayor's more unfortunate animosities, the one that resulted in, or perhaps resulted from, a series of scraps with Walter Jacobson.

The high-salaried anchor and commentator on WBBM-TV, the CBS affiliate, delivered a "Perspective" almost every night—a commentary that was exempt from most requirements of reporting or editorial accountability since it was clearly labeled personal opinion.

His perspective could get him in trouble. In a case that made national headlines, he was found guilty of libeling the Brown and Williamson Tobacco Corp. The mayor took cruel pleasure, after the courts had ruled, in referring to Jacobson as "Oh, you mean that convicted liar?"

Jacobson spent most of his airtime administration-bashing. He bashed Bilandic and he bashed Byrne and now he was bashing Washington. He was, like Sneed, favored by those who had spiteful tidbits to leak; he had researchers who could track down the details; and he had camera crews who could seek to document, or at least illustrate, his stories. Not popular among his colleagues, who in any case seem to resent the more highly paid among their fellow journalists, he was parodied as an agitated, bouncy little fellow, whose skepticism had completely deteriorated into cynicism even as his wit was turning sour.

The mayor was adamant about ambushes by Walter Jacobson or his surrogates. At first he reacted coldly, later angrily, finally not at all, whenever a Channel 2 camera crew would spring up on him with a hostile question—often asked by a production person, without a reporter present to take responsibility.

He felt that he was exceptionally accessible to the press, and that ambushes were demeaning. Besides, he resented being treated like a character in a drama scripted by a media sensationalist—and he considered Jacobson not a reporter but an entertainer, a performer of others' research who often didn't understand the nuances of his own material, an unfunny politically-oriented Johnny Carson.

The problem with that outlook was twofold: first, Jacobson might be as superficial as the mayor considered him to be—Jacobson would probably be the first to admit he was in the entertainment industry, not a "pure" journalist, whatever that is—but he was not a bad egg. He was accessible to reason; somewhere under his flippancy he cared about the issues and their long-term import for the city; and he was personally invested in Chicago, not a disdaining suburbanite who took his cheap shots and leached city services, then fled each night to his preserve outside the reach of Chicago property taxes. In other words, I felt, the mayor's lack of appreciation for Walter was based on a false perception, as it had been in the case of Harry Golden. Surely there was hope for improvement.

The second problem was that Jacobson reached a lot of people. I didn't know where he was "in the ratings," but ratings concerns are none of a press secretary's business. Let media buyers worry about station's rankings and shares—all I needed to know was that hundreds of thousands of people were within range of this man's voice. We went to great lengths, in various efforts, to reach much smaller assemblages of citizens and voters than were watching Walter every night. A hell of a lot of people went to bed with visions of Jacobson's sugarplums dancing in their head.

On several occasions I managed to force the chemistry to work—or at least to keep both elements in the same flask long enough to make something happen. On the other end, producer Gary Weitman was performing the same alchemy with Jacobson and political editor Mike Flannery, Jacobson's partner on the weekly interview program, "Newsmakers." Between us we tried to keep some semblance of a relationship alive, and tried to get the mayor to agree to appear on "Newsmakers" at least occasionally. If he didn't appear on it as frequently as he appeared on Channel 5's "City Desk," Channel 7's "Eyewitness Forum," Channel 9's "People to People," and Channel 11's "Chicago Tonight," then he should appear on it at least as often as he made it to the Spanish-language Channel 44's "La Mesa Redonda."

Our biggest success in that effort toward rapprochement was Walter's invitation into the mayor's apartment for an hour-long wide-ranging interview. Jacobson brought bagels from a Lincoln Park neighborhood deli, the mayor made coffee, and the two spent a morning chatting about problems and prospects for Chicago. Jacobson walked his cameraman through the apartment, giving Chicagoans their first glimpse of the private Harold Washington. And he flipped through a scrapbook of photos—Byrne, Vrdolyak,

McClain, Jesse Jackson and others—asking for reactions, a technique that gave the interview some political pungency beyond the pie a-la-mode personal profile.

The mayor agreed to give it a try when I argued that the program would be valuable beyond anything money could buy, in communicating the human nature of a man who was only a political symbol to most Chicagoans. No commercial could possibly have the reach of this program, in large part because Jacobson was understood to be no patsy of the mayor; and also because Channel 2, I was convinced, would spare no expense advertising their exclusive.

He was opposed to it for several reasons, not least because we were "rewarding our enemies," weren't we? But also because WBBM was the CBS station, and CBS was the network that had shafted him with the Ed Bradley interview at the 1984 Democratic Convention. He believed that to be a deliberate move by a network that had an ideological bent behind its actions. And there were other disincentives: WBBM—and CBS—recently had been the object of a boycott by Jesse Jackson and PUSH.

But I insisted that this was tailor made for the original concept: it was the next best thing to putting every Chicagoan face to face with Harold Washington for a personal conversation. No, I didn't think Jacobson would spring a surprise or take advantage of the hospitality with a cheap shot. Gary Weitman had gone out of his way to talk us through the program.

He overcame his misgivings and gave WBBM and Chicago viewers the rare treat of an hour-long visit. And if he was at times strained— what Jacobson considered a fair question about unpaid income taxes and jail terms the mayor thought simply rude—it was overall very successful.

Still, the mayor refused to do "Newsmakers" with Flannery and Jacobson. He said his principal problem was the seating arrangement on the program: the "Newsmakers" guest was positioned in a swivel chair between the two hosts, and forced to fidget left and right when responding to questions. Weitman had no problem placing the mayor left or right of the two hosts, if that was the issue.

But it wasn't. Although it had suited our purposes to swat softball questions and show Chicagoans how modestly the mayor lived, in the apartment visit, Mayor Washington still wasn't interested in being grilled by media picadors who were more concerned about tormenting the bull than they were about our issues. He wasn't afraid of the questions—in Flannery's other capacity as a political reporter, the TV newsman could grill him every day. But he didn't want to subject himself to a secondary role in their half-hour weekly mini-series.

Weitman and I thus enjoyed a second success when we set up a special "Newsmakers" program, taped in the mayor's office. It worked well for us both. From Channel 2's vantage it was an exclusive; few lengthy interviews had been taped in the mayor's office. And from our vantage it was the mayor being mayoral, as only the mayor could be. Though a viewer might subconsciously compare Eddie Burke and Harold Washington on equal terms, from one week to the next, seeing them propped up in the studio setting at Channel 2, only the mayor could be televised from the mayor's office, at the mayor's desk, in the mayor's chair.

The apartment visit and the infrequent attempts to schedule "Newsmakers" (we did in fact do an in-studio "Newsmakers" once in 1987, in a trough between the waves of antipathy) were well and good, but they had little to do with our daily problems with Channel 2.

The biggest problems for us—and the greatest liability for Channel 2's programming—were the live remotes. Whenever the mayor was making major news during the late afternoon or around ten o'clock at night, we could expect requests from TV and sometimes radio reporters to interview the mayor live, on site.

I was reluctant to promise live interviews, because I knew that I might not be able to control events with the precision that live broadcasting requires. Were the mayor ten minutes late to a taping, no harm done. But one minute late to a live shot can be disastrous to anyone who plots their work in one-second increments. An unexpected phone call, a problem in traffic, an add-on event squeezed between a committee meeting and a fundraiser, there were too many ways the mayor could be late.

On the other hand, I preferred the mayor to do live shots, rather than taped encounters. "Why?" he wondered out loud. "Why give them a chance to rake me over?" It took me several rounds before he agreed with my point: edited TV puts the entire show in the editor's hands, while live TV creates the opportunity for the subject to take charge. If you're clear about the points you need to make, and if you're confident about your abilities as a performer, live TV or radio provides guarantees that other broadcasting denies you.

His initial objections were intuitive, and sometimes intuition is misleading. On live TV he could feel the pain as they "raked him over." He often missed the TV news and so didn't have a sense of having been "raked over" except when it was live. But he agreed with the approach, and we looked forward to opportunities for live remotes. Especially when we traveled, and the live remote from New York or Mexico City or Rome depended on expensive satellite time, he subordinated his schedule to the needs of TV technicians, and cooperated every bit as much as if he'd been a paid actor in a made-for-TV movie. In turn, TV reporters made a complementary effort to stick to the subject at hand, and focus at least part of their story on the issues connected with the trip.

Except Walter Jacobson, on Channel 2. Every time we did a remote, it seemed, we'd get along fine while Flannery quizzed the mayor on the event he was covering; but then they'd go to the studio with a question from Walter, who would seek to befuddle the mayor with a surprise issue.

It happened once too often. Jacobson used a live remote interview to spring a question on the mayor with no purpose except to embarrass, a question that involved a city worker doing something he shouldn't be doing. And while there is a sense in which the chief executive is responsible for everything that happens throughout the administration, we counted it a cheap shot for Jacobson to use the pretext of a scheduled interview on a different subject to provide filler—or perhaps comic relief—for yet another bashing. The mayor took him to task for the sneak attack, at some length. It may have been good footage for Channel 2, but it was the last straw for live remotes for that station, except on the condition that Jacobson was out of the studio.

The mayor's attitude toward Flannery was unfortunately conditioned by his resentment of Jacobson. And in turn, Jacobson took the heat for a more general resentment of WBBM policies. The mayor had plenty to be resentful of.

One incident occurred when the mayor agreed to appear on Lee Phillips' show. Ms. Phillips is an inoffensive interviewer whose half-hour weekly program dealt with pastel subjects, and the mayor agreed to help promote one of her many worthy causes. The mayor had declined other WBBM appearances, but management was making every effort to work around his recalcitrance and achieve some controversial footage. For this interview someone from the news department slipped Phillips a zinger. Ask him about his problems with his appointments, they said.

Whether they meant our problems getting new board members approved by City Council, or whether they were questioning the quality of his staff, wasn't clear. Probably the former, but she interpreted it to mean the latter. Either way, she was out of her depth. The mayor, who had been enjoying the light conversation that characterized her program, was surprised by the question. If there was one thing even his critics conceded it was that generally he had assembled the city's finest cabinet of public servants. What problematic appointments was she talking about?

Oh, she improvised, people like Ruth Love, Amanda Rudd, Leonora Cartright, referring to three black women who had been appointed to head the school board, the library and the human services commission—by Mayor Jane Byrne. They had nothing to do with Mayor Washington.

Mayor Washington was usually unflappable, but this question was so out of character, so wrong-headed, and so stupefying in its implication that he glanced over toward me, breaking the plane of the interview, shaking his head in bewilderment. I interrupted the dialogue, walked into the set and suggested to Phillips that it was probably in her best interest to rewind and start the interview over. I didn't use these words, but we would be sparing her a good deal of embarrassment if we just played it straight. We did the interview over, without the extraneous material.

Another problem we always braced ourselves for was the ambush in the corridor. Mayor Washington enjoyed doing "At Issue," a talk show hosted by John Madigan for WBBM radio, and we got there about once every four to six weeks. But the radio offices were in the WBBM-TV studios, and for a time we weren't available for the radio program because the mayor didn't want to enter the building. Of course, he could be ambushed anywhere, by WBBM-TV or anyone else, and was; but it was the principle of the thing.

On one occasion the mayor was nonplused by Phil Ponce, the reporter who blurted his question after Ruth Love accused the mayor of being gay.

On another occasion the mayor was leaving Madigan's program when a TV crew confronted him without a reporter—a production person or intern was used to taunt him with questions they knew he wouldn't answer. The object wasn't to film the mayor's response to the question but to show the mayor discomfited by the attack, for use with Walter's "Perspective" that night.

John Madigan took the mayor's part, in his own commentary, "John Madigan Views the Press." He recounted the story Jacobson was chasing, a piece about chief of staff Barefield's wife leaving her job with the Board of Education, and agreed with Jacobson when he concluded "that 'clout' was undoubtedly at work."

But, he continued in his radio commentary:

> What I object to is what Jacobson did in following up on his "expose!" Two weeks ago today Mayor Washington was in this building to tape our weekly WBBM Radio "At Issue" program. He was here by invitation. Our guest!
>
> Channel 2 chose to ambush the mayor in a corridor after the taping. One of its reporters threw questions at him regarding Mrs. Barefield. Press secretary Alton Miller intervened. The mayor left the building without answering.
>
> Jacobson ran the tape that night, hit the mayor over the head for supposedly "hiding."
>
> A week ago yesterday Washington was the guest on a TV news panel at a TV academy luncheon. Jacobson was moderator. Some panelist asked him about Mrs. Barefield.
>
> The mayor responded by saying he thought the woman reporter "had gone beserk." And that he jumped into an elevator "to protect himself." An overstatement. And I don't blame Jacobson for doing his thing on the mayor again that night.
>
> But Washington is correct on the "ambush" charge. The mayor is unusually accessible. Channel 2 should have questioned him at City Hall or at several other available opportunities. Not sandbag him while he was an invited guest of CBS.

Despite the constant friction, Mayor Washington and Walter were cordial together, even chatty. At the annual TV Academy luncheon in 1987 mentioned by Madigan, the mayor spent a half hour or so rapping with Flannery, Jacobson and other reporters before going to the podium, even though in previous years Jacobson had been singled out and personally targeted in Mayor Washington's remarks—one year he "did" Sneed, another year Jacobson.

But the animosity he felt, I'm sorry to say, was real. He referred to Jacobson in still another TV Academy speech, in October 1986. "Reporters in the press room joke about a certain TV personality here in

Chicago, who is said to have a standard line to fall back on, whenever he runs out of questions. What he asks in a pinch, I'm told, whatever the subject you're talking about, is, 'Well, Governor, or Well, Senator, or Well, Mayor, when you get right down to it, doesn't it all come down to a matter of race?' "

Jacobson would truthfully deny that he ever ran out of questions, but he wouldn't argue with the general statement. He never had any qualms about calling a diamond a diamond, a club a club. To some this might appear merely realistic. To the mayor it was part of the problem. More, it was almost the heart of the problem, not simply because of the attitude, but because it was multiplied, exponentialized, by the media reach. He was concerned, he said "that the power of the media can take the distortions of such a world view, and enlarge it to truly frightening proportions. I'm not clear on the rationale for his unabashed black-and-white approach to the news," he said, "but I would suppose it is: (a) truly based in a racially polarized view of the world, not so surprising here in Chicago, I guess; and (b) justified by the self-described special needs of the TV medium, for controversy and provocative, arresting scenarios.

"But where does provocative and entertaining news leave off," the mayor asked, "and pandering begin?

"By pandering, I mean that crass appeal to baser instincts." Comparing it in a sense to pornography, he said, "If you have a certain degree of fear or misunderstanding in the community at large, and if you have a commercial medium that earns its living by appealing to that community, one effective way to compete with other broadcasters is by pandering to the most basic interests."

While we reject pornographic pandering, we accept pandering in more subtle forms, he said. "When the pandering is in the form of a crass appeal to our instinctual fascinations, we recognize it for what it is. I'm suggesting that in this case as well, we should recognize it for what it is, and avoid it."

I'm certain Jacobson was confident that he was only doing his job, and calling it like he saw it. But there was an intellectual and emotional gap between his approach and the mayor's style, and there would be no bridging them.

If the mayor's attitudes were causing suffering at Channel 2, it was not Jacobson who was hurting, so much as Mike Flannery, who was paired with him on the Sunday talk show, "Newsmakers." Walter had his commentary, and his anchor slot. Mike was the one who had to

cover the mayor, almost daily. And the mayor didn't distinguish between the two. Walter might hit him in the back, but when he turned
around the mayor usually punched Mike.

Although the mayor ultimately could never get past Flannery's association with Jacobson, during 1985 he came to trust Andy Shaw,
along with WLS-TV's Mike Jackson and Jay Levine; he respected
WMAQ-TV's Dick Kay as fair, and WBBM radio's Bob Crawford and
WMAQ radio's Bill Cameron as even friendly. He was increasingly
willing to try his "personal touch" with all these reporters.

Some newspaper people—Steve Neal, Mike Sneed, and the *Sun-
Times'* Fran Spielman—were beyond any such effort. Neal and Sneed
often wrote hostile stories using information that was tailored to
prove an antagonistic point, and were willing to print as fact biased
information from the political opposition even when they had no good
reason to believe what they had been told was true. There was no
point in working with them; in fact Mayor Washington seemed to enjoy finding ways of aggravating his problems with Neal. On one occasion, filming WMAQ-TV's talk show, "City Desk," he interrupted the
flow of conversation to publicly correct an impression that he thought
Steve Neal was attempting to create—that Neal met regularly with
the mayor. He forced Neal to acknowledge that they did not meet,
that Neal had not interviewed him for many months. On another occasion he embarrassed Neal before his colleagues, again on a public
broadcast, by blaming Neal for launching a false story that Mayor
Washington had once sponsored legislation calling for a nonpartisan
mayoral election in Chicago. The program was John Madigan's "At
Issue" on WBBM radio, and after that appearance the mayor asked
me to turn down any future talk show in which Neal might appear as
an interviewer.

At the *Sun-Times*, Spielman was clearly a spigot for Vrdolyak and
Burke—she seemed to us to have an individual career field staked
out, to "prove" incompetence and corruption in the city's minority
business policies—and though she may honestly not have known that
much of her material was unsupported by fact, her bias was considered irreparable.

Except for those three, no one else was considered beyond remediation. He never gave up.

He worked especially hard on the *Defender*, Chicago's black daily
newspaper, but with decreasing expectation that anything would
come of it. And when the *Defender* joined the chorus of media con-

demnation in the wake of a federal probe of City Hall, Mayor Washington was ready to give up on it altogether.

The *Defender* had published a hostile editorial the weekend before. I made a courtesy call a few days later, in February of '86, and tried to salvage a relationship with Sengstacke. I spent several hours with him in his office. He seemed friendly, and gave me a tour of the newspaper. Immediately following the cordial visit, however, someone at the *Defender* called Sneed, who wrote:

> ...INC. hears Al had a hot chat with head honcho John Sengstacke, who gave the green light to an editorial Saturday blasting Washington. "It's time we asked you, Mr. Mayor—What the hell is going on?" was the editorial's parting shot. So how come the shift in focus at the paper usually favorable to the mayor? Does it have anything to do with the fact that Miller once fired Leroy Thomas, now the executive director of the *Defender*'s editorial department? Isn't it true that Miller fired Thomas, a press aide for former Mayor Jane Byrne and Washington, in front of other press office employees and humiliated him? And isn't it true that for the last several months, Thomas has dictated a policy of virtually ignoring the Washington administration—prompting gripes from some *Defender* reporters who contend that they cannot even talk to Washington administration people unless they get permission from Thomas? Just asking.

The "Inc." phrasing is another example of the writer's slippery journalistic standards. No, it is not true that "Miller fired Thomas ...in front of other press office employees and humiliated him." He was fired—Ware and Washington suspected the loyalty of the Jane Byrne appointee and had made it clear that he was the one black employee in the press office who had to go—but with respect and privately. But then Sneed never claimed I did, did she? She merely asked a question: "Isn't it true...?"

I didn't know it when I urged the mayor to meet with owner John Sengstacke, but he later told me he had spent years vainly attempting to cultivate the man, to no avail. And though the mayor was personally close to the *Defender*'s City Hall reporter Chinta Straussberg, and sought to give her scoops on stories that might benefit from friendly treatment, we finally agreed that it was hopeless. Thomas would guarantee that if the story ever made print, it was heavily edited and not played prominently.

Our problems with the *Defender* were continual. Typical was the case of a groundbreaking photo from an event in the First Ward, in which Mayor Washington and Ald. Fred Roti, a member of the opposition "29," stood on either side of a black community leader. The photo was cropped by Thomas, the mayor removed, Roti receiving sole credit. The *Defender's* lack of support for Harold Washington became a communitywide issue among black Chicagoans after a letter-writing campaign and after Rev. B. Herbert Martin chained himself to the newspaper plant gate in protest of Thomas' editorial decisions.

The protesters had demanded that the *Defender* give Mayor Washington fair treatment. They represented the sentiment that the *Defender* should be a black counterpart to the *Reader*, an alternative journal with a solid black readership. It should live up to its name, they said, and be a defender of the embattled mayor, counter-attack the anti-civil rights policies of federal and local agencies. The *Defender* could pull ahead of the other news outlets on key stories, become the newspaper looked to by the white major media for their leads. The community protest resulted in a promise by Sengstacke to improve community relations, but little more.

Nothing worked, there was no rapprochement. The mayor guessed that the *Defender* had been bought off—Vrdolyak? I asked; Daley, he said—and that it wasn't worth the effort. I persisted, paid a visit to Sengstacke at the paper and was courteously received. Talk, but no change. We commiserated with Chinta on stories that never made print, but finally gave up on the *Defender*.

I never did satisfy myself about whether Washington was right, or whether our problems were more prosaic. I concluded at the time that Sengstacke was an absentee owner; general management of the *Defender* was just plain out to lunch; the paper had enough advertising and enough circulation just to keep things moving in a viable torpor; and Leroy Thomas' personal differences were allowed free reign. That still seems to me the likeliest explanation.

There was another factor that the mayor suggested may play a part. In a conversation about the *Defender* he said, "You know, not every black institution welcomed my election with open arms." The *Defender*, he said, had endorsed him only grudgingly, and with very faint praise, late in the 1983 election. "Some black institutions were doing very well under the old system, with a white mayor and a white city government. Some black institutions were in a much higher position, relative to their community, than they can ever be when you have a black mayor and a black corporation counsel and a black housing commissioner and a black woman running human services."

Mayor Harold Washington met Pope John Paul II at the Vatican, in July 1985. "Did you notice the twinkle in his eye?" the mayor asked.

Mayor Washington became the first major black elected official to endorse the Rev. Jesse L. Jackson for president, in October 1987.

(Photo by Joan Vitale Strong, courtesy N.Y.C. Mayor's Office)

Meeting the media together in New York Mayor Ed Koch's press conference room, following one of their periodic planning sessions. Washington enjoyed Koch, and respected him as one of America's most dynamic urban leaders. But he was mindful of New York's slippery political slopes and was careful not to be led into a premature endorsement of Koch's re-election.

Mayor Washington and Jerusalem Mayor Teddy Kollek hit it off when they first met in Israel in the summer of 1985. So Washington was pleased to play host when Kollek visited Chicago a year later to receive the Albert Einstein Peace Prize.

Then Vice-President George Bush may have seemed an unlikely fellow-traveler in Chicago's Columbus Day Parade. Yet Mayor Washington turned to him for help when HUD tried to take over the CHA.

When Holy Angels School was destroyed by fire, Mayor Washington sponsored a one-dollar lease of an abandoned public school building to the Chicago Archdiocese. At the announcement, the mayor and Joseph Cardinal Bernardin find a moment to confer, with Ald. Bobby Rush (2nd) looking on.

Above. When Bishop Desmond Tutu visited Chicago in January of 1986 he was welcomed with a series of events across the city. Mayor Washington provided a special touring bus, and together with Mary Ella Smith, accompanied him throughout the day.

Below. At the Democratic National Convention in 1984, CBS newsman Ed Bradley sandbagged Mayor Washington—who always refused to appear on the same screen with "Fast Eddie" Vrdolyak—by bringing the alderman into the mayor's interview. Washington chastised Bradley for the trick: "That's about as low as you can get." That occasion was always a factor in his attitude toward CBS's local affiliate, Walter Jacobson's WBBM-TV.

(Photo by Michelle Agins, courtesy Mayor's Press Office)

Above. He was proud to be one of few war veterans ever to serve as mayor of Chicago, and he was especially proud to host the nation's first major parade honoring Vietnam Vets. The former first sergeant joined General William C. Westmoreland on the reviewing stand.

Below. Mayor Washington genuinely enjoyed opportunities to meet with and work with Chicago's artists. In January 1985, he accompanied the Chicago Symphony Orchestra to London, where he struck up a friendship with CSO conductor Sir Georg Solti that would continue for the rest of his life.

(Photo by Michelle Agins, courtesy Mayor's Press Office)

(Photo by Michelle Agins, courtesy Mayor's Press Office)

Above. Harold Washington brandishing his shillelagh in his first occasion as mayor at the head of the St. Patrick's Day Parade.

Below. Down time, at the Hyde Park Hilton's restaurant during the re-election campaign of 1987. Mayor Washington would flip through the papers while I got his sign-off on the miscellaneous issues that had accumulated.

Above. Mayor Washington confers with chief of staff Ernest Barefield (left) and floor leader Ald. Tim Evans during a City Council meeting. *Below.* Mayor Washington was, beyond doubt, of all Chicago's chief executives, the mayor most accessible to the press. Wherever he appeared, he could usually be cajoled into an impromptu "gang bang" by the "barracudas."

Left. A rare photograph of Harold Washington with Edward Vrdolyak. Sworn enemies, both were dynamic, intelligent, witty men, and one-on-one they'd be likely to have a good time. But the mayor didn't want to send signals that "Council Wars" was fun and games, and avoided situations like this one. Parliamentarian Leon Despres is in the foreground.

Right, above. Ernie Barefield (left), Chuck Kelly (right) and I share a joke with the mayor before the Super Bowl victory parade in January 1986.

Right. Mayor Harold Washington had a good time at neighborhood festivals.

Right. Mayor Washington was welcome wherever he went, regardless of the current temperature in "Council Wars." In 1985 he rang in the New Year at the Devon senior citizens apartments.

(Photo by Michelle Agins, courtesy Mayor's Press Office)

Mayor Harold Washington and Mary Ella Smith, Cindy
Bandle and Alton Miller, hanging out.

The opening of the new Regal Theater was made all the
more memorable when Mayor Washington did a few turns
with Gladys Knight.

Chicago author Studs Terkel was an early supporter of Mayor
Washington, and a constant friend.

WLS-TV's Joan Esposito (left) and WMAQ-TV's Deborah Norville, two
journalists I never heard the mayor complain about. When Norville left for
New York the mayor responded to the suggestion of *Sun-Times* media
columnist Robert Feder and proclaimed "Deborah Norville Day."

A strategic moment in City Council. Corporation Counsel Judson Miner, who sat at the mayor's right, is the one without the sunglasses.

Every Christmas, Mayor Washington spent part of the day visiting children's hospitals to read holiday stories.

(Photo by Michelle Agins, courtesy Mayor's Press Office)

Above. Wherever he went, he was surrounded by throngs. He loved the attention, and generally ignored the concerns of his security detail as he waded through the crowds. *Below.* Wearing the hat he won from the mayor of Dallas after the Chicago Bears beat the Cowboys, and displaying a cheese steak he won from frugal New York Mayor Ed Koch after the Bears beat the Giants, Mayor Washington looked forward to Chicago's 1986 Super Bowl championship.

Right. Between appointments at City Hall.

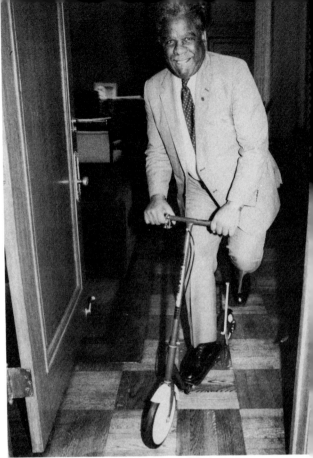

Below. "C'mon, Smiff," he'd say with mock gruffness when Mary Ella Smith showed up after work. "Let's get out of here—I've had enough grief for one day." The oversize white cards for speaking notes, and the folder with briefing papers, indicate that he still has at least one event on the schedule.

Left. At the governor's bill-signing, Jim Thompson's staff had forgotten to provide ceremonial pens. Upstaging Gov. Thompson (seated), Mayor Washington pulled one pen after another from his shirt pocket, from inside his coat, from his trousers. Even Lt. Gov. George Ryan (right) helped with the ribbing.

Below. During the final year of his administration, Mayor Washington did fewer impromptu interviews in TV studios, and more frequent interviews in his own office. He was always more comfortable on his own turf.

(Photo by Michelle Agins, courtesy Mayor's Press Office)

High Noon in the 26th Ward. After three years of "Council Wars," it all came down to the election of Ald. Luis Gutierrez (center), grinning while the mayor trades barbs with opposition demonstrators across the street. Security detail officer Rich Smiley (left), though alert for possible problems, lives up to his name.

When the mayor threatened layoffs, including members of his own staff, if his budget didn't pass, *Sun-Times* cartoonist Jack Higgins gave us a hard time.

All photos courtesy Mayor's Press Office unless otherwise noted.

It still seems ironic that the city's first black mayor should have so little luck with the city's only black daily newspaper; and so little interest in the other black community newspapers, which he noted we reached in our weekly mailings to the community press throughout Chicago, a mailing list that totaled some 500 small papers, newsletters, and community leaders of every hue and heritage.

We gave up on the *Defender*, but not on Chinta Straussberg. And with the other reporters, print and broadcast, he let me schedule a continual series of interviews, one-on-one, throughout 1985.

He enjoyed the encounters, and he conceded there was at least a short-term benefit from them. He knew that his loose, natural style, his conversation peppered with colloquialisms and, off camera, salty language, reached through at human levels where formally stated ideas from a podium or a press release would never reach.

And there seemed to be no little method in his occasional rapping and clowning, even at press conferences on serious issues where he was under attack, creating a "Kingfish" rhythm in the room, only to snap back to make a point when listeners were lulled off guard.

He manipulated his listeners with language, sometimes using $25 words, or words that are not commonly found outside Shakespeare and the King James Version, words that reporters would have to thumb through dictionaries to understand. He was kidded for his frequent use of the participle "burgeoning," and when he complained that the facts were as he had stated them, and not as the Eddies were "bruiting it about," an otherwise literate reporter quoted "brooding it about."

Sometimes he mispronounced words, though he used them perfectly correctly—a freestyle "potpourri" press conference, where reporters' miscellany was fair game, became "poopery;" "eschew," a word he used frequently, was "escue"—the sign of a person whose eye is educated by reading on a higher level than the ear is afforded in conversation with City Hall and Springfield types. He never stopped being fascinated by language for its own sake, and could become distracted in casual conversation as he searched for the *mot juste*, stopping to try the sounds and textures or precise meaning of several words, before continuing with a story.

Nothing was more effective in his courtship of reporters than the "Travels with Harold." While I worked with him he traveled to London, to Milan, throughout Israel from Bethlehem to the Golan Heights, to Rome, to Osaka and Tokyo, to Shanghai, Shenyang and

Beijing, to Mexico City, and to San Juan, Puerto Rico. We made quick overnight trips and longer excursions to mayors' meetings and speaking engagements, journalists' conferences and sales sessions with investment bankers and bond rating agencies. We were frequently in Washington, D.C. On all these occasions, reporters sought to accompany us.

The mayor's security was concerned that our departures and arrivals should not be known to the press. At the other extreme, I tried to arrange departure and arrival press conferences. I was generally successful, but there were times—when the trip was a nongovernmental, political fundraising trip to Los Angeles, Atlanta, or Washington—when the mayor agreed with Howard Saffold and seemed to make his sneak departure and secret arrival a test of my willingness to keep a confidence even against my professional instincts.

But with rare exceptions, we used the travels for all they were worth. Whenever we had a press initiative to promote, we joked about taking a trip. He was in demand as a speaker, all over the country, and there was hardly a week on the calendar where Ed Hamb didn't have at least one invitation in his files.

The trips were effective, first, because his contact with reporters could be more personal; rarely did we have more than four or five reporters traveling with us or meeting us at the destination. Instead of a gaggle of undifferentiated reporters approaching him as a bloc, he could deal with individuals, one on one.

Second, because the message we were sending, and the message the reporters were expecting, were generally the same. Both the mayor and the reporters would have done their homework on the same focused issue—whatever the trip was about—and both were more conscious of their complementary roles in putting the package together.

Third, because whatever the issue that took him out of town—whether meeting bond rating agencies in New York, or the Illinois delegation on Capitol Hill, or a conference of mayors in Nashville—it was an issue of some scope and scale, and not simply street fighting with Vrdolyak. Ironically, so far as public perception was concerned, he could be more "mayoral" outside of Chicago than at home. We learned the hard way that we should avoid live hook-ups with the studio at the time of the newscast, which would tend to encourage Walter Jacobson or WMAQ-TV's Carol Marin to ask a "Council Wars" question based on something that had happened in Chicago that day, instead of what we wanted to talk about.

Fourth, because professional needs on the road tended to insure that relationships were much more civil. For the mayor to become impatient with a reporter, turn taciturn, then close down an interview early is no disaster in your home territory, but it can spell the difference between success and costly failure when the whole reason for your trip, and your camera crew's travel expenses, is a solid five to seven minutes of quality time on the issue at hand. Reporters tended to take a little extra time guaranteeing that there was no friction between them and the man they needed for that night's story. The mayor responded in kind.

Additionally, while some of these effects were specific to the broadcast media, the elimination of discord with TV reporters had a positive influence on relations with print reporters as well.

There was another, even more profound advantage to these travels, particularly the trips abroad. At different times, reporters from all three channels, and both major dailies, accompanied the mayor overseas. I coordinated the land travel arrangements for the group, and reporters got to see the schedule that Harold Washington kept.

Many of them had accepted the characterization of Mayor Washington as an essentially lazy man who came to work late, went home early, and had no mind for details. Yet on the trip they could see the kind of schedule he kept, and they were hard put to keep up with him. Despite the deteriorated condition of his heart revealed by his autopsy, in the summer of 1986 he had us all winded by his vigorous climb to the Shrine of the Virgin of Guadeloupe in Mexico City.

This canard, that he slept late and was sloppy in his personal habits was epitomized in the Phil Lentz story in April 1985. Lentz wrote:

> There is hardly a politician in town who doesn't have an anecdote about a meeting where Washington did not appear, a phone call he didn't make or a promise he did not keep.
>
> Washington dismisses such complaints, saying a jammed mayoral schedule will lead inevitably to schedule conflicts. But the basis for many of the complaints, he says, is racism.
>
> "The mayor's late. Implication: Black man can't be on time; colored folks time, that crap all over again," he said. "It's just baloney."
>
> "You know something? I put in 14, 16 hours a day. I haven't been on a

vacation in three years. I'm not complaining, I love what I do. The only relaxation I get is Friday afternoons and I do my work at home so I can take my shoes off. They don't write about this. Oh, the mayor's 5 minutes late or the mayor didn't show up for some hotdog fest. Racism—you're damn right it's racism."

Still, the anecdotes and the perception persist. Though not publicly confirmed by either Vrdolyak or Washington, the story is reliably told about a meeting Washington requested with his arch-foe in the mayor's Hyde Park apartment at 9 a.m. one Sunday morning. Vrdolyak appeared on time, but despite persistent knocking on the door could rouse no one inside. Finally, just as Vrdolyak was about to leave, Washington appeared at the door, sleepy-eyed and dressed in a bathrobe. He had forgotten about the meeting he had asked for.

By repeating that absurd story, Phil Lentz perfectly proved the mayor's point—he was plagued with baloney, falsehoods that were fabricated to reflect character flaws, lies that were treated so uncritically that they could be reported as reliable, rather than as political poison pen letters.

Not only was the story not true, it could not possibly have been true. It would not be possible for a dogcatcher, much less the alderman from the 10th ward, to enter the block Harold Washington lived on without the notice of a cohort of police officers stationed outside, in the lobby, and in the command post on the sixth floor. Two-way radio reports would have blazed through the neighborhood, and in the command post Vrdolyak's every move would have been followed by the security TV cameras. To enter the apartment's lobby, he would have had to ring either the mayor's apartment or the command post—either would have amounted to ringing both places, and walked past the police guard stationed there. By the time he entered the elevator, even if he were visiting someone else who lived in the building, the mayor would have received a phone call informing him that Eddie was on the premises. And as the video cameras followed him down the corridor on the sixth floor, the door to apartment 65, across from the mayor's, would have opened and the alderman (and presumably the bodyguards who accompanied Vrdolyak wherever he went) would have received a courteous greeting from the officer in charge.

Of course, the premise of the story was ridiculous on the face of it. Harold Washington was not about to invite Edward Vrdolyak to visit in his apartment. The mayor was deeply offended by the credulity of anyone who read that story and believed it; he was unforgiving of the reporter who gave it currency; and he used that incident every time we spoke of the possibility that we were opening new doors of perception among the major media, and among white "undecideds." For months, even to the last day of his life, he cited that experience at midterm as a reason for distrusting the motives of reporters that I would tout as the "bright, unspoiled younger generation of journalists."

For the record, the mayor was usually up and reading his newspapers between 6:00 and 7:00—I could expect a call from him, or could call him without concern for waking him, as early as 6:30. Too frequently for my schedule he had a breakfast meeting at 7:30 or 8:00—I stopped trying to make the meetings with black businessmen on the South Side, because we rarely invited the press to them. His day was solidly booked, usually in half-hour increments. It was difficult to shoe-horn a press interview between the meetings with commissioners and staff, other political leaders and community representatives, but he was usually able to finagle some time. Until we agreed among ourselves—Barefield, Hamb and I—that we would give him two nights a week off, he was attending two or more evening events as well. He conjured up the energy for these things, sometimes by napping in the limo between stops. And after he returned home he could be called as late as midnight—later if something was about to break—and sometimes he called staff as late as 2:00 in the morning.

As for missing appointments, or being late, the only alternative would have been to have scheduled him for fewer events. As it was, he was rarely afforded enough travel time or enough time to complete an event in good form. And one emergency meeting with Barefield or Montgomery, even a telephone conference call to Sen. Paul Simon in Washington, D.C., could throw the rest of the day off schedule; either several events or appointments would have to be canceled, or he'd run half an hour late all afternoon. He expected Vrdolyak to take cheap shots at these vicissitudes. He was outraged that responsible journalists would give those shots any credence whatever. "They didn't do it to Daley," he said. "He was never on time. If a mayor's always on time, he's not doing his job. Yet and still, they say 'The mayor's always late.' Maybe it's the way I part my hair?"

14

The Press War

The turning point in the mayor's relationship with the media came on Christmas Eve, 1985. All the gradual progress of the past ten months was about to be blown away in what became known, in office shorthand, as the "Press War."

Nineteen eighty-five was ending well. We had won the People Mover fight, and persevered on the issue of affirmative action. We had done well in a sequence of parliamentary and public relations battles, from the CDBG controversy, to the G.O. bonds issue, to the 1986 budget. And although the mayor's appointments were still being held hostage in City Council committees, there was a growing public clamor for their release. We were winning the substantive contests, and we were winning the PR battle, in the effort to create a new spirit of acceptance and optimism for Mayor Washington's agenda.

It was as much a surprise to us as it was to the press and public, when we settled the 1986 budget dispute well ahead of the December 31 deadline. We credited our formidable organization of public education efforts and lobbying of constituency groups; but Mayor Washington was also suspicious that the device we had used to reach a compromise might be a Trojan horse. He repeated one of his favorite sayings: "When public officials stop arguing, you'd better zip up your wallet."

Our budget arguments had been based on a freeze of the property tax rate at the previous year's level. In recent years, Chicago's tax *rate* had been slipping downward, even as the *levy*—the actual dollar amount—was creeping up. That was because property value was coming on line faster than city spending was increasing. We had proposed a levy increase through a freeze in the tax rate, which would capture more of the property value growth.

Just when we thought we'd prevail in that argument, the Eddies revived an earlier proposal for a tax on commercial leases. Our City

Council negotiators jumped on the idea, and before it could be debated in the headlines and the business breakfasts, we had passed the budget in City Council.

The downtown business community would bear the brunt of this new tax, unless they could win the court case that would be sure to follow. The commercial lease tax probably did more to bring business leaders into an active civic role, as they fought to save their skin, than did any of the mayor's harangues.

Mayor Washington thought the business leaders probably had a good case; he had misgivings that we'd lose when it went to state court. But when the federal courts ruled for special elections in March, he was confident that we'd soon have a friendly City Council majority to pass substitute revenue measures.

So he was feeling pretty good, as the 1985 Christmas holidays brought to a close the year that turned the tide.

Christmas Eve, 1985: It was not a happy holiday for four aldermen who had figured in TV news stories of an FBI probe. I spoke with the mayor by phone that evening, because I knew we'd be asked for a reaction: especially since the aldermen involved were all members of the "21."

That fact was stressed in the first paragraph of the *Tribune*'s story on Christmas day: "The FBI is investigating alleged payoffs to Chicago aldermen who are allies of Mayor Washington in connection with the awarding of recent city contracts, two aldermen said yesterday. According to Ald. Perry Hutchinson [9th], FBI agents told him Monday, 'They are looking into some payoffs to black aldermen.' "

Two contracts were mentioned, the People Mover at O'Hare, and the collection of delinquent parking fines.

By the following day the *Trib* was quoting "sources familiar with the inquiry." Chicagoans would be hearing a good deal from those sources for the next three months: "The sources said the investigation is wide ranging and focuses on several aspects of the lucrative business of collecting delinquent fees and fines. 'It's going to be the case of 1986,' said one source close to the investigation." It would appear, from that comment and from the hysteria that subsequently developed in the press, that federal officials leaking information about the investigation were encouraging speculation that the probe would lead directly to the mayor.

"In an August interview, before his role as an undercover operative became known," the *Trib* story continued, "Raymond, again using the name Burnett, told a reporter for the *Tribune* that he had given money to Clarence McClain, a former city official and one of Mayor Harold Washington's closest friends. Raymond described the payment as a 'campaign contribution.' He told the reporter that he believed McClain could help introduce him to administration officials.... Raymond met with reporters from the *Tribune* [in August] to convince them that Systematic Recovery System could do a better job than Datacom." Raymond hadn't been mentioned in August *Trib* stories, so it's fair to guess that he had been one of the unnamed sources badmouthing the mayor and McClain throughout 1985.

McClain had been busy freelancing in an area of city management that he recognized was riding the wave of the future—at the federal level as well as the state and local levels—the collection of uncollected fines, fees and taxes. A few large firms were making their mark in this growth area, while cities across the country were trying to figure out whether they had the technological or managerial ability to develop an internal capacity to do this work efficiently and honestly; or whether it would make more sense to contract this out; and if the latter, whether for a percentage of the collections or a straight fee or some other arrangement. The potential for new development was— and is—enormous. For cities who needed the revenue, and for businesses who could profit from that need.

As Mayor Washington and Comptroller Ron Picur had pointed out frequently, his administration was the first to take such collections seriously. In previous administrations uncollected funds were not carried as an asset or a potential source of revenue; for all intents and purposes, they were written off as they would be in the private sector, as uncollectibles or bad debts. By attempting to estimate exactly what the potential might be, and by making a priority of collecting those outstanding fines and fees, the administration was entering a thankless realm of indeterminate guesswork—is there $150 million outstanding (going back to, say, 1980) or $74 million (going back to the beginning of the Washington administration)? Why not go back an even decade, to 1976? Or only two years, to stay realistic. To come up with a "total that's out there waiting to be collected," do you cite a percentage of what's "out there," based on the collection experience of other cities, or do you speak of the gross amount, including every parking ticket written to an Oklahoma farmer who vacationed here in 1979 and skipped town without paying his fine?

The political opposition, complaining that we wouldn't need tax increases if we'd simply collect what was owed, were certain to use the most inflated numbers—if all those farmers' tickets dating back to 1976 added up to $150 million, they'd prompt a headline reading: "City fails to collect $150 million".

The headline, and the story under it, would have nothing to do with the reality of establishing a collections procedure—including changes in state and municipal law to facilitate collections without taking every scofflaw to court, and technical changes in the design and wording of traffic tickets, and accounting changes in the way paid tickets were logged by the clerk of the court, and repairs on parking meters, most of which weren't working, and a dozen other related measures that were needed.

So there were plenty of cheap shots inherent in the issue. At the same time, some important management concepts were involved, and chief among them was the concept of privatization.

During the late 1970s and early 1980s, privatization was one of the urban responses to federal cutbacks and other financial pressures. Privatization meant farming out work previously considered municipal functions to private agencies. Not a new idea so much as an old one whose time had come back around, privatization was in reality a move backward—for better or worse—toward a time when government did not provide its current range of services.

Proponents urged that private agencies could collect trash, maintain public buildings and other property, collect parking ticket fines—in some extremes, even lock up criminals in private jails. These were touted as a way to improve efficiency, prevent municipal corruption, and get around the growing municipal workers' unions.

New industries were created by this new market. The management of solid waste had already been an area of geometrically expanding opportunity; now there was the prospect of it reaching all the way down to the actual pickup of your garbage. And dunning those who owed parking fines and water bills—that was just a matter of combining the solid sanctions of government (lose your license or your water) with a good computer mailing list, also obtainable from the government. To a sharp operator, privatization held the potential for millions in profit every year.

Some of the proponents had forgotten that one of the reasons municipalities historically have had to take responsibility for many government functions is that private sector management didn't work. Water companies, fire companies, in some cities utility companies, were less efficient and more prone to corruption than those which were created or reconstructed, directly responsible to the public trust. Follow that trend back through history far enough and you can make a case for privatization of libraries and schools—as some have in fact done.

Privatization in the area of collections of fines and fees is especially attractive to those preparing a city budget. Rather than show a hundred new employees on the revenue department rolls, offset by an iffy revenue projection, the planners can show simply a net income from collections, jobbed out to a contractor.

Also, in the 1970s—as in many cases today—the computer systems in use by municipalities were unsuitable for efficient collections. Cities which had invested huge sums in now obsolescent mainframes, for which maintenance and programming costs were astronomical and time consuming, had not realized the cost-efficiency and relatively easy programming of the new, smaller, faster generation of computers on the market. In many applications, a 1980s desktop computer can outperform the mainframes that were then in use.

To make matters even more problematic, many cities were using poorly trained personnel and faulty accounting systems as well as inadequate equipment for their collections. Parking tickets were never the top priority of police departments, stretched thin with other problems.

Companies structured to do nothing but collect past due fines and fees could not only show a marked improvement in collection rates, they could make the collections much less expensively. At one point the *Wall Street Journal* reported it cost New York City $26 to process a $15 parking ticket; Datacom Systems Corporation, one of the nation's first such agencies, could do it for $1.80. In return they asked for anywhere from a quarter to a half of the take. Exorbitant? From one perspective perhaps, but still a bargain to New York City.

Datacom, one of the country's largest of these new firms, was challenged by Systems Recovery Service, Inc., as they both bid to become the preeminent national collections company. SRS landed a contract to collect New York City parking fines. Whether or not the contract was won through payoffs to city officials, before long payoffs were indeed being made, to the tune of a quarter of a million dollars to one official.

On the strength of recommendations from New York, SRS then won a contract to collect water bills in Chicago. But their eyes were set on the lucrative parking fines collection business.

Both Datacom and SRS and miscellaneous other companies were interested in getting a piece of the action. Simultaneously, cities like Chicago and agencies within cities like the Water Department, the Clerk of the Court, and others involved in the complex collections process, were looking for expertise, for information, for successful precedents. The database of such information simply didn't exist.

Raymond had been hired by SRS to help secure a Chicago contract. The word was out—McClain didn't need to advertise himself, thanks to the Eddies, Fran Spielman, and miscellaneous other credulous reporters and adversely motivated political opponents—that Clarence was the man to see if you wanted a tour guide through the "reformed" City Hall.

McClain was simultaneously selling his services to Datacom and SRS. His success as a consultant was based partly on the truth, partly bluff: both competitors fell for the suggestion that a word from McClain could grease the skids. And both came to the correct conclusion that McClain knew his way around City Hall as well as any consultant they could hire, having worked there for several months in a high level position, and having convinced them (or not disabusing them of the notion, obtainable from Spielman or the *Trib*) that he was the mayor's "closest personal friend."

The service McClain provided to Raymond was to arrange a study of parking collections, to be prepared by the National Conference of Black Lawyers Community College of Law. The institution he selected, as described by Tuohy in the *Chicago Lawyer*, "regards itself as a place where black lawyers or law students can get special training on minority issues as a sort of complement to traditional law training."

The study they prepared has been fairly described as an informative analysis of the problems and prospects of city parking collections. Though it was said to have been commissioned to do a job on Datacom, it is considered neutral in its effect and could be used by either SRS or Datacom to buttress their sales pitch. Nonetheless, it seems clear that the avowed intention was to use the study in an information or disinformation campaign to favor SRS prospects.

McClain said the study cost $20,000 and the fee was paid directly by SRS to the school. "Sources said" that McClain received the money and that the sum was twice as much. "$40,000 Bribe Told," screamed the *Sun-Times* one Sunday, in the early editions. Was it a bribe? Well, no, because McClain wasn't an official. Subsequent editions of that day's *Sun-Times* substituted the clumsier "$40,000 Clout Fee Told," in the same three-inch letters.

At some point when the study had been completed, Clarence McClain arranged for Mayor Washington to meet with the two who prepared the study, Knox and Hammond. They met in an informal public setting, in a restaurant. Mayor Washington told me that McClain had suggested the meeting and may have been present when Washington arrived but that he didn't stay or sit in on the meeting. "Not that it would have mattered to me," he said, "but as a matter of record, I think it was just Knox, Hammond and me," at a restaurant near his apartment.

Mayor Washington flipped through the study, complimented them on the work, and told me later that he considered his function at that meeting one of congratulating and encouraging the school for the quality of their work. There would be a continuing need for educational institutions to study urban affairs, and he was glad that a black institution was participating in that field. He told me he had never read the study through in its entirety, but he knew that Barefield and others directly involved in the issue had read it. He had no idea who had commissioned or paid for the study, of course.

In the course of choosing a parking collections service, the leading candidate Datacom was attacked in City Council by a number of aldermen, including those whose Christmas Eve had been so unpleasant; and by members of the media who were mentioned but unnamed in the ultimate indictments: and by John Adams in the Revenue Department. Nonetheless, Datacom, not SRS, got the contract.

We were on an economic development tour in Japan and China when Barefield first heard of a potential problem with McClain. Charles Sawyer, acting revenue director and brother of Ald. Eugene Sawyer, came to Barefield with the story. Barefield handled the matter and gave the mayor an abbreviated report when we returned.

Barefield said that revenue director Charles Sawyer had come to him in late August, while the mayor was in China, with information that his deputy, John Adams, had accepted a questionable $10,000 loan or payment from the SRS lobbyist. Sawyer had urged that Adams be fired.

Barefield said he had wanted to hear Adams' side of it. He was aware of some tensions between Sawyer and Adams, he said, and thought that Sawyer might have been overreacting. When he talked to Adams, he was told he had received the money as a loan, but from McClain, not Raymond. Execrable judgment, he admitted, but not unlawful.

Barefield said that after discussion with Sawyer and Adams he split the difference; while he believed that Adams had done nothing illegal, he had been outrageously irresponsible. He had created the appearance of taking a bribe, and from McClain of all people. He would have to leave his job.

Adams had pleaded that his wife had medical problems, and had asked that he stay in his position until the first of the year, while he looked for a new job. He had been removed from supervision of contracts or participation in any bid process, Barefield assured the mayor. The mayor concurred in his decision and they moved on down the list of matters that needed the mayor's attention.

During the fall of 1985, Adams was on notice. A key controversy later developed as to whether Adams had indeed been terminated, or whether a demonstrably corrupt public official would have been allowed to stay in place had the FBI probe not disclosed the details.

During that period, too, Charles Sawyer accepted a campaign contribution for his brother's aldermanic office in the form of a reported $2,500 in tickets to a fundraiser—from SRS, from the same representative of that company that he had claimed had tried to bribe John Adams.

But Charles Sawyer's receipt of a campaign contribution was a legally accepted practice. Barefield was clear that Adams had been terminated. And the bottom line was that SRS was not getting the parking collections contract.

Now, during the Christmas holidays, what at first had seemed to be an aldermanic scandal had touched the mayor's own administration. The mayor called Barefield to 5300 and went through the details. This was the first time the mayor had focused on the matter.

Barefield reminded him of their discussion in September. The mayor remembered the Adams firing. "I thought he was out of here," the mayor said. He remembered getting a handwritten note from Adams asking for a reversal of the decision; he had turned down the request. "Why's he still around?" The mayor's first action now was that Barefield should terminate Adams immediately.

Barefield had more news: Sawyer had volunteered the information that he had accepted a campaign contribution from Raymond. It had not surfaced in any of the probe news and wasn't illegal, but it might be a "perception problem."

Mayor Washington was unhappy with Barefield for the mess that had been caused. The mayor had not questioned Barefield's judgment, or his decision, when the matter was first reported in abbreviated form, in September. In retrospect, he agreed, it should have been reported immediately to the Office of Municipal Investigation (OMI). Those were the standing orders for such cases, and they were reiterated to the cabinet in early 1986, when the scandal broke.

Later, when an independent investigator, former U.S. Attorney Thomas Sullivan, reviewed the matter, the Sullivan Report's sole adverse comment on the mayor's actions was that Barefield, "with the concurrence or acquiescence of Washington and Montgomery, acted [in September] in a manner which appears to have been designed to avoid or minimize publicity about a potentially sensitive matter."

The mayor's next decisions, made promptly as news reports continued to allege details of the scandal, were to order a belated inquiry by OMI, to order all city employees within reach of his executive order (i.e., all but aldermanic employees) to cooperate with OMI or forfeit their jobs, to fire two longstanding city employees named in the allegations, who were declining to cooperate with OMI, and to request Charles Sawyer's resignation.

But the fact was, Sawyer had done nothing illegal. The contribution had been duly deposited in his brother's ward organization account. Accepting and disclosing campaign contributions from contractors, and from vendors throwing money around in their efforts to win contracts, is a venerable tradition in American politics at every level, and certainly in Chicago. The mayor reversed himself, and put Sawyer on leave with pay while the matter was investigated.

In addition to the OMI legal inquiry, he also asked for an administrative review of all procedures in the Revenue Department, the Purchasing Department, the Comptroller's Office, and any division anywhere in government responsible for fiduciary transactions or decisions. And since his ethics ordinance had been languishing in City Council—tied up in Vrdolyak's committee—he ordered the preparation of an ethics executive order. It wouldn't have the teeth of an ordinance, but it would be a start. Under the executive order, such contributions as that accepted by Sawyer would still be legal by ordinance, but grounds for dismissal in the mayor's administration.

The mayor was frustrated and embarrassed by what he was reading. He was particularly irked that the name of Clarence McClain should arise in any context whatever, especially since any responsible official should know by now that McClain was to have no role in hiring or contracts. And he saw all the accomplishments of 1985, and the growing if grudging acceptance of affirmative action, all threatened by what he called this "schoolyard foolishness."

The mayor was unhappy with the handling of the entire matter, and held Barefield accountable. While he continued to depend on his chief of staff, and never ceased to consider him invaluable as the city manager Chicago needed, he didn't spare Barefield's feelings on this issue. Borrowing terminology made famous by Reagan's budget director David Stockman, he "took Barefield to the woodshed." But it never entered his mind to fire him, no matter how loud the demands that he do so.

◻ *Politics* ⸦══⸧

From the first day, the mayor's view of the scandals was colored by his conviction that he'd been personally targeted by "the Reagan mafia."

"Reagan and his mafia," he said, "consider the cities a 'special interest group.' They believe we Democrats have 'bought' our constituency with social programs. They're determined to undermine us among the poor, minorities, students, working people, by cutting off funds to these folks. That's what the big spending cuts is all about. It sure as hell isn't about budget balancing. And it isn't that self-help bullshit. It's politics, period."

He quoted a *New York Times* article in which Sen. D'Amato complained that the scandals in New York, Chicago, Washington, Philadelphia and elsewhere had "damaged our image. We'd been making very real progress," D'Amato said, "in rehabilitating the image of the city, and this situation certainly sets us back in the eyes of our colleagues." New York Gov. Mario Cuomo was also quoted as saying, "The good name of New York is being sullied at the very time the Congress is considering various budgetary cuts that could have serious consequences for all people who live in our cities."

"That's what this is all about," he said. "Get the mayors. Get Harold."

Mayor Washington saw the issue, too, in the light of the Reagan administration's scandals. They were trying to steer attention away from their problems by focusing on those of the Democrats in the big cities.

By the end of President Reagan's first term his administration was already being called the most corrupt in the nation's history, and what Ralph Nader has defined as a "typology of temptation" had proven endemic. From the cartoonists to Congressional probes, hundreds of federal administration officials were characterized as corrupt: investigated or arrested or convicted or forced to resign.

When the Reagan administration began what the *Tribune* called "an unprecedented federal campaign against municipal corruption," many people were concerned about the political implications: "The assault on municipal wrongdoing pits a Republican-dominated Justice Department against some of the nation's most prominent Democratic regimes, such as the administrations of Mayors Edward Koch in New York, Marion Barry in Washington and Harold Washington in Chicago. Not one of these well-known mayors has been accused personally of wrongdoing," the *Trib* admitted, "but the inquiries threaten the reputations and images of all three. There have been complaints the investigations were politically motivated and, in the case of Chicago, racially motivated."

And there was the local political angle as well. "Republicans campaign by indictment," the mayor told me. "It's a pattern. It's their style." He fully expected Republican Dan Webb to be his "Mr. Clean" opponent in the 1987 election, after he polished off Byrne in the primary. It had been reported that the story of Raymond the Mole had broken prematurely, due to published accounts of Raymond's legal problems in Florida that were released in December. The original intent had been to publicize the Chicago scandals later in the year. Mayor Washington was convinced that Reagan's strategists, in cahoots with local Republicans and the *Chicago Tribune,* were blatantly attempting to smear his administration in the heat of the 1987 campaign. To him, that explained the *Trib*'s apparent obsession with keeping the story tied to the mayor personally, and on the front page.

As Larry Green wrote in the *Los Angeles Times,* "There are even signs that the turmoil could lead to something long unimaginable in this one-time bastion of raw urban Democratic Party power—a Republican winner in the spring 1987 mayoral election. Republicans last won the mayor's office in 1927, when, some historians contend, gangster Al Capone really ran the city."

There never was any serious suggestion—apart from the Burke-Vrdolyak rantings, which in any case dated back well before this scandal—that the mayor was personally implicated in the scandals. But from the coverage one would draw the conclusion that everything tied together in a neat web. The mayor was at the center, "the mayor's closest personal friend" McClain was acting as his minion, and "the mayor's allies" in City Council were playing out the mayor's script. The daily diatribes seemed designed to convince the average reader that Mayor Washington had been caught in a local Watergate.

Salacious stories about videotapes of aldermen that showed "heterosexual and homosexual activities" were leaked to Sneed and to reporters—and tied to "the mayor's growing scandal." There were ominous references to "the cancer on the mayor's office." Charles Sawyer's injudicious sale of tickets to Raymond—which had not been a part of the probe and may never have been mentioned if Sawyer himself had not been forthcoming—were wrapped into the bribe accepted by Adams. Although the Eddies refrained from chiming in publicly, their operatives worked overtime to keep the pot stirred.

"Sources close to" former revenue director Ira Edelson called the September discussions with Montgomery and Barefield a cover-up. They discounted Barefield's idea that Sawyer had been mistaken and that Adams was telling the truth. Montgomery and Barefield were both accessible to reporters early on, and their statements were deconstructed and examined for contradictions. Montgomery said that "we had reason to believe that what Adams called a loan from McClain was actually a bribe from Raymond," apparently referring to what we had reason to believe *after* the story broke. That was seized upon as an admission that he had known, and covered up, that information in September.

All the stories were predicated on a series of truths. Taken together, they didn't add up to a cancer on the mayor's office, but they were irrefutably true. It is true that the aldermen were counted among the "21" who voted with the mayor. But as the media well knew, these four aldermen—Humes, Hutchinson, Kelley, and Wallace Davis—were not close to the mayor. They hadn't come in on his reform ticket; they were there when he arrived. They were old-guard Machine pols who had played the game with previous administrations, and who would by all accounts rather be enjoying the benefits of majority bloc membership if they thought their constituencies would tolerate a break from Mayor Washington.

Still the decisions that Barefield had made, regardless of his motives or beliefs about the merits, were inconsistent with the reform administration that Harold Washington had pledged.

And the mayor had been informed of Barefield's actions in September. He had signed off on them. He was therefore personally responsible.

So the media had carte blanche to pursue the issue. And they pulled out all the stops. The newspaper accounts and the TV stories tumbled across the printed page and blared out all through ratings month. In its competitive haste, the media issued stories that were rife with contradictions, misinformation and sometimes disinformation.

Channel 5's TV screens blazed with documentation "proving" that there had been no intention to fire John Adams; a budget planning document for 1986 shown with individual names pencilled in alongside the otherwise unintelligible budgetese for each position, for clarity in identifying each slot. John Adams' name was shown there, and the fact used as evidence that Barefield had no intention of firing him.

Channel 5 also interviewed one of Burke's political flunkies, Dennis Church, holding up a xerox of a handwritten letter from John Adams acknowledging that he was fired, claiming it had been "cooked," as he called it. This memo was part of the administration's defense that Adams had, indeed, been fired. But Church, who had worked in the Mayor's Press Office, was granted "expert witness" status for this broadcast, as he claimed to be able to tell from the absence of a time stamp on the memo, that it had never actually been delivered. As Church knew well, but Channel 5 did not, individual personal memos circulated on the fifth floor were rarely time-stamped.

Yet another Channel 5 piece quoted a second letter from Adams to the mayor, which was said to suggest, by implication, that Adams had been restored to his job. The letter actually indicated the opposite; it showed that Adams had accepted the fact that he was out of a job, with a grin-and-bear-it stoicism.

Sun-Times reporter Fran Spielman quoted John Adams as saying he had a meeting with the mayor in September 1985, in which the mayor promised he could keep his job. Adams vehemently protested her story. He subsequently issued a written statement contradicting Spielman. It said he had repeatedly denied to her that the meeting took place. She got the story exactly backward. Delores Woods remembers that the closest John Adams came to the mayor's office was to see her to ask for a copy of the mayor's official portrait autographed as a memento.

Above all, the daily front-page banner, just under the *Chicago Tribune* masthead, was the ultimate legitimization for all the smaller media. Watergate had come to Chicago, and no holds were barred.

I strongly resented the intemperance of the attacks; I thought most of the reporters had abandoned any sense of fair play. I wasn't dispassionate in my discussions with them, and I couldn't stomach their tolerance for the involvement of Burke's and Vrdolyak's operatives in what was supposedly a series of stories on a federal investigation. It seemed to me that the reporters were operating on the same antic wavelength that they'd come to enjoy when covering "Council Wars." Except now they were strongly implying and sometimes telling me outright, sometimes even with a certain jubilation, that the mayor had been caught breaking the law.

Many of these reporters had been collegial, if not friendly, with the mayor. Some of them went back ten years with him. I knew some of them to be scrupulously fair, even when they weren't favorable: Flannery, Kay, Shaw. Why were they now throwing caution to the winds, never mind courtesy, acting as though the mayor was at bay and it was only a matter of endurance before he broke down and confessed.

One reporter answered the question for me. After telling me that he *knew* the mayor had daily conversations with McClain, that in fact McClain was in and out of the mayor's office all the time, and that the mayor had personally intervened in the awarding of the parking contract, he related a conversation with an FBI source. He said he'd been given an earful on the mayor; and when he had asked, "How far can I go with these allegations," meaning how far out on a limb, the federal source had replied, "You can go as far as you can imagine. We've got this guy [the mayor] cold."

Clearly the hysteria would not have been so widespread, had trusted sources not given the green light. And the *Trib's* self-confidence was infectious; this was no Eddie Burke story—this was the FBI!

But many—Mayor Washington preeminent among them—saw little difference between the two, in this case. He was convinced the matter was politically motivated. Apparently the only aldermen that Raymond had sought to entrap were black allies of the mayor. In that sense, but only in that sense, there was a racial motivation too, he believed.

In a radio interview he was asked a leading question—whether he thought there were racial implications in the probe. He answered carefully, consistent with his avoidance of direct race references:

"I have no problem reading that at all. Obviously it was deliberate. The leak, and it was that, was deliberate. The finger pointing was deliberate. It was not an accident by any stretch of the imagination. And if perchance these people have been set up, that also was deliberate in terms of choice of people to set up. I look at it through the jaundiced eye of history."

The day after the stories broke, the Mayor commissioned the OMI investigation. During the week between Christmas and New Year's, Barefield, Montgomery, and Tom Coffey undertook to gather the facts and make sense of the allegations. Meanwhile the allegations kept coming; by the weekend of Dec. 28–29, McClain had been promoted to the headlines.

We agreed that we would be accessible to the media, within the limits of our information. Even before anyone on the fifth floor had a complete picture, Barefield and Montgomery were talking to reporters and sharing the sketchy information we had, making statements that might be slightly at variance with one another as new information became available.

On January 2 personnel action was taken on Sawyer and Adams, and the next day, just before the weekend, we announced that an SRS collections contract for water bills was being canceled because it appeared to have been tainted by the allegations.

The *Trib* led the pack in keeping the tempo fast and the temperature high. Although the mayor had not wanted to take the point—let Barefield and Montgomery take the heat, he said—it became clear that we'd have to do a press conference soon, even before we had all the information. In Watergate terminology, the mayor was being accused of stonewalling.

The mayor had spent some ten days reviewing information and watching the story develop—at the same time dealing with the tumult that had resulted from the surprise commercial lease tax, preparing for the arrival of Bishop Desmond Tutu in mid-January, and other normal business. We had decided that we'd do a mayoral press conference shortly after the New Year, but then decided that Barefield and I would make announcements of personnel changes and the suspension of the Water Department contract. I told the press we'd do a press conference on Wednesday, January 7.

To my frustration, it was not until that morning that everyone who had been assembling information could be collected together in one room—at the mayor's apartment—to review the information. It was clear that we knew nothing more than what had already appeared in the papers. All the action that was going to be taken in the near term had already been taken. Coffey had been urging a special prosecutor, a la Watergate. The mayor had told me, during the previous week, that he was leery of putting that much political power in one person's hands—a special prosecutor would have to be completely independent to be credible; could Mayor Washington trust anyone not to abuse that role? Besides, he hadn't wanted to reinforce the comparisons with Watergate. So he wasn't ready to talk about a special prosecutor.

It wasn't going to be much of a press conference.

While media relations had been steadily improving during 1985, I had broached the idea of scheduling regular press briefings for the City Hall reporters on the model of Franklin D. Roosevelt. The idea was to entertain a room full of reporters in an unstructured free-for-all, on background, not on the record. "That was before TV," the mayor said. I suggested we could accomplish much the same thing by inviting TV reporters in without their cameras. We could follow these informal sessions with regular press conferences, but first we'd give everyone a more relaxed encounter with their mayor. I had noticed that he seemed to get along with TV reporters much more easily when they were unaccompanied by their glaring lights. TV reporters were being cheated of the more laid-back mayor that their print colleagues knew. The TV reporters with whom I had discussed this idea in a general way were favorably inclined.

Now as the mayor and I contemplated his first press encounter on

"Raymond the Mole," we revived the idea. Barefield, Montgomery and I had experienced the ravening appetite of the media for confrontation on this issue. We'd all been called liars to our face. Voices were frequently raised in these "interviews" and press conferences, and some of the charges could only be described as wild. We were no longer dealing with just the City Hall press corps: dozens of young "investigative reporters" were now on the case, as well as most of the columnists. After all, this was "the case of 1986."

The spectre of the mayor being goaded in a public setting by that kind of treatment was something I felt personally responsible for avoiding. He could be testy when he was responding to a charge by Vrdolyak. God knows how he might respond to "some punk" quoting the FBI and calling him a liar. Whatever that response might be, I didn't want it on the six o'clock news.

I sold him on the idea of doing a press briefing in his office, followed by a press conference for the cameras. The press briefing would be on the record, and both microphones and notepads would be welcome. But no cameras. He would be conversing, not performing.

I suggested we bring the whole gang—there might be 40 reporters—into his office, seat them around his desk, and give them as much time as they needed to satisfy themselves that they understood what the mayor knew and what he didn't know about this story. There would be confused questions, questions with confused premises, repetition, perhaps mutual disrespect. Everyone would have an opportunity to vent.

Then, when the media were clear on details, we'd break, and meet again in the press conference room at 2:00, in plenty of time for the TV deadlines. We'd do a formal press conference, with cameras.

He had liked the idea when I proposed it the day before, but hadn't signed off on it—he wanted to hear from the entire group whether any new information had turned up, before he agreed to expose himself in any press conference, on or off the record. In our conversation at his apartment that morning, there was no new information. A good deal of time was spent in circular discussion—typical of most of our group discussions—and we were running into the time I had set aside for the press.

When we were finally able to break, the mayor and I headed for his limousine, and I called my office from the car. The press should be notified of a press briefing in the mayor's office, to take place as soon as we arrived—no cameras; there will be a press conference later in the day, time to be announced.

That was a mistake. Running as late as we were, I should probably have scrapped any hope of meeting the press that morning. I felt it was important to do the press briefing with unlimited time—take as long as it takes to sort all the charges out and put the mayor and the reporters on the same wavelength. And then I wanted a gap in time between that office meeting and the press conference, to cool any tempers that might need cooling, on either side. Finally, I didn't want the televised press conference to take place as late as 4:00 in the day, because I didn't want the cameras live. Everyone would benefit, I was convinced, if we took the time to get a coherent story out.

I perhaps should have scheduled the briefing for the following morning, which would have given us plenty of time to explain to the press what was being contemplated. Of course, I had already promised a press conference so the die was cast.

The meeting in the mayor's office itself was mild by the new standards of press coverage that were being set that week. But he was stunned by the reporters' ferocity. He had never experienced such a direct assault on his integrity, and he never completely recovered from it. From that morning forward, his relationship with reporters would never be the same.

I taped that encounter, and several sections of the transcript chronicle the deterioration of that relationship. On the tape, the questioners are occasionally identifiable, though often a question emerges from a clamor of voices.

> Paul Hogan, WMAQ-TV:...was [McClain] involved in possibly criminal activities?
>
> Mayor Washington: I don't know. I don't even know who is the subject of the FBI investigations. Some names have arisen.
>
> Q: You do know that the money came through McClain to Adams...
>
> A: That's the story we got, yes... Mr. McClain is not an employee of this government. He has not been for two and a half years. He has no right, or any "open sesame," and every executive, oh, from upper-middle to top who comes through my office—and they all are signed on by me before they get their employment—are cautioned about "influence peddlers" and are told clearly that anyone who attempts to approach them from outside the purview of government and the structure of things, are to be denied; they are to report it, and if they

take any action pursuant to any outside influence, undue or otherwise, they run the jeopardy of losing their position.

We've said this over and over again, we've said it at cabinet meetings, I have published on at least two occasions, through press statements, that statement more inclusive. Unfortunately the only time we've got it published in the paper is when Mr. Miller had to write a letter to a certain editor to get it in the paper. So we've repeatedly said that, and we've repeatedly admonished everyone in this government that you are not to respond to anyone outside this government and in the orderly process of what you're doing. That's a no-no. And I think my caution was well placed. In short, we've been prudent about this matter and we have tried to anticipate that kind of thing.

Q: Yeah, but if McClain was as it appears now to be the man who took the money from Raymond and gave it to your city official, isn't he as liable for—

A: Let me put it this way. Whoever it is, if they have committed criminal conduct, I hope they are apprehended and punished—whether they're in my government—

Q: Even McClain?

A: Mr. McClain or anyone else—in my government or outside my government. The difference is I have no jurisdiction over Mr. McClain, I have no control over his actions. Except as I would say about anybody, anywhere in the world, if they committed conduct which was criminal, then I would certainly castigate their conduct.

Bob Crawford, WBBM Radio: When did your administration, and when did you, first realize that the loan that went to Mr. Adams actually originated with Raymond? When did you realize that?

A: I am not at this point certain that that's true. I don't know.

Q: You still have some doubts about whether—

A: Not a question of doubts, I don't know.

Q: Okay, you still don't know. Now secondly—

A: Do you?

Q: Not for certain I don't, no. Except that Mr. Barefield said Adams told him the money actually came from Raymond.

A: You know, let's face it, what is fact in this case and what is speculation is yet to be determined to a great extent. And if you notice, when you ask me questions of fact I have to stop because I'm not certain that I have the facts, and obviously you don't have them, and I don't know what those facts mean when we get them. We're trying to be candid but not irresponsible in my selection of words and the statements I make.

Andy Shaw, WLS-TV: When you got that first report from Barefield, I'm just curious, couldn't you have just picked up the phone and called Clarence McClain and said stay out of this sort of stuff or something? Or couldn't you have gotten—I mean, this raises the question that comes back to you a lot and I know, I think you don't like it, but I'm not sure, but we're always trying to get you to clarify this relationship—

A: No, you're not always trying to get me to clarify anything. I've clarified it. Why should I have the responsibility of picking up the phone and calling someone not in my administration about anything. We have no connection in this administration with Mr. McClain. If Mr. McClain is involved in any unethical or illegal or criminal conduct he should suffer the penalties. He has no influence on this administration, never has to my knowledge; certainly not through this mayor or through anyone whom I know in this administration. You have made the connection, I haven't made any connection. He has been severed from this administration, period, hook, line, sinker, for over two and a half years. Period. And I have said it over and over and over again and I guess I'll have to say it over and over and over again. And maybe one day, the print media at least, will print it.

Q: But being severed from the administration is not the same as being severed from a role in the city in which we all live, and that's, he's not—

A: What I am supposed to do about that? I'm not condoning or condemning but if he's a private citizen, well how can I control that?

Q: Are we wrong if we refer to him as your friend—

A: Yes, you're wrong in the context of all these investigations. What kind of a designation is that? You know, I've picked up news stories when the only thing said in there was that he's a friend of the mayor, or "closest friend of the mayor." That's not true. I think I have the right to determine my friends and my close friends. I look around this room and I see a lot of people I've known a long time, but you're not my friends (laughter). And although I wouldn't resent most of you being called my friends, some of you I would.

Q: Is he your friend?

A: No. He's a former employee of mine—

Q: What is your relationship?

A: None.

Q: What is the last time you've talked to him?

A: None. [sic]

Q: What is the last time you've seen him?

A: Several months ago, in the hall. [Later clarified: he means the hallway of the apartment building where they both live.]

Q: And it's wrong also to refer to him as a political adviser?

A: Absolutely.

Q: Well then, doesn't it annoy you just the way he represents himself—

A: It annoys me for you to glom him on to me in any form or fashion at all.

Q: He says, he says—

A: Ah, there's the rub. But you don't come and ask me. You know, you just go on, and "he's my friend."

Q: But this is the strongest answer you've given—

A: No, no, strongest, weakest, you never printed it before. He told you that, and you printed it. Didn't I just tell you categorically that Adams was separated because he received dollars from a person who had— was perceived as an influence peddler whose name was McClain. Didn't I just tell you that? How many times do I have to say this?

Andy Shaw: Once more, at 2:00 this afternoon. (laughter)

A: Once more?

Q: At two this afternoon. Do you think that he pushes this perception—

A: (ignoring the questioner, continuing with Shaw) One thing I do have is patience, in abundance.

Q: Has anybody ever come to you and said that Clarence McClain is out there and is trying to make everybody think he's your friend so he can get all these contracts representing people—

A: Has anybody ever come to me and said that? No.

Q: Do you think that McClain pushes the perception that he's your friend.

A: Based on what I'm seeing which was printed in both papers [referring to the November promotional articles], I have to assume that.

Q: So why don't you just pick up the phone and say "Clarence, cut it out"?

A: (disgusted) You're kidding.

Q: I'm not kidding—

A: Oh, you've gotta be kidding. I've got a responsibility to call every person in the world who's throwing my name around—which might include some of you—you'd be amazed how many people say "Oh, the mayor said this," I don't even know them. They walk up to me and say "Hello, mayor," I say "Hello." (mimicking) "I was talking to the mayor the other day." And then they go and sell the Brooklyn Bridge to somebody. (laughter) I mean you've got to use a little common sense in terms of how you treat people in positions like myself. Why do you think I went to such trouble to tell my top administrators that they should be assiduously avoiding any contact with influence peddlers, and that if they did so they did so at their own peril? Why do you think I went through all that trouble? I mean, I wasn't born yesterday. I've lived here a long time. I have cabinet meetings, I say it over and over and over again because I know those things happen in the real world. And they happen to me hundreds of times a day and I don't know anything about it. And you have to understand that. And so don't let someone tell you they're my friend and go print that they're my friend. It's unfair to me—

Q: Why didn't they listen?

A: That's a good point. Why didn't they listen?

Questions: Mayor, mayor—

A: I think when the psychology of this whole thing is written, you know, and when some unarticulated premises in the minds of a lot of people are examined, you might find a lot of reasons why they didn't listen, and they may not be too proud of the reasons that made it impossible to understand what I was saying. Now is that vague? (no answer) That's vague, isn't it.

Q: Yeah.

A: Yeah, well deal with it. (some laughter, but not from mayor)

Q: Was it not until Christmas Day, your honor—

A: That's why I didn't want to go on TV, I wanted to talk to you. (he chuckles)...

Later a reporter from a black weekly newspaper indicates a different kind of problem for the mayor: complaints in his own base that his "allies" are being hung out to dry.

Q: What is your response to the charge by some of the black aldermen that Sawyer was just made a scapegoat of...

A: Sawyer? I just described what happened. Is that scapegoatism? What would you do? Walk down the street willy-nilly, hop-scotching down the line? No, you wouldn't. There is no cloud on him. We've tried to make it clear there was no cloud on him. But under the circumstances, until an investigation is completed, we thought certain steps should be taken. No one's accused him of anything. There was no cloud.

A white reporter, with the major media, continues on that question:

Q: Did he do anything wrong by taking a contribution from a contractor?

A: Well, we'll see.

Q: No, but since he—

A: The matter's open, the matter's open, the matter's open, the matter's open, sir... We haven't accused him of anything. And when the deal goes down, if there's no blame I'll be the first to say it, I won't hide it on page 36... it won't be a catchall phrase at the end of a long dissertation on roast pig on Channel Z 9-12. You'll hear it. (Interruptions, "Mayor, what's—") No, no we're talking about moral turpitude and we're talking about ethical conduct now, let's all keep it clean. (he chuckles) But you don't know what I'm talking about now, do you? "You're getting a little vague."

Q: Have you considered appointing an outside investigator...

A: We will do everything reasonable and necessary to make certain that this matter is laid to rest in all its parameters. At this point we have no reason to assume that OMI is not competent to do its job. If we have the slightest suspicion that more is needed, more will be given, period. We don't want anything hidden. We don't want even accusations of anything being hidden, nor do we want any suspicion that anybody's thinking about hiding anything. We're not. When I say we've got an open government we've got an open government and most of the things you know about this thing you got from us.

That last comment was true, in so far as we knew it. We had been forthcoming with everything we knew about John Adams, and we had introduced the issue as it touched Charles Sawyer. We had been more verbal than is usually appropriate in the firing of employees who had refused to cooperate with OMI.

Vernon Jarrett, *Sun-Times* columnist: ... Let me be blunt with you. Do you think this was an attempt to get Harold Washington?

A: Two and two is six, isn't it? You have to assume, you have to be mindful of that possibility, or shall you say probability. Be mindful of it. There's another scenario that might add up, I don't know. You have to raise the question, is it a political partisan thing? You have to raise the question about the wide swath of history, you have to raise all those questions.

Andy Shaw: You have to raise them, but how do you answer them?

A: Well, maybe you can.

Q: Is the fact that Dan Webb, who may have launched this federal investigation, may in fact be your Republican opponent in the next race at all a—

A: I wouldn't want to discuss this in the context of Mr. Webb because someone might assume I was accusing him of something and I'm not accusing Mr. Webb of anything; or Mr. Valukas (grins).

Q: Mayor, has OMI interviewed McClain?

A: OMI has no authority over private citizens, sir. OMI has no authority over aldermen. OMI has authority over executive department employees.. . .

Harry Golden, *Sun-Times*: Mr. Mayor, you noted that it's not appropriate for you to pick up the phone and chasten everyone who bandies your name about. On the other hand, this Mr. McClain is a special case—has he not been a source of irritation and potential embarrassment for two years?—

A: You have made Mr. McClain a special case. I didn't make him a special case. I made it clear to you he has absolutely nothing to do with this administration or me, no influence, he's not an inside dopester, he has no connection with this administration, none with me personally other than the fact that he was a former employee.

Q: His own actions propel him into the media. Such as his name, he propels his own name into this by making—

A: Why not go and investigate Mr. Raymond then? Why stop there? I mean, don't impose impossible burdens on me.

Q: (Fran Spielman? Debbe Nelson? both *Sun-Times*) Mayor, didn't McClain used to be a friend of yours? What made you change his status?

A: Mr. McClain was an employee who gave me good service.

Q: Wasn't he before that a friend of yours—

A: No, no, I met him under those circumstances and we parted under those circumstances. He worked for me. That doesn't put him down, that's what he did.

Q: (Fran Spielman) Then he's never been (unintelligible)

A: Oh, (Fran?) friend, friend—the way it's pressed about my closest friend, that's absolutely untrue. Friend—acquaintance. I made the analogy somewhat facetiously but we have gradations of people we know. Whether they're friends or not is for you to say or for me to say, not for some third party to say.

Q: At the beginning of your administration—

A: Just because you say someone's my friend doesn't mean he's my friend. And when you say "my closest friend" then you're really getting into somebody's head. Not mine.

Q: Mr. Mayor at the beginning of your administration—

Q: He's been saying it.

A: Well then he's wrong.

Q: And has he been wrong since he first, since you first came into office and he came into your friendship, he claimed to have frequent long private talks with you and—

A: When did he claim that?

Q: When you first came into office.

A: I never saw that. (another reporter finally succeeds in claiming the mayor's attention)

Q: Mr. Mayor, at the beginning of your administration you did call him your good friend and your loyal and trusted advisor.

A: Yes, this gentleman was working for me and he was giving me good service, and what am I supposed to do, put my toe in his rump? (general laughter, mayor not amused). He was discharged and that's the end of it. How do you talk about people that you know every day and work with. How do you talk about them? "Oh, I know X, I categorize him as Y and under certain circumstances as Q?" No, you use warm phrases to describe people that work with you; if you want them to work for you, you do. But don't assume from that anything more than I'm saying. And I don't know why this (his voice rises) *fascination* here, and you *won't let it go*! I keep talking about these unarticulated premises in your head. You ought to examine them. Don't examine me. Examine the premises. And maybe you'll find an answer to this. Which to me is not a mystery. And stop relating me to people to whom I'm not related. Next you'll say I'm a good friend of Arafat. Or Stalin.

Donal Quinlan: He lives in your building, he lives in your building—

A: So what. A hundred and some odd families live in my building. You might live there, I wouldn't know that. . . . (mayor stops; the aside is almost to himself) He lives in my building, isn't that something? That, you know, that's about, that's the greatest non sequitur I've ever heard in my life. So does the janitor. You know. So do some three-year-old children. What are we talking about here. You ever heard anything like that in your life, Vernon?

Q: May I ask a followup question, a specific question—

A: Yeah, who lives next door?

Q: You mentioned that you met him in the hallway, some months ago. Did he complain to you about having, about the suspension of Mr. Adams?

A: I have no dialogue with Mr. McClain. Period. "Hello, how are you? You're looking well. Take care of yourself."

Q: It would be a logical assumption that Mr. Adams would have related to Mr. McClain—

A: It's not logical based on what I'm saying. For Mr. McClain to come and tell me that. I just told you there was no relationship.

Q: But I mean at the time he bumped into you in the hallway, or at these other casual meetings, did he ever complain about the treatment of Mr. Adams.

A: No.

Q: And he never lobbied on behalf of SRS or any other contract?

A: Not to me, or anyone else I know of.

Q: Has Mr. McClain ever lobbied you to do business with somebody specifically?

A: No.

Q: Or steer business to somebody?

A: No.

Discussion followed about whether Montgomery had ever met with or knew Raymond—the mayor said he was assured that they had no business dealings but explained it's impossible to guarantee you've never "met" anyone, because as soon as you say you haven't, someone will produce a photo of the two of you shaking hands. He'd go to several receptions a night, and if there were 500 people at one of them, he'd have shaken hands with 490 of them. If the thrust of the question was did he know Raymond—or did Montgomery know Raymond—or did either have any business relationship, or did he remember meeting Raymond—the answer to all those questions was no.

A: (continuing) Let's don't get guilt by association. You know, next you'll say, like the other fellow did, "This fellow lives in your building, therefore."

Q: I didn't say "therefore," mayor, I say you shouldn't be surprised—

A: Well, it's implied.

Q: Well, you can't, you shouldn't be surprised—

A: Implied.

Q: You shouldn't be surprised—

A: It's implied, Mr. Quinlan.

Q: Were you surprised that we draw those connections?

A: I definitely am, Mr. Quinlan, I definitely am. They're repetitive, and persistent, in a certain sense insulting and disturbing that you continue to do that, notwithstanding that I have periodically taken you through this same—

Q: Is it surprising that Mr. Adams came up with McClain's name which you still are sticking to, that that's who he got the money from—

A: I'm not sticking to anything. I'm telling you what happened as I got it.

Q: Well, under these circumstances, why is it surprising?

A: Why is what surprising?

Q: That Adams says he got ten grand from McClain, he's suspected of steering a city contract, and we're asking about Clarence McClain.

A: Yeah, it's surprising that you continue to ask me about Clarence McClain when I continue to tell you I have no relationship with Clarence McClain. That's surprising. I begin to wonder why you continue to do it.

Q: Because it just came up again.

A: Yeah and it'll probably come up again next week. Why don't you just print what I wrote? I don't have any connection with Mr. McClain. Headline: "Denies it." Why don't you just say that. I've said it enough times.

Q: Mayor, regardless of any association McClain may or may not have with you, does it not behoove this administration to get the word to McClain to shut up if he's throwing your name around? (The mayor laughs a bitter laugh.) I mean, why don't you do that, why don't you or someone else—

A: Mr. McClain, shut up. Don't throw my name around. Stop it. (laughter) Isn't this getting a little ridiculous? (Chinta Straussberg, *Defender:* Yes.)

That afternoon at 2:00 we went into the press conference room to answer the same questions for the cameras, for the record. The print reporters had doubtless already filed the bulk of their stories, and seemed to be sated. The TV and radio reporters were calm and courteous. The mayor was relaxed—there were few questions he hadn't already heard, and he was clear as to the points he wanted to make. In many ways it was the easiest reactive press conference we ever experienced.

He was asked the McClain questions, and he took the opportunity to set the record straight:

> We said it definitely, we said it forcefully, and we said it often. We'll repeat it. Mr. McClain was severed from this administration over two and a half years ago pursuant to our finding for the first time that he was involved in some conduct involving moral turpitude back in 1970 before I even met him. He was subsequently separated from our political wing as well.
>
> Since that time Mr. McClain has had nothing to do with this administration in so far as I'm concerned and in so far as anyone in this administration who has talked to me about it. It is reputed that he has held himself out as being an influence peddler in this administration. If that is true it is incorrect. He has no influence to peddle with me and he'd better not have any influence to peddle with anyone else in this administration. And that goes beyond Mr. McClain.
>
> We made it very clear that no part of this administration is to be involved in negotiating or purveyance of contracts or favors or anything else. And any person in this administration who involves himself in that conduct does it at their own peril. I've told that to every high level administrator prior to being hired. I've repeated that at numerous cabinet meetings. It's pretty clear. Mr. McClain has no connection with this administration whatsoever. He was a former employee of mine who gave me frankly good service. In so far as being a friend, that was not the category of Mr. McClain. Mr. McClain was an acquaintance, an employee, who gave excellent work. The press has bruited it about on any number of occasions that he was my closest friend. They never got that from me, matter of fact I denied it. Yet and still they persist in printing it. I don't know why.
>
> Q. Political adviser?
>
> A: Neither. No connection. None.

The mayor had frequently been urged to repudiate Clarence McClain. He had always responded that he was "not into repudiation," and that it wouldn't make any difference what he said. The mayor's point was underscored shortly after the press conference, when Fran Spielman appeared on a TV talk show and repeated the bald lie: "I understand what he said publicly," she said, "but the point is ask anyone close to Mayor Washington and they will tell you that this man is a very trusted friend and will always be a trusted friend.... he hasn't sought to really cut McClain's access off to city officials."

Fran Spielman was a blindly biased reporter, as far as Mayor Washington was concerned. There was no recourse for it, none whatsoever, no court of law or of journals where any suit could be heard; so with difficultly he swallowed the issue and simply put her forever out of mind.

But he considered that the editorship of the *Tribune* was in a similar category, and the *Tribune* could not be so lightly dismissed. "You gotta pay attention to these snapping dogs," he said.

He was convinced that the "Bad Trib" had set its sights on a Pulitzer for running the mayor to ground. "They're a Pulitzer-machine," he had said in connection with a prior series. "They get their issue and then they turn a hundred little snapping dogs loose. If they've picked the issue right, they get their prize." Now he believed the *Trib* was going for its "Watergate Pulitzer."

At the same time, over the long haul, a stable relationship with the "Good Trib" was devoutly to be desired. As someone said, you don't do battle with anybody who buys ink by the barrel. He was anxious to restore at least an armistice with the *Trib*, and he understood that to mean an armistice with Jim Squires.

The *Tribune* scent for blood was particularly evident in its lead editorial for February 3, titled "A scandal that slowly rises." At this point there had been no new information for a month. It was clear that the federal and local "sources" had delivered all they had. That didn't prevent a fresh daily story rehashing the December details. If the scandal were rising toward the mayor's office, they were right about one thing: it was certainly slow. The editorial read:

> Reports of the City Hall payoff scandal are working away at the Washington administration like water torture. In the last few days, sources close to key figures in the investigation of a city contractor's $10,000 payoff to John E. Adams, the city's deputy revenue director, raise serious questions about how the administration handled what now appears to be a violation of state laws and city rules against official misconduct.

Sources say two top aides to Mayor Harold Washington—Corporation Counsel James Montgomery and Chief of Staff Ernest Barefield—knew five months ago that Mr. Adams had taken the money from the contractor, Systematic Recovery Service, Inc. That contradicts the mayor's contention that his administration did not know about the payoff until late December. It also contradicts Mr. Montgomery's and Mr. Barefield's claims that they did not know about it until the first wave of publicity surrounding the fact that Systematic Recovery's representative actually was a mole planted by the FBI.

More devastating is the claim by a source close to Charles Sawyer, acting revenue director at the time, that in an Aug. 29 meeting in the apartment of Clarence McClain, a controversial former adviser to the mayor, Mr. Montgomery stopped Mr. Barefield from firing Mr. Adams immediately because of Mr. McClain's ties to the mayor.

There are many unanswered questions:

Did the mayor's top aides think they could push a scandal under the rug?

When the scandal finally leaked out, did they decide to take options other than full disclosure?

Did Mr. Montgomery compromise his obligation as corporation counsel to enforce the law without equivocation?

Would the mayor's top aides make such an important decision without the mayor's approval?

The history of political scandal in this city has been exceedingly rich. But the examples Mayor Washington ought to ponder right now come from Washington, not Chicago. Twice in a decade, presidents found themselves trapped by their efforts to protect those close to them. Richard Nixon was dragged from power by the weight of the Watergate cover-up. Jimmy Carter, an avowed reformer, was severely damaged by his attempt to save his friend, Bert Lance. Scandal shows no respect for friendships and personal loyalty.

Mayor Washington has to answer the questions, and the answers have to bear up, or else he will learn the cruel lesson of political scandal the hard way. And the problem will continue to rise.

The *Tribune*'s ominous questions followed a faulty premise: a meeting that never took place. The mayor took it as a measure of the *Trib*'s carelessness with the details of this story, details that were momentous in their potential effect, that the editorial writer would go so far afield in his summations: there simply never was a meeting with McClain, Montgomery and Barefield. This carelessness indicated to him that the *Trib* was operating on generalized prejudgments of the mayor's complicity.

The mayor was convinced that the editorial had been personally written by Jim Squires. The implication of the fourth "unanswered question"—would top aides act without the mayor's approval—was clear, and though the *Trib* told us that Clarence Page had written the piece, the mayor did not believe that anyone at Page's level would have the temerity to call the mayor a liar. He was ready to take criticism for bad judgment, but not for corruption or dishonesty.

The editorial was also the clearest expression of the *Tribune's* apparent view of its role in this matter. With bitter references to the "dragging down" of Richard Nixon, and with its invidious comparisons of the cataclysmic Watergate scandals to the lesser Bert Lance embarrassment of "avowed reformer" Jimmy Carter, the *Tribune* seemed to be working out of a malevolent world view. The "bad Tribune" had reared up from the swamp, the "good Tribune" had fled, and the admission was plain as day: We're out to get you, mayor.

He told me he wanted to meet with Squires and the editorial board to discuss "the nature of the treatment" he was getting. I asked for a meeting for that purpose. We met at the *Trib* on February 5.

The meeting did not go well. Reporters present wanted to question the mayor about the allegations. The mayor made clear that he had not come to give the *Trib* an exclusive interview—he had expected an opportunity for candid discussion about their "unarticulated premises." He had no problem with the reporters being present, although they'd already heard most of what he had to say; but he wanted the conversation off the record. As he later told me, "They wanted me to take holy hell from them for five weeks and then turn around and give them a private interview?"

It would have been to our advantage to do just that; I had complete confidence in his ability to cut across the premises on which they were operating—the conspiracies, if he was right—and reestablish a dialogue with the "good Tribune" based on the simple facts. But he had made his frame of mind amply clear before we went in. "I'm not a noodle," he said. "You've got to stand for something."

Squires wasn't happy that the mayor wanted a background discussion. He dismissed the reporters and most of the editorial board. He apparently didn't want a full audience for the man-to-man confrontation that would follow; that's exactly what the mayor did want.

We were there, we said, because we were concerned that what had begun as a series of news stories had turned into a crusade.

The discussion was rocky. Both parties were hostile. The complete falsity of the McClain-Montgomery-Barefield meeting at McClain's apartment was cited as an example of how reckless both the reporters and the editorial staff had become on this issue. In reply we were told, "It really doesn't matter whether the meeting took place at City Hall or at McClain's apartment;" it required another round of discussion to clarify that no such meeting, anywhere, had ever taken place. McClain was not a factor in City Hall decisions.

But the confrontation was ugliest at the personal level. The mayor had come to ask the direct question of Jim Squires: You are running a daily diatribe, implying that the mayor and the administration are corrupt. When, sir, will you desist?

And when the question was finally put, the answer was blunt and cold: When we have gotten to the bottom of this matter, however long that takes, wherever it may lead.

The meeting ended on that note.

That week the papers reported that attorney Tom Sullivan had been signed on as special counsel to OMI, to investigate and prepare a report for the mayor on the allegations raised by the FBI probe.

This was not a parallel investigation, as some misunderstood it to be. From the mayor's standpoint, regardless of the legal prosecution and concurrent investigations of the FBI or any other law enforcement agency, he as CEO of a $2 billion corporation had a responsibility to know where the holes were and how to plug them. Sullivan was hired to report on what had happened in the Adams/Sawyer matter, but also to make recommendations on procedures and safeguards in the city's contracting procedures.

The report, said the mayor, would be available to the public. He would ask City Council to grant subpoena power to Sullivan.

A few days later a lengthy lead editorial in the *Tribune* discussed "The mayor's new investigator." Under that was an editorial dealing with the seizure of a Libyan aircraft by Israel, and another dealing with "Federal research funds." Tucked between the latter two editorials, unrelated to the lead editorial dealing with the investigation, was a smaller heading, "A Clarification."

This "clarification" was the *Tribune's* response to the mayor's visit. It read as follows: "An error in a Monday editorial may have left the incorrect impression that sources had told *Tribune* reporters that

Clarence McClain was present at an Aug. 29 meeting involving Mayor Washington's chief of staff, Ernest Barefield and Chicago Corporation Counsel James Montgomery. The sources did not say Mr. McClain was at the meeting. The *Tribune* regrets any misunderstanding caused by its error."

The mayor wasn't alone in his perceptions about the handling of the probe, by the press or by the federal government.

William Safire was writing about the concurrent New York scandals, in his *New York Times* column, but his perceptions apply to federal investigations in other major cities:

> Corruption in government is bad enough, but when that corruption mingles with prosecutorial panic and political ambition to breed abuses of power and denial of individual rights, citizens are in more danger than they realize...
>
> That sort of prejudgment is an offense to American justice, which holds that no man is a crook until convicted, and which must seek jurors not prejudiced by verdicts announced by my-skirts-are-clean fervor...
>
> In that hysterical setting, along came this story: "Federal prosecutors said Sunday that they would ask a grand jury next week to indict a key figure in the New York City corruption scandal...unless he agreed to cooperate in their investigation."...
>
> In this outrageous abuse of power, the prosecutor betrays his contempt for the grand jury system. The grand jury...is an assemblage of citizens, operating in secret, that is supposed to shield the accused from the potential misuse of power by government.
>
> Some prosecutors treat grand juries like rubber stamps and believe they can order indictments. Prosecutors' threats to witnesses are common, but a public prediction of a criminal charge unless a witness cooperates is new—as if both the press and the grand jury existed to do the prosecutor's bidding.
>
> Apparently [the U.S. Attorney] sees himself as the new Tom Dewey, riding a crime-busting reputation to the governorship and a Republican presidential nomination. In the exposure of fraud and bribery, the unidentified prosecutor apparently figures, anything goes.
>
> Anything does not go. Bribery and fixing must be rooted out, but not in a way that rips up our liberties. The corruption is not so much in the men on the take as in the men on the make.

Andrew Greeley wrote in the *Sun-Times*, Apr. 20, 1986:

> Is no one concerned when the federal government tricks people into committing crime?
>
> Are we prepared to accept a situation in which the government uses known criminals to lie, bribe, cheat and deceive in order to seduce someone into criminal behavior for which they can then be arrested?...
>
> What happens to the public's confidence in the law enforcement system, the courts, and ultimately the law when government prosecutors, having learned that political trials can lead to the governor's mansion, become the allies of criminals in dishonesty and deception?...
>
> I thought that we all had the right to be considered innocent until proven guilty. Now it seems that the federal government has the right to decide in advance that someone is guilty and then go out and trick them into providing evidence for a conviction.
>
> And in case there is any doubt about it, the United States attorney will tell you the whole story on his nightly televised press conference—after the case has been leaked to the media a few days before.

The *Chicago Lawyer* editorialized in its January 1987 issue:

> For a working journalist leaks are a good thing... But the fact that leaks help a journalist do his job does not mean that the leaking of information is ethical or lawful. We all know that—even journalists know it—if we stop to think for a moment....
>
> The leaking of information by prosecutors about pending investigations falls into the category of improper behavior. Prosecutors are given enormous powers in our legal system to obtain information about possible criminal activity. They can subpoena witnesses and documents before a grand jury. Often they need not actually exercise these powers in order to obtain the same results. They have the power to indict or not to indict, or to exercise discretion in the selection of charges, or to request that immunity be granted. In some cases, prosecutors can also wiretap.
>
> These vast powers can lawfully be used by prosecutors only in the service of criminal justice. If no indictments result, prosecutors have no mandate, and no right, to circulate information obtained through the legal process... Even after indictment, prosecutors are expressly constrained...

Thomas F. Roeser, a leading Chicago Republican who was certainly not an ally of the mayor, though perhaps could be counted a friend, raised the political questions in his *Sun-Times* article on Jan. 27, 1986:

> Blacks won the mayoralty fair and square. Now, a new political identity they won for themselves may be destroyed for the most mischievous of collaborative reasons—malicious partisanship and what I would not be stunned to discover as collaboration between segments of two parties [Vrdolyak-Burke and the Republicans] and prosecutorial elements. Small wonder it is still true to say that the price of being black in America is, for some, the price of paranoia.

> So let us begin to give scrutiny to the extent and nature of the "corruption" regurgitated by the [federal] Super Jaws. Let us question its intentions, recalling that a federal government that has failed to deal with its own deficits, subsidies to the well-off, welfare-engineered breakup of families, its own undeclared wars may well give us nothing in return for a few media-hyped convictions than Chicago as another Belfast."

Dr. Mary R. Sawyer, in her study titled "Harassment of Black Elected Officials: Ten Years Later," analyzes what she considers a recurring pattern, consistent with the mayor's concern for those who campaign by indictment:

> Typically, several different tactics come into play simultaneously. Perhaps as invidious a form of harassment as any is the interplay that takes place between the news media and law enforcement agencies. The scenario usually begins with a rumor started by an investigative office, or by an ill-founded news report. The rumor may trigger a media story alleging wrongdoing, which then triggers a criminal inquiry, which then becomes the subject of further news stories, which then give rise to a grand jury investigation, which leads to more stories and editorials based on leaked and often fallacious information. This spiral of inflammatory stories and criminal investigations sometimes culminates in an indictment. The indictment typically results in acquittal, or in a conviction which is ultimately overturned on appeal—which then receives a three-inch announcement on page 17 after the story had been front page headline news for months on end.

In the mayor's experience it had been twice as bad—page 34. As usual it was Mike Royko who made the mayor smile by putting the issue in perspective, in the *Chicago Tribune*, Feb. 25, 1986:

> Let us consider the current scandal. There are actually two separate

scandals, neither of which is going to cause a leak in the roof of City Hall, much less blow it off.

First we have the three or four aldermen who are suspected of taking money from Michael Raymond, the embezzler, con man, thief and suspected murderer of old ladies, who has found employment with the FBI.

On a scandal scale of one to ten, the aldermanic bribes would be, oh, at best a three or four. . .nowhere near the stature of such recent power-houses as Ald. Tom Keane. . . .

When Keane was caught, he was acknowledged to be second only to Mayor Daley as a political power. Those who are now under investigation don't have as much power as one of Keane's precinct captains. . . .

The second part of the scandal involves one payoff allegedly taken by one middle-level administrator in Mayor Washington's staff. Despite the panting of the press, I rate that as a two or maybe a three. . . . He is an obscure paper-shuffler. Why the great grabbers of City Hall lore used to pocket more in one week than this amateur took in his one breathless, sweaty venture into pocket-stuffing. It's almost embarrassing to think of this as a true Chicago scandal. . . .

A day in the press doesn't pass without still another hot rumor about who in City Hall knew when that obscure paper-shuffler took his bribe, who didn't know, who didn't blow the whistle. Or amazing disclosures that maybe the Mayor is quitting or weeping or chewing the edge of his desk.

The reason for that, of course, is that Harold Washington took over a City Hall brimming with people who hate his innards. And they are eager to grab the phone to pass on the latest bit of hot information.

Why don't the veteran city employees like Washington? I'm not sure what the reason is. Maybe they just don't like the way he parts his hair. I'd hate to think that it had to do with some kind of bigotry against Baptists.

David Protess, professor of journalism at Medill School of Journalism, and Paul McGinn, managing editor of *Chicago Lawyer*, conducted a content analysis of the news coverage. They wrote to the mayor with their findings.

"An analysis of press coverage of the FBI probe into the awarding of city contracts documents that both the *Sun-Times* and *Tribune* lacked balance in their reporting," they wrote.

The analysis, they said, included a comprehensive study of all the articles published during the first two months of the scandal, from December 25 to March 1.

They found that "both newspapers devoted far more column inches to allegations than to responses," and that they named Harold Washington far more often than the facts of the stories warranted, suggesting that he might be an eventual target of the investigation. The *Sun-Times*, they showed, named the mayor 276 times, more even than Raymond the Mole. The *Trib*, which kept the steady drumbeat going longer than any other in the media, named the mayor 446 times.

In opinion pieces—editorials and op ed columns, the tendency was even greater to make the mayor the central focus of the alleged corruption. He was named 99 times by the *Trib* and 87 times by the *Sun-Times*, far ahead of the runner up (in both papers), Clarence McClain, named 20 and 17 times, respectively.

More to the point, less than half of the stories which appeared in the most crazed period, February 1–March 1, contained new information. According to *Chicago Lawyer*, "only 43 percent of the *Tribune's* stories had new information during that 30-day period, and 49.6 percent of the *Sun-Times* stories," revealing that each paper used just over half their stories to rehash old information and allegations for a full month.

They also noted that both papers relied heavily on unidentified sources in their stories—the *Tribune* 59.6 percent of the time, the *Sun-Times* 27.8 percent.

Although the *Tribune* continued its daily dose for a time, by late February most of the media had become more interested in the looming special aldermanic elections than in "Raymond the Mole." When the indictments didn't materialize—in January the "sources" were promising them in February, but spring turned to fall and they still hadn't arrived—many in the press became sullen whenever the subject was raised. Two different reporters who had each offered me a variation on the same friendly advice—quit City Hall, get out while you can—were now muttering that they had been misled on the story.

The appointment of Sullivan provided the climactic factor. It was a cap on the continuing story, an opportunity for the media to get out of it. It must have been difficult for editors and station managers who had implicitly promised the public that they were on the case, to drop the Watergate circus just as casually as they'd raised it. But the truth is, they were out of fresh material, and had been for weeks.

Whatever the rationale, except for the *Trib*, the stories slowed to a trickle at about the time Sullivan was appointed. But it wasn't dead, only asleep. We were due to be revisited by the Adams, McClain, Barefield's "bad judgment" and all the rest, in October.

In the mayor's public announcement when he appointed Sullivan he said that he wanted a full disclosure, to clear the air, and let the chips fall where they may. When we read the Sullivan report in October, we saw that it simply reiterated what the press had already amply written. There were no surprises, no sensational disclosures.

The only adverse comment from the mayor's standpoint was the editorial observation by Sullivan that the mayor may have exercised bad judgment when he accepted his chief of staff's word for what had happened. The mayor was annoyed by Sullivan's interpretation, but hell, it was far less caustic than what the media had been printing and broadcasting for weeks. So it was completely in our interest to get the report out and get it aired, now, before the 1987 election campaign was any further along.

But when he received the report it came with a reminder from Sullivan that as an OMI document it was privileged and could not be released. The testimony collected from individuals in the course of the investigation was protected by law. The intent of the law was to insure the effectiveness of investigations by guaranteeing those who cooperated that their assistance would be confidential. Sullivan announced that neither he nor any of his staff, nor anyone from OMI, would make any comment or statement about the investigation or the report that resulted.

The mayor was stymied, and not least because the Eddies immediately complained of a "coverup," a position the press parroted. It was implied that the report detailed McClain's secret role at City Hall, and suggested that other instances of corruption were revealed.

Consistent with Sullivan's reminder, the mayor had to tell the press that the Sullivan Report was "classified." The municipal code, which the mayor cited in making his announcement, was "Section 1, Chapter 25-46 [which] says, and I quote: 'The investigatory files and reports of the Office of Municipal Investigation shall be confidential and shall not be divulged to any person or agency, except a law enforcement officer or agency, and for investigative or prosecutorial purposes.'"

He directed Judd Miner to request a declaratory judgment from the Circuit Court of Cook County, to permit us to make the report public. At the same time he requested city employees to waive any right to confidentiality that might be deemed to exist, in order to expedite its release.

Despite the legal obstructions, the media joined the Eddies in charging the mayor with a coverup. "The mayor claims the law prevents its release," said one article. Any cub reporter could more accurately have stated simply, "the law prevents its release."

The mayor was between a rock and a hard place, heading into an election. Judd had advised that it was unlikely we'd get an advisory order. I remember the mayor's rueful grin, the shake of his head, as he considered the bind we were in. The report was a hot potato, and the longer we were stuck with it, the longer it was going to burn. As a politician he was tempted to interpret the law as loosely as his critics were, and get the damn thing out. As a lawyer, and as mayor, he felt he had an obligation to protect the legal process against even such a universal clamor. In the end, the politician won, but he couldn't bring himself to acknowledge that.

While we were wrestling with the issue, Art Petacque of the *Sun-Times* approached me with the advice that it was to the mayor's advantage to get the thing out—a point where we had already arrived. Petacque, unlike most reporters with an interest in the report, had not been among the "barracudas" that attacked the mayor on this issue throughout the spring. In making his case, he made it clear that if he were to get a copy of the report, he'd play it straight, no cheap shots.

His call was helpful to me in making the same case to the mayor. The mayor had dealt with Petacque before and had reason to think he'd be fair. We knew that the report contained no surprises—no McClain connection, no secret misdeeds, only the Revenue Department infractions that had already been reported and the bad judgment of Barefield.

As I said to Petacque when we talked about the report, echoing the mayor: "We're not looking for any special treatment, Art, just a fair shake." No promises had been made or requested, on either side. I left the Sullivan Report in a plain envelope on the front seat of my car when I went to the Downtown Sports Club, near the *Sun-Times*, for my regular workout. When I returned to the car it was gone.

Petacque's scoop on the Sullivan report inspired one of the few calls I had ever received from Sneed. She was under enormous pressure from her editors to come up with a copy for the *Trib*, and apparently her regular connections had come up empty. The mayor didn't want her to have a copy but I convinced him that this was one of those situations where what helps your enemy doesn't necessarily hurt you.

Of course, by releasing the report in this way we accomplished only one advantage: we got the damn report out. We didn't accomplish the other advantage: the mayor took no credit for releasing it, only recriminations for sitting on it. As far as the public knew, it had been released despite his desire to keep it a secret.

Both receivers of the report kept that perception intact. When the stories hit, even Petacque's fair treatment read like an expose, a fresh installment of last winter's shocking scandals.

Mayor Washington tensed and took the fresh blow with a smile. "It was not clear who had leaked the report," the *Trib*'s City Hall reporters wrote, "but the mayor said he was glad to have it out, and City Hall insiders said it was to the mayor's political benefit to face the report's criticisms now, rather than have its information trickle out in the months preceding the mayoral primary election next February."

The report, as the mayor pointed out, contained nothing new. Everything it said had already been in the newspapers—and more; that is, it substantiated far less than the wide-ranging allegations we had already endured. The mayor called it "the first lucid account I've read," and it was that.

It was most interesting for what it did *not* contain. There were no scandalous stories of graft and corruption at City Hall, no indication of a pattern of corruption in what the *Trib* had called for months "the widening investigation at City Hall."

Throughout the period when he was promoting his affirmative action programs, the mayor had defended his administration for its elimination of *institutional* corruption, through numerous reforms. He acknowledged that no chief executive can ever guarantee there will never be a case of *individual* corruption in his administration; all he can do is promise to punish it when it's found out.

He had done that. The report confirmed it. And after all the sturm and drang, all we got for our money was the sad story of a single case of individual corruption of a Revenue Department bureaucrat, and a judgment based on hindsight of how it might have been handled differently.

He agreed with the report that the entire matter should have been handled differently.

But the report showed, as he pointed out, that no one had accused Barefield or Montgomery of any illegal act. The report, in fact, went out of its way to make that clear, as well as the fact that they were not accused of "official misconduct" as defined by state law. It concluded that the contradiction between Barefield's story and Charles Sawyer's story could not be resolved. And it accused Barefield of being too soft-hearted.

Still, the mayor was treated to a final slap of the story that had appeared, under a variety of headlines and with a variety of emphases, throughout the winter:

"Though Washington held numerous press conferences and insisted that he and his aides were forthcoming about the case," the *Trib*'s story said, "a comparison of the report with their public statements indicates they were often misleading and contradictory about the case.

"For instance, while the mayor repeatedly asserted that McClain, who resigned in disgrace in 1983, had no role in the government, his top aides were busily trying to cover up the fact that McClain had secretly wielded influence over a city contract."

The report showed just the opposite. It showed McClain working at the periphery apparently *attempting* to have influence on a city contract—but without any success whatever. SRS never got the contract he was hustling for. Charles Sawyer blew the whistle on Adams and McClain the day he learned of the connection. A far cry from the allegations that the man who (in case readers had missed the earlier stories) "resigned in disgrace in 1983," had spent the past two years pulling the mayor's strings and selling clout.

The reporters—Mike Sneed was back in the bylines for this series—hung their entire case against the administration on the allegation that a warning from McClain had delayed awarding the contract to Datacom. McClain, the report said, had urged the city to look at a study which would show that Datacom would be a poor choice. In fact there was a delay to consider this possibility—anyone claiming to have urgently important evidence against a vendor could cause an alert city official to go slow—but it was examined and rejected, and the city proceeded to sign with Datacom.

As to the "contradictory" and "often misleading" public statements: as the mayor repeatedly tried to make clear to reporters, he was in the dark about the details just like everyone else. A few re-porters, apparently obsessed with the conviction that the mayor was a felon, consistently refused to separate new information from hind-sight and sought to trip the mayor on variations in his remarks, as they rushed to judgment.

But the mayor didn't expect the press, which had invested so much ink in proving McClain's dominant role, to help him out. He was just happy to have these stories running now, in October, rather than sometime in February, just before the primary.

There was still one more shoe to drop—the indictments them-selves. It was widely speculated, by a press now sour on the story, that they might be timed to interfere with the mayoral elections. The federal investigation had messed up our last Christmas. Now we won-dered when the indictments would come down; we were fully pre-pared to see them break, once again, on Christmas Eve. As it happened, when the indictment finally came down, the prosecutor took care to avoid any interference with the election, although the timing was bad.

It was not until 11 months after the first reports, in the heat of the mayoral campaign, that U.S. Attorney Anton R. Valukas, standing with officials of the IRS and the FBI, ominously positioned before a table covered with matte black machine guns confiscated in a mar-ginally related investigation, announced the indictments.

Two months before, Michael Raymond had been charged with murdering a 66-year-old woman for her money, in Florida. And he had been sentenced on a Nashville weapons conviction.

The *Sun-Times* of Nov. 22, 1986, used a photo of the mayor with one of his crumpled-up expressions—perhaps listening to a question, perhaps belching privately as he waited for the TV crews to get their cameras rolling—and labeled it "A disturbed Mayor Washing-ton...," under headlines that roared, "7 indicted in City Hall payoff case."

But it was the *Tribune* coverage that day, by Tom Burton and Maurice Possley, that made the mayor comment, "I don't know whether to laugh or cry."

Chicago Aldermen Clifford P. Kelley [20th] and Wallace Davis, Jr. [27th] and five other men were indicted by a federal grand jury Friday on a wide range of charges in the first wave of indictments stemming from a 2-1/2 year FBI undercover investigation into alleged City Hall corruption . . .

Also charged were Michael Lambesis, chief investigator for the Cook County Circuit Court clerk's office; Carmen Aiello, a former chief supervisor in the city water department; Herman Mitchell, a former precinct captain in Davis' 27th ward organization; Raymond Akers, Jr., a lobbyist for Waste Management Inc.; and Paul Vesper, an associate of Lambesis who owns an Arlington Heights electronics firm.

Davis, Kelley and Aiello were charged with accepting payoffs from Michael Raymond . . . But Friday's indictments reveal that the inquiry extends far beyond the bill-collection business and that payoffs were far larger than had been known publicly.

The indictments, containing several counts unrelated to Raymond, also display a strategy by prosecutors to de-emphasize the informant, who is charged in Florida with murder and is a suspect in several other deaths. . . .

The array of charges unrelated to Raymond range from several alleged dealings by Kelley with Akers, 32, and Waste Management, the giant Oak Brook-based waste-hauler, to the alleged extortion of West Side businesses by Davis, to several weapons charges involving Lambesis and Vesper.

Actually, the same story indicated that the weapons charges were not unrelated: those accused "were charged with selling Raymond illegal weapons, including an Uzi submachine gun, automatic pistols and a silencer [and that they] knew Raymond was a convicted felon who was not entitled to bear arms."

Many media observers agreed with the mayor that the investigators and the reporters had labored mightily to produce a mouse. And now they were trying to dress it up to look like a hamster, at best. These "City Hall payoff" items were a far cry from the front page stories on Clarence McClain, John Adams, Ernest Barefield—"and maybe the mayor"—they had run all spring. And the "inquiry [that] extends far beyond the bill-collection business" with "payoffs far larger than had been known publicly" was in fact a lumping together of a miscellany of cases.

The article went on to detail indictment specifics dealing with Waste Management. Buried halfway through the story was the acknowledgement that "Kelley and Davis are members of the City Council bloc allied with Mayor Washington. But they are thought more to be allies of convenience rather than long-time close associates of the mayor, so it is believed that the political fallout for Washington will not be too great as he prepares for a re-election fight."

As he reviewed the story, the mayor muttered "Page 34." He observed that the "sources" were still being relied upon:

"But others with closer ties to the mayor, including former top aide Clarence McClain and the city's former deputy revenue commissioner, John E. Adams, still are under investigation, sources close to the case have said."

Finally, buried in the story back on page 12, after months of page one banners screaming out from every street-corner vending machine: ". . . Valukas, who announced the indictments, stressed that the mayor is not a target of the investigation." Period.

The mayor looked at me and shook his head. "Page 34," he said. "It's unbelievable."

A *Sun-Times* story the following day seemed to plead patience for the investigators and the media, and to promise more information for a city selecting its next mayor:

> The indictments Friday of two aldermen and five others were part of the U.S. attorney's plan to bring pressure on relatively minor figures in the City Hall corruption inquiry in the hopes that they will provide key evidence against more powerful aldermen and corporate executives, investigators said. . . . These future indictments, which could be announced before Christmas, could include the names of several of Mayor Washington's closest allies, sources said. . . .
>
> The second wave of indictments could come as early as next month, and most of the individuals to be indicted then are included in a report on municipal corruption completed last month by special mayoral investigator Thomas P. Sullivan. . . .

The adventure with "Raymond the Mole" cost us several casualties. The most significant was Jim Montgomery, who had been in one too many adverse stories.

Jim and Bill Ware between them had carried the load for the administration during the first two years. Jim had been in the fore of every battle, and had learned to stomach the wild accusations along with the valid criticisms. Now Jim was being pressured out by stories that he had accepted free transportation for a family vacation.

He had accepted the job as corporation counsel with the understanding that he would be permitted to fulfill his commitment as co-counsel on a $22 million civil rights lawsuit in Las Vegas. That case was coming to a head, and it provided a good occasion to make his departure.

Efforts had long been underway to isolate the mayor—from Barefield, from Montgomery, from Ware—and each crisis provided a fresh opportunity to make a move. Early in the "Molescam" period Mayor Washington asked me to sit down with Thomas Todd, a leading black activist and attorney who was recommending an orchestrated outcry from the black community. He had strong opinions on how we should be handling the media.

Al Johnson was also present. Todd kept saying that the mayor should be removed as a spokesman in the scandal stories, put in the background. "So should you," he said to me, several times. I detected an overtone of resentment—I'd almost say he was begrudging me my "high visibility" in the media since the onset of the scandal stories. In any case, I thanked him for his advice and promised to keep in touch. That was the last time I heard from him, and I certainly wasn't going to be the one to initiate the next contact.

But what impressed me at that meeting was his flat statement, spoken with the assurance of one who is in charge: Montgomery had to go. Now Barefield is next. When I later discussed the episode with Barefield, after the mayor's death, he nodded knowingly. It was part of a constant effort, he said, to separate the mayor from the administrative team on which he relied. Todd and others had applied the pressure, but the mayor wasn't having any of it. He would stick with Barefield.

Another casualty of that period was Tom Coffey, head of intergovernmental affairs. Tom had come in conflict with the kitchen cabinet, but that wasn't enough to do him in. Mayor Washington was good about supporting an aide under fire. The intramural politics—a dispute with the fundraisers—was only the final straw.

What finished Coffey off was the mayor's wrath at the way he dealt with the media. Every other day the mayor would identify another story or a fresh item in "Inc." in which Coffey was featured, or his contributions promoted, or his enemies chastised. He was never quoted directly, but his involvement was transparent.

The mayor didn't understand why I wasn't upset with Coffey's press agentry. He supposed I would have had more sensitivity to encroachments on my turf, or that I would have resented his taking individual credit where group credit was due.

I replied by making the case for Coffey that his job as lobbyist, unlike just about any other cabinet level job, required him to play the media as one of the tools of his trade. I felt that Coffey and I were sufficiently coordinated that we weren't working at cross purposes. The fact was that we didn't clash because there was no way I could do the job Coffey was doing, in the management of the Springfield and City Council legislative agenda.

The mayor acted as though I were naive or blind to Coffey's efforts to undermine me; he later told me that if he hadn't known better he would have assumed that Coffey and I were in league, that I had joined the Coffey camp.

That was part of the problem, in retrospect: that the mayor perceived a "Coffey camp." In Coffey's job, at his level of involvement in the constant wars we fought, and given his likely role in the campaign to come, the mayor needed to know there was a complete commitment to his judgment and will. Any nuance of more complex commitments, at least within his innermost circle of advisers, was anathema to him.

The mayor had wrestled with the question of cutting Coffey loose as early as the previous fall, and had talked about it through November and December. He was apparently under a good deal of pressure to act, from within his kitchen cabinet.

It was my first experience with any change at the top. When I first heard the mayor talking about "cutting Coffey loose," I didn't take it seriously. The mayor fretted about it for so long that I decided it was his way of venting frustrations. On some occasions he was abrupt with Coffey, verbally slapping him down when they disagreed, unusual behavior for the easy-going chief executive. I was so tied up with with my own preoccupations that I may have missed other tensions which gave rise to the mayor's changing attitude. But I got used to the situation, took it as an object lesson, and never considered that the mayor would actually take action.

It may have been that Barefield was also counseling against it. For whatever reason, the mayor was moving slowly. And when Raymond the Mole came on the scene, I figured the termination would have to be permanently shelved. But Mayor Washington had decided that he had to make his move well before the 1987 campaign had gotten underway, and not even the "widening scandal" was going to change his mind.

In February the mayor finally asked Barefield to sever Coffey. Barefield asked my advice on how to handle the termination. Ironically, in my career as an arts administrator, I had more experience firing people than he had in government. Earlier he had practically had to pry Norty Kay's fingers off the ledge, one by one, when Coffey had fought to keep his wordsmith on the payroll. My advice apparently wasn't worth much, because Coffey wouldn't accept the word from Barefield. He made a strong case to the mayor for retention. Failing at that, he negotiated himself one of the best severance packages I ever saw at City Hall.

Among the severance agreements was that we'd keep a lid on the fact that he had been asked to resign. Faithful to the deal, the mayor opened himself to the perception that his top people were losing faith in his administration in the depths of the Molescam scandal. Indeed, we did nothing to counter the claims being made in some quarters that Coffey had resigned in protest against the mayor's handling of "Molescam."

In my last conversation with Coffey, as we got our story straight, he urged that for the mayor's sake we should not stray from the agreed line. "It won't do Mayor Washington any good, right now, if people think I'm leaving under a cloud, of any kind." The logic escaped me: how would anyone think otherwise but that he was washing his hands of a mayor in trouble? "In the long run there are no secrets," he said. I agreed. It was one of the best lines I'd heard at City Hall.

I realized as I saw Coffey make his exit that ability and brains were no guarantee of secure employment in high places. There was no question he was one of the most able strategists in the mayor's camp. But the mayor was concerned that Coffey had his own agenda. He needed an IGA director who would never cause him to second-guess motivations. I think it was a mistake, a loss comparable to that of Jim Montgomery.

But the biggest casualty of that period was the dissolution of any relationships we'd begun to build with the media. In early 1985, when I'd inherited a list of friends and enemies, I learned to live in what astronauts might call a non-biotic atmosphere. I had learned to breathe through a mask, while I tried to help improve the atmosphere. I believed that 1986 would truly bring a "new spirit"—and after the special elections I envisioned we'd throw away the masks altogether.

By that metaphor we were suddenly submerged in methane. No reporter could be trusted. No bridges were going to be built. The mayor became bitter, his interactions with the press became forced and hypocritical—he didn't believe in the goodwill of any but the out-of-town reporters—and he made himself much less accessible to almost all journalists. Vernon Jarrett, the increasingly outspoken black columnist at the *Sun-Times* who emerged as a Washington partisan during January and February, was a rare exception.

No conversation with me conveyed the mayor's sentiments better than a remarkably candid conversation he had with Ann Marie Lipinski of the *Chicago Tribune* in November of that year. I had recommended her as a reporter of a different stripe—remember Harry Golden, I advocated—and promised that the piece she was doing on the mayor and the media might help break the ice; I felt we needed to unfreeze our relationship with the *Tribune* before the election. I had come from an industry where an angry director can throw a typewriter at an angry producer, and then both can work together to create a Broadway masterpiece. I had learned from the mayor, too, that nothing in politics is cast in stone. In a matter of months, with Raymond the Mole behind us, the "good Tribune" could be our most valued ally.

So he agreed to the Lipinski interview, which I taped. A partial transcript picks up in the middle of a conversation on so-called investigative journalists who, he said, "do no more investigating than picking up the phone when Eddie calls."

Mayor Washington: . . . Pam Zekman [of WBBM-TV] is the only shining light in the whole mess, you know, I mean, really the only one who deserves to be called an investigative reporter. The rest of them are a bunch of slugs. Vicious. Look, take Jim Ruddle and track him through the whole Datacom process, and you'll find a man who has to be suspect, the way he was talking he was actually telling people not to pay their traffic tickets. . . . So the commentary level on TV is just, I guess, of all the lot, the worst. Radio? It has a lot of redeeming features, mainly because of the talk shows. I'd say of the three media, radio is probably the best.

Q: You said a minute ago that you've more or less given up on dealing with some of the—I assume that you meant the major editors and station managers, you're not talking about people down in the press room. Was there a turning point for you, I mean, at what, when did you decide that, when did you just want to cut bait with them?

A: Oh, around the time of the handling of the big expose a year ago. I thought I was dealing with a bunch of beasts out there.

Q: We're talking about Raymond?

A: Yeah. It went crazy. We were always aware, I only instinctively and Miller intellectually aware of the fact that in a press conference, in a real serious issue, you don't get from the electronic media the kind of incisive questions you need to get the story out. It's a confrontational thing, that kind of thing. From the print you get more analytical questions. Mr. Miller said, let's do this: Let's have a two-stage press conference. Let's have all the media in but no cameras in the first phase, and let the story unfold. And then go back into the other room and bring the cameras in and you'll probably get a more calm and collected approach. That makes a lot of sense to me.

Before he could announce it I got a letter from NBC, talking about the First Amendment, which they probably haven't read. Crazy stuff, you know, they came in here just as belligerent with their sketch artists and all that sort of stuff and just acted like a bunch of animals, animals. It took an adroit person like myself, with whip and chair, just to control that operation. You weren't here, it was a horrible situation. [Then] we walked over and had a nice, decent, sensible press conference.

And so, for about two weeks Walt Jacobson and NBC and these people were just going bananas, they were going crazy. I said look, why am I catering to these slugs? I mean that's not what I'm about at all. I'm through with this. Are you getting all this on tape (laughs). Use some discretion. Professional discretion. (serious again) I said why am I going through all this, this is insane. I'm just not going to submit myself to that, my integrity requires more, I shouldn't treat myself that way. We're going to be strictly at arm's length. If you act like an ass I'm going to treat you like an ass, which means I'm going to leave you alone. That's about where I am.

Q: But from their view, to deprive them of the camera is to take my tape recorder and my notebook away. It's their tool.

A: That doesn't deprive them of anything. No, we said, we're going to walk over there [afterwards] and have a press conference, you can bring whatever you want.

Miller: Plus, they could bring their mikes, they could bring their tape recorders and their notepads, just like you could. They could bring them in here and be just like reporters, and not like TV entertainers. But if what happened in this room had been on tape . . .

HW: Yeah, and here's what came out of it. You had a cartoonist sitting here, you had a rather rainbow [seating configuration] around me, no one was closer than, say, six feet. I look on Channel 2 and there's Flannery standing up over me with his finger in my eye. If he'd been there

I'd have broken his neck. And this is what—to give the impression that I'm besieged and, you know, insane stuff. To me that's not reporting, to me that's not the First Amendment, to me that's not responsible or anything, that's just a pack of wolves acting silly. And demeaning the whole process of government and the relationship between government and the media. That's bad, that is really bad. And that's what kind of modified my attitude about going out of my way to cooperate with them. I'm not going to do that.

Q: So in practical ways how has that affected the way, when you say you're not going out of your way—

A: I just structure the whole thing more. I'd stop in the middle of the street and give an interview, I'd give a speech and come out and analyze the speech, you know, I'd—you call me at home I'd answer your questions. Your time is my time, my time is your time. I said that's silly, I'm not going to do that any more. I still have potpourri press conferences, I still have three, four a week, don't I? I still talk to media on the street about important issues. I've just sort of slowed down. Certain interviews I don't make, I don't keep. I'm not going to sit down with anything less than a responsible reporter and take my time and talk to them. (laughs)

Q: I was struck going through some of the clips by a quote of yours. You were addressing the TV Academy Luncheon back in October of '84 and someone had asked you, when will it all end, meaning the infighting between minority and majority sides. And you said, "When you roll up your sleeves, put on your boots, get in with the mayor and end it. You give me no help." Is it the media's job to assist the mayor and assist the administration in getting out his message or—

A: It's the media's job to do as I said before, to print the stories. When I say give me some help I mean tell what's happening. I don't need any help in the sense that they need to boost me. The press didn't get me here, if anything they tried to keep me out. It's not a question of asking for their help to sustain me in office, but asking for the assistance of the media in portraying factually what's happening so the people will know what's going on. After all, I was elected on a mandate, I had a platform, I had a program, my Washington Papers, the transition papers, this is my standard of operation. People have a right to know whether or not we're progressing under that. You read the papers in the City of Chicago, you'd never know it. They don't even talk about it. I daresay most people would be stunned if they saw a headline saying 90 percent of our transition goals had been achieved. I've said it a million times, you never see it, not even incidentally. But let Eddie Burke say something nasty about me or anybody else, and, Headline! You know, Eddie Vrdolyak gets a pimple on his neck—headline! It's insane. This is what cheapens government and you want to know why you can't improve government: people don't want to get into that mess. "Beirut on the Lake" is a figment of the imagination and to the extent it exists it came out of the media's mind. They foment it, they want it, they covet it, they love it and they're the only ones that gain from it.

Q: That line, of course, raises the issue of how the national media has treated you. The *New York Times*, the *Wall Street Journal*, the *Washington Post*—

A: What do they think of the press here? They probably think you all are crazy.

Q: Have they treated this administration differently than the local press has?

A: Very objective. They want to know what's going on, period.

Q: "Beirut on the Lake," though, came—it was a front page *Wall Street Journal* story.

A: I don't rate the *Wall Street Journal* as the national media, period.

Q: It is.

A: I don't consider it that. I don't rate it with the *Washington Post* or the *New York Times* or the *St. Louis Post Dispatch*. No, I don't rate it that way.

Q: How do you rate it?

A: I don't rate it. It's a businessmen's newspaper. Nothing wrong with that, but that's what it is.

Q: Appealing to a very influential sector of—

A: Yeah. Slavishly doing so. "Beirut on the Lake."

Miller: They won't even do editorial boards. They're not interested.

Q: To what extent do you let the media set an agenda for you. How much responding do you do to what the press is caring about or writing about?

A: Depends on what you're talking about. If the media, if Walt Jacobson gets on TV and says workers aren't working and you see pictures and all, we look at it. We don't assume because he's a jackass, he's always wrong. We go check it out. That goes across the board, that media can be a source of enlightenment for this administration or any other, if you're talking about the functioning and operation of government. So obviously we respond to it in that sense. Editorial policy? It depends, it depends, most of it I don't agree with. What other area could you be influenced by the media?

Q: Just in the various subjects they decide to explore.

A: Oh, yeah, well, we respond to them, check them out if they have any validity, you know. It would be unwise not to. There are certain investigations that go on that arouse your interest and I think you're unwise unless you at least check them out and refer them to the relevant agency for factual accuracy and for programmatic viability and all that kind of stuff. Yes, you can't function in government without doing that. There is an interfacing, there is a relationship and it's a healthy one and it's in that area that you're talking about that I think that perhaps the relationship is best—that the media does point directions by virtue of what they write and think. That's the good side of the media.

Q: The rare good side.

A: Hmm, no, I didn't say that either. That's the good side. The question is, is the bad side so bad that you begin to wonder whether or not the good side is worth it? I sometimes wonder. I sometimes really philosophically speculate on whether or not the Founding Fathers would tolerate the media today, or would they rewite the First Amendment. I think they probably would rewrite it. I don't think they had in mind this commercialization of the flow of information to people, that's not what they had in mind at all. I'm certain they'd put some brakes on it. If they had thought that the defense of people and the sanctity of one's integrity rested on the slender fiber of the libel laws, they'd probably go bananas.

Q: How do you think it would be rewritten?

A: I'm hard pressed to say, but I'm certain there would be some brakes put upon the freedom of the press to do as they damn please and get away with it. I can't imagine that they would have agreed with the Sullivan Decision which eventuates in a situation in which you can say anything you want about an elected official, damn near, and get away with it. I don't think they had that in mind.

Q: I'm sorry, what specifically are you referring to?

A: The standards of libel to which an aggrieved party must make in order to get recourse from someone who is libeling him. Which in effect says that the media can say anything you want about a public official and get away with it. And I don't think that was the point of it all. I think that's part of the reason why they're so arrogant and so ruthless in their handling of just simple ordinary everyday stories. I don't think the Founding Fathers would have tolerated "Inc." I think if they'd thought "Inc." would have come around, they would not have written the First Amendment at all. They probably would have prohibitioned gossip. I don't think it's healthy. It's dangerous, it debilitates, it minimizes and it doesn't do so in a healthy way. On the other hand, ordinary everyday factual stories in the media or investigative reporting on the standard of a Pam Zekman, is healthy business. And then if you're socked, you can't fight it, I mean, that's what it's all about.

Q: Did you feel this strongly about these issues when you first took office?

A: Um hmm, I was always on the side of the media, I supported shield laws and all those kinds of things. I can see the value of the sacrosanct —quote, "sacrosanct"—media. I don't think I would—I'd probably be picking cotton on somebody's plantation, sans the 13th, 14th, 15th Amendment, if there weren't a media. I understand that.

Q: But your appraisal of the Chicago press corps, was it like this when you took office?

A: Not quite because I had no everyday relationship to the editorial aspects. To working reporters, I probably knew them better because that's who you see, that's who you work with. I had a high opinion of the working journalists and still, as you can detect, comparatively, still do—comparatively. You don't really see them until you work with them every day. By the same token they don't see me, unless they do it every day.

Lipinski asked a question about the *Tribune* reporters who had written a long biographical article in the *Tribune*'s Sunday magazine. The mayor had called them "cotton heads" and suggested they "should have been bullwhipped."

A: Reporters are like any other institution, lawyers, doctors, accountants, they feel they have to protect each other. They don't impose standards on each other. They do not discipline each other. Sometimes I think they don't even talk to each other. They circle the wagons to fight off—quote—the enemy. And so you can make a legitimate criticism of reporters and all at once you're getting attacked from all sides, or you don't get an audience because they don't want to talk about it. They're "one of the clan." You know that and I know that.

As a lawyer I understand that very thoroughly. But as a lawyer I don't have that kind of influence on the people, that the media has, or the people in the media have, or the working journalists have. It's just that simple.

I think my observations are temperate, very temperate. I think my responses to the *Trib* thing were on a level of which I had a right to because it was a personal thing, it was personalized by the article. They weren't interested in government, they were interested in doing a hatchet job because I wouldn't sit down with that slug and waste my time telling him about my life. Period. And that was get-back, that was pretty clear. They almost threatened me. I wasn't certain that was what it was, [or] I'd have bent his nose out of shape. (laughs)

Q: Why don't you address the magazine piece on its merits, then? I mean, Cheryl [Devall] asked you on that show to list the mistakes which you claim are numerous—

A: Where'd you get the idea of Cheryl or anyone else that I have to respond to that pressure. If you print something you have the responsibility to make it accurate. The fact that I don't respond to it is irrelevant. I can't seem to get that across. "Well, if you'd talked to me it would've been right." No, no, no, you switch that around. And it's a waste of my time to even talk about it because they're not going to change. This poor little kid doesn't understand that. She's lost.

Q: Meaning Cheryl?

A: Yeah, totally lost. She can't understand that, you know, we just can't talk. You don't take it upon yourself to write about me, get it wrong, and then accuse me because it was wrong. I don't have any responsibility to straighten anything up. Nor do I have a responsibility to come in and help you circulate your newspaper by straightening up the story. I'd rather go to another newspaper and straighten it up. But I get that same thing. I get it from you in a temperate way. But that's the typical response of a reporter. "Well, if you'd talk to me the error wouldn't have been made." Or, "I'm in a rush, I couldn't do everything," or, "I called but I couldn't catch the people to get it straight." And that whole article is just replete with this—deliberate, I think— warps and twists of simple little facts that could have been checked. They put together conversations and situations that never happened, they had people in places that they never were, saying things they never dreamed of, all through that article.

Q: But you are, you do respond to it. You're responding to it on one level—

A: I'm not going to respond to it factually because I don't want to see the retractions in that newspaper.

Q: Where will we see them?

A: I might not even bother.

Q: Because I think you said at one point on a radio show that you were going to make a formal response to the—

A: No, I might not even bother.

Q: You decided not to—

A: I decided I'd rather talk about the mess you got, than help you clean it up. (a bitter laugh)

Q: Does the black press in Chicago treat you better?

A: Better than what?

Q: Than we do, than the white media.

A: You know they do. Period.

Q: Why do you think that is?

A: You Polish? (she: Um hmm) Would the Polish media jump on a Polish person and beat her across the head? Would they beat up on you?

Q: If I had it coming.

A: No, I doubt it. (laughs) If they did I'd jump on them. No, no, that's life.

Q: Are they doing their job? I mean, I certainly wouldn't want the *Daily Zgoda* not to write a story about me because I was Polish, if I had, if there was a story that needed to be written.

A: You're kidding. You gotta be kidding. Otherwise you're the purest person I've ever seen in my life. Nobody wants to be beaten up.

Q: Well, I wouldn't hold the *Daily Zgoda* to a standard that I would not hold the *Defender* or the *Trib* or WBBM—

A: You would expect the *Daily Zgoda* to state your case clearly, concisely, historically and pleasantly. You know you would. And that's only right that they should, why shouldn't they?

Q: Why should they? Why should they apply a different standard to you?

A: That's life. That's the way things are. The family looks out more for you than someone else will. Why shouldn't they. That's understood in life, and your family's opinion of you is accepted with that in mind, and understanding, that they are and you are entitled to that bias, that's just life. Whether it's Irish, Polish, Jewish, come on, that's what life's all about. (pause) Nobody but a journalist would be confused about that statement. (laughs)

The mayor had a hard year in 1986. Molescam wasn't the only crisis we had to deal with. And the prospects of smooth sailing with the press seemed more distant than ever.

But while we were dealing with Raymond the Mole, life went on.

The Bears won the Super Bowl the same January of 1986 that we were fighting with the press. The media, the mayor's office and maybe even the federal investigation seemed to agree on an armistice for the duration, and the mayor went to New Orleans with a sizeable Chicago delegation to enjoy the victory. Back in Chicago we tried to help keep the bonhomie alive, with a victory rally to celebrate the team's triumphant return. But the weather was bitter cold, the throngs of happy Bears fans slowed the motor caravan to a frozen crawl, and except for a few players the team never got off their bus.

That month, too, Chicago played host to South African leader Bishop Desmond Tutu. The groundwork had been laid in mid-1985, when we got a call from organizers of an American fundraising tour. Confirmations were difficult to make—Tutu's schedule was tight, and the organizers were resolute about planning his every hour in the United States around the potential for philanthropy. Every dollar raised went to Tutu's work in South Africa—the organizers were working pro bono—but we had to think hard before we could make the moral commitment to them, or assure them the Chicago trip would be worthwhile.

When we finally made the commitment, there was just one day when he could swing his itinerary our way. We grabbed it, organizing a tightly choreographed series of events that filled the time from daybreak to his afternoon departure—breakfast and lunch fundraisers, rallies, and some private time with Mayor Washington. He was in and out of town in about 20 hours, and his people raised the dollar goal they had targeted from Chicago.

For our purposes, the one-day visit, like the Bears game, was helpful in breaking up the McClain-Mole monody that the press had been performing. Every little bit helped, and we kept on the lookout for similar events to schedule. But beyond its PR utility, the visit provided another kind of respite for Mayor Washington. He said months later that the quiet courage and the soft eloquence of the diminutive Desmond Tutu had been an inspiration at a troubled time. "That little guy puts his life on the line," the mayor said. "He's right in the middle of the 'Third Reich', over there. And we think we've got troubles. It kind of puts Vrdolyak in perspective, doesn't it?"

All the special events in the world wouldn't move Raymond the Mole permanently off the front page. In the final analysis it was probably the Chicago readers who moved it off, when it became clear they were tired of reading the same story, day after day. Anyway, something more interesting was coming along: showdown at high noon, the 1986 special elections.

When it's all sorted out, Thursday, Nov. 7, 1985, will probably be identified as the beginning of the end for all three Eddies. That was the day that Judge Charles Norgle ruled on a new ward map for the city of Chicago. The legislative and PR successes aside, the climactic battles of "Council Wars" were won in the courts and ultimately in the precincts of one ward. The stage was set by a judge's decision.

15

The Special Elections

If Chicago's unique political identity could be traced in those meticulous cuts that vivisected the city into 50 wards, its political identity crisis was perfectly symbolized by the ward map dispute of the early 1980s. The precision of those lines was precisely the problem.

In 1981, following the 1980 census, Jane Byrne's City Council had approved a ward map which had been painstakingly designed to discriminate against blacks and Latinos. It was challenged in federal court by the minorities, who won their case against the city. A new map approved by Byrne's City Council and used in the 1983 elections was in turn struck down by a federal appellate court the following year, because it did not sufficiently correct the problem.

By that time "the city" was no longer the Byrne administration, and corporation counsel Jim Montgomery had become as invested in the fight as the plaintiffs' leading attorneys, Judson Miner, Raymond Romero and Bridget Arimond. However, the City Council majority bloc, the "29" under Vrdolyak's leadership, represented "the city" as defendants. They took the case to the U.S. Supreme Court which in June 1985, upheld the appellate court by declining to hear an appeal.

There would have been no "Council Wars," except for the illegal ward map, Mayor Washington frequently chided. "If the map were drawn right in 1981, I would have been elected with a reform City Council in 1983." He never stopped believing he could have his majority—now, not in 1987—by staying on the case. He, Montgomery, and Miner were sometimes, it seemed, the only optimists who insisted there could be not only a new map, but special elections in 1986, as well.

Or perhaps they weren't alone. Vrdolyak may have been the fourth "optimist." Although he swaggered and swore that there would be no court action in time to make a difference on special elections, he did take precautions. In keeping with the sometimes laughable psychopathology of the circumstances, when the defendants saw which way the case was going they asked their lawyers to switch to the side of the plaintiffs (a move the court disallowed). They saw how the wind was blowing, and wanted to be able to tell any credulous Latino voters they could find, in the elections which were likely to come, that they had not been dedicated all along to their disenfranchisement.

Now, on this sunny Thursday in November, under pressure from the courts, a compromise had been achieved. Both parties agreed to boundaries which, if the judge concurred, would literally change the shape of Chicago, redistricting seven wards. We called a press conference to make the announcement, getting out ahead of the defendants' attorney William Harte who, consistent with their plea-switching ploy, was calling the new map "my plan."

The stage was finally set when Judge Norgle accepted the compromise and ruled that remedies would not be postponed until the 1987 elections. Even though less than a year remained in the term, there would be special elections in all seven wards, concurrent with the regular March 1986 primaries.

Ironically, Harold Washington had already played a role in the ward remap decision a few years earlier when, as a U.S. congressman on the Judiciary Committee, he authored an amendment in the historic Voting Rights Act of 1965.

The significant change that he inserted provided that where previously a plaintiff in a voting rights case had to prove *intent*, now it was only necessary to prove *effect*. As applied to Chicago's ward remap case, the burden wasn't on Judd Miner and Ray Romero to prove that Byrne's minions had deliberately sought to deprive minorities of their representation; all that was necessary was to show that their ward map had that effect. Mayor Washington was proud of that legislative accomplishment, and whenever the subject was appropriate he would drop his own name in that connection.

The decision on special elections was announced in early January 1986, while Raymond the Mole stalked the headlines. But if its historic significance was muted by other events, it was clearly recognized by the pols on both sides of "Council Wars."

For Harold Washington, it would mean the difference between taking charge, or coming out a loser. For the Eddies, it would mean the difference between continued success in their efforts to stymie the mayor, or losing control of City Council. The Eddie who had the most to lose was not Vrdolyak or Burke, but Parks Superintendent Edmund Kelly.

Kelly was something of a living artifact of the old Machine. But if Daley could sometimes be made to symbolize the bright side of an authoritarian machine, Kelly represented the dark side.

In the late '60s Daley had assigned Kelly to rebuild the 47th Ward machinery, and rewarded his able lieutenant by giving him the parks job in 1972. Kelly built a patronage army that consistently delivered for the Machine—the "Fighting 47th" was the only ward on the North Side to oppose the tide for Byrne and stick with Bilandic.

Though it was not a marriage made in heaven—Kelly talked about running for mayor, and Byrne talked about reforming the park district—after Bilandic's defeat he did not long delay in making his accommodations with the new mayor.

He had weathered a career of complaints against his management of the parks. He had become practically an entire career field for the activities of the Better Government Association, who did a series of studies and exposes of the parks, over the years.

In 1977 the BGA and investigative reporter Pam Zekman, then with the *Sun-Times*, revealed that rock music promoters represented by a Kelly-connected attorney had a lock on permits for concerts at Soldier Field.

BGA also found what they considered evidence of a massive skim of tickets for those concerts, citing one "Pink Floyd" concert with an estimated 80,000 in attendance, where the Park District reported only 64,000 tickets had been sold. According to BGA, one of those participating said of the scheme, "its purpose was to create a pool of unreported cash...to be divided later between rock promoters and Chicago Park District officials." The concert promoter and two associates were later convicted.

In 1979, the year Jane Byrne brought her reform candidacy before the voters, BGA reported that the "Fighting 47th" was enjoying the spoils of victory: a direct precinct-by-precinct correlation between park district jobs and vote-getting performance of precinct captains. WBBM-TV, working with BGA, showed that "at least 311 Park District job holders live in the 47th Ward and earn a total of $4.7 million a year in salaries"—four and a half times the number than if the park jobs were evenly distributed across the 50 wards of Chicago.

A *Sun-Times*/BGA series showed how Chicago parks, particularly in minority neighborhoods, had been allowed to deteriorate, contrasted them with the beauty of the parks in the 47th Ward, and further noted that the 47th had more park district employees than all the city's predominately black wards combined.

Those employees had plenty of free time as an election approached, BGA reported. Working undercover they clocked four 47th Ward precinct captains, their combined earnings totalling over $100,000 in park district salaries, who at election time worked an average of less than 20 percent of their day on the job.

Kelly's army was proud to serve, and grateful to their captain, BGA said: in the period studied, park employees contributed over $22,000 to his war chest, and spent another $16,000 on advertisements in his testimonial ad book.

In 1986 Kelly represented what Harold Washington enjoyed calling "the last bastion of patronage." Actually he had singled out Kelly even before he became mayor, in fact made his removal a campaign issue. The Democratic committeeman had reciprocated by leading his precinct workers out of the fold, delivering the "Fighting 47th" to the Republicans in the general election.

His three-year contract as park district superintendent had expired in February 1985, but the other two Eddies had provided for him, by blocking Mayor Washington's appointments to boards and commissions. Incumbents remained sitting until replaced, which meant that Byrne's, Bilandic's and Daley's lame-duck appointees were still in charge of many key agencies.

In January of that year, Sydney R. Marovitz, whose term on the parks board had expired in 1983, nominated Kelly for a new contract; Iola McGowan, whose term had expired in 1981, seconded. Jack McHugh (expired 1984) and William Bartholomay (due to expire that year) concurred. They voted 4–0 (the fifth board member had died six months earlier) to give Kelly an unprecedented four-year contract.

In the fall of 1984 Eddie Burke had publicly pledged that the mayor would never be allowed to replace Kelly in the job. That was a strategic and tactical error for the Eddies: their anti-appointments strategy had now become a personal defense of Ed Kelly, the indefensible.

Throughout the spring of 1985, a growing clamor was raised along the lakefront. It went beyond the parks issue straight to the heart of the matter: the stalled appointments were "hostages," they cried, and whatever you thought of Harold Washington, you had to let him do his job. Indefatigable lakefront activists were drawn into the battle. As the Eddies learned, you don't do "Friends of the Parks" director Erma Tranter like you do Clarence McClain.

So we had the "goo-goos"—supporters of good government—unequivocally with us on this one; although they might not take sides on "Council Wars," they agreed with us on the need for special elections.

We had Latinos aligned in growing numbers. And we had the courts. The remap order provided for "supermajorities" approaching two-thirds for Latinos in four wards; and for blacks in two. The seventh ward would be redesigned only slightly and the black–white split would remain about 50–50.

Washington didn't see much hope for change in that 50–50 ward, the 18th, where Vrdolyak ally Robert Kellam still held the edge.

In the 31st Ward, incumbent Miguel Santiago, the city's only Hispanic alderman, had been installed as an acknowledged puppet of the Vrdolyak organization. In the steadily maturing political climate of his ward, now buttressed by a somewhat stronger majority of Latinos, he was clearly vulnerable.

The Puerto Rican alderman had been an object of ridicule from the moment he was introduced. A few days after taking office in 1983 he assembled the press to level criminal charges against a reform activist. He had been threatened with bodily harm, namely having his feet set ablaze. Under patient questioning the truth became clear: he had been warned that the community would "hold his feet to the fire," as they evaluated his behavior.

With all Santiago's weaknesses, however, Mayor Washington didn't hold high expectations for any of the other candidates in the 31st, and didn't spend much of his time there. He had some concern that he'd lose more points than he'd gain by actively campaigning against an incumbent Latino alderman. "Bad as he is," he said of Santiago, "he's probably got it locked."

That left five wards that would make the difference. Any four of them would change the mathematics of "Council Wars"—29–21 was stalemate, 25–25 was victory, since the mayor, in his role as City Council president, could vote to break a tie.

But he was going for all five. "I don't want to break those ties," he said with a grin. "You can hide behind 26 votes. With 25 you're up there buck naked." Every tax measure, every controversial vote, would be not only the action of the new City Council majority, or even the policy of the Washington administration, but the personal stroke of the tie-breaking mayor.

In the 22nd, staunch Washington ally Jesus Garcia was going to be a clear winner. In the 15th and 37th, both with solid black majorities, it was plain that whoever the new aldermen were (eight were running in the 15th), they would vote with Washington.

The 25th was iffy. Mexican-American Juan Soliz was the strongest candidate. As a state representative he had become cozy with the Vrdolyak camp: he had started his career with us, but defected after he claimed Washington reneged on a deal to pay his campaign expenses. The mayor's version was that he had offered to help, but not to cover everything. He considered Soliz was looking for a public excuse to side with Vrdolyak. "Soliz has been bought, period," he said. Worse, Soliz would be tough to beat. Better not count on that.

Everything might very likely come down to the 26th Ward.

In the 26th, Luis Gutierrez was a Washington ally who was going up against a young Vrdolyak ally, lawyer Manuel Torres. A street-crossing guard named Blasinski complicated the election as a write-in candidate.

Gutierrez was a ball of fire, feisty, choleric. Torres had a sullen quality that advertised a distaste for the give-and-take of a campaign. It was as if he'd been promised he wouldn't have to spend much time debating, or meeting with the press and public. Or perhaps he had been advised that he would do well to display maturity and an almost swaggering self-confidence, against the boyish enthusiasm of Gutierrez. "Don't play Torres cheap," the mayor warned. He was concerned that 26th Ward voters, even those who preferred Gutierrez over Torres, might prefer Eddie over Harold.

The February elections produced only one surprise, but that one was a doozy. As we might have predicted—Soliz and Kellam and Santiago won their races for Vrdolyak, and our allies took the 22nd and 37th. The run-off in the 15th would produce a Washington winner either way. The pending City Council count was 25–24, in favor of Vrdolyak. But what about the 26th Ward?

When the dust had settled, the vote count gave our Luis Gutierrez a razor-thin but still determinative majority. He had beaten Torres by only 20 votes out of more than 10,000 cast. Even though the gadfly Blasinski got 11 write-ins, Gutierrez still held a bare absolute majority.

And then the Board of Election commissioners claimed to have found another 11 write-in votes, in the back of a box in a warehouse. Counting those votes, no candidate had received a clear majority and a run-off election would be required. It was set for April 29.

It was the April 29 run-off election in the 26th Ward that decided the fate of the mayor's first term, and perhaps the 1987 election. As Rupert Murdoch's *Sun-Times* headline aptly blazoned, it was indeed "High Noon" for Harold and Eddie.

☐ *How to Steal an Election* ▭

Mayor Washington considered that he was waging two campaigns simultaneously that spring. He not only had to help win the 26th Ward for Gutierrez, he also had to do battle with the Board of Election Commissioners, in preparation for the 1987 mayoral reelection campaign.

"We can win this election," he said, "but they can steal it. And if we let them get away with it, they can steal it again in 1987." It was a war he wanted to fight on the beaches of the 26th Ward, before he was forced to fight it on the steps of City Hall a year later.

So I learned how to steal an election. By watching and listening, through the special elections and through the months of litigation and the mayor's public awareness campaign, I discovered how tenuous our right to vote can be, when there's a Machine at work.

Chicago's aldermanic elections are nonpartisan. Not that a candidate isn't identified with a political party (almost always Democrat), but that the entire field of candidates meet in one election. The one who tops 50 percent wins, and if there is no winner the first and second place finishers compete in a run-off.

Just about every imaginable aspect of an election is covered by a statute or case precedent, pretested in the courts, and tested again in the alleys, the polling places, the Board of Election Commissioners at City Hall, back in the courts, and even in transit among these battlefields of the ballot.

And in addition to the litigious approach, there's also a larcenous one, equally notorious in Chicago, that works beyond the reach of the law to guarantee elections.

The phenomenon isn't unique to Chicago, of course, nor is it a recent invention. In ancient Rome, we're told, a "wealthy candidate would quietly arrange for his election...with a band of political 'go-betweens.' These professional gentlemen would proceed to mark out the Roman tribes into smaller and more wieldy sections, arrange voters into clubs and fraternities, compound with each section for its votes, marshall the faithful henchmen to the [polling place], and duly pay over the stipulated honorarium upon delivery of the election."

Chicago's 50 wards are subdivided into roughly 60 precincts each, with about 500 registered voters per precinct. In a well-managed precinct like the ones on which Daley's Machine depended—and some are still just as well maintained as they ever were—precinct workers can reasonably be expected to have logged the name and address and perhaps the whiskey preference of every voter in the precinct.

In each precinct, a precinct captain (usually a city employee with plenty of unofficial time off) directs the operation of assistant captains, who typically will have personal responsibility for anywhere from 50 to 100 voters and their families. That's a door-to-door responsibility that continues all year round. A good assistant captain will care for his or her bailiwick, anticipate the general needs and be solicitous of individual problems.

This is as good a point as any to stop and offer one cheer for the old Machine.

City services in theory are allocated according to city management principles; needs are prioritized and public resources are evenly distributed. In theory the process is independent of clout. Everywhere except in the real world.

When you, the constituent, need a sidewalk repaired; and when there's an assistant precinct captain to pass the word along; and when the committeeman who gets the word is either himself the alderman, or pulling the alderman's strings, there's a pretty direct connection from citizen to City Hall. And though the pool of city services is not bottomless—it's a finite, zero-sum game, and if you get more than your share, someone somewhere is getting less than theirs— there are things you can do to improve your chances of getting the sidewalk fixed.

For one thing, you can participate in rallies and fundraisers for Machine candidates. You can placard your house and your place of business with campaign posters and literature. You can contribute handsomely, particularly if you're working at City Hall, or with Police or Fire, or the Park District, or the public schools, or any of the eight municipal taxing bodies. You can be active in circulating the petitions that are required for candidates to be listed on the ballot. You can enthusiastically play your part on election day, not only by voting right but also by serving as an election judge.

An argument can be made that the Machine provides not only an efficient system for the delivery of services but also the most immediate practical application of democracy yet developed by mind of man. After all, doesn't it merely provide free-market incentives to the otherwise ephemeral principles of responsible citizen participation in government?

The major problem, of course, is that the system tends to have a coercive, even extortionate, influence. By design, it works only for those who support the Machine candidate, which has the not too subtle effect of encouraging you to "vote right."

Worse, the system contains within it both the incentive and the means of stealing an election. And when a powerful Machine can influence the Board of Election Commissioners, the state legislature and even the courts, as well as the party apparatus, the Machine can achieve that ultimate of power, the kind that can't be overthrown from within.

The operation begins even before there are technically any candidates, while signatures are being collected on petitions. A specified number of valid signatures, duly collected and certified, are required to put your candidate on the ballot. He or she must collect a great number of extra signatures, because of the certainty that some will fail to hold up under examination. Candidates have been unlawfully put on the ballot who failed to collect enough valid signatures, because the petitions were not challenged or because of unfair election board rulings. And elections have been decided before they've begun, by candidates who successfully challenge enough of their opponents' petition signatures.

Petitions are invalid if they are photocopied, or unsigned by the circulator or not notarized, if the circulators or the signatories are nonregistered or nonresidents, if the addresses are incomplete, if there are duplicate signatures, or if the signatures have been "roundtabled"—falsified in a group "autograph session" by forgers who are seeking to provide some variety by passing petitions around a table. There are other technical requirements that a grass-roots opposition movement might overlook, and which a well-financed Machine can take the trouble to discover and point out. And once you've collected your opposition signatures, it's not inconceivable that the Board of Elections can lose or alter the sheets. Knocking candidates off the ballot is the easiest way to influence the results of an election before it begins.

As election day nears, the most important responsibility of the assistant precinct captain is to go door to door, politely inquiring of neighbors how they intend to vote. If for the Machine candidate, the voter is noted as a plus; if for the opposition, it's a minus. Where there's uncertainty, it's a zero. The pluses, minuses and zeroes become important to each precinct's election strategy. Basically, the truly legitimate and efficient way to win the election is to be certain that all plus voters make it to the polls on election day. Discouraging the turnout of minus voters works just as well.

By watching the mayor, and listening to election law pros like assistant corporation counsel Rich Means who advised Mayor Washington, or Arlene Rubin of Project LEAP (Legal Elections in All Precincts), I learned that there are three major areas of concentration for a Machine trying to steal an election: preventing registration of opposition voters; influencing votes on election day; and falsifying the results of an election.

Registration chicanery has been somewhat frustrated since its heyday, when, except for a single day, a month before the election, new voters had to go downtown to sign up, and the process was made as cumbersome as possible. Election reformers first persuaded election officials to deputize local public librarians as registrars; and then, in 1982, succeeded in creating "deputy registrars" and provided for registration throughout the community, as well as at the Board of Election Commissioners. Still, reducing opposition registration is the best way to guarantee that the incumbent stays in power.

The law intends that Illinois voters are registered in perpetuity, according to their home address. So long as they don't move or change their name, and so long as they vote once every four years, they shouldn't have to re-register.

However, there's no practical guarantee that a suspected opposition voter will stay registered. The same law provides a means of striking absent or phony voters from the rolls. Designed to remove those who once voted from the graveyard, or from an address that turns out to be a vacant lot, the law permits election judges to challenge a registration. One election judge from each party will canvass each precinct, verifying that voters live at the addresses provided on the list.

To help steal an election, however, very often both canvassers will represent the Machine, regardless of what they said when they were assigned; and very often the person removed from the rolls is a bona fide voter—for the opposition. The fact may be apparent from campaign literature in the window, or may be assumed based on race or ethnicity or neighborhood.

After a challenge from the election board commissioners, the voter is supposed to get a pink slip under the door, so she has notice and time to straighten out the problem. But that sometimes gets "lost." A mail notification is supposed to be sent from the Board of Election Commissioners, but you know how the mails are these days. A person may not find out she's been removed until she shows up at the polling place on election day—when it may be too much trouble to get things straightened out.

Periodic moves to legislate re-registration of *all* voters are sometimes presented as a good-government move; but they may have ulterior motives. When you clear the rolls and start from scratch, the Machine usually has more resources than the opposition can muster to motivate voters to re-register.

After registration maneuvers, and before election day, the Machine can busy itself manipulating absentee voting. To avoid the rush and crush of election day, and vote by mail, all a voter has to do is claim intent to be out of Cook County on election day. If he should later change his mind, the absentee ballot is still valid of course, and he won't be charged with perjury. The Machine can improve turnout among its supporters by facilitating the process. The 16,000 potential votes in nursing homes can be happy hunting grounds for Machine absentee voting—the staff will often be glad to help, the more so since no nursing home is in total compliance with Chicago's deliberately arcane building code, administered by Machine inspectors. As a public service, of course, a precinct captain will assist the absentee voter in filling out his ballot.

When designing the ballot, the Board of Election Commissioners can insure that the Machine candidate gets the favored position on the ballot. This can be achieved in a number of ways, including an alteration in the size of type or the layout of the ballot itself. A Machine candidate who would otherwise appear on the bottom of the name list can be pushed up to the top of the second column, if the type size is enlarged so that fewer lines will fit per column.

The Machine can further prepare for election day by insuring that polling place judges are all Machine hacks, or that those who aren't don't know what they're doing and must defer to the Machine hacks.

The five election judges in each precinct are supposed to be civic-minded neighbors of specific party affiliation, who receive a small stipend in return for helping out at the polls. They are confirmed and formally appointed by the Circuit Court, from lists provided by the two leading political parties; their nominations usually originate from the party precinct captains. They have specific duties, requiring some training, although the law requires that only one per party per precinct needs to be trained and certified.

It's pretty hard to find Republicans in some Chicago precincts, and hard to be sure that the "Republicans" who show up are really Republicans. Then, if the Board of Elections is Machine-dominated, the training can be spotty, or the judges' manuals unreadable. They may even accidentally omit an entire section, as happened in 1987 when critical information concerning the color of the different party ballots and their location in the supply box was dropped from the manual, to the advantage of Vrdolyak, then running on a third-party ticket.

Untrained and inexperienced election judges are likely to be susceptible to advice or intimidation, especially since the Machine's precinct captain will be on hand as a poll-watcher, with all the answers. As it is, the election judges are all too likely to defer to the precinct captain anyway, who not only has loads of political experience but who is also, lest we forget, one of your most politically-connected neighbors. Why bother looking up the rules in a cumbersome manual?

There are supposed to be three Democratic and two Republican election judges in each precinct with an even number; the reverse, two and three, in each precinct numbered odd. As already noted, however, in Chicago's one-party system they might all be Democrats under the skin. And even if they're really Republicans, chances are dim that they'll be particularly interested in protecting the rights of insurgent Democrats in the Democratic primary. Perhaps needless to add, even (or especially) when there's an opposition movement within the Democratic party, the Democrat judges are Machine or "Regular" Democrats.

A favorite Machine tactic is for judges to sign up, receive training, and then on election morning call in sick. The Machine will insure that "volunteers" are available to pitch in. When voters are lining up at 6:00 a.m., and the original judges aren't available, the volunteers will just have to do.

The final action the Machine can take, just before the polls open, is to move the polling place from its customary location in the neighborhood. Voters on their way to work will show up at the usual location, then decide it's too cold or too wet to walk to the new site. (Legitimate questions have been raised about why Chicago's primaries, the elections where all the important decisions are made, have been set for February, the coldest, wettest month of the year.) This is a particularly effective way to screen out factory workers and others who have to vote as soon as the polls open at six, in order to be at work by seven.

And then the election judges, especially when they're filling in for others who have called in sick, can be slow about getting the polls open. The judges can be late, or keys to the building can be lost, or unfamiliarity with how to set up the voting machinery can slow things down. Thousands of votes can be lost because voters can't wait for the judges to get their act together. Lucky for democracy that there are so many absentee ballots available to be counted.

Sometimes, particularly in problematic precincts, the Board of Elections might send over an inadequate supply of ballots and other materials. Naturally this will cause still more delays—perhaps at lunch hour or in the afternoon rush.

A number of poll-watchers or challengers may be present, from each party represented on the ballot, and from civic organizations, to deter irregularities. But the polling places can be selected and set up to make poll watching very uncomfortable, and all but the most committed can be daunted by the fact that the only place they can perch to effectively observe is on a hot radiator, or in a cramped space. Rich Means remembers a polling place set up in a Park District field house, where the smallest, darkest, coldest room was selected out of a number available.

The poll-watchers are there to satisfy themselves that the election is not being stolen. They are entitled to make sure that each judge does a good job, and no more than a good job:

—That the judge who is instructing voters on how to punch their ballot, is not misinforming ("You a Democrat? Just punch 3 and you're done") or instructing the voter on a choice of candidate;

—that the judge who is checking the name and address of each voter, does so in a loud and clear voice, so the poll-watcher can check off the name or identify someone trying to vote twice; and that the judge doesn't misdirect a voter by telling her she's come to the wrong polling place;

—that the judge validating the voter's signature against the signature in the precinct binder isn't playing games—the poll-watchers are entitled to doublecheck to their own satisfaction;

—that the judge who issues the ballots in a primary election gives the right color (i.e., right party) ballot, and that the ballot is properly initialled—otherwise it will not be counted; and that the voter is directed to the proper party voting machine; if a Republican ballot is voted in a Democrat machine the vote won't tally; if a non-Machine Democrat is misdirected to a Republican machine, he'll fail to find his candidates listed, will often assume that he's the one at fault, and will leave without mentioning the problem and without voting for the opposition;

—and that after the voter emerges from the voting booth, the judge who's there to deposit the punched ballot in the ballot box does not mutilate or pocket the vote.

Votes are cast in Chicago, as they are in about 40 percent of elections across America, by punching a machine-readable ballot, in a mechanical (non-computer) voting machine that aligns the card in a frame. The voter selects the candidate's name or referendum issue from one or more pages of a fixed name list and pushes a metal pin through the corresponding hole in the frame. Generally a number of elections take place on the same day, all performed with the same voting card. The voter flips through different pages on the name list to make selections for each race, each time punching the indicated number in the frame. The underlying card stays put until the balloting is complete, at which time it's returned to a carrying envelope and deposited in a locked box.

It is possible that a suspected non-Machine voter could be given a prepunched ballot. It is also possible that she is directed to a voting booth where the frame has been altered so that the alignment changes—she's punching 9 according to the frame, but 10 on the card.

But the most frequent violation, Means says, is illegal assistance. The election judges make the determination as to who is eligible for help in voting. While the law specifies that two judges, one from each party, may assist, any person of the voter's choice, even the precinct captain, may render the assistance. They may help an illiterate or non-English speaking voter, or one who is physically disabled, to vote the party line. The mere presence of a political partisan in the voting booth may be sufficient to determine the voter's selections. A good poll-watcher will insist that the voter who forgot his glasses should go home and get them, and not be assisted in punching his ballot. At the very least the poll-watcher is entitled to an affidavit for each act of assistance, and insistence on that affidavit can make a dent in the practice.

As should be evident, a good opposition poll-watcher is bound to get on a Machine judge's nerves. Each polling place is assigned a police officer to keep order. To facilitate their caretaking responsibilities, the election judges have the legal right to request the policeman to arrest anyone they decide is causing a problem at the polls. All involved are explicitly immunized against prosecution for false arrest. It's a lot better today than it was in the early Daley days, before the civil service reforms of police commissioner O.W. Wilson. Then each ward had its own police district, and the command structure was inevitably responsive to the Machine organization in that ward. But it's still likely that the police officer on duty is a Regular Democrat, at best hearing and seeing no evil.

During the day, Machine partisans can help create an unhospitable environment for opposition voters, to keep their turnout low. Gang members have been used for that purpose. The memory of coercive past practices can be another reason for lessened voter turnout.

The polls close at 7:00 p.m., but the Machine is still at work. Though poll-watchers have a right to remain for the vote count, the judges may illegally request their removal, which request the police feel obliged to enforce.

Votes are counted by feeding the cards through a counting machine. If more than one candidate has been punched for any office, the ballot is invalid for that office. If any ballot has been mangled so that it won't feed into the machine, that "spoiled" ballot must be remade by the judges. When feeding the cards through, a judge might invalidate a vote by sneaking a punch onto the card; or may remake a ballot to his own liking; or may attempt a somewhat more sophisticated ruse by feeding four or five "properly" marked ballots through repeatedly, while discarding other ballots to keep the vote total correct.

Another practice—Rich Means told me that this one produced the most vote-fraud convictions—is the casting of ballots for voters who never show up at the polls. Back when the bell-ringing lever-operated machines were used, a police witness told Means, the action after the polls closed in one precinct sounded like a pinball parlor. Today it's quieter but just as effective.

The process then requires for the counted ballots to be sealed.

Later a percentage of them will be hand-counted and the results compared to the computer count, which should be statistically similar. The machine produces a printout of the tally, and copies are made available to each party's poll-watchers, who generally telephone the results to their political organizations.

The machine also produces a coded cassette tape. The tape, and the sealed ballots, are forwarded immediately to the ward's receiving station. The transporting of ballots is supposed to be public and supervised. At the receiving station the cassette is placed in a telecommunications device which sends the results directly to the computer at the Board of Elections at City Hall. Broadcast reporters monitor the incoming totals, precinct by precinct, and keep Chicagoans up to date on the results.

A good political field operation can be ahead of the Board of Election Commissioners, as poll-watchers telephone results directly from the polling place to their party headquarters. As a practical matter, a sampling of key precincts can give a clear indication of how things are going. On primary election night in February 1987, when we were watching the coverage from the mayor's apartment, he was frustrated because our number crunchers couldn't tell him how we were doing. We didn't have enough poll watchers who were allowed to stay in the polling places until the final count to provide accurate numbers. He needed good numbers before he could leave to greet his supporters and claim victory over Jane Byrne.

Despite repeated calls, our people couldn't help; the media were all dependent on the Board of Elections, which was slow; but Vrdolyak, who wasn't running in the primary, was on the TV screen announcing that his people were calling it Washington over Byrne. The mayor visibly relaxed, mentioning that Eddie was the only one likely to have reliable numbers at that point. We were able to focus on preparing his acceptance speech and when official numbers came through, confirming Vrdolyak's tally, we left for the rally.

Since the 1970s, Chicago's Project LEAP, the League of Women Voters and other civic groups have done much to eliminate the institutionalized vote fraud that made Daley's Chicago famous around the world. In the old days, as LEAP's Arlene Rubin has written (the ironic "sic" is her own), "Patronage was the driving force: to keep his [sic] work job, the precinct captain had to meet a vote quota. The result? Office holders who were not elected. Their jobs were stolen for them."

They were effective in eliminating the more blatant offenses, but in its place was administrative fraud at the Board of Elections. LEAP's Arlene Rubin catalogued a list of infractions:

"The BOE had to be enjoined to stop accepting trays of absentee ballots from precinct captains. . . . Open Meetings Act violations; undistributed student absentee ballots; poll-watchers barred from receiving stations or the central computer area; absentee ballots from able-bodied citizens (except for their twisted arms) not out of the city on election day; favoritism in poll sheet [final count] availability [to opposition poll-watchers]; write-in ballots mysteriously found in a warehouse; arbitrary and last-minute polling place changes; slipshod counting and security for last-minute absentee ballots; misdirected, late, or erroneous supply delivery. . . ."

The write-in ballots mysteriously discovered were those 26th Ward ballots that forced a run-off. Even after the "final" tally, I was learning, the Machine can still get away with larceny.

So now it had all come down to the 26th Ward. The mayor and Eddie Vrdolyak eyeball to eyeball. For good measure, Burke was in there too, and the Eddies were backed up by Jane Byrne, Rich Daley, Ed Kelly, Tom Hynes. All our eggs were in that one basket, right next to Eddie's.

They had brought all their best precinct captains in, all their most experienced campaign workers from all over the city. We had our own troops, including veterans like Uptown publisher/activist Slim Coleman and lawyers like Tom Johnson. It was not only the most costly aldermanic election Chicago had ever seen, it was also probably the most intensively "worked." Had it been a World War I battlefield, the 26th Ward would have resembled the pockmarked surface of the moon.

With all that in place, it was a source of considerable pride that Gutierrez won the run-off with 53 percent of the vote. Yet the mayor was careful not to gloat. Election night we turned the lobby of 5300 into a makeshift television studio and gave live interviews to all three 10:00 news teams. Mayor Washington was careful not to brag or bluster about the win: he was particularly sensitive to tribal irascibilities—black, Irish, Croatian, whatever—and he also refused to accept the premise of many questions that assumed "his" aldermen were now in charge. "I don't own any aldermen," he repeated. "I am not a boss."

And yet, he wasted no time in using his 25–25 edge to reorganize City Council. He refused to make sweeping moves, which caused criticism among several of the old "21" who wanted across-the-board retribution, with *every* former Vrdolyak ally punished and the two Eddies completely eliminated from all committees. He made a point of accommodating Vrdolyak loyalists who were prepared to switch loyalties. He wanted cooperation, not control, and ultimately, if possible, consensus approaching unanimity.

He would not, for example, countenance removing Eddie Burke as chairman of the powerful Finance Committee. Instead, the new majority created a Budget Committee, gave it most of the Finance Committee's powers, and installed Washington floor leader Tim Evans at its head. Burke retained his limo, and his bodyguard.

And when it came time to redress grievances at the Park District, rather than retire Ed Kelly as general superintendent, the Washington team created the new position of executive director, with Washington's former consumer affairs commissioner Jesse Madison in the job. The superintendent reported to the director.

In general, there was approbation for the new City Council's action on appointments, which began to flow out of the various committees and onto the floor for confirmation. But there was a curious reaction to Kelly's change of status.

The mayor was surprised to see, over the next few weeks, as the consequences of his electoral victory played out, that a tone of resentment crept into the media. Ed Kelly had been the parks baron for a generation, and if parks in some neighborhoods had suffered, parks in others had blossomed for years. Thousands of kids had earned their first jobs—and had their first experience of the Machine—working summers in the parks under the patronage of Ed Kelly.

Even columnists who were obliged to acknowledge he was corrupt "in a technical sense" would apparently discover a sentimental side of the issue as he was threatened with political extinction. Mayor Washington was referring to *Sun-Times* commentator Tom Fitzpatrick when he told the media, "One newspaper columnist actually became Kelly's flack during that campaign.

"It's as if we touched a nerve," he said. "It's as if somehow Ed Kelly—imagine!—represented the true spirit of Chicago; and anyone who challenged his right to blunder his way through his private preserve, the Park District, was playing dirty pool."

"I was frankly surprised by the columnists and commentators," he told reporters at the Academy of TV Arts and Sciences luncheon, "who took Kelly's part, as though some revered Chicago institution were being lost forever."

He didn't have much time to spend looking over his shoulder. The appointments and the City Council reorganization were high priorities, but the biggest pending legislation was the passage of the 1986 budget. We were halfway through the year, and the budget—which had been passed as required by statute prior to the first of the year, but ruled illegal—had still not been adopted. The budget deliberations for 1987, in fact, were about to begin.

There was still an $80 million gap in the 1986 budget, which had to be made up through some combination of taxes, fees, and spending cuts. The new 25–25 City Council advantage wasn't worth a nickel if it wasn't worth that $80 million. Yet we had a devil of a time going over the top.

Ald. Burton Natarus [42nd], a white lakefront alderman with a strong admixture of black CHA residents among his constituents, was the designated hitter for ward committeeman George Dunne, who was also the chairman of the Cook County Democratic Party.

Mayor Washington told me he felt a kind of kinship with George Dunne; he felt they two represented the best of the Chicago political Machine. The Machine rewarded loyalty as well as ability, he said, and in a perverse way it saved its biggest rewards for those who combined those attributes with an independent streak. "The one thing you won't learn from the Machine is courage," he said. "You have to develop that somewhere else." He believed that Dunne, like he himself, had stood the test and faced up to the challenges that develop all those qualities.

He also admired Dunne's style. As committeeman, and as Cook County Board president since 1969, Dunne exercised complete control over his staff and supporters. "My operation's a sieve," Mayor Washington complained. "With George, you don't say a word unless he points you out and tells you to. He gets a pass [from the media]. Me they give holy hell." It was true that Dunne enjoyed simultaneously both a reputation for personal accessibility and for professional discretion. No leaks from his shop.

Dunne had bucked the tide in his support of minorities within the Democratic party. He had backed black candidates for the legislature and for statewide office well before it was politically expedient to do so, recognizing that the future of the party lay in the acceptance of blacks as just the latest "ethnic" group in a party fabric that was a quiltwork of other ethnics.

When Mayor Daley died he vacated not one but two seats of power. While the mayoral succession devolved upon Bilandic, Dunne was elected to Daley's other position, chairman of the Cook County Democratic Party. But when Vrdolyak mounted his successful campaign to unseat him in 1982, supported by Mayor Byrne who was understandably apprehensive of Dunne's identification with the Daleys, Dunne had to retreat to his role—limited but still influential—as committeeman of the 42nd Ward.

Dunne backed Richard M. Daley in the 1983 primary. When Daley placed third in that race, Dunne became one of the few white politicians to sign on with Washington, the winner of the Democratic nomination. The following year Washington was ready to test his political strength by attempting to vote Vrdolyak out as party chairman and restore Dunne to the office, but the votes weren't there.

By mid-1987 they would be, and after kicking Eddie Burke out of his preeminent City Council position, and Ed Kelly out of the Park District, the removal of Eddie Vrdolyak as chairman of the Cook County Democratic Party, with George Dunne taking his place, would bring the mayor great satisfaction. "It made the set complete," he said in late 1987.

But now, in 1986, he needed a small favor.

Burton Natarus, Dunne's alderman in the 42nd, had always been among Mayor Washington's "21." There had been times when voting for the mayor's social programs and property tax increases could not have been easy for him. The 42nd Ward included Chicago's Gold Coast and the "Magnificent Mile" of Michigan Avenue retail stores, some of the most valuable real estate in the world.

It also included some of Chicago's poorer citizens, living in the nationally infamous CHA projects, Cabrini-Green.

But the decisive factor in his alignment with the Washington "21" was the fiat of his committeeman, George Dunne. Now that Natarus was among not 21 but 25 he might have been expected to relax under all that protective foliage. But he had been increasingly unpredictable ever since City Council reorganization began, when he had threatened to vote against the mayor unless he was awarded the chairmanship of the Transportation Committee.

Now, to the mayor's surprise, after all the normal push and pull of legislative tradeoffs, at the critical vote on September 12 it was Natarus who was having a prolonged and vocal anxiety attack about the final passage of the 1986 budget. By identifying himself as the holdout, we assumed, he was grandstanding for constituents who he thought might be thankful at election time, for his efforts to forestall the tax increase. We knew he wanted to make a point; we never believed he would jeopardize passage of the budget as he did.

But because he had grabbed center stage, he became the focus of an effort to crack the mayor's new working majority; and he put himself in a position to be *blamed* as the 25th vote that made the tax possible.

We redoubled our efforts to bring him around. Barefield and budget officials worked with him to demonstrate the need for the increase, which is to say, to help provide him with a rationale that would be convincing to his constituents.

A number of black aldermen became impatient. The usual reason for such balky behavior at budget time was the cutting of side deals: what was Natarus negotiating for himself? Why was the Gold Coast alderman getting special consideration while long-time loyalists, dependably compliant, made do?

While we struggled to identify a new ally among the former "29," and continued a holding action on the other 24, and kept up the effort to bring Natarus around, we also revived a PR campaign, discontinued the previous December, to sell the need for a tax increase.

The mayor's usual approach was to threaten layoffs of city workers, which can create intense pressure on recalcitrant aldermen from all those precinct captains. In this case he added a new twist to show his sincerity, by announcing he would cut his own staff first. A Jack Higgins cartoon appeared in the *Sun-Times* showing Harold Washington as the Lone Ranger alongside Tonto, his press secretary: "Do as I say or he gets it!" he was saying, pointing a gun at my head, with "Don't worry Alton, it's empty," muttered under his breath.

In fact he was perfectly ready to temporarily lay off his entire cabinet to dramatize the situation. Barefield had asked every department to develop contingency plans for massive layoffs, and the mayor would have gone through with it had he been pushed to the wall. But as I told a reporter at the time, we knew it would never be necessary. Natarus would come around before we got even halfway to that point.

As a *Sun-Times* editorial put it, "We won't deride Mayor Washington's threat to lay off 11,000 employees as a bluff. Considering the urgency, he is entitled to grasp at any strategy that might work. But we don't believe for one minute that our city's leaders will turn this city over to the looters, muggers, rapists and arsonists who would romp once police and fire services were sharply reduced.... Mayor Washington will not let this happen, and the City Council will not let this happen."

I asked him why he was confident on this issue, and he answered, "George Dunne." He was irked that Natarus was playing hard to get, but he wasn't as concerned as he would have been if the alderman had been anyone but Natarus. Now he was merely puzzled. What was Natarus all about? What did this really mean?

The mayor was scheduled to lead a delegation to Mexico City on September 16, to help celebrate Mexican Independence Day and to receive official thanks for Chicago's aid to earthquake victims there. We had hoped to get the budget resolved before we left, but it was proving impossible. Fortunately for the Mexican trip, other aldermen were planning to be out of town, and the critical City Council meeting was postponed until the end of September.

While we were in Mexico, Barefield delivered the bad news on possible layoffs. In two press conferences on successive days, he laid it on heavier than the mayor would have preferred. The Mexican trip was clouded by concern for how the legislative strategy was being handled. And despite his self-assurance, the mayor wondered out loud more than once—what was with Natarus? Could George Dunne be sending a message?

When we returned to Chicago he immediately moved to deescalate the layoff scares. The latest announcement, while we were in Mexico, had been a warning from Barefield that police and fire could be cut in the first or second wave. The mayor had been questioned by the *Sun-Times'* Harry Golden, accompanying us on the trip. Out of touch with the tone of Barefield's layoff announcements, the mayor was quoted more firmly than he had intended, in support of the statements. Eddie Burke was getting pretty good play out of his characterization of the plans as "hysterical." Natarus was quoted as hardening his position: "The mayor has made a pretty strong statement, but I'm not inclined to change my position one iota at the present time."

That wasn't like the alderman. The mayor ruminated—could Dunne possibly be another Lipinski—a carefully cultivated white political leader now turning away from him, toward Daley? Could it be connected with the dumping of Ed Kelly, or a down-in-the-marrow reaction to the mayor's new control of City Council? When I asked whether he had any real reason to think we might have such problems, he acknowledged that he didn't. But it was plain he was concerned.

Again the mayor met with Natarus. Again the meeting caused some resentment among black aldermen who may have considered they should have bargained harder for their own needs.

"That's the problem with being a winner," the mayor told me with a rueful smile. "On a good day, it's a lot easier being an underdog. And then when you have an alderman getting cute like this," he said, using a hackneyed legislator's phrase, "you drive up the price of pussy."

He didn't have much to offer Natarus, and he couldn't do much to change the city finances, in the unlikely event that the real problem was the tax hike.

And yet, now that he was again in direct conversation with the mayor, the alderman was much more tractable. Once again the mayor felt he had achieved a commitment to proceed. The City Council meeting was scheduled for September 24.

That day we worked the floor to be sure no one else had been lost along the way. Burke was up to something, and we couldn't be sure there wouldn't be more surprises. If we couldn't do it today, the mayor would have to begin making the cuts, which would be disruptive to the city and potentially damaging to our bond rating. Worst of all, it would send signals that the special elections had not ended "Council Wars." Mayor Washington believed nothing could hurt him more in the general election than a continuing stalemate in City Council.

The traditional rhetoric ping-ponged from alderman to alderman across the council chambers—against taxes but for fiscal stability—when suddenly we were hearing disturbing language from Natarus. Could it be? It seemed he was asking for yet another delay in considering the matter, more time to look at budget figures.

We had to stall the vote to see what was going on. Tim Wright of IGA, whom the mayor had begun depending on after aldermen complained about Jacky Grimshaw, frantically worked the floor in a last-minute search for any other 25th vote that might be available. Natarus' speech was rambling, but it was evident he wasn't ready to vote with us: Yes, as his remarks focused on the subject it was becoming clear that he was asking to have the issue delayed yet another week.

Mayor Washington was standing at the podium, gavel in hand, grasping at straws in his asides to Judd Miner, who was seated where the corporation counsel customarily sits at the mayor's right; and giving instructions to Tim Wright or listening to advice from Ald. David Orr and Ald. Tim Evans, wondering how long we could keep the issue in limbo while he decided what to do. He muttered to me, as I moved between the podium and the press corps, that Dunne must be the problem. It was a suspended moment, an emotion almost tangible that the critical vote was slipping away from us. Dunne was the problem? Perhaps. So might he be the solution?

There was only one way to find out. I asked the mayor if he'd mind if I called Dunne and put him in the middle of this. Let's put the proposition to the test, I said.

He looked askance at me. What I was suggesting was hardly professional. If I'd been a seasoned legislator, or a life-long politician, the idea never would have occurred to me. "I can try to reach him right now," I said. I had all his numbers from some earlier crisis—I had discovered that in times of urgency you will be given the home number for Bishop Tutu in Johannesburg, or White Sox owner Eddie Einhorn at home, or George Dunne in his car; I'd made a point of collecting them in miniaturized print, in my pocket address book.

"Sure," he said, but he was preoccupied with other tactics: if the meeting were postponed, what was the soonest we could reconvene? What was Dunne up to? What the hell did Natarus really want?

Leon Despres, who sat to the mayor's left as parliamentarian, handed me the phone under the desk, beside the podium. I called Dunne's office. The mayor needs to talk to your boss, I said to his secretary; she told me he was at a board meeting at the Brookfield Zoo. I called the zoo and was put through to the executive offices. The board meeting was taking place in some out of the way location at the zoo, but they managed to get him to a phone. "The mayor is calling for you, Mr. Chairman," I said, and handed the phone to my boss.

He motioned to Natarus to join him at the podium, and spoke briefly to Dunne. Simple, to the point: I really need your help on this budget, old buddy, it's come down to one vote.

I stepped away from the podium. Harry Golden and Andy Shaw and others had been motioning to me from the press box, and I went to see what they wanted. Like everyone else in the City Council chambers, vamping for time, they just wanted to make conversation.

"Who's Natarus talking to?" Andy Shaw asked. "George Dunne?" He grinned at the joke, but he was right on target. I didn't see any particular stigma—everyone knew Natarus conferred with Dunne on major issues. I told him yes, he was.

When Natarus returned to his seat the voting proceeded, and we passed the 1986 budget 25–25, with the mayor breaking the tie. It was critical that the budget be passed that day. We couldn't have weathered the continuing pressure from other aldermen, and would have been forced to finish the preelection year with serious cutbacks or a deficit, which would have undercut one of the mayor's proudest accomplishments. Worse, it would certainly have affected the bond rating upgrades which we had been counting on, due in the fall. It was one of those moments where another ten minutes could have spelled the difference between accomplishment and failure.

After the vote, the mayor motioned me back to the podium. "Don't mention the call to Dunne," he said. He was being protective of Natarus the man, who didn't like to be thought of as having strings; and of Dunne the politician, who shouldn't have to take the heat for the property tax in some future campaign against Vrdolyak. But I also think he found the tactic distasteful.

I told him I'd already mentioned it to Shaw. "Well, don't let it get out," he said. "Don't tell our people." And on this issue he went so far as to tell the only outright lie I'd ever heard him tell, some days later, when he was asked a direct question about it. The official line was that Natarus had needed to check some final figures with the budget office, and having satisfied himself, changed his vote. Although some writers speculated that Dunne may have been on the other end of the line, Natarus was given the benefit of the doubt. Andy probably thought I'd been kidding or making small talk. Today, a full cycle of municipal elections later, we're all far beyond any consequences of the call.

Later when I asked the mayor whether he thought Dunne had in fact been up to something he shook his head. "Burt gets that way sometimes," he said. He campaigned hard for Natarus in the 1987 election, and the Cabrini-Green vote guaranteed the alderman's 54 percent majority.

16

Election of 1987

The mayoral election of 1987 was certainly as remarkable as the election of 1983, and almost as revolutionary.

In a sense, the campaign of 1983 never really ended. Even before Mayor Washington was inaugurated, the Eddies made their all-out effort to launch a parallel city government. And then Jane Byrne announced in the summer of 1985—to preempt the field—that she would challenge Mayor Washington in 1987. The special elections of early 1986 continued the process. And even the Illinois gubernatorial elections—and federal midterm elections—of November 1986, were a part of the continuum.

Throughout his first term, Mayor Washington gaily boasted that he would be mayor for 20 years. But he deliberately created ambiguity about whether he would run as a Democrat or as an independent. Privately he made it clear that he would never leave the Democratic party. It was essential for his national agenda, as well as common sense locally, that he remain a recognized Democratic leader.

But publicly, he enjoyed confusing the speculations of all the Steve Neals. He also knew he was costing the Eddies and Byrne money and, he hoped, some sleep, by keeping them in limbo as to his final strategy.

Throughout 1986, while the pundits pondered and badgered him on the question, he kept reminding them there was another equally important election coming up in November.

He was initially optimistic about a change in the governor's mansion, and looked forward to a state government that would be more cooperative with the city. "It's coming together," he said. "By this time next year you won't recognize the political landscape."

He predicted the political future: Eddie Burke no longer Finance Committee chairman, Eddie Vrdolyak run out of office and out of the Democratic party, Ed Kelly dumped and the Park District reformed, the "29" disbanded and the City Council doing the business of the city. Vrdolyak no longer chairman of the Cook County Democratic Party, and a cooperative ally, George Dunne, at the helm. At the state level, Jim Thompson no longer governor, a sympathetic Gov. Adlai Stevenson, working with Democratic house speaker Michael Madigan and Democratic senate president Phil Rock to coordinate state policy for the benefit of Illinois cities. He looked forward to a Democratic victory in the 1988 presidential elections, as well.

He never supposed it would be easy, even though Stevenson had come within 5,000 votes of beating Thompson in the election of 1982; and even though "Big Jim" was now running for an unprecedented fourth term, and was considered vulnerable on his record. He told me, "Adlai Stevenson is the only person who runs a looser campaign than I do," and considered nothing certain.

But even in his fantasies he couldn't have guessed what was going on away back in the Virginia headquarters of the idiosyncratic Lyndon LaRouche. The ultraconservative political experimenter had been busy with plans that would make a mockery of the Illinois election of 1986. He had exploited Illinois election law which provided that each party's primary candidates for lieutenant governor run separately from candidates for governor; and he had engineered one of the quirkier demonstrations of Illinois voter predilections.

He entered two completely inexperienced and unqualified "LaRouchite" candidates whose names were red, white and blue, against opponents with ethnic-sounding names: Fairchild against Sangmeister, Hart against Pucinski. The electorate apparently voted by ear; it is hard to imagine a majority of Illinois voters preferring the policies of the bizarre LaRouche. The result of that primary election was that Stevenson was paired on the democratic ticket with a follower of Lyndon LaRouche.

Rather than run with Fairchild, Stevenson created a third party which he called the Solidarity Party. His predicament was cause for sniggering, and not only among Republicans. His chances for an upset looked slimmer every day. But if Mayor Washington wasn't optimistic about the man's prospects, he was sincere when he praised Stevenson's character and his courage in running on the Solidarity ticket and when he asserted Adlai would make the better governor. Jim Thompson's victory surprised no one.

The campaign that concerned the mayor more directly was the

effort to change election law, so that the mayor's race would be nonpartisan. The ambiguities that the mayor had tried to create were having their effect. As Hank Klibanoff told it, in the *Philadelphia Inquirer:*

"A little more than two months remain before the Democrats and Republicans hold their Feb. 24 party primaries to nominate their candidates for mayor—and still the political scene here remains utterly cluttered with comedic uncertainty.

"Who's running and who's not, changes about three times a week. And the speculation runs rampant every day. The air is so filled with trial balloons it's a wonder that airplanes are being cleared to leave O'Hare."

The confusion stemmed from the many options available to the candidate. The leader of the movement to eliminate those options was Congressman William Lipinski.

Lipinski had been a colleague of Mayor Washington in the U.S. House of Representatives. He was also one of the city's most effective ward committeemen. As a leading white ethnic political leader, universally regarded as honest and hardworking, and not identified with the opposition tactics of the Eddies, he was one of the most promising white politicians with whom Washington could begin to forge new alliances.

The mayor had carefully cultivated him, through bridge-building efforts by Tom Coffey. The mayor enjoyed a better-than-cordial personal relationship with him, and more than once shared the podium and the limelight in city improvement announcements affecting Lipinski's constituents in the 23rd Ward, and the 5th Congressional District. Lipinski's former secretary, now his designated alderman for the 23rd, Bill Krystyniak, was invited to accompany the mayor to Israel and Rome. On that trip we talked optimistically of Krystyniak's being the first to break the "29," even before special elections looked likely. Krystyniak volunteered that he never understood why Washington and Lipinski should be at odds.

But the bridge fell apart. Overnight—as though released from an unpleasant family duty—Krystyniak was almost jeeringly making his opposition loud and clear in City Council. When the city sought to coordinate an announcement of federal funds for southwest Chicago, customary whenever such funds were released, Lipinski ducked the press conference and preempted us with a leak that credited the efforts, instead, of Republican Governor Thompson.

The mayor told me their relationship completely fell apart after the special elections, when Lipinski asked to be named park superintendent succeeding Ed Kelly: "I said ask for anything else, Bill." The mayor said he had no choice—it was essential that he have a loyal friend with compatible interests, not an ally of convenience, in the park superintendent role. "And I'm going to pay holy hell if I don't appoint a black," he said. Still, he was surprised at Lipinski's total reversal, the dramatic suddenness of his enmity, and the intensity of his next move.

Lipinski became the sponsor of a drive to change state law, calling for nonpartisan elections for mayor in 1987.

Chicago's mayoral elections are partisan: to run in the primary, candidates declare their party affiliation, and run against qualified fellow party members. Democrats against Democrats, Republicans against Republicans, (if there is more than one Republican willing to run). The candidate with a plurality—not necessarily a majority—is that party's candidate in the general election.

In "normal" times, the Democrat race is the only one that matters. When Harold Washington won that race in 1983, even with his 37 percent plurality, as a life-long Democrat who had paid his dues to the party and who for many years had played his role in Daley's Democrat Machine he had a right to expect the party to rally around him. In "normal" times, even though 1983 might have been a better year than usual for a white Republican candidate, Washington would have walked, not run, from the primary to the fifth floor at City Hall. For better or worse, the system had served the city and the party well.

That was then. Now this arrangement had become a mathematical problem, a "multiple choice" question that the Democratic regulars had failed in 1983, and hoped to avoid in 1987.

The game is fixed, they charged. Any strong black candidate can win a plurality in the Democratic primary. That gives him an unfair advantage. Why not "make it fair" by changing the rules? If every candidate runs in a single nonpartisan election, with a run-off to decide between the first and second place (except of course if first place wins a clear majority), we'll be guaranteed a mayor with a popular majority.

All the stops were pulled for this campaign to change state law. Steve Neal contributed when he wrote repeatedly that Harold Washington had sponsored such legislation while he was serving in

Springfield. The mayor finally had the opportunity to call him on that misstatement, when they were both guests on John Madigan's WBBM radio interview program, "At Issue." But by that time it had gained such currency that it was being repeated by other public figures—Congressman Rostenkowski repeated it on a radio program —and other journalists who treated it as fact. A few journalists, notably political correspondent Bruce DuMont of WTTW-TV, acknowledged their error. Others, including the originator, Neal himself, let it simply sink out of sight. The mayor resented the falsehood because it created an impression of cowardice or hypocrisy on his part.

Vernon Jarrett patiently dissected the matter, in his *Sun-Times* column of July 27, 1986: he noted that the mayor had been irked by Bruce DuMont's flat statement on the TV program "Chicago Tonight," "that none other than Washington himself had once advocated this same kind of nonpartisan election."

DuMont, "a highly regarded Chicago radio and television journalist" as Jarrett notes, told Jarrett, "I have heard that statement repeated for so long by reputable journalists until I assumed it is an accepted fact."

Jarrett continued:

> DuMont pointed out that one source for the statement was Steve Neal, reputable *Chicago Tribune* writer, who had made a similar presumed statement of fact in his regular columns and on radio talk shows...
>
> DuMont spent a goodly part of Thursday and Friday trying to answer Washington's challenge to "find any record of any such bill with my name on it." In fact, Washington doesn't recall "anybody even sponsoring such a bill" when he was in the Illinois House or Senate.
>
> DuMont checked with the Legislative Reference Bureau in Springfield, but no one there could remember such legislation. "I checked with old-timers and other knowledgeable people, but no one could recall the bill or Washington's suggestion of one," DuMont said....
>
> [Jarrett concluded] DuMont showed his professionalism when he retracted his statement during his Thursday evening "Inside Politics" program....

The practical effect of the nonpartisan election that Lipinski was pushing is best shown by considering the actual results of the 1983 election. Had it been nonpartisan, Daley would have been eliminated and Washington and Byrne would have topped the roster, subsequently facing each other in a showdown. The "white hope" would have been the strongest white, not the weakest as it turned out.

Partly from political necessity and partly from the personal affront, Mayor Washington bristled at the move. "I *am* a majority candidate," he insisted. "I won 50 percent plus of the vote. I ran one-on-one in 1983."

That response skirted the central issue when the matter was considered from a racial point of view. The candidate he beat, under the existing system, was an unelectable Republican.

But that didn't have to be. It wasn't out of the question that a strong Republican could emerge; or that a strong Democrat could change parties. For that reason, most Republicans who saw the Reagan years as boon times for party building joined the mayor in opposing the nonpartisan election. And a good deal of speculation centered on the question of who might switch parties and become the Neo-Republican to take him on. Ed Kelly was most frequently assumed, by Northwest Side Democrats if not by most Republicans.

In any case, it was precisely the "racial point of view" that most offended Mayor Washington. For all his pragmatism as a politician, and his unabashedly African-American ethnic identity, he was sensitive to the suggestion that he was "only" a black mayor, not a real mayor "who happened to be black."

Mayor Washington argued against the prudence under law of changing a rule that affects the incumbent. He cited various precedents but most frequently the 22nd Amendment to the U.S. Constitution, which provided for change in the presidential succession but did not apply to then incumbent Harry Truman.

He chided proponents for their devious interest in "changing the rules in the middle of the game," arguing that it didn't matter whether it was theoretically good or valid in principle, if the motivation was racist.

He offered arguments that nonpartisan elections would be detrimental, perhaps lethal, to the two-party system in Chicago. Even though his Progressive Democrats had been locked in a struggle to the death with the Regular Democrats throughout his incumbency, he was sure this argument would get a receptive hearing not only among local Republicans, but also among national Democrats who could put some pressure on Lipinski, Rostenkowski, and others—

they might be ward committeemen in Chicago, but they had responsibilities as congressmen and party leaders in Washington.

He argued that any such change would reflect very poorly on a Chicago that had already been through the mill of public opinion. Whatever you may say for a nonpartisan election, he argued, and however
pure your own motives might be, you know it's a racially inspired attack on the status quo, and therefore never mind the rationale, it's
wrong.

But at bottom, his strongest reaction was just plain personal.
He talked about it with journalists that October:

> Everyone in this room knows that the motivation for nonpartisan may-
> oral elections in 1987 has nothing to do—not even indirectly—with a
> desire for election reform in Chicago. It's targeted on me, personally,
> we all know that, most of its proponents freely admit it.
>
> I'm not saying it's racially motivated. Let's let that one pass—every
> man and woman knows their own heart, but no one can be sure of any-
> one else's, and I judge people not by what I think they think, but by
> what they do. In this case, I won't presume to judge.
>
> But questions of race aside, there can be no doubt that this effort to
> change 150 years of electoral policy is targeted on a single individual,
> yours truly.
>
> Regardless of any other merits of the issue; whether you think it's a
> good idea or a bad idea, or part good, or part bad, or an idea to be post-
> poned to 1991, or an idea to be debated; no matter what plane you ele-
> vate the discussion to, you can't get away from a basic fact: this was a
> movement targeted at Harold Washington.
>
> You can't write about my motives for fighting this move, with every
> means possible, without taking into full account that basic, primal
> matter of fact—no man is going to stand idly by while someone men-
> aces him with a baseball bat.
>
> You can't talk theory, dressed up for political philosophers, with all the
> proper legal phrases, unless you keep in mind that from where I stood,
> all this is about is a personal attack, staged by alley fighters. I was not
> going to get drawn into a Socratic debate about political theory by peo-
> ple trying to pull off a political mugging.

But it was not impassioned argument or personal conviction that
knocked Lipinski out of the box. Political chicanery did the trick.

The same election statutes that Lipinski was seeking to change are
specific about referenda put before the voters. One article states that

no more than three referenda may be included on any given ballot. Another provides alternative ways of getting a referendum listed: you may collect 140,000 signatures on petitions, or you may pass an ordinance in City Council. While Lipinski & Co. were out hustling 210,000 signatures, Mayor Washington's forces introduced three items for nonbinding (and irrelevant) referenda in City Council. The nonpartisan mayoral election move was dead.

A number of Washington strategists took credit for the idea to stack the ballot with three innocuous referenda. In fact, it was the brainchild of one of the mayor's less-heralded strategists, attorney David Canter.

Reaction to the nonpartisan ploy occupied only part of Mayor Washington's political agenda during the last half of 1986. He was also active in efforts to change the management of the Board of Elections—specifically to oust the Machine's BOE chairman Michael Lavelle and appoint new commissioners; he was still dealing with the Sullivan report, the pending federal indictments, and other fallout from Raymond the Mole; and he was gearing up his campaign organization to deal with a one-on-one race with "the strongest candidate that Eddie could field."

"When it all comes down to fifth street," he said, "I'll be running one-on-one against whoever they believe is the strongest white candidate." As it worked out, he was right twice.

Jane Byrne had declared early—in mid-1985—that she would run for reelection. Her preemptive move had the desired effect; no other white candidate wanted to run the risk that Daley had dared, and be branded a spoiler. The mayor beat her with a clear majority in the Democratic primary.

A number of candidates started out in the general, but when it came down to "fifth street"—a poker term referring to the final cards played in five-card stud—the only opposing candidate of consequence was Fast Eddie Vrdolyak.

The mayor warned me, as the preelection maneuvers were gearing up, that a "movement campaign" was completely different from a "Machine campaign," and that I should plan to "hang loose."

By all accounts, including his own assessment, the grassroots movement that had sprung to life around his 1983 candidacy was one of the most disorganized political efforts in the history of American big-city elections. Florence Levinsohn's book *Harold Washington: A Political Biography*, was written from inside the campaign. She quotes one observer, Chicago political fixture Don Rose who had been around since the hairy revolutionary movements of the 1960s, as calling it "the most inept large scale campaign I've ever seen." Levinsohn continued:

> Rose isn't alone in calling the campaign inept. Most observers, inside and outside the staff, agree. They say: Washington did not trust his staff, perhaps justifiably. He knows more about campaigning than ten of them together. He hired a campaign manager and then undercut him regularly and finally eased him out. He arbitrarily changed scheduled dates without consultation with those in charge of the schedules. He intimidated his press staff so they didn't feel safe speaking for him. He permitted chaos to reign by never permitting anyone to pull together the various centers of influence. He did not create a strategy group until close to the end of the campaign. So go the charges. Some are documented.
>
> The veteran campaigner, Rose, volunteered to work for nothing. He could prepare the media materials. He could handle the press. He could even be campaign manager. His offer was rejected.

Rose had worked with Washington in his first mayoral campaign, in the special election of 1977. Rose and the mayor had had a falling out then. The mayor almost (but not quite) acknowledged that he had possibly been at fault—the story is he had misinformed Rose and led Rose to inadvertently mislead the press on an important matter—but, he told me, he couldn't forget that Rose had broken with him publicly, rather than work it out. "That's not someone you want with you in a tight spot," he said.

The mayor never really believed in handlers and press wizards anyway. In my case, I'm sure, it was my awareness that Washington was his own best press secretary that fostered the professional bond between us.

On the other hand, he respected Rose's credentials as a life-long champion of liberal causes. A number of main-line white liberals had urged that he bring Rose into the campaign, and he agreed with them that having Rose aboard would "send a message." He also believed in co-optive hiring: the more people from that profession you could afford to put on the payroll, the fewer there were available to the other candidates. The fact that they were highly accessible to buddies in the media, and might leak campaign information, was more than offset by the advantage of having all that "spin control" out there working for you, from issue to issue. And you didn't really have to tell them anything you didn't want to read in the paper.

So Rose was hired for the 1987 campaign, and the mayor's advisers were once more reassured that this election would be an improvement over 1983.

For one thing, the mayor agreed with those funding the campaign who insisted on hiring a competent professional to keep track of the funds and direct the staff. He assured them he wouldn't interfere—indeed, though he could become irritated about misspent funds, and sometimes even penny-wise about some campaign costs, in general he had little interest in keeping track of the money, so long as someone did, and so long as there was always enough.

The person chosen was Ken Glover, an executive with Drexel Burnham on Wall Street, a young black professional for whom the mayor had great respect. Glover had been instrumental in the reelection strategy since 1984, if not earlier, and had presented Mayor Washington a detailed game plan in an August 1984 memo.

But there was a slight hitch—Glover couldn't leave New York until December, so Jacky Grimshaw, who was to be Glover's assistant, would have to be the acting campaign manager for the first few weeks of the campaign.

The mayor also agreed to form a strategy group—though he never promised to take them seriously. In fact, he didn't so much form the group as acknowledge it, as it coalesced around his candidacy, over in the campaign office.

As always, he continued to depend on individual advice based on individual expertise, and when in doubt to follow his own instincts. Slim Coleman remained one of his most dependable strategists; Vince Bakeman was the only person he trusted for straw polling of minorities; Jim Andrews and David Canter for the numbers; me for press. So long as these folks were attending those strategy meetings, he felt he had all the exposure to their collective wisdom that he needed.

He had originally believed that it would be necessary for me to take a leave of absence from City Hall and work out of the campaign office, on the campaign payroll. "The press will beat holy hell out of you if they catch you doing campaign work on city time," he said. I was set to make the move, even looking forward to the temporary change, and the new upswing of my learning curve that would follow.

A *Tribune* story made the announcement in early November: "Alton Miller, the mayor's press secretary, is expected to leave his City Hall job in December to assume the full-time duties of political spokesman, administration sources said. Miller's support comes directly from the mayor, who values his political and strategic advice, those sources said. Other members of Washington's braintrust are apprehensive, however, that Miller's lack of political experience and his strained relationship with the Chicago press could hurt Washington's candidacy."

At about this time I had a fortuitous conversation with Paul O'Connor, son of legendary political commentator Len O'Connor whose book *Clout* had helped introduce me to Chicago politics. Paul had served as press secretary to Gov. John D. Spellman of the state of Washington, and he'd been through a gubernatorial campaign.

"Watch out," he said. "The campaign will want to eat you alive. The press secretary is one of the few people who stand between their rolling battlefield bureaucracy and the mayor. Eliminate you, and maybe Barefield, and they can exercise complete control over the candidate—a campaign bureaucracy's dream."

In the course of a lengthy, seemingly clairvoyant description of the situation I was just discovering, he confirmed most of my own impressions. He was talking about Washington State, but he could have been describing City Hall in Chicago. His insights fortified my growing apprehension that I was staring into the maw of a corporate monster; that I might, in one of the mayor's favorite expressions, "go into the campaign and get swallowed up, sink down into the earth, never to be seen again."

The mayor and I both came to the same conclusion at about the same time. He saw that I was about to be signed onto someone else's team, which was exactly what he didn't want for his press secretary. He didn't want it regardless of whether it was Barefield's "benign" bureaucracy or what was sure to be the hostile environment of the campaign bureaucracy.

For my part, I realized that what I was planning was about to complicate my life beyond recognition. I was about to move from my city-subsidized research staff, and my city-supplied computer database filled with information we'd been gathering on Byrne, on Hynes, on the Eddies, on all the issues; my city car with its telephone, my irreplaceable secretary, Tumia, my immediate proximity to every city department head—all for what? So I could relocate two wet, cold blocks away from the mayor's office that I would be trying to serve. Plus, if the campaign was going to match my salary, it would be another $10–20,000 drain on the war chest, not counting the cost of all those accoutrements.

Besides keeping me at hand, he also made the point that he wanted his scheduling to continue to be coordinated by the mayor's press office, not by the campaign. Although it was clear that campaign priorities would dictate where he went and when, Delores Woods would continue to control his appointments, minute by minute; and the press office would continue to brief and organize the public events with scheduler Ed Hamb, whether they were "governmental" or "political." From the standpoint of press office operations, Hamb would continue to be the point of contact. Whether he was directed by the campaign or by any other usual agenda wouldn't matter to the functions the press office briefers would perform. We'd just take whatever he gave us.

The mayor was still concerned that the press would lambaste us, and it was Harry Golden who came to the rescue. He scoffed at the idea that the press would give us a hard time. Every mayor in memory had retained his City Hall staff, he said. The press wouldn't scold us if we did, they'd ridicule us if we didn't.

Jacky Grimshaw made a strong pitch for a separate campaign press secretary and the idea was rejected. Though there were press aides there, the mayor was determined that he wouldn't have two press secretaries—the idea of having a separate campaign press secretary was as bad as having a separate security detail, he said. Ken Glover would serve as press spokesman for the campaign organization, when a spokesman was appropriate. David Axelrod would often be available to the press for his insights. Beyond that the mayor didn't see a need for further press representation, so long as the campaign was coordinated with the press office.

That coordination was not good. To begin with, there were serious divisions within the campaign organization. Jacky Grimshaw, who had been Tom Coffey's assistant and now was acting as IGA director, wasn't getting along with Ken Glover. He believed she was subtly undermining him, he told me in a series of phone calls early in the campaign. Others told me that Jacky and a few staff members she had put in place constituted a hostile independent element within the organization.

Second, Jacky wasn't well organized. The field operation was in trouble. To make matters worse, she was getting increasingly testy, as she came under attack by the mayor's allies and other campaign staff members.

Third, I had an attitude problem. Throughout my work with the City Hall bureaucracy, I had mixed feelings about the management-by-consensus of my friend Barefield. I had managed to develop a tolerance for our long, rambling meetings, though I resented the late hours I would have to work when I returned to my office, making up for lost time. All the mayor's players had jostled for position, and we were all comfortable in our roles.

Now we were in the thick of a campaign for reelection and many of the players who had helped in 1983 were suddenly on hand, understandably assertive about their right to play a key role. For the most part, their energies were safely absorbed in planning and policy meetings where issues small and large were exhaustively examined.

I couldn't stomach those long, rambling gab sessions; the campaign seemed to thrive on them. I admired the patience of Slim Coleman and Ernie Barefield, who spent as much time in real work as I did and who yet were always ready for yet another round of these midnight assemblies.

I could barely tolerate the long and often pointless meetings of MPAC, the Mayor's Policy Advisory Group chaired by Ernie Barefield, which had been meeting in City Hall nearly every week for two years. At times we had upwards of 30, 40 people—department heads, key aides, outside advisers—sitting in these morning sessions for hours, to listen to debates of departmental agenda details that held no priority for most of us. I discerned that we were all enduring these meetings for the sake of Ernie's consensus approach to management. By getting us all in one room at the same time, he was trying to avoid normal management problems of communications and coordination. But at what expense?

As often as possible I took advantage of the mayor's early morning schedule to skip these meetings and get filled in later, usually palming them off on my deputy press secretary who seemed to appreciate the "honor." I told the mayor what I was doing, that is, what he was saving me from, and he agreed. He was concerned that the MPAC group had grown from the small circle of top advisers he had intended it to be, and he had assured me he would reorganize its functions after the April election.

Now the campaign organization was inflicting us with the same stuff. Besides the investment of time required, it was painful for me —as it was also for Ed Hamb, the scheduler, who had to agonize through their process of scheduling by committee, with every constituency group having their say in the consensus—to watch this group attempting to reinvent many of the processes we had developed over the past two years. While I appreciated their conviction that they knew more about political campaigns than the Barefield bureaucracy, I also knew that over at City Hall we'd been waging a continuous series of campaigns throughout the first term. We knew all about it.

I resolved all my problems with the campaign by deciding they were unresolvable, and ignoring them. I sent delegates to cover meetings—it was always possible to find someone on my staff eager to participate. My rule of thumb was that if the mayor didn't need to attend a meeting, I didn't. I would be on the receiving end, as the mayor was briefed on their recommendations, rather than be one of those delivering the consensus to him.

For the most part, Mayor Washington followed the drift of the campaign team on each of several levels. He showed up for meetings called by Bill Berry and the other top funders, and listened to their considerations. He sat in on some of the media strategy sessions. And he was occasionally available to the larger, general campaign conversation groups. He was continually in touch with the ideas of all these forums, by talking individually with those who had attended.

He was notorious for playing one against another—idly, not maliciously—and encouraging each person to speak his or her mind about what was going on. In this way, I suspect, he was reassured that he knew where all the passions lay, and could better evaluate information dispassionately. Even more, he was fostering an environment where the only true and trustworthy anchor for the entire enterprise would be the rock-solid man in the center, the mayor himself.

Though he understood my aversion to the long general sessions, and even sometimes called me out of meetings when I did choose to attend, he directed me to make the key media meetings; although I had no role to play in the development of the effective TV spots David Axelrod was producing, he wanted my disinterested opinion before they were aired.

And he wanted me at the daily morning strategy sessions in his office, involving Glover, Barefield, Axelrod, and occasionally a few others.

Early in the campaign, on November 7, there was a general meeting at the Lenox House hotel. Those invited included Bill Berry, Jacoby Dickens, Al Johnson, and Bob Hallock, all from the mayor's kitchen cabinet; Ald. Tim Evans, Ken Glover, Vince Bakeman, Don Rose, and Jacky Grimshaw from the campaign office; and Barefield and me from the mayor's office. The mayor ran the meeting.

He began by spelling out the purpose. There had been no government structure with which to interface in 1983; now there was, and we needed to figure out how best to do it. "Our people are technically able," he said, meaning most of the campaign staff as well as City Hall aides, "but they're politically naive. We need a 'transmission apparatus' to translate political decisions into governmental activities that will work as campaign events."

The "Committee to Re-Elect" would be the corporate body, with Jacoby Dickens acting as CEO. An executive committee of some 25–30 key players would have responsibility for management between meetings of the whole committee. And the campaign office, with Glover as chief operating officer, would run the day-to-day campaign.

How best to interface with the government apparatus? A "bridge group" would be needed. Barefield would be the bridge to government. Bakeman would be the bridge to the miscellaneous advisory groups that needed input. Other consultants would play a role. In this bridge group the diverse energies and agendas of the "movement" could have free play, and good ideas could be distilled out for the campaign's use.

Most of the work of that November 7 meeting had already been accomplished in private sessions between the mayor and others in the room. But it was a signal event for the formal integration of the re-election campaign.

In the short term, however, the session was even more memorable for an indiscretion that took place sometime during the next three days. In the course of the meeting it had been discussed that Cecil Partee, the first black elected to citywide office when he became City Treasurer in 1979, intended to run for reelection. That office, along with that of City Clerk, forms a three-person "top of the ticket" in the quadrennial mayoral elections. The mayor was endorsing Gloria Chevere, from the Puerto Rican community, as City Clerk. He would have benefited from having a white "running mate" for the Treasurer's office—the tricolor ticket would have made a wonderful "unity" statement before we'd ever said a word. But the discussion was no deeper than a wistful observation: it was clear Partee was in the race to stay, and there would be no effort to remove him.

The meeting was Friday. John Kass called me Monday to say that someone at the meeting had leaked information about Partee. Going off the record, I confirmed that Partee had been discussed. Then, reviewing media calls with him as I did every day, I told the mayor that Kass had called on that subject. The mayor wasn't happy that a Partee story was being written, but I didn't attribute much significance to the call or to the issue, which had been in the air for weeks.

The next day both the *Sun-Times* and the *Tribune* carried stories about Partee. Basil Talbott, Jr., in the *Sun-Times*, wrote that "Some mayoral strategists, speaking anonymously, said Washington would prefer an ethnically balanced ticket.... The Washington aides conceded there is little chance of fielding a fully balanced ticket if Partee insists on running."

John Kass' *Tribune* story said that the mayor "has been asked by his political strategists to replace...Partee with a white, lakefront liberal," and confirmed that "sources close to Partee said he learned of the move two weeks ago."

The next day there was consternation among the strategy group. The stories, which also dealt with announcements of other splinter movements, fostered the impression that there was division in the base, that some blacks were threatening a schism. Worse, for the mayor's inner circle, there was concern that someone had deliberately sought to sabotage the campaign.

There were other leaks that had become increasingly annoying. Talbott had done a story on our field operation that depended on inside information about the mayor's distribution of petitions. He did a second story on a mammoth petition drive we were planning. Sneed had run an item saying that Rose and I were feuding—if we were, it was a one-way feud that I hadn't been aware of. I suspected, and told Rose as much, that someone else was attempting to stimulate a fight by spreading these stories.

Not long after, as Ken Glover was coming on board, Don Rose was dumped as the campaign's media man, in favor of a former protege of his, David Axelrod. The mayor was impressed with Axelrod, and had his old misgivings about Rose; it was completely his decision, made in the face of the lakefront liberals' advice.

We eased the public blow as much as possible: our story was that Rose had earlier been "tentatively" signed by the committee before Glover was in place; now Glover was making his first executive decision, in reconsidering the position and hiring his own choice, Axelrod. Rose would remain connected to the campaign, as a general consultant.

I was later told that Rose believed he'd been canned as a suspect in the Partee leak. He and all political consultants were always suspect in leaks—it's an occupational hazard in that career field. The sometimes overlapping loyalties of media-connected, campaign-connected press consultants can make the labyrinthine plot lines of LeCarré novels look straightforward by comparison.

But his being fired had nothing to do with that. The blunt point is that Mayor Washington didn't like Rose very much. The 1977 incident was a contributing factor, and the clincher was a *Tribune* Sunday magazine story which came out the same week that the leaks were reported, in which Rose seemed to be calling the mayor a "whore."

Interviewed by the authors, Rose recalled Washington's beginnings as an independent politician. He was quoted as saying that "members of the [anti-Machine] group had trouble understanding how Washington could be so critical of the Daley organization and still remain a member. 'Some of them thought he was a worse whore [than other Machine politicians] because he knew better,' Rose said."

When that item appeared in the November 16 edition, even though Rose called the mayor to apologize, the end was in sight.

Beyond his personal relationship with Rose, the mayor had a general skepticism about the political experts and the would-be handlers who swarmed around his campaign. He deferred to the wisdom of those who pretended to know what color "power tie" he should wear, how dark his suit should be, and whether or how he should cut his hair; but unless Ken Glover called him early in the morning to remind him, he was likely to show up with the same soup-stained paisley cravat, finger-stained at the knot, that he'd worn the day before.

He paid attention when advisers counseled against hard-hitting "comparative" (i.e., negative) campaigning, pitting his record against Byrne's, and instead urged him to be mayoral and statesmanlike, above the fray. Based on research conducted in May 1985, at the height of "Council Wars" (and just after Jane Byrne announced she'd be running again in 1987), they advised that Mayor Washington's

"negative remarks about Byrne and/or Daley [were] offensive to bor-
derline supporters which may weaken his position with what could
have been Washington supporters," and they "strongly recommend[ed] that the Mayor *completely* refrain from any sexist or negative remarks that would be interpreted as being associated with
sex/gender when addressing Jane Byrne."

He heard them. But he had trouble assimilating the advice. He
said it was too close to the same "discredited advice I got from lakefront liberals since day one," and he was straining at the leash. Day
by day he was becoming more and more uncomfortable with a campaign where you took it on the chin and smiled and postured like
someone's idea of what a mayor looks like, while the other side made
its points.

Axelrod had laid down the shape of the campaign in a December
memo, drawn up even before he was certain the mayor would be running in the Democratic primary. His campaign strategy depended on
several premises.

First, the mayor should run on the excellent record of his first term
(despite a Steve Neal story to the contrary, based on an advisory
memo from the mayor's pollsters). Second, whenever possible Vrdolyak should be employed as "our best organizer among both blacks
and targeted whites. And the closer we can tie Vrdolyak to Byrne and
Hynes, the better." The memo suggested the two themes could be in-
terwoven along the lines of "We've accomplished a lot—despite the
Vrdolyak crowd." And third, it urged a close identification of the
mayor with Chicago's thriving neighborhoods, and with "average citizens" providing personal testimonials to the mayor's achievements.

All this would be established to build a positive foundation, before
negative campaigning would begin. Advertising that stressed the
Byrne record against the Washington record would not start until the
final weeks of the campaign. "It probably would be beneficial for the
general [campaign after the primary was won] if we never had to get
low down and dirty with the primary media," Axelrod urged.

Sound advice, the mayor acknowledged. And yet it was foreign to
his nature to be in a campaign and under attack, and not come out
with his sleeves rolled up.

He bitterly resented the fact that he had spent the better part of the
past two years responding and reacting to attacks from the Eddies.
He had yielded the initiative to them, and was usually positioned as
the one who had to reply. Now when candidate Vrdolyak attacked

him he ignored it. Vrdolyak wasn't a real candidate, he repeated. He was shilling for Byrne. "Watch them operate," he said. "She'll take the high road and Eddie'll take the low road, but they're both in it together, joined at the hip, cheek to cheek, jowl to jowl." Sometimes he seemed to believe it himself, that Vrdolyak and Byrne had cut a deal.

It was clear that Axelrod's strategy was sound. It also had the distinction of being the only immediate strategy in the campaign, complementing Glover's PERT chart, and Slim Coleman's comprehensive calendar of events and suggested events for field operations, which he had prepared that fall.

But it was equally clear that it wasn't working for the mayor. On January 10 I gave him a memo on the subject. "I understand the Jan.–Feb. period breaks down into Jan./'Sell the record,' Feb./'Hit the opposition,'" I wrote. "I would suggest that we drop this kind of thinking and not hold back from the comparative (attack) style until Feb." I listed almost 20 opportunities to make points and attack Byrne, from upcoming groundbreakings to the release of our crime stats for 1986. And I suggested a formula for attack that I thought combined the best elements of all the suggested strategies.

Each time we go on the offensive, I said—and we should go on the offensive daily—we should follow this "template": First sell your record by outlining your accomplishments in the specific area being dealt with. Then show how you did it *despite* the opposition of the Eddies. Then contrast your achievement in that area with the dismal Byrne record.

This would produce all the adrenaline of the attack, but it would be couched in positive terms—what *we* accomplished—and it would have the extra advantage of linking Byrne and Vrdolyak at every mention.

He liked the approach. It happened to be timed just as he was most frustrated by his advisers' programming. He was aching to hit back. He was dying to attack.

Finally he broke his leash. One morning in the car from Hyde Park, when he was fulminating about the passivity of his campaign, I took the opportunity to suggest that we had a series of attacks on Jane Byrne, ready in the press office. He decided to seize the moment, and in that morning's strategy session informed Glover of what he was going to do. He had been increasingly querulous, over the previous few days, about his campaign posture. Now he wasn't asking when do we get started, he was telling.

We had to assemble the materials hastily, and schedule the press conference on the fly, as he was about to go into a City Council meeting. He wouldn't use the mayoral press conference room for political hits, and there wasn't time to do it at the campaign office, so we created a makeshift visual by spreading receipts dating from the early 1980s on tables in the vestibule behind the Council chambers—an area I always referred to as backstage. We didn't have a proper sound system or podium; the glare of the TV lights and the bristling microphones poked in from all sides lent something of a crisis air.

The receipts had come from Mayor Byrne's reimbursement records, on file since her term of office, and they showed how her city petty cash funds had been used for personal expenditures for her and her family. As always in such cases, the more trivial the expenditures, the more subject to ridicule they could be. It was not a moment of electoral grandeur. It was a hearty cheap shot, and as such made lively headlines.

The campaign was jostled slightly off track, but it quickly adjusted to the new mode. Byrne had been making points by accusing the mayor of traditional fundraising practices—it was sufficient to accuse the "reform" mayor of doing the perfectly legal and customary, so long as it could be made to suggest hypocrisy and phony reform.

In response, Jim Wascher in the campaign office had prepared a detailed analysis of Byrne campaign funds. Glover and I set up a proper press conference, with bold graphics and detailed charts, to illuminate the contrast between her funding and ours. Again, it was good press—they'd been waiting for us to unleash. "We're having fun now, aren't we?" Glover repeated over and over that morning.

The 1987 campaign requires its own book of chronicles, and it's sure to get it.

Someone will detail the adventures we enjoyed when the lake overflowed and flooded Lake Shore Drive. Byrne almost chortled with the "good news"—she had been elected on the strength of that snowstorm a decade earlier, and she seemed to take this new natural disaster as her due. But the indefatigable Streets and San commissioner John Halpin was on the phone to me at two in the morning when the flooding began, and after we did some planning, I called the mayor. We were out early, on site, and we not only got great lakefront exposure but took the credit for Halpin's miraculously successful effort to reopen Lake Shore Drive hours or days ahead of predictions.

Someone will tell of Hynes' glass jaw—how he tried to run by being above the fray, then overreacted when we staged a series of sharp attacks on him that shocked, perhaps dazed him, and drew him into a fight he wasn't prepared to handle. One of the mayor's lakefront supporters was distressed by our attack—"Don't dirty him up," she said, as though Hynes was a natural resource that shouldn't be sullied by politics. And a Chicago reporter that we met on a plane weeks later said it was "too bad that Hynes had to be tarnished like that. We need some heroes, don't you think?" No, the mayor didn't think. Pretty faces shouldn't get into the ring, is what he thought.

Someone else will have to sort out the allegations concerning Vrdolyak's alleged "meeting with the mobster." The *Sun-Times* headlined Steve Neal's story of a Vrdolyak rendezvous with an alleged mob boss, which was offered without evidence, even after Vrdolyak detailed his actual whereabouts. We never believed it happened, not because it couldn't have but because we had heard the same stories—which were turned down by at least one *Tribune* columnist—when they were apparently being circulated by Hynes' political operatives. He who lives by slander, dies by slander, we figured.

The mayor beat Byrne in the primary. Overnight she became a supportive ally. He then confronted Eddie Vrdolyak and Cook County Assessor Tom Hynes, each running as a third party candidate. Together with a Democrat-turned-Republican, Jane Byrne's former budget director Don Haider, the four candidates met in debate.

In the debate Vrdolyak outperformed all three of his opponents combined. Sassy, clever, earnest, well-informed and above all natural, he did what he had to do: identified himself as the only other viable candidate in the race.

Mayor Washington looked miserable, and he knew it. "My own campaign did something to me that Vrdolyak could never do," he told me. "They cut my balls off." Indeed, there was a gelded quality to the muted performance he gave, swollen briefing book in hand, as he fulfilled his promise to lay low and make no mistakes. He had been drilled and grilled on the issues, or rather, on how to reference subject areas in the expanded looseleaf book he was given. A ream of single-spaced pages made him unquestionably the best-informed and most boring chief executive that ever had to face three bushwhackers in debate.

The master-debaters, as we called the assassins of spontaneity who briefed him for his debate, got what they wanted: no big mistakes. But Mayor Washington took a lot of kidding from friends and from his staff on how successfully he'd been subdued. "These folks might know how to get me elected," he joked, "but they're sure going to cut in on my creature comforts." He meant they had trimmed his sails and hurt his style.

The final weekend of the campaign was the most remarkable. Tom Hynes dropped out of the race with 40 hours remaining before the polls opened, making it one-on-one with Vrdolyak, unless you counted Don Haider which only 5 percent did. The mayor threw away the campaign organization's consensus schedule and asked Ed Hamb and me to set up the final days for him. The three of us talked it through at a soul food restaurant on Roosevelt, and we went to work.

We worked the geography and the constituencies, up one side of Chicago and down the other. The mayor was a whirlwind, and Ed was reminded of the frenetic pace of the 1983 campaign. Mayor Washington was supercharged with a new vitality, now that he finally was in the ring with Vrdolyak alone.

The Rev. Jesse Jackson was on the scene, and the two of them walked the long stretch of CHA buildings, greeting the residents and trying to crank up the voter turnout. I remember taking a moment, during that long walk, to return some phone calls from the limousine. While crowds chanted around the two leaders, and the car slowly paced their walk down the endless service drive, I nodded off in a quick catnap. The mayor's driver, Wilbourne Woods, woke me with a gentle comment when the mayor was about to get back into the car. I wondered how the hell the mayor could keep on going.

17

Making the Issues National

The mayor won reelection with 54 percent of the vote. We called it a mandate, but privately the victory was tinged with bitterness. He believed that if Hynes had not dropped out at the last minute—if he'd dropped out two weeks earlier—we could have run a real campaign against Vrdolyak instead of holding to our policy of not even acknowledging he was a viable candidate. That might have cut into the 40 percent that Eddie was able to win.

That 40 percent hurt. Even the presumably progressive 43rd Ward (where I lived) went for Vrdolyak—in fact, the stats were approximately the same as Eddie's own 10th Ward. "We have to face it," the mayor said. "We've leveled off at about 53, 54 percent. That's about all we're going to get." I hoped he was wrong, that he had learned the wrong lesson from the campaign, that we could continue to build steadily through the next term and he could be what he always wanted to be—a truly consensus, mandated mayor.

He didn't waste time worrying about it. He had other things to worry about.

Throughout the second half of his first term, he became increasingly sensitive to what he called the "power grabs" of Republicans at the state and federal level. In years past, a certain balance of power was written into the charters of such city-based institutions as McCormick Place, the largest convention center in the world. Although both the mayor and the governor made appointments to such boards, the mayor held the majority, or chose the executive director.

Now he detected a strategic shift, as one institution after another came into contention. He believed that white Democrats were making deals with Republican leaders to divest the city of many of its prerogatives. If Chicago were "going black," they seemed to be saying, Cook County was still solidly white. If these institutions could be made regional, or given over to a state authority, they could be "saved" from the changing demographics.

In fact, Chicago wasn't "going black." As the mayor was fond of saying, by the year 2000 it was supposed to be one-third each, black, white and Latino or Asian. Coalition politics, dominated by progressives—that would be the mayor's base into the year 2003.

But the immediate political problem was to stave off the takeover attempts. McCormick Place, Navy Pier, O'Hare and Midway Airports, the stadium authorities, the Port District, the Park District, the Chicago Housing Authority and the Chicago Public Schools—in the mayor's world view, all were going to be considered fair game by disgruntled whites, by Republicans, and by their media allies.

It was a political ploy, he believed, with deep ideological and racial roots. It was supported by the Reagan administration as part of a more general attempt to undercut black Democrat mayors. It would be fueled by racially-based anxieties of white property holders, including national corporations based in Chicago. And it would ultimately serve an unholy alliance of the Eddies and Gov. Jim Thompson.

While he would continue to hold forth at the local level, he saw the need for operations in a wider theater of war. He would take his issues to the national level, in the context of the 1988 presidential election. Housing, education, jobs, health care—these were all local issues on which he could speak from hands-on experience. But they were ultimately issues that could be resolved only by federal policy. Of those four key issues, housing was the one he decided to make his main theme—more by necessity than choice.

It was thrust on him when problems with the Chicago Housing Authority threatened to become a major campaign issue in late 1986.

The mayor's CHA boss Renault Robinson told us he was going to miss a HUD deadline for anticipated funding. The U.S. Department of Housing and Urban Development had already given him extensions; this missed deadline would mean lost funds.

The *Chicago Tribune* began a new series of stories on municipal management, assisted by a steady stream of information from their contacts with HUD—in the Chicago regional office and in Washington. Initially we were concerned that the exposés were deliberately targeted on the electioneering incumbent, but we soon realized that the CHA stories, lurid as they were, would not be a serious campaign issue. The reasons were simple: the problems had arisen under Daley, and worsened under Byrne. Vrdolyak and his supporters had also had a hand in it. The Republican Don Haider had started out in the Byrne cabinet. The only candidate who might have been able to turn the CHA problems into political capital was County Assessor Tom Hynes, and he was trying to run a nonconfrontational campaign.

But if the CHA mess wasn't a serious liability in the campaign, neither did it go away when the campaign was over. In fact, it was just beginning.

Once during "Council Wars," when we were talking about press coverage of the issues, the mayor said with a laugh that he felt like "What's his name, Errol Flynn,"—he mimicked swordplay— "fighting with both Eddies and all the press as well."

The fight with HUD over the CHA was another duel that he said we were fighting two ways—with the Reagan administration and with the *Chicago Tribune.*

There was a mixed cast of characters for what would become a long-running drama for us (for the record, all were black):

Renault Robinson, who had been appointed to the CHA board by Jane Byrne, and in August 1983 appointed to the chairmanship by Harold Washington. He had been an organizer of the Afro-American Patrolmen's League, which had worked to reform the Chicago Police Department after the murder of Black Panther Fred Hampton. He had been an outspoken critic of former CHA mismanagement from his position within the system. He was considered a staunch political ally of the mayor. The mayor called him a "folk hero among the residents of the CHA." For a few months, in the long-standing tradition of CHA chairmen, he had personally managed the housing authority; but in the middle of the bitter winter of 1983–84, with boilers breaking down and management decisions turning sour, he had been forced to hire Erwin France as interim manager, while a national search was made for a professional.

Zirl Smith was the housing professional who had been hired in the spring of 1984, to run the day-to-day operations of the CHA. He was hailed by the *Trib* and many civic leaders as the professional whose skills were overdue. Robinson, who was on a collision course with Smith probably from the day Smith was hired, felt he was a bureaucrat who made all the right sounds but couldn't deal with the realities of the CHA.

Rev. B. Herbert Martin, usually described as the "mayor's pastor," a minister and community activist who also benefited from city contracts. He had been appointed to the CHA board shortly after the mayor gained control of City Council, and in January 1987 was the mayor's choice to succeed Robinson.

Brenda Gaines, deputy chief of staff in the Washington administration, formerly Washington's housing commissioner, who was loaned to the CHA for most of 1987 as their interim replacement for Smith.

James E. Baugh, the Washington-based HUD executive who was HUD's highest ranking official for public housing, with the official title of "general deputy assistant secretary of public and Indian housing." He had known Zirl Smith for years.

Gertrude Jordan, who headed HUD's regional office in Chicago; she had strong ties to Gov. Thompson, with whom she worked before coming to HUD. She also apparently had developed personal or political ties to Robinson and to Rev. Martin.

All the relationships were complicated, and the mayor was always uncertain as to who was really working for whom. Clearly, he said, Baugh had been commissioned to embarrass the mayor, and to help the Reagan administration in their nationwide campaign to discredit Democrat incumbents' management of public housing. That move was not simply political but ideological as well, a key element in a campaign to dismantle public housing programs altogether.

In addition, on a professional level, there was apparently a turf war going on between Ms. Jordan in Chicago and Mr. Baugh in Washington. That didn't make Jordan the mayor's ally, but it complicated analysis of options.

On a personal level Ms. Jordan seemed to have a problem with Brenda Gaines. And she seemed sympathetic to Rev. Martin.

None of these observations were very serviceable when it came to solving the problems of the CHA, or even in deciding who it was we were confronting. We never did finally resolve all the questions we were raising. But we did make the decision to fight HUD for control of the CHA, and we did refuse them the day-to-day management authority they were seeking to take from us.

Mayor Washington didn't have a comprehensive solution for the CHA. He even said once he didn't believe there *was* a solution. The

CHA didn't have a problem, he said, they *were* the problem. But at the same time, for better or worse, those ugly buildings were home; they were the "neighborhood," for 145,000 neighbors. And they were precincts full of voters.

"They're obscene," he said, "an abomination. They should never have been built in the first place." He echoed the conventional wisdom that the high-rises by their very design were unsuitable for habitation by anyone but young singles and the elderly. And by crowding them together in a forbidding solid wall for three miles along the Dan Ryan highway, they became a monument to the public policy of mass segregation.

"No parent is going to be able to supervise kids from twenty stories up," he said. "No rest rooms, no place to play. They built those elevators exposed to the elements up the side of the building, the elevators are going to break down, and so the kids are going to relieve themselves in the hallway; so the buildings stink. There's never enough money for maintenance; talk about community pride, even professional managers can't keep them in repair. It's custom made for gang recruiting. They're horrible, horrible."

He was half-serious about reviving a plan to sell or lease the top floors of the buildings—those particularly unsuited for family life—to U.S. agencies, especially the military. "You put the army up there," he said, "and those elevators would run."

The only long-term solution was to do away with them, redevelop the land they were on for lower density living.

But not until there was some guarantee of housing for those who would be displaced. Naturally, they would have to be moved in advance of any demolition plan. No solution was worth listening to if it didn't consider that problem up front.

Chicago, like other cities, was facing a growing shortage of affordable housing. Like the old joke says, those buildings were unsafe, unsanitary, almost uninhabitable—and we needed more of them! The problems with the CHA were thus only a small band of a spectrum of housing issues, from the plight of the homeless, to the shortage of single-resident occupancy (transient) dwellings, all the way up to the average homeowner who could no longer afford her home. All homeowners, in every bracket, were going to be affected by the looming problems, but they would be especially serious for those currently living in public housing.

Mayor Washington pressed the point that the loss of housing was largely due to the phasing out of federal housing programs by the Reagan administration. Not only were the programs not keeping up with new housing needs, but the existing buildings were being lost at the rate of 70,000 units a year, according to HUD's own figures.

Mayor Washington said it, and he meant it literally, that "nobody can make the CHA work—the only solution is just to get rid of it. What you need in the meantime is someone with Renault Robinson's skills to keep it all together. You got a lot of brothers and sisters in there that don't have anything at all if they don't have confidence in Renault." His immediate priority was not to solve CHA problems, but to contain them, for the 145,000 citizens of what would be, separately incorporated, Illinois' second largest city. In the permafrost of his defensiveness with the media, he was preoccupied with the PR problems. Management efforts were directed at damage control, not root causes. His first priority was to "defend Chicago" against a great raid on the CHA.

In trying to defuse CHA as a campaign issue, our position was that the federal government, playing footsie with previous Machine administrations in Chicago, was principally responsible for the mess things were in.

That in its development, it was a mid-century twist to the turn-of-the-century "black belt"—a horrendous concentration-camp approach to black containment. All sides, he felt, should begin from that premise.

That though it was the *second largest* public housing program in the country, the CHA had never placed higher than 12th in the list of recipients of HUD funding.

That though the CHA had well over 50 percent of the Illinois public housing, it received just about a third of state public housing funds.

That previous managers of the housing authority had used it as a patronage haven and a bond market, and that the federal government had winked at 20 years of such mismanagement by Charles Swibel and others.

That HUD itself was riddled with corruption: in May it was reported by the *Sun-Times* that a HUD director of property management for the Midwest region, based in Chicago, was "permitted to resign quietly after investigators learned his agency had awarded $710,000 in improper, no-bid contracts to a firm his wife secretly helped set up." Before the year was over, Baugh would be under federal investigation. The *Washington Post* carried a series of stories that tied him to a $399,000 contract awarded to a firm connected to D.C. businessman John Clyburn, also under investigation, who employed Baugh's wife.

We had already learned how difficult it is to outshout a newspaper with the circulation of the *Chicago Tribune*. The mayor was determined, though, that HUD would not take over the CHA.

At least, not without a fight. At the same time he was sorely tempted to take a different tack. Some days, he said, he really believed his best course would be to lose this fight and let HUD assume the legal liabilities and the cost of maintaining the CHA. But on other days he considered the political downside, as well as his ideological preferences, and stiffened his resolve.

Still, it was sometimes nearly impossible to steer a straight course, given the management turmoil at CHA and the internal politics among board members, between board members and resident councils, between various coalitions in these groups and Gertrude Jordan, and between Rev. Martin and Brenda Gaines.

A sampling of the management problems can be gleaned from coverage by the *Sun-Times* of May 3, 1987:

> [Board members] Renault Robinson, Leon D. Finney, Jr., and Earl Neal made "pivotal personnel and financial decisions...often without informing other board members...
>
> "Half of the stuff I didn't know until I read it in the newspapers," [former CHA board member] Letitia Nevill said.
>
> Neal...admitted he did not pay attention to the capital spending that drained the CHA's operating budget, provoking the current crisis...
>
> Finney said he became alarmed about the CHA's financial practices in 1985, pressured Smith for details, and was stonewalled. He said he did not go public with his concerns because he was intimidated by a news media that was pro-Smith and anti-Robinson.
>
> "I predicted that we were going to be in deep trouble if we could not hold the staff accountable and we could never hold staff accountable because...if you spoke out against Zirl, the news media branded you as meddler," Finney said.
>
> "We could never get an accurate accounting out of Zirl or out of the accounting department. I asked when can we wrap our hands around this whole mess? How much is in operating, how much is in capital? It

was always a promise, 'We'll get it to you.' We could never get the truth."

George Cramer, the CHA's former chief fiscal officer, was fired by Smith in 1986 after alerting board members to improper fund transfers ordered by Smith. "If corrective measures had been taken... when the board got word that there was mismanagement going on, perhaps we wouldn't be in the shape we're in today," said Cramer, who was rehired by board members the same day.

"I've never experienced anything like CHA in my life. I've seen better controls at a corner candy store than at this place."

The containment of the CHA crisis proceeded in several simultaneous arenas. The mayor forced some management changes; first Smith's resignation in favor of Brenda Gaines' interim appointment; then Robinson's resignation, when he proved reluctant to let Brenda do her job. I had just finished a rationale for keeping Robinson on the job when the mayor phoned me and said he'd decided to cut him loose, and asked me to prepare a resignation statement for Robinson and a followup response that the mayor could deliver.

The mayor also decided to personally intervene in the public relations skirmishes. Where earlier he had wanted a low personal profile, he decided he had to get out in front. Rev. Martin had commandeered the public relations staff at CHA, and they were working at cross-purposes to Gaines.

The flashiest arena in which we confronted HUD was in Washington—at HUD and at the White House.

Early on July 7, 1987, as we were flying to New York City where the mayor would deliver a late morning speech on affirmative action to the NAACP, he asked me to make three reservations for the D.C. shuttle.

"We're going to Washington," he said, "to see George Bush."

A prominent black Chicago Republican, attorney Jewel Lafontant, had agreed to set up a meeting with Vice President George Bush, to see what might be done to call off the dogs at HUD. All the arrangements were to be made in strictest confidence—he hadn't wanted to use the staff at City Hall because he didn't want any leaks. The security staff didn't know. His scheduler didn't know.

"You and I and Howard Saffold," he said. "We have to get there by 3:00."

I told Saffold what was happening, and he did whatever he had to do to reassign his security team without telling them the mayor was going to D.C.

In New York, while the mayor made his first major speech attacking the administration's nomination of Judge Robert Bork to the U.S. Supreme Court, Saffold arranged for a car to get us to LaGuardia, and I arranged for a car to meet us in D.C. Tickets for the shuttle could be bought on the plane; I would put them on my American Express. If we caught a 1:00 shuttle, we should arrive in Washington in plenty of time.

He finished his speech at about 12:30, and brushed past the New York press. The police vehicle taking us to LaGuardia was a compact car, and the three of us were cramped in the back seat. But we were grateful for the small size, because the driver had to thread his way between lanes to get us to the airport by 1:00.

As it turned out the plane was on the ground for a full hour, and we landed in D.C. after 3:00. In Washington, when the car I had arranged wasn't immediately apparent in front of us, I hailed us a cab. The mayor had made the rendezvous personally with Ms. Lafontant, and had said we'd meet at the White House gate. I had to guess which gate Lafontant would assume he meant, and directed the driver.

We were late, but the vice president was running even later, so no harm done. Saffold and I cooled our heels—it was a blisteringly hot day—in a White House waiting room while the mayor conferred with George Bush. When he was finished we exited through separate doors, then ran into the vice president as he was leaving. We later heard he had an appointment in Ohio to help promote the administration's campaign to appoint Robert Bork.

Did the meeting with George Bush help? We calculated that it couldn't hurt. It would be helpful even if all it meant was that HUD understood the mayor was in this fight to stay.

I traded in our New York return tickets for our trip back to Chicago, and we came home that evening. On the plane we ran into Joel Kaplan, one of the *Tribune* reporters who had been covering the confrontation with HUD. I was sure our cover was blown, but he was only mildly surprised to see us. After all, the mayor traveled to Washington fairly frequently, and how could he know this trip had not been announced. Our secret stayed safe until we decided to announce it weeks later, along with a litany of other extraordinary measures we'd employed, while we "left no stone unturned in the search for so-lutions."

During the fight with HUD, Barefield joined CHA board members and attorneys in a series of meetings with HUD officials, in D.C. and in Chicago. When the CHA board went into its final confrontation with Baugh and his staff in Washington, the mayor asked me to make the trip with them. He was concerned that we weren't achieving a resolution, and he was particularly concerned that Baugh's bullying tone, together with the beating we were taking in the *Tribune*, might overcome the stamina of the board. It was the board, in the final anal-ysis, and not the mayor, who had the ultimate statutory authority to resolve the matter.

He was in particular concerned that Rev. Martin might waver—he was even concerned that Martin had negotiated a separate peace. He wanted me to stay in touch with him throughout the day, by tele-phone, and apprise him of our progress. In particular, he wanted me to give him an opportunity to intervene if by any chance Ernie or the board should appear to be caving in under the pressure.

Since my phone calls would have to be placed from within HUD headquarters—from the citadel of the opposition—I decided to equip myself with a portable telephone. I knew they could be rented at Hertz, when renting a car. I didn't need the car, and tried to leave it in the Hertz lot to save time at check-in, but that proved too compli-cated to arrange. I took the car, the phone, and extra battery packs, and caught up with the delegation at HUD.

At several prearranged times during the day I kept the mayor up to date. Sometimes I called during the middle of meetings, sometimes from the corridors, even from the sidewalk—there's a *Tribune* photo that shows me in the background as the delegation departed HUD, making a phone call from the street.

The mayor needn't have worried. His board members were solid as a rock, and Rev. Martin was among the most eloquent and most defi-ant. Although the mayor had been momentarily concerned about the commitment of publisher Bruce Sagan, a white liberal who was not considered an entirely known quantity, it turned out that there was no one more philosophically and emotionally solid on maintaining CHA independence than this man.

Baugh took the position, and reiterated it through endless negotiat-ing sessions, that we had no choice, that HUD held all the cards, that he was humoring us even to be giving us a hearing. But in the end the compromise that HUD accepted was essentially that which we had begun by offering. HUD had backed down from its threat to take over the CHA, and the mayor had agreed to restructure its management in the way HUD had wanted to. The process of turning around the mismanagement of this huge agency, this city-within-a-city, on which so many souls depended for the bare essentials, as well as their quality of life, had begun.

One problem that didn't end with the HUD resolution was the mayor's increasing disappointment with Rev. Martin. Mayor Washington had reluctantly let Renault Robinson go when he fussed with Brenda. Now Martin was feuding with Brenda, and it was turning into a pissing match involving other board members, residents' councils, the media, and Gertrude Jordan. Rev. Martin was reported seen at meetings which Jordan attended, without informing Brenda they were taking place. And it appeared Martin was also a source of leaks that were embarrassing the administration.

The mayor made it clear—to Barefield, to Brenda Gaines, and to me—that Rev. Martin was not long for the CHA board. Although the move would have to be done at an auspicious time, it was clear he was out of there.

In time Martin would indeed resign from the CHA board, following a series of political maneuvers centered on board factionalism and CHA management. But by that time he would have performed his final function as "the mayor's pastor," conducting services at his grave.

Among the tactics we'd employed in the showdown with HUD was to get Mayor Washington named chairman of the housing task force of the U.S. Conference of Mayors. Now he intended to cultivate that position into a meaningful role. He sought to book speaking engagements, to prepare white papers, and to convene small groups of mayors, to develop that issue.

He would gain a certain prominence among Democrats on Capitol Hill, and among the public at large, if he were successful in his confrontation with HUD. Besides that, if he could show that Baugh, for all his bark, had rubber teeth, he might help encourage other resistance efforts in other cities.

He had made housing a key article of his Second Inaugural address. He had promoted the issue widely. Now it would become a constant theme as he laid the groundwork for his involvement in the 1988 Presidential elections.

His problems with Reagan's federal policies were fundamental and at times almost obsessive. There were occasions when he dismissed the Republican agenda as purely political, even crassly financial; Chicago-style power grabs writ large. But more often he would wax bitter on the philosophical premise of Reagan-Republicanism, as he perceived it—the irresponsible abandonment of the *real* problems confronting America.

"What this guy is saying," he said to me on the plane, on the way to a speech he was making in Columbus, "is that the people walking the streets because they have no place to live, that's not 'his problem.' Housing falling apart all over the country, not 'his problem.'

"He's the fucking president. He's the chief executive of the nation. He's not a figurehead, he's the CEO. Can you imagine what would happen if I were to say—you pick the issue—'that's not my problem'?

"He's washing his hands of us, all our nasty little detail problems. But what does that mean? Does that mean these are our problems, these are our fault? We're on our own? Mayors have to be responsible, where the president isn't? Good luck and God bless you? Like the man said, if we were a foreign government we'd get foreign aid.

"And the Republicans at the state level are no better."

It was at the Labor Day Parade, in September 1987, that he motioned me over to where he and Jesse Jackson were talking. He threw an arm around my shoulder.

"Al, you know Reverend Jackson," he said. We had worked together briefly in the mayor's campaign, and there was a mutual respect between us. "I don't want to announce this yet, we'll talk about it, but I'm going to endorse Jesse for President." I nodded.

"I want to do it someplace—not City Hall—wherever we all think it might make the most sense." He waited for my reaction.

I said the obvious: "We should pick a site that makes a statement. Some place that captures the significance of the endorsement in terms of the real issues. Some place with symbolic and historic value." Jesse was right on the same wavelength. "Symbolic and historic significance," he repeated.

We exchanged phone numbers, and within a few days I was meeting at PUSH with the Rev. Willie Barrow and various progressive political and labor leaders.

A site on the Chicago border was recommended—a G.E. plant in

Cicero, where layoffs were threatened because G.E. was planning to close down some operations. I wasn't crazy about leaving Chicago, but the site had everything we needed: a receptive crowd of black, white, brown, good media backdrops whether we did it indoors or out, and symbolic value.

I made a trip to the plant and checked the location out, then prepared a full briefing for the security detail. The fact of our endorsement was to stay secret until we were ready to release it, and since the campaign I had found new leaks in my own staff.

The morning of the announcement we telephoned Jesse and suggested a rendezvous at a small soul food restaurant halfway between Hyde Park and Cicero. David Frost had been doing a series of presidential candidate profiles, and he was traveling with Jesse that day, so a half hour before the mayor made his endorsement, Jesse Jackson, David Frost, Harold Washington and Alton Miller were jammed into a plastic-covered booth in a small diner that offered "Coon Dinner on Tuesdays," which was choked with security personnel, Frost's TV technicians and their equipment, and an occasional stunned neighbor who had just come in for some ham hocks and greens.

The mayor had no misgivings about endorsing Jesse, or about endorsing him as early as he did. He was one of few prominent black Democrats who supported Jesse—then or later. But he owed Jesse, and more importantly, he believed in him. "He's a force for good," was his standard reply whenever he was questioned about his endorsement.

I've found that Chicagoans either don't know Jesse Jackson, or they feel they know him too well. Perhaps it's the old truism that a prophet is not without honor, but in his own country, and among his own kin, and in his own house.

Almost anywhere else in the United States, Jesse is respected as a powerful force in American politics, and as a mind to reckon with. I have always been surprised by the contempt that familiarity has seemed to breed among many, black and white, in his own town. Perhaps they remember him too vividly from his dashiki days. Perhaps they resent what they consider his shameless hustle of white businesses, during his several efforts for black economic and political empowerment.

The only ambivalence that Mayor Washington ever evidenced was when it came to sharing the limelight with Jesse. He made it clear to me that in politics you sometimes have to boss or be bossed. When he was still consolidating his local base, during his second year in office, it had been necessary to show national Democrats as well as local constituents that there was only one progressive leader in Chicago. Rather than endorse Jesse he had straddled the question by "supporting" him but running his own favorite-son slate of delegates for the Democratic convention.

But he indicated to me that Jesse had come to respect the mayor's political requirements, and the two had always achieved accommodation and cooperation. He was grateful to Jesse for his support, and he was absolutely unhesitant about accepting it, whether he was being questioned by a Jewish activist on the lakefront or a white ethnic in Kelly's ward or a black South Sider.

So I was surprised at the mayor's unsolicited comment to me, almost by way of reassurance, that he and other blacks who were backing Jesse had the candidate's promise that when they decided, he'd withdraw from the race. The mayor mentioned this several times, and each time it was almost a non sequitur from our previous conversation, as though it had once again occurred to the mayor to make a record of it. He was under pressure from other national Democrats, including just about every black elected official, not to endorse Jesse. I think he was reassuring me that what Jesse's black supporters were doing was not irresponsible from the standpoint of the party's national agenda in 1988.

Whenever questioned about his candidacy, the mayor would make all the obligatory references to "when" Jackson won the nomination, never "if." If a reporter asked him to name a second choice—that is, if the reporter implied there was a symbolic choice in Jesse, and then a real choice in Dukakis or Simon or Cuomo—the mayor never fell for the premise. He'd made his choice, he'd say: Jesse.

But if a reporter, particularly one from a national publication, accepted the answer and then shifted the line of questioning into the mechanics of politics—if, for example, she asked whether Cuomo could be lured into the race—the mayor would proceed along a different conversational course, what some reporters would call a realistic rather than idealistic mindset, and discuss the convention in post-Jesse terms.

After listening to him several times, and calling his attention to the subtle shift, I saw that twinkle in his eye, and the twitch of a smile as he thanked me for reminding him he had slipped. Clearly he was doing it on purpose, and it was a sophisticated rusticism he was practicing, to send signals to the reporter that although he would not be quoted in any way other than total support for Jesse, he was not averse to talking turkey.

The mayor died early in Jackson's campaign. Knowing the mayor, and having seen his genuine respect for his younger colleague, I doubt that he would ever have enjoyed dealing with such a problem as presuming to tell Jesse it was time to withdraw. On the other hand, the conditions were spelled out up front, he said. And if Democratic party officials had ever been required to come to terms with Jesse, it would certainly have been Harold Washington who would be asked to bell the cat.

More importantly, Mayor Washington would have been of service in the post-convention campaign.

He had met with Gov. Mike Dukakis at the U.S. Conference of Mayors meeting in Nashville the previous summer. He had spoken with all the Democratic presidential candidates, and while his first choice was always the non-candidate Cuomo, and his public preferences were Illinois leaders Jackson and Simon, his meeting with Dukakis, of all his meetings with candidates, was the one he enjoyed most. Dukakis may have been briefed on the mayor's interest in housing issues, and his preoccupation with municipal financial management; in any case, where the mayor spoke in generalities with the other presidential aspirants (not counting Simon and Jackson—he didn't have to set up special meetings with them), he talked brass tacks with Dukakis. The mutual respect was obvious.

So I have no doubt that had Harold Washington lived, there would have been a clear line of communication between the Jackson faction and the Dukakis campaign. And I'm personally convinced that while there may have been no difference in the national outcome, the slim margin in Illinois would have been reversed. Governor Thompson would have been damaged politically by the loss of Illinois to the Democrats, and Mayor Washington's own clout in Springfield would have been decisively strengthened.

Finally, the mayor's partnership with Jackson would have multiplied the effectiveness of both men at the national level, in the continuing effort to restore a viable, practical, humane liberal agenda in the Democratic party.

Incidentally, Jesse Jackson asked me to join his presidential campaign as his press secretary shortly after the mayor died. I met with his chief aide, Frank Watkins, and with Gerald Austin, his campaign manager. I flew with him and his sons in their six-seater campaign plane to Montgomery, Alabama, and then to a number of towns in Iowa, early in the campaign, as we prepared to work together.

I prepared a paper for him dealing with his Israel/Palestinian Arab policies, and drafted a letter for him in response to an unfavorable magazine article. He had welcomed me aboard, and announced my hiring to WLS-TV's Andy Shaw, when I got a message that the deal was off. I was told a few days later by Gerry Austin that Bob Johnson of Johnson Publishing, major campaign backers of Rev. Jackson, had instructed him to drop me. "They say they won't withdraw their support from him," Austin said, "but they won't go out of their way to boost him. It's reverse discrimination."

It was a fact of life. I'd been used to wearing the jacket whenever the mayor had to stall or cancel a press interview. On one occasion, when "creature comforts" caused a change in his schedule, he had missed an interview and left a Johnson (*Ebony* magazine) writer waiting. We had a devil of a time scheduling their photographer to come to his home for a two-hour shoot—it was almost impossible to schedule anything for more than an hour. Still, it was part of my job to take the heat whenever he had to duck out. Now that rap was following me beyond his lifespan: I found the irony amusing—I was an equal opportunity scapegoat for the media's problems with the mayor. In any case, having had a sample of the breakneck pace of the Jackson campaign, I'm grateful to Bob Johnson or whomever kept me free to write this book.

18

Good Times

I worked for Mayor Washington for one thousand days
(a thousand and ten, to be exact, but we took a few
days off), and the sense of adventure never wore thin.

Some of the fondest memories are of the simplest moments. Those
memories are particularly rich because I never took those moments
for granted. There was never a time when I wasn't consciously—
self-consciously—enjoying the adventure. I suspect many of us who
worked with Harold Washington had the same experience.

▭ *Restaurants*

Restaurants figure prominently in those memories. The mayor was
scheduled tightly throughout the day, and unless he had a luncheon
speech somewhere, lunch wasn't on his calendar; he usually made do
with a salami sandwich from the little shop on the 10th floor of City
Hall. But whenever we had two outside events with a half hour or
more between them, it didn't make sense to return to the Hall, and
we'd usually end up getting a bowl of soup somewhere.

He used that down time to catch up with the day's newspapers,
paging through the *Defender,* the *Trib* or the *Sun-Times* while I went
down the checklist of issues in my Day-Timer. About half our conversation was specific to current issues, the remainder a more general
discussion of life and the times.

Those restaurant visits were great opportunities to mix with voters, too. He was welcome wherever he went. In quarters where he
might have polled less than 1 percent of the vote in 1983, everyone in
the restaurant was excited to see him, to ask for his autograph, to
have a picture taken with him. Frequently we encountered folks like
the elderly woman in a Ukrainian neighborhood who turned around
from the cash register suddenly and found herself face-to-face, ex-
claimed, "It's Mayordaley Washington," and threw her arms around
him in a big hug.

Once I realized we'd be making a lot of stops at restaurants, I had Tumia Romero contact aldermanic offices and prepare a 50-ward restaurant list, so we always had the names of recommended places to eat, no matter where our city travels found us.

He couldn't have been one hundred pounds overweight without overeating, it's clear, but I can't reconcile that with my experience. Most days he seemed to be starting without breakfast; lunch was rarely more than the salami sandwich, maybe with a bowl of soup, and a Coke. He would joke about the big meals he fixed for himself at home in the evenings, when his work was done, so I assume his over-indulgence was too much, too late. Once when I showed up at his apartment late with a speech he needed, he gave me a plate full of ham hocks and greens, leftovers from his supper.

Any nutritionist would be appalled by his basic eating habits. I cringed every time I watched him smear two full butter patties on each small piece of hard roll. And I winced at the thought of all those calories in every Coca Cola that he so casually washed down. The few times we ate a full restaurant meal, especially at Izola's or Gladys' on the South Side, his tastes ran toward the substantial meat and potatoes specials, with an emphasis on deep-fried. Even in Loop restaurants, dining with a corporate leader or a media executive, the mayor was likely to unfold his napkin with a shake, tuck the corner into his collar, and spread that butter on those rolls.

You don't tell your boss he's fat, or that the cultural patterns that shaped his eating habits should be reexamined. But his pals like Howard Saffold and Delores Woods did make an effort to keep him mindful of his diet. Whether their influence extended into his late-hours culinary activity is doubtful.

▭ *People* ▭

Mayor Washington enjoyed public attention, and not just because his admirers were voters. He enjoyed people, wherever he met them, and particularly in neighborhood settings. In black neighborhoods, every time another woman rushed up to him to give him a squeeze—"Got to give my mayor some *sugar!*"—he was genuinely delighted. "The old ladies, especially, they like me," he told me, pleased. "I don't know what it is I got, but the old ladies, white and black, it appeals to them."

I was touched to see him interact with black men down on their luck. His security detail would perk up, but without real alarm, when he would be approached on the street. Without a hint of condescension, the mayor would shake the man's hand, respond to whatever he might have to say, perhaps close with a restrained, "Hang in there, my brother." It was clear that he was sensitive to their special need for a sense of dignity that a patronizing attitude, even a slightly solicitous manner, would offend.

From time to time, passing through a crowd, someone—always black women, of varying ages—would hold out a lottery ticket. Without pausing to give it any attention he would simply touch it in passing, a discreet lick of his fingers over the outstretched ticket as he moved to shake another hand or pat another shoulder. The first time I saw that I asked what it meant. "Luck," he told me, slightly reticent. "Some folks believe that the king can cure your illness, or bring you luck in the lottery."

He enjoyed his celebrity, and was especially pleased to be recognized in other cities, even in the streets of Jerusalem and Mexico City. In Mexico City and Puerto Rico he was frequently told that he was a daily hero in the "Council Wars" fight, through the coverage of Chicago's WGN-TV, Channel 9, which was seen via cable across the continent. On the other hand, he was amused and a little miffed when two black attendants in New York's LaGuardia airport, seeing an entourage and a waiting limousine, asked him in a familiar manner whether he knew who all the fuss was for. He grinned and told them it must be somebody really important.

He enjoyed crowds. The members of his security detail were the ones who hated to see him in crowds, he said, because then they had to go to work. "I can't spend all my time protecting you," he would joke with Frank Lee or Al Rowe. "I've got better things to do. People expect me to run their city." And he was half serious when he groused, from time to time, that being followed around by a security detail who never gave him a minute's peace was the most onerous thing in his job description. "If these guys had their way," he'd sometimes mutter, "I'd never leave 5300. And I'd never meet anyone. And I'd never be elected."

Though it gave the detail some grief, for his part, he enjoyed wading through well-wishers, shaking hands, smiling till he laughed, trading quick oneliners as he passed. From the Tillman campaign in 1985, through his public appearances in his final weeks, it seemed to me that we were always wading through throngs. Given the temporary insanity of the 1983 campaign, it is not surprising that from time to time Saffold could sufficiently impress his boss with a sense of his vulnerability and persuade the mayor to wear a bullet-proof vest. In fact, it's surprising that he couldn't be talked into one more often.

The mayor didn't spend much time with the families of people who worked with him. It was as though it would have been an awkward personal burden for him to become too acquainted with the wives and husbands and children of the staff from whom he had summoned so many hours. He wasn't solicitous about our family life because, I suppose, he really didn't want to know. But when he was with our loved ones, it was as though they were—temporarily—a part of his own family.

On the night of his climactic victory over Jane Byrne in the 1987 primary, we waited at his apartment until Byrne's concession, then headed to the victory rally. I had told Cindy I'd probably be finished by midnight, but we were clearly running much later. I thought I might be able to call her from the car on the way down, to say I'd be late. Instead, I was furiously writing the mayor's acceptance speech in large block letters on 5 × 8 cards, even as we turned into the driveway at the hotel. It was midnight by the time we finished the rally, and Mary Ella, the mayor and I were wedged in the back seat of his limousine, heading back to 5300 where I had left my car. It was the first time I had been near a phone all night. Still exhilarated from the victory, I wanted to find some way to include Cindy in the excitement. "Mayor," I said, "you'd be doing me a big favor if you'd tell my wife where I am." I dialed her and when she answered—she'd been watching the rally on TV—he got on the phone and told her, "This is your mayor speaking. I hope you don't mind that I had to borrow your husband today, but I'm hereby giving him special dispensation to be late tonight." I'm not sure how she responded but he chuckled, and warned her, "Now that's only good up to about a half hour from now. If he's any later than that, it's not my fault."

Though he didn't spend much time with the families of his staff, he had a soft spot for their kids. He always enjoyed children, whether with their parents or in a classroom or hospital ward. He was natural and unaffected in his conversation with them. I was surprised at his easy manner, considering that he had no children of his own. He told me, with evident pride, that he had come to realize what a role model he was. I thought he was making an obvious statement, but he repeated it with a kind of wonder. He said that was what had caused him to quit smoking, when he really focused on the fact that every move he made and every word he said would be imitated by some youngster, somewhere.

I never saw Harold Washington with a cigarette. He had made the decision to stop smoking in 1984, he told me, and never went back to tobacco.

□ *Travel* ⸏

Mayor Washington enjoyed travel for its own sake, and he enjoyed most of the destinations. Travel costs were minimal because usually the organization that had requested him as a speaker picked up the tab for four roundtrips in first class, a hotel suite for the mayor with an adjoining room for security, and two other rooms, usually in less pricey parts of the hotel, for Kelly and me. Meals, other than the dinner at which he spoke, were put on the hotel tab. Or Mayor Washington would peel off a bill from the wad he always carried—I don't believe he owned a credit card—and pick up the check for his entire group, including the security detail.

As I told him one morning, at breakfast in the restaurant of New York's Waldorf-Astoria, he had gotten me into a whole class of hotels that I never expected to stay in. The King David in Jerusalem, the Imperial in Tokyo, the Jianguo in Beijing, the Beverly Wilshire when we went to Los Angeles for Hugh Hefner's fundraiser at the Playboy Mansion. On the other hand, in New York and Washington, Miami and Hartford, Nashville and Seattle, Carmel and Columbus, and most other U.S. trips, we stayed in upscale but soulless modern hotels, far from whatever local color the city might afford. He got a kick out of my practice of showing up late for breakfast, having already eaten somewhere else in town. I would get up two hours before anyone else, and do an early morning tour before our first appointment, which was usually a breakfast meeting of the mayor's party in his suite, to go over the day's agenda.

In Israel, Mayor Washington was wary of the political liabilities in some sectors of his community. He had long since established himself as a friend of Israel, in the U.S. Congress and elsewhere; and he was enthralled by his visits to biblical sites, including Nazareth, Bethlehem, Capernaum and Jerusalem. He was fascinated by the geopolitical education he was getting from his meeting with President Chaim Herzog and Prime Minister Shimon Peres, and he genuinely enjoyed Tel Aviv Mayor Shlomo Lahat (he loved repeating that name, which he did on the slightest pretext, for the rest of his life), and the inimitable Mayor Teddy Kollek of Jerusalem.

And yet he was concerned lest there be a perception that he was being "used" by the Jewish lobbyists who were making arrangements for the trip. The only Arabs we were meeting were people, like the mayor of Bethlehem, who had been approved by Israeli officials.

Once we arrived in Israel, and the circumstances were evident, he asked me to make certain that we include an independent Arab leader on his agenda. That proved awkward for our Jewish sponsors, who were personally cooperative but professionally obligated.

So I made an an independent contact in East Jerusalem, through an Israeli Arab reporter who had come to cover the mayor's visit. Not wishing to cause an incident, the mayor kept his side trip a secret. He was able to fool the press traveling with us on the bus by sending Saffold on without him. Everyone assumed, until the bus actually pulled away, that since Saffold was there, the mayor could not be anywhere else. The mayor and I paid our visit by cab, crossing into the Arab quarter for several hours of discussions.

The high point of that trip to Israel and then Rome—which included a visit to the Wailing Wall, a tour of the Golan Heights, and an introduction and a gift from Pope John Paul II—was when he piloted a boat across the Sea of Galilee. We traveled from Tiberias to Capernaum, on our way to the Golan Heights, by boat. When he was asked as we left Tiberias if he'd like to take the wheel, he jumped at the chance, and didn't relinquish it until we were pulling in at the dock. He couldn't walk on the water, he acknowledged reluctantly, but he could steer a course across it.

In the Mideast and in the Orient, on our trips to Japan and China, he kept his watch on Chicago time, and made a point of staying abreast of developments back home. I was his point of contact, calling Cindy before I went to bed halfway around the world, having her read me the morning headlines as she was waking; and calling Barefield to exchange information on events at City Hall. The mayor's relationship with Barefield was one of true friendship, as strong as any I ever witnessed between the mayor and his aides; but Barefield's slow, deliberate manner of speech could drive him crazy—especially on a static-ridden international phone call. So he asked me to screen Barefield's information and boil things down to a list of options. Barefield, on his end, had usually already done just that, so the mayor was able to keep up with important breaking issues even from thousands of miles away.

On all our trips, a lot of improvisation was called for. Whenever IGA's Washington lobbyist Ron Gibbs set up an agenda we were in good shape; but most of our trip agendas were an amalgam of different departments' checklists, and there was no real coordination. In Puerto Rico, probably for political reasons, our Latino advisers had neglected to set up—or even to seek—an appointment with Gov. Rafael Hernández-Colón. When we realized the gaffe I walked into the governor's office cold and was able to get Mayor Washington onto his schedule. In Mexico City we missed a rendezvous with a local representative who was scheduled to guide us through a development partially funded by Chicago contributions. We had print reporters and several TV camera crews walking with us that day, and everyone needed to get the event over so they could file. When we realized we were on our own, afoot in a strange neighborhood with an hour to kill—even the bus had left, with instructions to rendezvous in an hour—the mayor and I bluffed our way through the situation, choosing the first construction project we found and rapping with the workers there on the progress they were making. The footage was pretty good; we never did link up with the people we were supposed to meet, but Ald. Jesus Garcia knew his way around and it turned into a productive day of site inspections.

We had the reverse problem there too—our planners had downplayed a meeting scheduled for the mayor in Mexico City's City Council chambers. It was described as a short visit with minor dignitaries, in a closed office. They said the press shouldn't bother to cover it. Our reporters were happy to have a free hour or so to play tourist. We went into a small office, met a dignitary or two, were then ushered into another office, smiled and took photos with another dignitary—and then walked from a waiting room into a gilded, velvet-lined hall, finding ourselves in the center of what seemed to us a Fourth of July celebration in Mayor Washington's honor—bands playing, flags waving, a standing welcome in council chambers, a key to the city, a flowery speech thanking him for his courage and dedication to reform in Chicago. It would have been worth the price of the trip, just to have that moment recorded for Chicagoans of Mexican ancestry to see the respect their mayor had earned in the home country.

But the most memorable improvisation was at a meeting of mayors in Rome. We had been told that the mayor would be making an address on transportation, and a formal presentation—essentially a recitation of statistics—had been developed by a staff writer in one of the departments. But when we arrived for the meeting we found that the group had understood they'd be hearing from the mayor on the subject of political management of urban issues. Like everyone back in Chicago, what they wanted to know was all about "Council Wars."

The mayor paled as he realized he was about to be introduced to deliver an address he hadn't prepared. I began scrawling the speech, outline fashion, in half-inch letters on the backs of the reading cards on which the original speech had been printed. He did his speech by reading a card, elaborating where appropriate, then pausing for the translator, while I finished the next card and handed it to him. Ever after, he loved to tell the story about the speech he delivered with the ink still wet, written even as it was being delivered, in Rome.

☐ *Speeches*

Of all the various functions I performed for Mayor Washington, writing speeches was probably the most satisfying.

When I started with him, I wasn't sure whether he wanted me to write his major speeches, like the State of the City speech which would be delivered a mere six weeks after I came aboard. Several times I had suggested to the mayor that he might prefer to stick with Brian Boyer for these major addresses; my nose certainly wouldn't be out of joint. The mayor left the question open, waiting for me to decide how I wanted to handle it.

The question was decided on our first trip to Washington, D.C., for a series of meetings with Illinois lobbyists and legislators, to promote his federal agenda. The agenda had been planned by IGA, and that office had prepared his briefings and remarks. Reading them on the airplane, the mayor felt they were off point, and gave me a sketchy outline of what he wanted to say. When we arrived at Loew's L'Enfant Plaza Hotel it was dinner time. Some ten people had made the trip from Chicago, and we all met in the hotel dining room. The mayor reiterated for them what he had found lacking in the briefing, and I had the benefit of their comments. Then I left them, with my airplane notes from the mayor, a few additional notes from the dining room, ordered a room service meal and a typewriter, and did several pages of speaking notes for the mayor's use the next morning. That was the first real speech I had written for him—beyond the short responses to media charges or the Eddies' attacks.

After the Washington trip, and my first real speech, I decided I'd write his 1985 "State of the City" myself. I knew the tone of a "New Spirit" that I wanted to set. And even though I was new to the administration, I had reams of information on existing departmental policies (such as I understood them), and the tactical insights of Slim Coleman. I used the occasion as an opportunity to develop the mayor's philosophic outlook on "Council Wars"—basing the argument on conversations I'd had with the mayor.

I enjoyed speechwriting. One taste and I had become a junky. Anyone who tries his or her hand at political writing runs that risk. Speechwriting is amazingly addictive.

Everyone who's ever worked in any bureaucracy is familiar with the phenomenon of policy by press release—the decision isn't final until it's been phrased in an official announcement and made public; up till that deadline, things remain in flux. The policy-making potential of a speech is even greater, when it becomes the personally affirmed word of the boss.

At his request, I wrote speeches for Mayor Washington personally, not to be vetted by any committee. He didn't want them circulated for comment. If he felt they needed to be reviewed, he'd call in a department head and talk through the issues.

We agreed it was important that he have one principal speechwriter, so that his speeches would have an internal consistency that goes beyond surface similarities.

The speechwriter's art is collaborative. In a good working relationship, the speaker is writing his own speech, using a speechwriter instead of a pen. In the same sense that St. Paul is said to have dictated not the words but the essence of certain letters, to be more explicitly elaborated by his amanuensis, a politician's speechwriter is not a ghost writer but a facilitator. Whenever I was asked whether I had written a certain speech, I answered, and truthfully, that Mayor Washington writes all his own stuff.

In the act of speechwriting, the job qualifications of a press secretary are put in high relief. In everything he or she does, a press secretary practices the art of synthesis; of grasping an impossibly wide range of issues, raw data, impressions, priorities, and then making choices. Not his or her own choices, but choices for the boss. The act of synthesizing must come out of an identification with the boss's ob-

jectives and philosophy and life style—but to be an effective and af-
fective art, it must come out of the speechwriter's gut as well.

As in much of a press secretary's job, the challenge is to be both
personally assertive and professionally accessible—simultaneously.
And to make your contribution without being intrusive—the idea
isn't to shape the boss's thinking, but to discover it, coax it out if necessary, help to focus it, and reflect it powerfully. And in the process,
to test for weaknesses and help discover flaws, challenge assump-
tions, point out gaps between intention and effect. Communication is
not a matter of getting the idea out, but of getting it in. It's not
enough that the speech sends the right ideas, but that the target audience receives them.

That collaborative relationship is a prerequisite for a press secretary generally, and for a masterful speechwriter in particular. I didn't
understand then, and still don't, the willingness of some speechwri-
ters (and some politicians) to let the author, not the speaker, take public credit for the speech—as though their boss were an actor or
anchorperson reading a script. I put that in the same category as I
put those PR people who appraise the results of their work by the degree of their own visibility in the process.

I understand that before my time, Brian Boyer produced all his
speeches. After Mayor Washington's death, while editing *Climbing a
Great Mountain: Selected Speeches of Mayor Harold Washington,* I
discovered that the structure of Boyer's speeches, and the metaphors
on which he depended, were similar to mine. But that's because the
structure, the metaphors, the speeches, were neither Boyer's, nor
mine, but Mayor Washington's.

The writing of a speech began with a conversation. The mayor
gave me, in five minutes or less, the effect he hoped to produce. He
sometimes detailed what he considered to be the fundamental arguments supporting his primary points. I took that and put it into the
desired form and length, usually by outlining it first. Then I gave him
both the speech and the outline.

I developed his arguments, using his speaking patterns, his own
imagery and phrases, as well as his ideas. When appropriate I provided back-up support—current stats on the subject, or references to
others' work in the same area. That information usually came from
my staff, who collected data and policy recommendations from city
departments.

I was usually careful to check with the appropriate cabinet members before presenting policies to the mayor, but there were occasions when I'd deliberately avoid the more orderly, more cautious tendencies of the bureaucracy. Dr. Linda Murray, in the city's Health Department, could suggest ways in which we could accelerate our public health programs, whereas the already overburdened chief of staff might not want to make any such commitments. But once the mayor announced it as policy, Barefield would find a way to implement it.

During the preparation for the 1985 "State of the City," I learned to deal with another element of speechwriting: Mayor Washington didn't deliver a formal text well. He was as stilted in reading a speech as he was lively in speaking off the cuff. Yet he felt it necessary to read such formal speeches as his "State of the City" and inaugural addresses. Bill Ware had warned me that he needed plenty of time to absorb the speech, or his delivery would suffer.

I understood the difference between thinking with your eye and thinking with your ear. Mayor Washington, like any poker player or politician whose strength lies in reading people, had an ear for detail. I asked if he'd mind if I gave him a cassette of the speech—I wanted him to hear to intended rhythm and emphasis. He jumped at the idea, so I read the speech into a tape recorder—not very well, but clearly— and he "studied" the cassette recording along with the text.

When he read the speech on April 10, Ware told me it was the mayor's best delivery of a written text that he had ever heard.

That's nice to hear. But the best reviews I ever got for the speeches were those from the mayor himself, usually issued in that momentary calm in the elevator as we were leaving a cheering crowd, as he handed me the curled-up cards he'd used at the podium, usually with a big grin: "That was a selfreader, Al."

▭ *Arts and Letters* ▭

Mayor Washington did an inordinate number of events with the Goodman Theatre, where Cindy worked. As one who was concerned that his schedule be balanced across constituencies and issues, I was embarrassed that he showed up in so many Goodman photos, attended so many Goodman parties, issued Goodman proclamations, and the like. At first I shied away from them, deemphasized the connection. And then I realized that he got a kick out of loaning me a little "clout." It was part of the "psychic income" that he enjoyed, that he could do favors like that. Rather than play it cool, I let him know how much I appreciated his Goodman appearances. "My stock's going way up, mayor," I told him truthfully.

The fact is that he enjoyed the arts, and artists. I made a point of not being cast as the administration's unofficial arts connection—we had a solid Commissioner of Cultural Affairs in Fred Fine, and I wasn't going to middle him with my access to the mayor. The mayor himself, unprompted, courted and was courted by Sir Georg Solti of the Chicago Symphony Orchestra; Leonard Bernstein, whose politics the mayor found as compelling as his music; the distinguished impressaria Sarah Zelzer; the legendary Maria Tallchief; the American Ballet Theater artist Natalia Makarova; architect Harry Weese; writer Studs Terkel; and many others.

He would have enjoyed these personalities regardless of their career fields, but his interest in the arts went beyond the fun of meeting people. He could surprise you with a literary reference, out of the blue. For example, he called Rev. B. Herbert Martin his "Becket," when "the mayor's pastor" had proved a disappointment on the CHA board, and was slated for removal. He came up one morning with a passage from Machiavelli on the pros and cons of reform. During a cabinet meeting he used a reference from Shakespeare's *Henry V*—the St. Crispin's day speech—referring to them as "We few, we happy few," in the throes of "Council Wars."

▢ *Perks* ▭

I appreciated the courtesies he extended to Cindy all the more because I was vaguely aware that I was doing something wrong in the perks department.

I didn't even have an expense account. I was as careless as Mayor Washington about my own finances, and never even got reimbursed for three airfares from New York to the White House; or for a hundred-dollar box of Cuban cigars I bought in Montreal airport, for the mayor to present to Teddy Kollek; or for several hotel bills that I had to put on my credit card because of screw-ups by someone back in Chicago.

Just about my only perk was the city car I drove. It came along just in time. When I was hired, in 1985, my beat-up 1973 Honda was on its last legs. It had become a bucket of bolts, but I considered it the perfect city runabout, and I was reluctant to give it up. Long since fully paid for, it cost me next to nothing in maintenance and gas; I could park it anywhere (both because it was small and because I was careless about getting tickets on my out-of-state plates), and I never needed to worry about theft of the car or its contents—I even left it unlocked—it simply wasn't worth stealing. Why would I want to give up all those freedoms just for a better looking model?

My city car was a perfect replacement. It cost me nothing in car payments. Gas and maintenance were provided by the city. I could park it anywhere, and I never needed to worry about theft. I even left it unlocked. During the day I would pull it into my own parking space at the LaSalle Street entrance of City Hall, and if it needed gas or a wash, Tumia would call Streets and San and they'd take care of it. I left the car wherever I needed to catch up with the mayor. I'd ride back with him, telephoning Tumia to let her know where Streets and San would find the Dodge. When I got back to the Hall, a shiny, just-serviced, car would be waiting for me.

Mike Royko once wrote that the real reason for being mayor of Chicago, despite all the headaches and thankless tasks, was that you never have to look for a place to park. I would add that a press secretary can take advantage of some of the same.

But otherwise I was a real amateur about city perks.

I was probably a disappointment to my neighbors, too. I wouldn't know how to begin getting special attention for my sidewalk or alley, or other city services. When friends asked for help with a city matter, I would go through channels—partly because I didn't know any other way, and partly because I didn't want even an appearance of impropriety.

But I do secretly regret not taking advantage of some of the more legitimate perks that might have come my way, if I'd only been paying more attention.

Invitations arrived for social events that I probably would have enjoyed, if there had been a let-up in the tensions of "Council Wars," or "Raymond the Mole" or the special ward elections, or the reelection campaign. Movie screenings, theater openings, ethnic fests, events at Navy Pier—I tried to remember to bring them home to Cindy. If she picked out an occasional event, it would be better than stacking up the invitations to yellow on my windowsill at the office.

Most of the city perks were intangible. During my first week on the job, Cindy walked over from the Goodman Theatre to City Hall, to see my new office. When she entered City Hall for the first time in her life, the police guard said as she passed, "Hello, Mrs. Miller." She was impressed, and so was I. And I was equally impressed by the fact that I could run into any Chicago cop, in any part of the city, and find myself on a personal basis. Like Woody Allen, I've never been particularly comfortable with the manifestations of authority in society, and it was a new experience, a pleasant one, to break through that apprehension.

When traveling with the mayor, airport security checks were waived, and waiting was always comfortable. But even when I was traveling alone, or meeting him at the airport, I was able to drive to O'Hare and leave my city car at the sidewalk, knowing that between Tumia and the airport officials, it would be parked in an employee lot, and ready for me when I returned.

It's easy to see how public officials become insulated against the inconveniences of public amenities. Still, I wouldn't have missed it for the world.

☐ *Radio Days* ⊏══════════════════════════════⊐

Mayor Washington's most pleasant hours with reporters were spent not so much in making news as in casual reflections, on radio talk shows. In particular he enjoyed the half hour he did every month with Bill Cameron on WMAQ radio. Bill had been a friendly reporter during the mayor's Springfield days, and the mayor never forgot that. Bill would usually be joined by Harry Golden of the *Sun-Times,* and Jim Strong or Manual Galvan of the *Tribune,* for a free-wheeling rap session on current events. Mayor Washington did a similar show for John Madigan and Bob Crawford of WBBM radio, but not as often. We weren't able to get on a regular schedule with Madigan until he accepted that the mayor wouldn't appear on the show if Steve Neal were invited to be among WBBM's guest reporters.

The mayor said he did the radio talk shows for the "three bites" you were able to get from each. You made news the Thursday or Friday you taped, with brief sound bites broadcast as news that day; then the story was usually recycled into daily newspaper stories, sometimes even a Sunday think-piece; finally, the half-hour radio broadcast on Sunday was the icing on the cake. But I suspect his reason for enjoying these programs as much as he did was the camaraderie he felt with the reporters. In a radio studio he could loosen his tie, put his elbows on the table, sip from a cup of coffee, lean back and gab. Occasionally the affiliated TV station would want to get a two-for-one, by bringing cameras and lights into the radio studio. But we established a ground rule for his radio appearances: No TV. Not because it would have made bad TV, but because it would have ruined the radio ambience. "Let's face it, Mayor," I said, "you don't want to make news. You want to make history, but you really don't care about making news."

Mayor Washington also enjoyed the hour-long call-in shows he did every month—once for a consortium of black radio stations ("The Mayor's Report"), and again for WBBM ("Ask the Mayor"). Anyone who listened to those detailed discussions of ward-by-ward and block-by-block city problems knows that Harold Washington understood not only the big picture, but also the nuts and bolts of city management.

☐ *Management*

He was proud of his management style, though he frequently had to defend it. The Eddies had promoted the notion that he was sloppy and unlettered in the details of city management. In fact, he was an ardent student of management principles, and could talk turkey with Chicago CEOs as well as government leaders across the nation. His idea of light reading included case studies of management in action, in books like Caro's *The Power Broker,* the classic on New York's Robert Moses; or Clark and Ferguson's *City Money.*

He was a lifelong legislator and compromise-maker, but he was no ward politician. He had broader horizons than any Chicago mayor in memory—he was better traveled, better read, arguably better schooled in hard-knocks politics—and yet he was probably more approachable and down-to-earth with the labor union representatives, the management consultants, the financial advisers and the bureaucrats on whom he depended, than any of his predecessors had been. No middlemen were in the Washington program; he wanted to know the specifics behind every key decision that was made. A careful analysis of the work of "Bottleneck Bill" and "Bottleneck Ernie" would probably show that Harold Washington himself was the cause for the slowdowns when they occurred, because he reconsidered so many decisions that were brought to him for signoff.

Even before he was elected, he had commissioned a comprehensive set of detailed recommendations, department-by-department, on Chicago reform. He had a transition team produce a second document, with action steps that could be tracked as part of a management-by-objectives plan. He complained that his senior staff were technocrats "without a political bone in their body." But he was proud that he had assembled such a team, and promised them unswerving support when it came time to take the heat, so long as they were unflinching in "cleaning up the mess we inherited."

He was proud of the fact that he wasn't a boss, and particularly proud that he had ended the handshake labor deals and instituted responsible collective bargaining contracts across city government.

He was always ready to remind you that the same people who claimed to know the city budget inside and out—from 1987 Republican candidate and media darling Don Haider, to Finance Committee Chairman Eddie Burke—were the very people who had spent Chicago into a $100 million deficit. Although they postured as fiscal prudes during the Washington years, it was clear that they had voted for (or planned; Haider had been Byrne's budget director) higher taxes under Byrne than they ever opposed under Washington. They were the ones who had driven the city workforce to over 42,000 positions. He took the heat for reducing that by some 8,000.

That's what he did for a living. He took the heat. As much as he loved bonhomie, he loved a vigorous debate. He was the happy warrior when he was comfortable with the cause. He was proud of the fact that he had been elected by a victory margin of white and Hispanic votes, but he insisted that his being a black mayor was what made the difference. What he did no white mayor could have done, because no white progressive could have been elected without that solid black base he brought into the equation.

He was a politician by trade, and proud of it. Mayor was his job title, but his profession was politics. Politicians, he asserted, were the people who took all the good ideas of the philosophers, and all the anxieties of the handwringers, and brought them together to a state of action. As a mayor he was a manager: he appointed, he delegated, he reviewed, he decided. As a politician, he went one better; he took the heat.

☐ *Shades* ▭

Mayor Washington was well known for the unqualified support he gave to those who worked for him, and some would say he cut too much slack. That support wasn't limited to the big issues, like resisting efforts to oust Barefield. It extended to smaller items, too. Like the issue of my sunglasses, which began in my very first week on the job.

When I wasn't wearing them against the glare of TV lights, my sunglasses were usually stuck to the top of my head, the way I've worn them for years. The photos and TV clips in which I appeared almost always showed me hatless, with these cheap sunglasses in place. The gossip columnists began referring to me as "Shades," and folks in the mayor's office teased me about them. And before long, strangers on the street or in the crowds attracted by the mayor at events, smiled when they recognized my sunglasses, giving me a thumbs-up, telling me to "give 'em hell," or "keep on keepin' on." Time and again I heard the comment, "don't let 'em take your shades away!"

It didn't take me long to realize the value of so simple an icon. By the end of my first week on the job, Walter Jacobson and Mike Flannery were teasingly introducing the query, "Why do you wear those sunglasses?" as one of the issues of their interview program with me. Soon after that *Sun-Times* cartoonist Higgins first caricatured me with the glasses.

Why did I wear them? I didn't really have a clever answer to the question. The truth is too simple: even in the winter I wear sunglasses against bright light. If I tilt my sunglasses back on top of my head I don't lose them; if I put them anywhere else, I end up buying a new pair every week.

Sometime in that first week, an earnest Ald. Ed Smith came up and asked me not to wear them. "One of my constituents called me to complain about it," he said. "It's too casual. It doesn't show the proper respect."

I told him I appreciated his comment. And I did—Ed Smith, alderman in the 99 percent black 28th Ward, is probably the most sincerely motivated alderman, even the most "proper" in the original gentlemanly sense, that City Council has seen in a long time. I knew that he wouldn't have stuck his neck out to venture that opinion if he hadn't been genuinely concerned about appearances for the mayor's sake.

But I wasn't dressing for anyone's taste but my own. I tried to keep it friendly and light-hearted when I told him, "I'll stop wearing my sunglasses when you get Dorothy Tillman to stop wearing her hats." He told me, no, he was serious. I said, still friendly but insistent, that I was dirt serious. He should explain what I said to the constituent who called.

The mayor never had a problem with my wearing sunglasses, and when they became a temporary *cause celebre* he went out of his way to characterize them. He asked me idly why *do* I wear them, and I replied that there was no particular reason, but it had become an issue, so I couldn't take them off. He seemed to see a point to that. He said, with a smile, "They're the chip on your shoulder. I got no problem with that."

The shades did have two practical functions. First, I never had to worry about mussed hair—people see the glasses, not the haircut.

Second, it served to help people tell me and Judd Miner apart. Both the corporation counsel and I on countless occasions were stopped by strangers who recognized us from TV or newspapers, but misidentified us—"You're—don't tell me—you're Judd Miner—no—," pointing to the glasses—"You're Alton Miller."

Actually, my first name is distinctive enough to have caused another confusion. During the week I was hired, a serial killer named Alton Coleman was in the news, and apparently for many people the imprint of our names was crossed. To this day I'll still encounter a stranger on the elevator, or bus driver, who will smile, wave a greeting of recognition, and say with utter sincerity, "Hello, Mr. Coleman."

▢ *Philosophy*

Mayor Washington was generally as private about his religion as he was about the rest of his personal life. Some official biographical sketches list his religion as Roman Catholic. As a small boy he attended a Catholic boarding school in Milwaukee; he received the last rites of the church. His father was an associate pastor in the African Methodist Episcopal church, and Harold tagged along when Rev. Roy Washington made his political or spiritual rounds.

He would frequently remind me that the church has historically been the preeminent social and political force in the black community, as well as the fount of its spiritual strength. His periodic meetings with black ministers were as much a matter of paying respect as of sharing information. He once told me, and he wasn't kidding, that he had an "understanding" with the black ministry—City Hall is his, but the communities are theirs.

He had no problem with the Rev. B. Herbert Martin's designation as "the mayor's pastor," but the fact is that he made a point of going to a number of churches, sometimes several on the same Sunday. Traveling with the mayor, I saw the inside of many places of worship, mostly black churches on the South Side.

Mayor Washington did go on the record about his religious philosophy, and the role it had played in his public life. For a private person, it's a pretty strong statement of his more spiritual side. But both his religious beliefs and his philosophical orientation turn out to be applications of a strong internal ethic to political practicalities. They also reveal a man who was not ashamed to identify with the mainstream, rather than the margins of social movements.

The "Statement of Faith" was broadcast on the Chicago Sunday Evening Club, on WTTW-TV, Oct. 20, 1985. He told the television audience:

> Religion in my family was never just a matter of what a person believes. It was always measured in what a person practices.
>
> As the son of a minister, the grandson of a minister, as a young man secure in a family that was secure in its church, it came naturally—no pious pretensions, just a responsibility to do good.
>
> Jesus was a carpenter. He wasn't just an itinerant preacher who filled the air with phrases—he was a builder and doer, and the Bible rings with his references to the life and work of plain working people...
> And Jesus was a healer. He took care of the sick, the blind, the halt, the lame. And he told us, too: Take care of their needs. He told us, loud and clear: Don't think for a minute their problems are none of your business. They *are* your business: 'even as you do unto the least of these, you do unto me.'
>
> If there's one thing that our modern science and technology have taught us—and it's something that religion has always said—it is that there is no part of this planet that is not connected to the future of Chi-

cago as a whole. There is no human being whose problems don't, somehow, connect up with ours, somewhere down the road....

We have to do God's work here on earth. If we don't, who will? We have to make all the parts work together, to create a harmony of the whole. The Jews have a word for that special harmony, that we Christians have borrowed—as we have so much of our fundamental faith. That word is Shalom—Peace. But it's not a static phrase, not simply the absence of striving. It's the ideal of a harmonious working-together of the whole world.

His political philosophy took a lifetime to elaborate. He was an unabashed liberal progressive who had grown up in the bosom of the Regular Democratic Machine. He was anti-war and pro-defense: "I'm just about the only war veteran in Chicago politics," he would say, and while he fought the "obscenity of our nuclear buildup," by contrast to the short-changing of America's cities, he favored the maintenance of strong armed forces. His Veterans Day observances were with both protestors and traditional veterans organizations, and he was especially proud to have hosted the first national parade for Vietnam veterans.

In another signal way, he placed himself squarely in the mainstream, in a conversation he had with the *Sun-Times'* Lynn Sweet. She had asked him why people should care about party loyalty in the Chicago mayor's race.

Oh, I think it's good to stand for something. I think there is more than just a scintilla of difference between the Democratic and Republican philosophy, whether you're talking about the national, the statewide, the county—or local. Although I confess to you, the closer you get to home, the less significant party labels become.

But if you're talking about a philosophy as I talk about a philosophy, Jeffersonian philosophy, if you're talking about that in the broadest aspects, then it means something whether you're working in your house or whether you're working in China.

It's a consistency, it's a continuity, it's a universal way of looking at life. And that's to me what the Democratic party stands for. When I say party, I'm not talking about a bunch of people standing for office. I'm talking about a philosophy, a platform, a vision, a standard which you shoot for. Now I don't know that everybody sees it that way. I think most people who are Democrats probably do, who have given any thought to it.

I started off as a Democrat really before my formative years. I started off as a kid when my dad was one of the first black democrats in Chicago. It was only later when I began to look and compare and equate, that I realized that there were differences between the parties, significant differences, historically, and that the differences were important in this world in which radicals don't win. They may shake up the goddamn groundwork but they don't win, and the ones who win are those who make the quantum changes and shifts, and move.

So I made a decision. I'd rather be one of those who work within the vineyards of the legitimate aspects of it, than be the revolutionist who was pushing them to do so. And that's why I went that way.

So I have grafted onto the Democratic structure my own philosophy, which I think most people who think about the party say so. Hubert Humphrey, for example, beautifully phrased just exactly what I'm trying to say. And others. Franklin Delano Roosevelt said it. And others have said it.

▢ *Unpleasantries* ▭

As the careful reader has already discerned, Mayor Washington had no love lost for Mike Sneed, and laughed bitterly at the very idea when I told him she had come to me asking for a chance at rapprochement, shortly after he took control of City Council. He was particularly upset with her snide references to Mary Ella, but he also was upset by one particularly hurtful item that had appeared back in 1985, involving Bill Ware.

At the time, only three people knew of the anecdote involving my sunglasses on the afternoon that I was hired by Mayor Washington. Bill Ware, who suggested I take them off before meeting with the mayor; myself; and Steve Neal, to whom I'd innocently told the tale in one of our first meetings. Neal probably had given that tidbit, along with miscellaneous other droppings that he couldn't use in his own article on me, to Sneed.

In the meantime Bill Ware was going through the ups and downs of the illness that would finally end his life. He was absent from the office for long stretches, then back for a few days, then gone again. Despite his ailments, he was trying to keep up with the demands of his job, coping with intra-office infighting, and trying to fend off the published rumors that he had AIDS. He didn't know me well and couldn't be sure where I was coming from; hopefully he assumed I was friend, not foe, but he had no reason to be completely confident.

There was some friction between us. Tom Coffey had pressured him to give my larger office to IGA, and Ware had acceded. I had strongly protested in a memo, and my argument was so vehement that Ware had had to renege on his agreement with Coffey. I suppose it was a measure of his decline, that a newcomer to City Hall could stare him down.

It was the last morning he ever came to City Hall. Sneed had run an item that day, out of the blue, that chided Ware for the sunglasses incident. Ware must have assumed that I had an open channel to Sneed and was using her to needle him. Perhaps that made me responsible for some of the other harrassment he'd been suffering in the columns? I went to his office to anticipate any confusion Sneed might have caused, but Ware had left. Martha Redhed didn't know when he'd be back. She thought he was going out of town. The only message he had left was that I could use his parking place. As we later learned, he was going to Sloane-Kettering in New York, to die.

On rare occasions, though, the mayor found he could laugh at Sneed. One of his favorite stories was the tale I told of the Sneed Dinner Club. There was a period when I was featured almost daily in Sneed's column, with items about how I parked my city car too close to stop signs. I don't know who parks Sneed's car in Wilmette, but in my Lincoln Park neighborhood, any place but a fire hydrant is fair game, and I wasn't about to reform to please one of my "Sneed-scoop" [sic, one of her terms] neighbors. No big deal, but it was annoying to read about it nearly every morning.

There were several members of the cabinet that the mayor suspected of carrying stories to Sneed. I told him I had a plan to test the premise.

I told just two selected colleagues, one day at a time, that I was about to be disqualified from the Sneed Dinner Club. What was the Sneed Dinner Club? Oh, I thought they knew—it's a group of top mayoral aides who get together once a month for dinner. Whoever has been mentioned most often in Sneed's column eats for free. They were accusing me of purposely parking my car in front of that stop sign every day, and walking away with the honors.

Two days after I passed that fib along, the Sneed items stopped—forever. It was months before she found any reason to write about me again. The mayor loved it. And he was a little more careful about what he told both cabinet members.

☐ *Race*

On the subject of race I was too often presumptuous of a certain innocence, no doubt the product of my Washington, D.C., background. Several times during my first weeks I referred to the mayor as color-blind—in making his appointments, for example—and though the spirit was right, the facts were wrong. No mayor of Chicago is likely to be color-blind, ever. Color-adjusted might be a better term. We can't be Pollyannish, as Harold Washington would say, about a subject so important.

Still, I could follow my faulty instincts into ridiculous positions. Once, coming out of the elevator on the fifth floor with Mayor Washington, I pointed to a statue of George Washington standing in the hall. "If Thomas Jefferson had been the first president," I volunteered, "you'd probably be Mayor Harold Jefferson." The remark came out of some theoretical discussion of some days earlier, about black migration from the South into Chicago.

He gave me one of those askance looks I got during the first weeks, when he was still trying to figure me out; more of a professorial disputation than a personal reaction.

But the next day, irked by some "unarticulated premises" he had brushed up against in the media, he carried on for a few minutes about some theoretical white ethnic racists "whose ancestors were probably serfs to some Polish knights." I could hear the pain in his voice, and I perceived that he was answering my insult of the day before. Why was it an insult, I asked myself; it was a given that his forebears had been slaves. And then I took the next step; I tried to imagine—completely without success—a man as proud and independent as Harold Washington ever being anyone else's chattel property. Trying to combine those thoughts in one idea was like an optical illusion; I couldn't make them fit. I could imagine how it must have been simultaneously infuriating and humiliating to be reminded of that impossible paradox. A day later, I found a way to apologize for the insensitivity of my idle chatter.

On the lighter side, I had another encounter with racism, secondhand. Lynda Gorov of the *Sun-Times* told me my name came up when she was interviewing black activist Lu Palmer, who complained of all the Jews who were advising Harold Washington. When she asked for examples he said, "Well, for instance, Alton Miller." I took it as a compliment, but Lutherans are not among the sects of Judaism. To the best of my knowledge, from the Jewish standpoint, they're not even part of the solution.

▭ *Good Times* ▭

For all his problems with the media, he enjoyed reporters, and welcomed opportunities to mix with them socially. The travels were good for that, but so were occasional parties like the one for Basil Talbott, who was leaving his Chicago beat to cover federal politics for the *Sun-Times*, in Washington, D.C. Mayor Washington lingered long after he was scheduled to be somewhere else, meeting with many journalists that he enjoyed, some of whom he hadn't seen socially for years. He couldn't have known it, but he was making his own good-byes, as the party took place two days before he died.

Some have floated the idea that Mayor Washington had premonitions of his death. I find the idea ridiculous. He had been given a clean bill of health not long before, and although he had weight and blood pressure problems, I'm convinced he had no thought of his own mortality. In particular, he had no concern to establish an "heir to his legacy." Whoever he or she was, his successor was probably skipping rope in a playground somewhere—he was serious about being mayor until the year 2003.

No, for all intents and purposes, he said, he was mayor for life. What would he do later? "Shit," he said, settling back in his chair with a big smile. "I'm going to be mayor for life, and die at my desk."

19

Thanksgiving Day

Thursday, Nov. 25, 1987. A somber holiday. The mayor's entire cabinet was at work, organizing the details of his lying in state, a special memorial session of City Council, a motorcade, his funeral service, his interment, and the political futures of his survivors.

Staff members assigned themselves to various work groups. Some congregated in Brenda Gaines' office, where they consulted protocol and tradition to put together invitation lists and seating charts and ceremonial procedures for the public events of the next few days.

Others were meeting with Mike Holewinski, the mayor's liaison for the Police and Fire Departments. He was coordinating security for City Hall and for the funeral, the traffic plans, which would include a long route through Chicago's South Side neighborhoods, and other details involving police and security.

A number were at work at the political office, two blocks from City Hall. Presumably they were working on the question of mayoral succession, planning a course of action designed to elect Ald. Tim Evans at the next City Council meeting. I had been at enough of those meetings at the political office. I pictured Jacky Grimshaw and Vince Bakeman fussing with Ernie Barefield, and shuddered for Tim Evans.

None of us had recovered from the shock of the day before, of course. And yet no one wasted much time expressing feelings. We all knew how each other felt. We all felt the same. Now we had to pull off another major campaign, the mayor's last. Like all the campaigns and crises, we were surprised but not intimidated, unprepared but not unequipped.

It was a situation the mayor would have enjoyed. Guiding all this activity was nothing more organized than a passion. Enthusiasm for the challenge, and respect for the boss, was doing what a management-by-objectives work plan was supposed to do. If ever there were an argument for communal administration, this was it.

I remember thinking that with Harold Washington we had learned to work like sappers, coolly and deliberately operating through one crisis after another, with bullets whizzing past and the flak bursting all around us and the screams of the wounded assaulting our concentration. Even though some of us might not be good friends, we had learned to guide on the boss and stay the course, despite adversity and confusion and self-doubt. Now we had to do it one last time, without him.

We kept our thoughts to ourselves, for the most part. But the awareness washed over us in waves, that our center of gravity was gone forever.

I moved from group to group, pleased to see almost all my staff in one cluster or another, sometimes stopping to put in my two cents but mostly silently absorbing as much as I could of the planning, aware that everything was subject to change every half hour. I tried to distinguish between events that had been firmly fixed and events that might be modified.

I brought my best guesses to the reporters, reminding them that things were in a state of flux. With the continuing assistance of Fire Department press aide Jerry Lawrence, I established camera pool agreements, media seating at the funeral service, arrangements for still photographers, special passes for photos of the lying in state.

I was only too happy to go with the flow—whatever was customary, after brief discussion, I okayed and authorized with a memo. The press was pretty much making up my mind for me, based on precedent and their experience with this sort of thing. Except for a minor hassle here and there—at one point I was told the church was completely ruling out any photos or press coverage of the funeral service, but we worked that out—things proceeded smoothly.

I was asked to draft a lengthy memorial resolution, to be read and adopted by the City Council in their special session. Only a few weeks earlier I had outlined a speech which the mayor delivered before a rally of supporters. I called the speech "We Made the Hard Choices," and I composed it in a style that could be adapted to many uses, for various audiences in Chicago, and also on the road during the 1988 presidential campaign. In it he listed, one by one, the issues for which we had all stood strong, the battles we had won, the principles to which he thought the national Democratic party should be dedicated. Now I adapted it to one more use: instead of each line of the litany beginning "We made the hard choice to...", it became, "Whereas he made the hard choice to...". It concluded with the customary commendations. I thought it was fitting that his memorial resolution should have been, in a sense, the message he'd been selling, the statement he would have delivered in person if he could.

That Thanksgiving Day, I found a moment to take Barefield aside. I told him I planned to call it quits at the end of the year. I would stay for a month's transition, until January 1, but no longer. I intended to make my announcement now, so that it wouldn't later be misunderstood as a reaction to the new mayor, whoever that might be. I gave the story to Lynn Sweet of the *Sun-Times*—it was the least I could do, having stood her up for lunch the day before.

Then I went home, where Cindy was preparing our Thanksgiving turkey. We had a quiet dinner, and I had a chance to talk to my daughter Julie in Ann Arbor, my folks in Texas, my brothers in Ohio, Cindy's mom in California. I was thankful for family, and thankful that Cindy and I had each other, but I wasn't thankful about much else.

It was during the next week that I gradually began to feel a welling up of thanksgiving for the thousand days I had been given.

For the first time in a thousand days I was aware that being press secretary was a job, not an adventure. I was suddenly conscious, as I moved from chore to chore, that without the personal commitment to Harold Washington, the great grey bureaucracy around me was about as hospitable as the stomach lining of Jonah's whale. On the last morning of the mayor's life I was eagerly looking forward to a 12-hour work day. Now seven hours seemed interminable. How did people do this for a living, I wondered? Why would anyone stay? City Hall was bad enough. Without Mayor Washington it was grim. Without any mayor at all, it was intolerable.

Nature abhors a vacuum, and she sometimes takes revenge. Self-appointed sentinels of Mayor Washington's legacy had stationed themselves at every crossroads and were probing in the confusion to discern friend from foe. New claques sprang to life. One morning they'd be formulating ad hoc policy in my office, or Gaines' or Grimshaw's, around a table cluttered with coffee cups and cigarette butts; disoriented, hunched in aimless talk like overnight mushrooms, in sudden loose rings with nothing at the center; the next morning they'd be gone, and a new ring of mushrooms would materialize down the hall.

People who had worked together in a smooth, self-confident flow of cooperation through five hard years were now clotting in separate corners, unsure of one another's sentiments, uncertain where their loyalties should lie. Some were figuring out how they could keep their positions. Some were figuring out how they could improve them. Some were wondering who they were supposed to give their resignation to. One of the most overworked people during that interim week was the office manager who knew the answer to questions of accumulated vacation and leave time, and could tell you what you needed to know about getting out when the getting was good.

We all had our Harold Washington dreams during the next few weeks, as our subconscious safety nets tried to let us down easy. In mine, the mayor had brought me to a boxing match, a Golden Gloves type thing. Like my father, who had taught me to face challenge, Mayor Washington wanted me to learn to box. I wondered why he would want me to be a boxer, to get beat up and battered around—in real life, I had never particularly identified with the culture of boxing. And then in the dream I realized: the knocks were another way of learning, beside the book-learning and the talk-learning I had learned with all my life. Not only would I learn to mix it up, bob and weave, and how to dish it out. I'd learn how to take it. And if I didn't learn how to take those knocks, I could never learn to fight.

The general confusion of the cabinet and staff was all the greater because of the controversy surrounding the election of a new mayor. Succession law provides that the vice-mayor (Ald. David Orr) serve as "interim mayor" until the City Council has elected one of their own to be "acting mayor;" the interim mayor takes office automatically, but the election of the acting mayor is subject to bitter parliamentary dispute.

Overnight, the worst horrors of "Council Wars" were revived for television audiences. Literally overnight, because the City Council election assembly became an all-night aborted filibuster. While crowds of protestors ringed City Hall and chanted their opposition, a hasty alliance of Machine aldermen, white and black, the old "29" and elements of the "21," elected a new black mayor who had voted with Washington but also had been, like Washington once upon a time, a powerful Daley supporter in the Machine. Ald. Eugene

Sawyer, brother of Charles Sawyer who had accepted a contribution from Raymond the Mole, was now Mayor Sawyer.

His election outraged most of the original "21," who were supporting Ald. Timothy Evans. The four Latino aldermen voted as a bloc, against Sawyer. Mayor Washington's white Lakefront coalition split. Ald. Anna Langford and Ald. Bill Henry voted alongside Ald. William Krystyniak and Ald. Victor Vrdolyak (Eddie's brother; Eddie himself had abandoned the City Council when he ran for mayor), and against their former allies.

The person credited with orchestrating Sawyer's election was the same instrument of Bilandic's succession 11 years earlier, Ald. Edward Burke. The entire evening was closely covered by the press, and when Sawyer faltered, Burke had been witnessed virtually commanding the unwilling candidate to take the job—at the top of his lungs. Some are born mayor, some achieve it, and some have it thrust upon 'em.

A few days after Sawyer had been elected, Jacky Grimshaw called in the TV cameras for a statement. She punched the Washington button pinned to her coat and announced she worked only for him. She didn't clarify what she meant, or why it mattered. Then she held a second press conference a day or so later, to protest her firing by Mayor Sawyer. The irony was that had Washington lived, Grimshaw would have suffered Coffey's fate, for the same reasons. Just as he'd done with Coffey, the mayor had spent weeks building up his resolve. He had said repeatedly, to me and several aides—Barefield, Tim Wright and Ron Gibbs, among others—that she was soon to be gone.

Barefield tried to hold onto his position, as did a number of top aides, who believed they could best continue Washington's agenda by staying in place. Sawyer needed his own chief, so Barefield was out, but most did keep their jobs, working their little patch of the vineyards even though the great estate had fallen.

I worked with Sawyer for four weeks, until January 1. He asked me to stay on for the balance of his term—Judd Miner, Sharon Gilliam, Kari Moe, some of Mayor Washington's best people were joining the Sawyer administration—but I was looking forward to starting fresh.

I couldn't get used to the new landscape. Most of all, I couldn't get used to the new cast of characters that now swarmed around City Hall. No one was certain who was authorized to represent the new mayor's administration; for a few days we endured the spectacle of discredited former Washington employees—hangers-on that the late mayor had finally kicked out of City Hall—throwing their weight around, styling themselves with makeshift titles, claiming to speak for Mayor Sawyer. Mercifully, within a few days of their slouching in, they were asked to slouch back out again, by Erwin France.

France had come to replace the earnest Barefield. He was a smooth operator, a black Henry Kissinger of Chicago city management, who had been winning city contracts for more than two decades, and who had enjoyed the greater or lesser confidence of five mayors. Now his portfolio was expanded to include a wide range of day-to-day operations. He worked for months as a high-paid consultant who exercised all the prerogatives of a surrogate mayor.

In place of the soft-spoken Charles Kelly as the mayor's principal buffer against the world's walk-up business, we had Steve Cokely. Cokely first came to my attention a couple years earlier, as an aldermanic aide who made a headline or two by labeling Columbus Day a "racist" celebration. He was later forced to resign from Sawyer's employ after it became known that only a few months earlier, as a follower of Minister Farrakhan, he had produced a series of tape recorded sermons claiming, among other highlights, that Jewish doctors were deliberately infecting black babies with AIDS toxins. He had the distinction of being the only person, in my three years of government work, ever to provoke me to shouting, during one confrontation in the mayor's office.

In place of Mayor Washington's cohort of Lakefront legal advisers, from whom I'd learned enough smatterings of law to get myself passing grades in a bar exam if the profession loosened up a little, I was seeing a new group of attorneys. One of the new key players was Lisa Rubel. Someone had tipped the press that Sawyer had accepted a "finder's fee" for an aldermanic service a few years back, and that caused a flurry of adverse press. Rubel was among the lawyers brought in to deal with Sawyer's defense. She had been one of the people from whom our secrets were carefully guarded; now she was a colleague, with the run of the office.

As an aside, there was a general feeling on the fifth floor—no confirmation but a recognizeable M.O.—that the tipster was someone in Eddie Burke's office. The allegation was part of a scenario in which Burke had forced Sawyer to take the job, and now was guaranteeing that he'd be too damaged to hold on to it. Whether there was any truth to that charge, there was a lively irony in the fact that Burke's Rubel was brought in to clean it up.

Sawyer was completely overwhelmed by events. Mayor Washington was still "the mayor" in his conversation—none of us had lost that habit—and for an entire month he declined to use "the mayor's" desk. He worked from the coffee table and overstuffed armchairs, the desk and chair draped in black behind him.

Sawyer had been a powerful alderman—leonine in his self-confidence, he was also the committeeman in what Mayor Washington had once described as the "best-run ward in the city." Now he was drawn, his shoulders sagged, his head drooped. Although he'd always been a soft-spoken, gentle man, he had stood tall and had acted with assurance. For the entire month I worked with him he sniffled with a cold that he had caught on the night of December 1.

He told me that he had not wanted the job as mayor. He said he had suggested to Tim Evans, in the late afternoon of December 1, that they postpone the City Council meeting. "If Tim had done what I asked, he'd be mayor today," he said in his quiet way. "He said he wanted to go ahead, because he had the votes. I knew better, but he wouldn't listen. So I said to myself, fine," he told me, shrugging his shoulders, "let's get it on."

As was widely reported at the time, and as Sawyer repeated to me, it was Evans again who inadvertently resolved the issue in the wee hours of the morning. Sawyer had been wavering, throughout an evening of fits and starts, aware that if he accepted the offer of his former adversaries he would earn the eternal enmity of most of his former allies. But live TV cameras were prowling the halls, and when one of them broadcast an interview with a cocky Tim Evans daring Sawyer to make his move, he was steeled for action. He was finally declared mayor at 4:01 a.m.

There is no shortage of people who still claim to speak for Mayor Washington, who will declare how he would have felt or what he would have said, in any situation. My ouija board is out of whack, and I don't know what he would have felt as he watched his old buddy Sawyer beat his old buddy Evans out of the job. He wouldn't have been comfortable watching Burke's side come out on top; but if he agreed with Sawyer that Evans didn't have the votes, he wouldn't want Dick Mell to have it, and he wouldn't have wasted time crying about it.

He was a strong adherent to the principle of political trade-off; or, as he put it, that "nobody does nothing for nobody for nothing." He would have expected Sawyer to take it on his terms, not Eddie's. He would have wanted to know, not what did you give up for it, old buddy? But, what did you get?

The next mayor might be white, might be black, might be "Latino, Asian or other," might be male, might be female, but the one thing the next mayor would most certainly be, would be the person with the most votes. Political ability and not the passing of any sceptre would make the decision for Chicago.

Whatever he *might* say, I know what he *did* say, in response to reporters' questions about succession during the previous several months: he said that he had no successor. He had been no one's successor, and no one was named in his public testament, either. Although he was tolerant of the sentiment, and paid it lip service, that he had been drafted by the "Movement" and that the same movement would just as easily produce another Harold—he knew that all his political accomplishments hung on him; that without him, there would be no center. And for all the hangers-on, who would claim to have been the ones who propped him up, within days, and increasingly over the months ahead, it would be clear that they were only a numerous and diverse collection of Christmas tree ornaments, collected by a master, with no Christmas tree on which to hang.

Sure, he had heirs. He had been defining a new politics for Chicago, and in a sense everyone who followed him had inherited a new set of standards. As he was fond of saying, he had changed not only the dialogue, but the behavior. Not only would white and black progressives be vying for the privilege of representing his legacy; the bosses of the Chicago Democratic party would soon be selling their slate of candidates as the slate that Mayor Washington had blessed, that he had called "a slate made in heaven." Even Burke and Vrdolyak would be ameliorating their rhetoric and allowing as how they had perhaps overstated from time to time when they challenged Mayor Washington.

Like every transitional figure, in every age, he had one foot firmly planted in the bad old days, in the world he had worked to reform. He was personally shaped by the old standards, scarred by the hard knocks of the old political conspiracies and campaigns. And when he met the Eddies, he beat their ass on their own terms, in the old way, not in some abstract "reformed" sense, in some city on a hill. He fought the way they fought, and he outfought them, and he did it in Chicago.

But if that rear foot would never be lifted, he was facing forward into a new Chicago, where his other foot was already aggressively making its print. One thing was certain: he had stretched Chicago into new forms. Never again would any mayor—whoever that might be—get away with holding back on freedom of information, or circumventing public hearings on important issues. Never again would any mayor, white, black, brown or yellow, get away with contracts channeled to a favored few, or jobs concentrated in certain wards, or appointments to top positions that were not balanced by race, ethnicity, gender. Those parameters were changed forever. He stretched Chicago, and it would never be able to return to its former shape again.

And he taught all those who watched him work, or worked beside him: know who you are, stand for something, don't be afraid to take the knocks. He taught us those lessons the only way we could stand to learn them: he stayed there beside us. He made it worth our while.

□ Index ══════════════════